IBM® System/370 Assembler Language Programming

IBM® System/370 Assembler Language Programming

Keith H. Nicaise

TAB Professional and Reference Books

Division of TAB BOOKS
Blue Ridge Summit, PA

IBM, MVS, MVS/XA, MVS/ESA, ESA/370, System/360, and System/370 are registered trademarks of International Business Machines, Inc.

Burroughs B5000 is a trademark of the Unisys Corporation.

Appendix A is reprinted by permission from *System/370 Extended Architecture Reference Guide*, © by International Business Machines Corporation.

Appendix B is reprinted by permission from *System/370 Extended Architecture: Principles of Operation*, © Copyright 1990 by International Business Machines Corporation.

TPR books are published by TAB Professional and Reference Books, a division of TAB BOOKS. The TPR logo, consisting of the letters "TPR" within a large "T," is a registered trademark of TAB BOOKS.

FIRST EDITION

FIRST PRINTING

Library of Congress Cataloging in Publication Data

Nicaise, Keith H.
IBM System/370 assembler language programming / by Keith H. Nicaise.
p. cm.
Includes bibliographical references.
ISBN 0-8306-7380-6 ISBN 0-8306-3380-4 (pbk.)
1. IBM 370 (Computer)—Programming. 2. Assembler language (Computer program language) I. Title.
QA76.8.I123N53 1990
005.2'25—dc20 89-48452
CIP

TAB BOOKS offers software for sale. For information and a catalog, please contact TAB Software Department, Blue Ridge Summit, PA 17294-0850.

Questions regarding the content of this book should be addressed to:

Reader Inquiry Branch
TAB BOOKS
Blue Ridge Summit, PA 17294-0214

Vice President and Editorial Director: Larry Hager
Book Editor: David M. Gauthier
Production: Katherine Brown
Book Design: Jaclyn J. Boone

Contents

Acknowledgments

The author is indebted to Touro Infirmary and its administrations and employees that have served that institution. Much of the contents of this book is the direct result of the author's twenty years of experiences at Touro.

Special thanks are due to the fellow employees who served as students and for their patience, suggestions, and criticisms of the presented material. These courageous guinea pigs are Niru Munshi, Jack Brunet, Zac Dodge, Joseph Ferrara, Kenneth Ibert, James Rosenberry, and Frank Sunsin.

Many thanks to Professor Lloyd Bingham of Tulane University and long-time associate Leonhard Spohrer for their influences on the contents of this text. Of course, such appreciation is also due many other individuals for similar contributions.

The author also thanks the IBM Corporation not only for permission to reproduce material but also for their contributions to the computing industry. All computer professionals owe thanks to IBM for providing the tools and research that contributed so much to the current profession.

To
Anastasia,
Ryan
and
all past, present, and future assembler language programmers

Introduction

This book is designed to serve three kinds of computer-literate individuals. The first kind is the student or programming professional who wants to learn the basic principles of assembler programming. For these individuals the "Number Systems," "Basic Architecture," "Introduction to Assembler Language," and "Getting Started" sections provide a basis for their needs. For the more serious student and beginning assembler programmer "Comparison and Branch Conditional Instructions," "Formatting Instructions," "Dump Analysis—Batch Applications," "Bit Manipulation," "Loop and Indexing," "Byte Manipulation," and "Execute and Linkage Instructions," sections are offered. For the experienced assembler programmer "String Manipulation," "Subroutines," "COPY and Macro Instructions," "Dump Analysis—CICS Applications," "Input/Output Channel Programming," "Stacks," "Redundancy and Error Correction Techniques," "XA and Bimodal Programming," "Floating-Point Instructions," "Cross Memory and ESA/370 Instructions," and "IBM 3270 Data Streams" sections are available.

Many books on this subject are either very shallow in the scope of material presented and/or are basically restatements of the material supplied by the computer hardware manufacturer. In an attempt to address these areas of concern, this book provides the basic material with concise definitions of machine and assembler instructions, system macros, etc. Such explanations are illustrated by supplemental examples embedded within the text and more detailed examples in an appendix. It has been my experience that such a presentation enables the student to grasp the concepts of assembler programming more easily. If you need more rigorous explanations of obscure special cases you are referred to specific reference material. For the more advanced student, the use of such references is encouraged but is not normally required for a general understanding of the routine usage of the facilities of the assembler and operating systems.

Another purpose of this book is to dispel the idea that assembler programming is too difficult for the general programming professional. It is probably true that assembler is a more complex and powerful language than some other computer languages, but the serious student can, perhaps with somewhat more effort, become proficient in the usage of assembler programming. Once such proficiency is attained there is no substantial difference in the difficulty of programming in assembler languages; in many applications assembler is the easiest language to use. In all cases, much more efficient programs—in processor and memory resources—can be produced in assembler language than in any other programming language.

Those programmers who choose not to adopt assembler as one of their programming languages will find basic assembler knowledge beneficial in their profession.

The contents of this book are adequate for a multiple course college level text in assembler programming or other computer science subject.

It is expected that the student has been exposed to at least one higher language (e.g., FORTRAN, COBOL, PL/I, Pascal, BASIC, etc.) or hardware architecture in order to receive the maximum understanding and benefits from this text.

The organization of this text is designed to introduce the material in a logical order for the general student. Special needs and backgrounds may alter that sequence. For example, many non-assembler programmers are adequately familiar with binary and hexadecimal arithmetic. Hence, little or no time need be spent on chapter 1. Also, the "Dump Analysis—Batch Applications" might be presented too early for those who will continue past this point and those who are not writing programs for actual machine processing. The author chose this placement to emphasize the importance of these procedures. The programmer who has some knowledge of assembler programming may select only those chapters that will provide the information to expand skills in specific areas.

1

Number Systems

Because most people have 10 fingers (or digits) the ***decimal*** (or ***base 10***) number system developed. Computers, on the other hand, are constructed of electronic components that rely on two states (off/on or open/closed). These electronic properties have been exploited to store information within the computer. Hence, the most natural and convenient way to represent information internal to the computer is by means of the ***binary*** (or ***base 2***) number system.

Although systems programming and hardware interfaces have been established that permit the computer to accept and present information in decimal numbers as well as alphabetical and special characters, it is still sometimes convenient to understand the internal representation of such data. Because assembly language programming brings us closer to the actual internal operation of the computer it is, perhaps, more important to understand the internal processes for assembler programming than for programming in a higher level language.

As the first step in understanding the internal architecture and operation of digital computers, we will provide the basics of binary arithmetic and notation. To formalize the concept of binary and other nondecimal-based number systems, consider exactly what the customary Arabic numerical notation represents. For example, the representation '1234' is used to denote the value of:

$$[(1 \times 1000) + (2 \times 100) + (3 \times 10) + 4)]$$

or

$$(1 \times 10^3) + (2 \times 10^2) + (3 \times 10^1) + (4 \times 10^0.)$$

Using such a representation we may develop a number system based on any positive integer. Consider for a moment the digits of a number system. You will note that for a base of n the digits are 0 through n-1. The digits of the binary number system are therefore 0 and 1. The expression *binary digit* is abbreviated to *bit*. Binary values are represented by such notation as 10110_2 which represents

$$(1 \times 2^4) + (0 \times 2^3) + (1 \times 2^2) + (1 \times 2^1) + (0 \times 2^0) = 16 + 4 + 2 = 22$$

Although such representations are easily and efficiently handled by the internal circuitry of computers such representations overwhelm the human. For that reason a compromise has been established that allows the human to better relate to binary numbers. This compromise is to convert binary numbers to *hexadecimal* (or *base 16*) numbers. Hexadecimal numbers are constructed in the same manner as the shown representations of decimal and binary numbers. Note, however, that hexadecimal digits range from 0 to 15. To remove the inconvenience of not having a single character convention to represent hexadecimal digits above 9 those respective digits are defined to be represented by A, B, C, D, E, and F. Thus, $A2C_{16}$ denotes:

$$(10 \times 16^2) + (2 \times 16^1) + (12 \times 16^0) = 2560 + 32 + 12 = 2604.$$

The relationship between these three number systems is demonstrated by the following table.

Base 10	Base 16	Base 2
0	0	0000
1	1	0001
2	2	0010
3	3	0011
4	4	0100
5	5	0101
6	6	0110
7	7	0111
8	8	1000
9	9	1001
10	A	1010
11	B	1011
12	C	1100
13	D	1101
14	E	1110
15	F	1111

CONVERSION OF BASES

By using the number table note that a single hexadecimal digit converts to four binary digits (as you might expect since $2^4 = 16$). By using this relationship, you can convert long strings of binary digits to a smaller number of hexadecimal digits; for example $1010000111110101_2 = A1F5_{16}$. Now you have a notation that is much more manageable but does not require the tedious effort to convert between decimal and binary numbers.

Although it is rarely necessary to manually convert between decimal and either binary or hexadecimal, a thorough discussion of number systems should probably include the techniques for such conversion. The following discussion addresses only the conversion between decimal and hexadecimal. To convert from decimal to binary, first convert to hexadecimal and use the demonstrated relationships to convert the resulting hexadecimal value to binary. To convert from binary to decimal, first convert to hexadecimal and then to decimal.

To convert from hexadecimal one method is to apply the following mathematical aid:

$$\begin{aligned} wxyz_{16} &= (w \times 16^3) + (x \times 16^2) + (y \times 16) + z \\ &= 16\{16[16 \times w + x] + y\} + z \end{aligned}$$

Although this example is for only four digits you can inductively apply it to values of any number of digits. A non-algebraic demonstration of this technique follows using the value 1234_{16}.

$$\begin{array}{rr} & 16 \\ \times & \underline{1} \\ = & 16 \\ + & \underline{2} \\ = & 18 \end{array} \qquad \begin{array}{rr} & 18 \\ \times & \underline{16} \\ = & 288 \\ + & \underline{3} \\ = & 291 \end{array} \qquad \begin{array}{rr} & 291 \\ \times & \underline{16} \\ = & 4656 \\ + & \underline{4} \\ = & 4660 \end{array}$$

Reversing this process converts from decimal to hexadecimal, for example 4660_{10} is converted by:

$$\begin{array}{r} 291 \\ 16\overline{)4660} \\ \underline{32} \\ 146 \\ \underline{144} \\ 20 \\ \underline{16} \\ 4=R_1 \end{array} \qquad \begin{array}{r} 18 \\ 16\overline{)291} \\ \underline{16} \\ 131 \\ \underline{128} \\ 3=R_2 \end{array} \qquad \begin{array}{r} 1 \\ 16\overline{)18} \\ \underline{16} \\ 2=R_3 \end{array} \qquad \begin{array}{r} 0 \\ 16\overline{)1} \\ \underline{0} \\ 1R4 \end{array}$$

Which yields: $4660_{10} = (R_4R_3R_2R_1)_{16} = 1234_{16} = 1001000110100_2$

REPRESENTING SIGNED VALUES

The preceding discussion has addressed the representation of unsigned (positive) binary values. While almost all modern computers represent positive values in a manner similar to the above descriptions, negative numbers are represented with varying techniques. The following discussions will be narrowed to the IBM System/360 architecture that has been carried forward to the IBM System/370, 43xx, 9370, 30xx, and other compatible systems produced by other manufacturers.

In general, integer binary values are represented in 16 and 32 bit formats. The first (high-order) bit of these formats is used as a sign indicator. If this bit is a 0 the remaining value is expressed in the previous manner. However, if this bit is a 1 the value is negative and the remaining bits are in ***2's complement*** form.

To better understand 2's complement form, it might help to remember 10's and 9's complementary representations from elementary mathematics courses. To obtain the 9's complement of a decimal number, each digit is subtracted from 9. To obtain the 10's complement, the number is subtracted from the power of 10 that is one digit longer than the number. For example the 9's complement of 12345 is 87654 while the 10's complement is 100000 − 12345 = 87655. Note that the 10's complement is always one more than the 9's complement.

In an analogous manner the 2's complement of a binary number is obtained by subtracting that number from the power of 2 that is one bit longer than the number. An alternate method is to compute the ***1's complement*** and add 1 to the result. The 1's complement is obtained by subtracting each digit from 1, or by substituting each 1 with a 0 and each 0 with a 1.

Examples:

1.	Value	0000000 00000001
	1's complement	1111111 11111110
	+	1
	2's complement	1111111 11111111
	Signed value	11111111 11111111
2.	Value	1111111 11111111
	1's complement	0000000 00000000
	+	1
	=	0000000 00000001
	Signed value	10000000 00000001
3.	Value	1111111 11111000
	1's complement	0000000 00000111
	+	1
	=	0000000 00001000
	Signed value	10000000 00001000

REPRESENTATION OF NONNUMERICAL DATA

It has been demonstrated that any integer value can be represented in the binary storage methods of electronic circuitry. Now let us consider how the computer represents nonnumerical information such as text, to do this each character is coded as a unique bit pattern. To select such a bit pattern it is simply necessary to decide how many unique characters are to be represented and then use the appropriate number of bits necessary to provide the desired mapping. The IBM System/360 architects chooses 8 bits to represent characters. Up to 256 characters can be represented in this number of bits.

Although previous character representations have been based on 4, 5, 6, and 7 bits; most architectures currently have settled on the 8-bit representation. Such pieces of data are called *bytes.* There are two major standards for character representation, EBCDIC and ASCII, used primarily in IBM S/360 and non-IBM S/360 architectures, respectively.

EBCDIC is an acronym that represents *E*xtended *B*inary *C*oded *D*ecimal *I*nterchange *C*ode. This code is an extension of BCD or 6-bit Binary Coded Decimal. The term *Hollerith code* is also used to designate such codes in honor of their inventor, Herman Hollerith. Hollerith codes normally refer to card codes but are also used in describing text data within FORTRAN FORMAT statements. Dr. Hollerith was the founder of the Hollerith Tabulating Company which later became International Business Machines.

ASCII is an acronym that represents *A*merican *S*tandard *C*ode for *I*nformation *I*nterchange. There are several different ASCII codes but the term usually refers to the 8-bit standard used by most modern computers. The main exception to this statement is when dealing with communication equipment—where it is suggested that detailed specifications be obtained.

Reference

IBM Form Number SA22-7085. *IBM System/370 Extended Architecture: Principles of Operation.* Appendices A and G.

2

Basic Architecture

The IBM System/370 class computers consists of three major components or subsystems. These are:

a. The *Central Processing Unit* (CPU). This unit controls all processes executed by the system. There may be multiple CPUs within a given configuration. Presently the maximum number of CPUs are the six contained within the IBM 3090 Model 600 but this number is expected to increase in future systems.
b. The *Input/Output (I/O) Channels.* Information is transferred between main storage and I/O devices (usually I/O controllers) by means of I/O channels. While the channels are controlled by the CPU, once started, they perform their tasks independent of the CPU.
c. *Main Storage.* Main storage (or memory) is a large array of monolithic circuits which is used to store data and programs. These circuits are created in a manner for efficient storage of binary data as discussed in the above *Number Systems* section. In addition to main storage most systems also contain *cache* memory which is high speed storage that provides a means for accelerated performance but is not related to programming. Also, some large systems contain *expanded storage* which is slower than main memory but much faster than most I/O storage devices. To access data or instructions within expanded storage they must first be moved to main memory.

The remainder of this section will be concerned mainly with the components and operation of the CPU.

REGISTERS

Registers are composed of very high speed storage circuits that operate on small quantities of data. The System/370 CPU contains 16 ***general purpose*** registers, 16 ***control registers***, 8 ***floating-point registers***, the ***program status word*** (PSW), and other registers. Our discussion will be concerned mainly with the general purpose registers.

The general purpose registers are 32 bits in length. These registers are identified by the numbers 0 to 15. All may be used as ***accumulators*** and registers 1-15 may be used as ***base registers*** and ***index registers***. The bit positions within each register are numbered, from left to right, as 0 to 31. Some instructions can use two adjacent registers as an even-odd pair. In this case the pairs are identified by the numbers 0, 2, 4, 6, 8, 10, 12, and 14. The bit positions are numbered 0 to 63. Some instructions also access individual bytes within a register. In that case the bytes are referred to, from left to right, as bytes 0 through 3.

ADDRESSING

Initially the System/370 addressing could address up to 16,777,216 (1000000_{16}) bytes of memory. The extended architecture (XA) mode extends this to 2,147,483,648 (80000000_{16}) bytes. To retain compatibility with the initial addressing scheme the CPU has two distinct addressing modes. These modes are called non-XA and XA modes or 24-bit and 31-bit modes, respectively. Unless specifically noted our discussion will be restricted to the initial, 24-bit, addressing mode.

In some older machines, where addressing was generally restricted to memory sizes of less than 32,768 (8000_{16}) locations, the absolute memory address was included within each instruction. With the availability of much larger memory sizes such an addressing scheme became inefficient. The System/370 addressing scheme is implemented using base registers and ***displacements***. That is, instead of providing the absolute address a relative address is provided that is added to the contents of a general purpose register (not register zero) to construct an ***effective*** address. This relative address is called the displacement and can range from 0 to 4095 (FFF_{16}). Thus two bytes containing the register designation and the displacement are sufficient to address the largest memory size.

For example, if register ten contains the value 100000_{16} the CPU interprets the two byte address of A123 to designate storage address 100123_{16}.

MACHINE INSTRUCTIONS

Program execution is carried out by the CPU Interpretation of instructions stored within main memory. These instructions are stored exactly as data are stored, that is, by a sequence of binary digits. The components of an instruction are:

a. An operation code. Normally one byte in length but there are some extended operation codes that consist of two bytes. The code always begins at the first byte of the instruction. This code is decoded by the CPU and the specified operation is performed.
b. Operand. A description of the operand(s) that participate in the execution of the operation. There are three types of operands.

    1. Operands located within registers. The operation code specifies the type of register, the operand specifies which register(s) will be used.
    2. Immediate values. This is an absolute value contained within the instruction. Immediate operands are 8 bits in length.
    3. Operands within storage. The operand field of the instruction specifies the address (in base-displacement form). The length of the operand can be implicitly determined by the operation code or, for some operations, must be explicitly included within the instruction.

INSTRUCTION FORMATS

There are nine basic instruction formats. These are described below and illustrated in Machine Instruction Formats of Appendix A.

a. RR (Register-to-register) instructions contain two register operands. RR instructions are two bytes in length. For example, the contents of one register may be added to the contents of the same or another register by means of the *Add Register* (AR) instruction.
b. RX (Register-storage, indeXed) instructions contain a register, an index register, and a storage operand. These instructions transfer data between registers and storage. Storage is accessed (i.e., an effective address is generated) by the conventional base-displacement technique but, in addition, can be modified by adding the contents of another general purpose register to that address. The length of these instructions are four bytes. An example is the *Add Halfword* (AH) instruction which adds a two byte value stored in memory to the contents of a general register.
c. RS (Register-Storage) instructions also transfer data between main storage and registers but do not provide the indexing feature of the RX-type instructions. Instead of the index operand a third element may be present. These instructions are four bytes in length. An example is the *Store Multiple* (STM) which transfers the contents of consecutive registers to memory. In this case, the terminal register identification is the third element.
d. SI (Storage Immediate) instructions contain an 8-bit immediate operand and a storage operand. These instructions are four bytes in length. An example is the *Move Immediate* (MVI) instruction which replaces the byte at the effective storage address with the immediate value.

e. SS (Storage-to-Storage) instructions contain two storage operands and one or two length fields. These instructions can move storage contents or perform arithmetical operations between values contained within main storage. These instructions are six bytes in length. An example of an SS instruction that contains a single length field is the ***Move Character*** (MVC) which moves up to 256 bytes from one memory location to another. An example with two length fields is the ***Multiply Packed Decimal*** (MP) which multiplies the contents of one memory location by the contents of another memory location which can be of different length.

f. S (Storage) instructions contain a single storage operand and the operation code implies a second operand. These instructions are four bytes in length. These instructions have an extended (two byte) operation code. An example is the ***Store CPU Timer*** (STPT) which stores the contents of the CPU timer in the double word designated by the storage operand.

g. E (Extended) instructions contain only an extended operation code—all operands are implied. These instructions are two bytes in length. At the present time there is only one E-type instruction—the ***Update Tree*** (UPT). This instruction is beyond the scope of this discussion.

h. RRE (Register-to-Register, Extended) instructions are RR-type instructions with an extended operation code. These instructions are four bytes in length. These are privileged instructions and are beyond the scope of this material. Privileged instructions are restricted to execution only when the CPU is within the supervisor state.

i. SSE (Storage-to-Storage, Extended) instructions are SS type instructions with an extended operation code. These instructions are six bytes in length. These are also privileged instructions and will not be discussed in any more detail.

INSTRUCTION TYPES

Although instructions are grouped by the individual formats they can also be grouped into five types. These types relate to the kind of data they process and the functions they perform.

a. *General* instructions perform binary integer arithmetic and non-arithmetic functions such as branching and logical operations.

b. *Decimal* instructions perform arithmetic and conversions on data stored in the decimal formats. These data formats are described below.

c. *Floating-Point* instructions perform arithmetic on data stored in floating-point formats. These formats are briefly described below.

d. *Control* instructions are used to modify control registers and other facilities that relate to the operational states of the system. These are privileged and semi-privileged instructions and are beyond this discussion.

e. *I/O* instructions provide communication with I/O channels. These are also privileged instructions and will not be included in this discussion. Those who might pursue this subject should note that the operation of the I/O system differs considerably between non-XA and XA architectures and, therefore, should direct those pursuits in the proper direction.

BINARY INTEGER DATA FORMATS

Most of the information needed in understanding this format was presented in the first section (Number Systems). The only additional information that needs to be presented is exactly how these data are processed by the general purpose instructions. Normally these data are processed in *full word* and *half word* formats. A *word* is composed of 32 bits, or four bytes. In earlier models of the System/370 architecture these data were required to begin at memory addresses that were multiples of 4 and 2, respectively. In later models, instructions were permitted to access data not aligned on these boundaries but performance was degraded. In current models these restrictions no longer exist. There are, however, instructions that do require alignments of their operands. These instructions will be discussed later.

DECIMAL DATA FORMATS

There are two formats for decimal data.

a. Zoned decimal.
b. Packed decimal.

Zoned decimal data is primarily used for external purposes. It is basically EBCDIC format (FO_{16},...,$F9_{16}$) to represent the decimal integers. The first hexadecimal digit is called the *zone* and the low-order digit is referred to as the *numeric* bits. This terminology is related to card codes. These separate hexadecimal digits are sometimes called *nybls.* The zone portion of the low-order byte represents the sign. Normally the hexadecimal C denotes a positive number and D designates a negative number. Zone decimal data do not participate directly in decimal arithmetic but must be converted to packed decimal data. This conversion is normally accomplished by the PACK instructions.

In the *packed decimal format* the zone fields are removed and two digits are packed into each byte. The low-order four bits of a packed number contains the sign—again, normally C or D but may also be A (plus), B (minus), E (plus), or F (plus). The successful completion of a packed decimal arithmetic operation always produces a sign of C or D. Packed decimal values can be up to 16 bytes, or 31 decimal digits, in length. Examples are:

12345C = +12345
07890D = -7890

FLOATING-POINT DATA FORMATS

Floating-point calculations are normally utilized on value whose magnitude have a wide variation. These data are represented in a format similar to the so called 'scientific notation' used by scientific and engineering calculators. Thus a given precision (i.e., a given number of significant digits) is preserved.

A floating-point number consists of two parts:

a. An ***exponent***, sometimes called the ***characteristic***, which is a seven bit unsigned value. This value (0-127) represents a signed value from negative 64 to positive 63. This technique is called ***excess-64 notation.***

b. The ***fraction***, sometimes called the ***mantissa***. This part consists of the precision of the value to be represented. It is actually the hexadecimal fraction obtained from dividing a given value by 16 raised to the above exponent.

While the complexity of the floating-point representation will not be presented in further detail, until the special section Floating-Point Instructions, we will present the following decimal example as an analogy.

$$123.456 = .123456 \times 10^3$$

In this example the characteristic is 3 and the mantissa is 123456.

3

Introduction to Assembler Language

Assembler language is the programming language that is closest to machine language. Thus, it is commonly called a *low level* language. It is composed of statements that represents instructions and comments. Comments are intended for the human reader of the program and are ignored by the assembler. Instructions direct the assembler to produce machine instructions, control output format, etc. There are three types of instructions:

a. *Machine instructions* are the symbolic representation of the machine instructions that were introduced in the last section.
b. *Assembler instructions* are used to provide the assembler with information or to direct the assembler to perform certain functions during the assembly process. For example, to define register(s) to use as base register(s) or to define data constants.
c. *Macro instructions* instruct the assembler to substitute predefined sequences of code which can be composed of machine or assembler instructions, other macro instructions, or comment statements. For example, most I/O operations and other common tasks are performed by macros supplied by IBM and other vendors. The programmer might include macro definitions within a given program or include macro definitions within macro libraries.

Appendix A contains examples of machine and assembler instructions. Macro definitions will be introduced as they are needed or can be obtained from references in the bibliography.

CODING CONVENTIONS

Assembler source statements consist of 80-byte records. Instructions are coded in the *statement field,* continuation indicators (any non-blank character) are placed in the *continuation indicator field,* and continuation statements must begin in the *continuation field.* The position of these fields can be altered with the *Input Format Control* (ICTL) assembler instruction but the defaults are normally used. Defaults are bytes 1-71, 72, and 16; respectively.

Most statements can have up to nine continuation records but some can be continued indefinitely. An example of this later type is macro instruction statements. For a complete listing, see the appropriate Assembler Language Programming Reference manual.

There are two types of statements: The comment statement and the instruction statement. The comment statement contains an ('*') in the first position and any EBCDIC characters in the remainder of the statement. Instruction statements contain up to four entries, separated by at least one blank. Entries are defined here and must be entered in their specific sequence.

a. The *Name Entry* is usually optional and contains a label to identify the statement. If present, it must begin in the first position and be a valid assembler symbol (to be defined below).
b. The *Operation Entry* is the symbolic code for the machine, assembler, or macro instruction. This entry is required and may begin in any position after the starting position.
c. The *Operand Entry* contains one or more operands associated with the instruction. This field is optional, depending on the requirements for the specific instruction. If more than one operand is used the individual operands are separated by commas.
d. The *Remarks Entry* is optional. It can be any EBCDIC character string and can include blank characters. Note that, with the exception of operand fields that include blanks that are enclosed within single quote marks, blanks are not allowed in other entry types. If a remark entry is included within a statement that does not have an operand entry, a comma must be substituted for the missing operand entry.
e. The *Continuation Indicator* is a one-character field. If blank the statement is complete. If not blank the statement is continued—beginning in the continuation field of the next record. Care should be taken to prevent remark characters overflowing into this field.

An example of a machine instruction statement is listed below.

Name	Op Code	Operands	Comments
LABEL1	MVC	ALPHA,BETA	MOVE BETA TO ALPHA

In Assembler H, assembler symbols consist of at most 63 alphameric characters. The first character must be alphabetic (#, $, and @ characters are defined to be alphabetic). In most cases an underscore ('_') is permitted within a symbol, for exceptions see the Assembler Language Programming Guide. While up to 63 characters are permitted, it is strongly recommended that this maximum be limited to eight characters except for very unusual reasons. One reason for this recommendation is that other assemblers restrict symbols to be no more than eight characters. In addition to that reason, long symbols tend to be awkward and lead to listings that are difficult to read.

The program will be much more readable if the above fields start in specific relative positions within the input record. The normal convention is that bytes 1 to 8 are reserved for the name entry, bytes 10 to 14 is used for the operation entry, and the operand entry begins in byte 16. The remarks location is often selected by the individual user but byte 35 is a reasonable location. Operand entries occasionally exceed whatever space is allowed and overflow into the space reserved for the remarks entry, in which case the remarks entry is included in whatever space is remaining in the statement field.

BASE REGISTER INSTRUCTIONS

Machine instructions reference storage by a base register plus a displacement from this register. The assembler normally generates displacements for symbolic references that are included in the operand entries of assembler statements. In order for the assembler to know which registers are intended for base registers and the value these registers will contain, the USING assembler statement is used. It is sometimes necessary to inform the assembler that such specified registers are no longer valid. The DROP assembler instruction is used to discontinue base register usage.

The USING instruction requires at least two operands. The first operand is a symbolic expression that defines the contents of the (first) base register at execution time.

At least one and as many as 16 operands follow the above operand. These operands can be either absolute or symbolic expressions but must have a decimal value of '1' through '15'. Thus:

USING address,$register_1$[,$register_2$,...]

If multiple registers are specified the assembler assumes that they will contain the value that is 4096 larger than the preceding register operand. The above brackets ('[','] ') are used to denote optional operands and are not coded into the statement. For example

```
         USING  START,12,8
START    L      10,ALPHA
         ...
         DS     4096C
ALPHA    DC     F'100'
```

The example shows how to inform the assembler which registers are used to establish addressability but it is necessary to assure that the base register(s) contain the proper value. It is sometimes known that a register will have a certain value but this is often not the case. Note that if no register contains a known relative value there is no way to specify a storage location (except for the first 4096 bytes of storage) that could initialize a base register. Fortunately, there exists a special form of an instruction that will load the address of the next main storage location. This instruction is the ***Branch And Link Register*** (BALR) instruction. When this instruction is executed the low order 24 bits of the general purpose register that is specified as the first operand is loaded with the memory address that follows the location of the instruction. Control is normally transferred to the address contained in the second register operand. However, if the second operand is zero no transfer is performed. For example:

```
BALR   5,0         LOAD BASE ADDRESS REGISTER
USING  *,5         ESTABLISH ADDRESSABILITY
```

Note that we have introduced a new concept. The special symbol ★ indicates the current address and is called the location counter reference. The left most column of the listing of assembly statements is called the location counter. This is a relative value, initialized by a START or other assembler instruction, that indicates the relative displacement of the storage addresses.

Note: The BALR instruction is valid only for the non-XA addressing mode. The instruction alters bits 0-7 of the first operand register. The ***Branch And Save Register*** (BASR) is an equivalent instruction for XA addressing mode.

The DROP instruction is used to communicate to the assembler that the current base register(s) is (are) no longer to be used. This instruction has an operand for each register to be removed from base register usage. It is of the form:

DROP $register_1$[,$register_2$,...]

For example:

```
        DROP  5
        LH    5,XTABLE
        ...
XTABLE  ...
```

TERMS AND EXPRESSIONS

In the above discussions we have used some terminology that has not been fully defined. We will now define these and introduce additional concepts.

The basic element of assembler language is called a ***term***. A term can be used by itself or in combinations to form an ***expression***. Terms are either ***relocatable*** or ***absolute*** depending on whether their value changes, or does not change, upon program relocation.

A symbol is an example of a term. For example:

```
ABC        DC     2CL4'ABC'      RELOCATABLE TERM

FIVE67     DC     H'5,6,7'       RELOCATABLE TERM

SEVEN      EQU    7              ABSOLUTE TERM

ABCPLUS7   EQU    ABC+SEVEN      RELOCATABLE TERM

DIFFER     EQU    FIVE67-ABC     ABSOLUTE TERM

Y          DC     X'12345F'      RELOCATABLE TERM
```

The assembler instruction Define Constant (DC) is used to define constants. These constants are assembled into the output of the assembly but can be altered at execution time. The Define Storage (DS) defines an area of main storage but does not assemble a value into storage. The Equate (EQU) assigns a value to a symbol.

The DC and DS assembler instructions can have as many as four subfields within its operand field. These subfields are:

a. A ***duplication factor*** which instructs the assembler to duplicate the operand multiple times (including zero). This field is optional. For example the 2 in term ABC above.
b. A ***type*** subfield which defines the type of data to be defined. A complete listing of these types are provided in Appendix A. The type subfield is required.
c. The ***modifier*** subfield(s) of which we will presently only consider the length modifier. The length modifier defines a length to the data. For example, the L4 in the operand of ABC. This subfield is optional and, if present, always begins with the character L. If not present, the length attribute of the symbol is symbol of either the type or value subfields. For example the length attribute of FIVE67 is 2 (a halfword) and that of Y is 3 (6 hexadecimal digits).
d. The ***nominal value***(s) subfield(s) specify initial value(s). This subfield is optional for the DS instruction but required for the DC instruction. If present for the DS it is ignored by the assembler. The values are enclosed in single quote marks or, for address constants, parentheses.

Self-Defining Terms specify values explicitly. Such terms are absolute. They can be expressed in decimal, binary, or character format. For example:

```
10

X'F'

B'1011'

C'A'
```

Literals are a means of defining data constants without specifying their values in DC instructions. Note literals are not terms—they can be specified only as a complete operand of a machine instruction. A literal always begins with an equal sign '=') and contains subfields that are quite similar to the operand subfields of the DC instruction, for example: =5XL2'15' defines the value $00150015001500150015_{16}$.

4

Getting Started

We have already discovered two of the tasks necessary to begin a program—loading a base register and establishing addressability. This section will introduce other common functions.

SAVING AND RESTORING REGISTERS

In MVS, the programmer is expected to exit the program with the contents of the general registers restored to the values that were present when the program received control. This is usually done by the SAVE and RETURN macro instructions. A common prototype is provided below.

```
         SAVE    (14,12)          SAVE REGS 14,15,0,1,...12
         BALR    12,0             LOAD BASE REGISTER
         USING   *,12             ESTABLISH ADDRESSABILITY
         ST      13,SAVEAREA+4    SAVE CONTENTS OF REGISTER 13
         LA      13,SAVEAREA      POINT TO CURRENT REGISTER SAVE AREA
         ...
         L       13,SAVEAREA+4    RESTORE REGISTER 13
         RETURN  (14,12)          RESTORE REGS 14,,,12 & RETURN
SAVEAREA DS      18F
```

As you can see from Example 1 in Appendix D the SAVE macro generates an STM machine instruction which stores 15 of the registers in an area which is referenced by register 13. Register 13 is saved within the user's program because it must be at a known location that can be referenced at exit time. The above procedure is called the standard linkage convention, a software standard that facilitates communication between programs. Likewise, the RETURN macro restores the registers from the save area pointed to by register 13. Of course, register 13 must contain its entry value to restore the other registers from the correct storage location. The RETURN macro also returns control to the operating system.

Although there are no requirements to save the contents of register 13 in the precise manner given, it's a recommended procedure in case subroutines are called via the standard linkage convention.

In DOS, the registers are not saved at the entry in the root (main) program but the same linkage convention is used for subroutines. In fact, if an attempt is made to save the registers in DOS, a program exception will probably occur—depending on the contents of register 13.

INPUT/OUTPUT MACROS

Most programs require either input, output, or both. IBM provides the following macros to support the I/O functions:

a. OPEN, to prepare a data set for processing.
b. GET, to retrieve records.
c. PUT, to write records.
d. CLOSE, to terminate processing of a data set.
e. DCB, to specify data set and processing characteristics.

There are additional I/O macros but the above suffices for our purposes. The following are the basic formats for OPEN, GET, PUT, and CLOSE.

OPEN	(dcb_1,$option_1$,dcb_2,$option_2$,...)
GET	*dcb,address*
PUT	*dcb,address*
CLOSE	(dcb_1,,dcb_2,,...)

Where:

dcb = the name of a DCB macro instruction.

address = the main storage address where the record will be received or from where the record will be written.

option = INPUT or OUTPUT (other options are available but will not be discussed here). If INPUT, the option can be omitted—the dcb operand will then either be followed by two consecutive commas or the terminal parenthesis.

The DCB macro has many possible operands but, to simplify this discussion, samples are provided below to read card images (CARDS) and print output lines (PRINTER):

```
CARDS     DCB  DDNAME=SYSIN,        Data Definition NAME (from SYSIN)     X
               DSORG=PS,            Data Set ORGanization (Phys. Seq.)    X
               MACRF=GM,            MACRo Instruction Form (Get, Move)    X
               EODAD=eof-add        End Of Data ADdress

PRINTER   DCB  DDNAME=PRINTER,                                            X
               MACRF=PM,            (Put, Move)                           X
               LRECL=133,           Logical RECord Length                 X
               BLKSIZE=133,         BLocK SIZE                            X
               DSORG=PS,                                                  X
               RECFM=FBA            RECord format (Fixed,Blocked,type-A)
```

THE END STATEMENT

The END statement indicates the end of the assembler source program. It consists of the operation field ('END') and can contain an operand. If an operand is present, initial program execution will begin at the location defined by this operand. Else, execution begins at the first executable statement.

REGISTER USAGE

While all 16 general purpose registers can be used, the operating system can alter registers 0, 1, 14, and 15 when performing such requests as I/O. Therefore, if the contents of these registers are of value, they should be saved prior to issuing such a request. Also, as we will see later, some machine instructions alters specific registers not explicitly referenced as an operand.

5

Comparison and Branch Conditional Instructions

The condition code is a two bit value that is set by various machine operations. For example, arithmetic operations normally set the condition code to indicate that the operation produced a positive, negative, or zero result. Other conditions such as overflow of register contents modify the condition code.

In non-XA machines this value is stored as part of the program status word (PSW). In XA machines this portion of the PSW is used for the expanded address and the condition code is relocated to a fixed storage location. It is seldom the concern of programming where the condition code is actually stored—its value is determined by Branch Conditional (BC and BCR) instructions.

COMPARE INSTRUCTIONS

Various compare instructions are used to compare two operands and their result is that the condition code is set to reflect the relative value of the operands. Comparison is either arithmetical or logical. Arithmetical comparisons consider the sign of values (either binary integers, floating-point, or packed decimal). Logical comparisons consider only a string of bits. As examples, for an arithmetical comparisons of signed binary integers 8001_{16} (= $-7FFF_{16}$) < $FFFF_{16}$ (= −1) < 0000_{16} < 0001_{16} but for a logical comparison 0000_{16} < 0001_{16} < 8001_{16} < $FFFF_{16}$. Some compare instructions are:

a. CR (Compare Register) compares the contents of two general purpose registers. The comparison is arithmetical.
b. CP (Compare Packed Decimal) compares the value of two packed decimal operands. The comparison is arithmetical.
c. CLC (Compare Logical, Character) compares the value of two charac-

ter strings. The comparison is logical and is terminated by the first byte that is different than the corresponding byte in the other operand.

d. CLI (Compare Logical, Immediate) compares the value of the immediate operand to a byte in storage. The comparison is logical.

e. CH (Compare Halfword) compares a register to two bytes in memory. The comparison is arithmetical.

The value specified by the first operand is always compared to the value specified by the second operand.

BRANCH ON CONDITION INSTRUCTIONS

There are two forms of the branch on condition instruction. The RX-type instruction (BC) is used to transfer control to a location specified by the base register and displacement of the second operand. The RR-type (BCR) is used to transfer control to a location whose address is contained in the general purpose register specified by its second operand. In either case the branch is dependent on the value of the bit mask specified as the first operand of the instruction and the value of the condition code.

To understand this operation it is necessary to observe that the mask contains four bits and the condition code can have four values. We number the mask bits by their binary values (from left to right—8, 4, 2, and 1). These mask bits correspond to the respective values of the condition code (0, 1, 2, and 3). Control of instruction sequencing is transferred if, and only if, the value of a mask bit is on (1) that corresponds to the value of the condition code. For example:

```
BC    8,LOC      BRANCH IF CC=0

BC    4,LOC      BRANCH IF CC=1

BC    2,LOC      BRANCH IF CC=2

BCR   1,5        BRANCH IF CC=3

BC    13,LOC     BRANCH IF CC=0 OR CC=1 OR CC=3

BC    15,LOC     ALWAYS BRANCH

BCR   0,8        NEVER BRANCH
```

The last two examples are special forms that really do not depend on the value of the condition code. When the mask is 15 (1111_2) one of its bits will always correspond to the value of the condition code. When the value of the mask is zero, then there is never a corresponding value, and the branch will never occur.

EXTENDED MNEMONIC INSTRUCTIONS

It is difficult to remember the resulting condition codes for various machine instructions. To simplify coding of the corresponding branch on condition instructions the assembler has synthetically extended the operation codes to represent common conditions. These are listed in Appendix A-3. When coding these instructions the mask code is not coded—the assembler generates the mask dependent on the operation code used.

The following examples generate exactly the same machine instructions as the above examples.

```
BE      LOC         BRANCH IF EQUAL
BM      LOC         BRANCH IF MINUS
BP      LOC         BRANCH IF POSITIVE
BOR     5           BRANCH IF OVERFLOW
BNP     LOC         BRANCH IF NOT PLUS
B       LOC         UNCONDITIONAL BRANCH
NOPR    8           NO OPERATION
```

6

Formatting Instructions

Like the simple Unpack Packed Decimal (UNPK) instruction, the Edit (ED) and the Edit and Mark (EDMK) instructions convert from packed decimal to zoned decimal data formats. The ED and EDMK instructions, however, provide a means to control the format of the output. This control includes leading zero suppression, punctuation, floating currency signs, and sign indicators. While these are very powerful instructions and, once understood, are easy to use; their description is complex and will be broken down into various steps.

These instructions are SS-type instructions. The first operand must contain a pattern that directs the editing process and the second operand contains the packed decimal value to be formatted. The description of the pattern is given below. Each operand is processed left to right. Each byte of the second operand is required to have a decimal digit in its left four bits and either a digit or a sign value in the right four bits. The result replaces the first operand. There is a single length—that of the first operand.

FILL AND DIGIT-SELECTION CHARACTERS

The first byte in the pattern is called a *fill* character. The remaining bytes of the pattern can be composed of characters that either direct the formatting of the output or that are used in punctuation of the output. The first case we will consider is the *digit-selection* character. As each digit from the second operand (source) is examined a byte of the pattern is examined. If this byte is a digit-selection character then the pattern position is either replaced by the fill character or by the zoned decimal value of that digit. The fill character is used if a significant digit has not been found. If a significant digit has been found, the zoned decimal value is used. The digit-selection character is the hexadecimal value 20_{16}. For example:

```
            ED      A,B             GENERATES 'b123'
            ED      C,D             GENERATES 'bbb1'
            ...
A           DC      X'40202020'
B           DC      P'123'
C           DC      X'40202020'
D           DC      PL2'1'
```

Note that we have included a digit-selection character for each digit of the source field. Also, the notation 'b' is used to denote a blank character (40_{16}).

SIGNIFICANCE-STARTER CHARACTERS

Although the above is sufficient to format positive numbers, it would probably not yield the desired results if the source is zero—since a significant digit would not be encountered the output would be completely blank. Normally, a low order zero would be expected. This is accomplished by the *significance-starter* character. The significance-starter character performs the same function as the digit-selection character but it also forces a trigger, called the *significance trigger*, on—just as if a significant digit had been found. The effect of turning this trigger on is to convert the next digit to be processed into zoned decimal. The significance-starter character has the value 21_{16}. The significance trigger is sometimes called the *S-trigger*. Thus:

```
            ED      A,B             YIELDS 'bbb0'
            ...
A           DC      X'40202120'
B           DC      PL2'0'
```

PUNCTUATION

It is customary, in commercial processing, to insert commas between each group of three digits—starting from the integer units position and moving to the left. Also a decimal point is used to denote decimal fractions (e.g., 1,234.56). The edit instruction supports this requirement by allowing embedded EBCDIC characters within the edit pattern. During the edit process these characters either remain in place or are replaced by the fill character depending on whether the significance trigger is off or on, respectively. These embedded characters can have any value other than 20_{16}, 21_{16}, or 22_{16}. Thus:

```
          ED   A,B          YIELDS 'ƀƀƀƀ12,345.67'
          ...
A         DC   X'40206B2020206B2021204B2020'
B         DC   PL5'1234567'
```

Note the hexadecimal values of $6B_{16}$ and $4B_{16}$ which are the EBCDIC representations for the comma and period, respectively.

SIGN PROCESSING

When the edit instruction encounters a sign (A_{16} to F_{16}, in the right half of a source byte) the significance bit is either forced off or on depending on whether the sign is positive or negative, respectively. In the case of a positive sign, this results in replacing all pattern characters with the fill character until the significance trigger is again turned on. But for negative values, the pattern character either remains unchanged or (for the digit-selection character) is replaced by a digit from the source field. For example:

```
          ED   A,B          YIELDS 'ƀ123ƀCR'
          ED   C,B          YIELDS 'ƀ123-'
          ED   D,E          YIELDS 'ƀ567ƀƀƀ'
          ...
A         DC   X'4020212040C3D9'
D         DC   X'4020212040C3D9'
C         DC   X'4020212060'
B         DC   P'-123'
E         DC   P'567'
```

Note the EBCDIC values of —, C and R are 60_{16}, $C3_{16}$, and $D9_{16}$, respectively.

FIELD-SEPARATOR CHARACTERS

Multiple, consecutive packed decimal fields may be processed by a single edit instruction. To re-initialize the significance trigger a ***field-separator*** is employed. When this character is encountered in the edit pattern the significance trigger is turned off and the character is replaced with the fill character. The value of the field-separator character is 22_{16}. For example:

```
         ED     A,B          YIELDS 'ƀ123ƀƀƀ56-ƀƀƀ0ƀ'
         ...
A        DC     X'4020212060222021206022202120 60'
B        DC     PL2'123,-56,0'
```

THE EDIT AND MARK INSTRUCTION

The Edit And Mark (EDMK) instruction performs all of the functions of the Edit instruction but, additionally, the address of the first significant digit is inserted into general register 1. This address is the location within the output field (first operand). Register 1 is not modified when significance is forced by the significance-start character. If multiple fields are processed, the register is modified each time the first significant digit is encountered which results in the address of the last encountered case.

This instruction is used in cases such as applying a ***floating*** currency symbol or a negative sign prior to the first significant output digit.

Because register 1 is not modified by the result of a significance-start character, the register is normally initialized to the address of the digit that would be forced by the effect of that character.

A sample of such usage is:

```
         LA     1,A+6        POINT TO FORCED SIGNIFICANT DIGIT
         EDMK   A,B          FORMAT RESULT
         BCTR   1,0          DECREMENT ADDRESS
         MVI    0(1),C'$'    INSERT FLOATING CURRENCY SYMBOL
         ...
A        DC     X'4020206B2021204B2020'
B        DC     PL4'123456'
```

MINI EXERCISE

Write a program segment to format a packed decimal field of five bytes that is assumed to contain a decimal point two digits to the left of its least significant digit. If the value is negative, enclose the output in parentheses—with the open parenthesis immediately preceding the most significant digit.

7

Dump Analysis — Batch Application

When a program abnormally terminates (ABENDs) a dump can be obtained. This dump often simplifies determination of the cause of the failure. In other cases the operating system provides messages that pinpoint the cause of the problem without the necessity of further diagnosis. These system messages should be examined as the first step of problem determination.

The remainder of this discussion assumes that the system messages are not adequate to determine the cause of the failure. We will use the first sample dump in Appendix E in this explanation.

THE INSTRUCTION ADDRESS

The first step in dump analysis is to determine the location of the ABEND. The instruction address contains either the address of the next instruction to be executed or, very rarely, the address of the instruction being executed. The instruction address is contained in the low order portion of the 64-bit Program Status Word (PSW). In XA mode the length of this address is 31 bits and non-XA mode it is 24 bits. The address is that of the instruction being executed only when a failure occurs during the execution of an *interruptible* instruction.

The value of the PSW is printed on the first page of the storage dump and also on the system console.

MVS DATA AREAS INDEX

The last page of the MVS storage dump contains a listing of data areas. Items that are normally of interest are REGISTERS, MODULE name of application program, and PCLINK STACKS/SAVE AREAS.

SYMPTOM DUMP

Much of the above data is summarized on the system console output that is printed prior to the dump ($SYSMSGS). Therefore, it is recommended that this report be examined before going to the actual dump. This data includes:

a. PSW AT TIME OF ERROR.
b. ILC (Instruction Length Code).
c. INTR (Interrupt Code).
d. DATA AT PSW (A hexadecimal display of the twelve bytes beginning six bytes prior to the instruction address).
e. ACTIVE PROGRAM LOAD MODULE xxxxxxxx (Failing module name, normally the application program name).
f. ADDRESS xxxxxxxx (The hexadecimal load address of the above module).
g. OFFSET xxxxxxxx (The relative hexadecimal displacement of the instruction address).
h. GPR 0-3, GPR 4-7, GPR 8-11, and GPR 12-15 (The contents of the general registers 0-15, displayed in hexadecimal digits).

ANALYSIS OF FAILING INSTRUCTION

If you have an assembly listing of the program, find the offending instruction using the above OFFSET value. The reason for the failure might be apparent from the context of the instruction.

If no assembly is available or its reference does not suffice, we must now examine the failing instruction. The following explanation proceeds as if no listing is available. If a listing is available the procedure is somewhat less complex.

a. First determine the beginning of the instruction. Assume that the instruction address identifies the instruction following the failing instruction. That is, subtract the instruction length code from the instruction address.
b. Decode the operation code. Use the 'Machine Instructions by Operation Code' table in the *System/370 Extended Architecture: Reference Summary* or other equivalent table.
c. Examine the operands. This often requires the evaluation of storage addresses based on the base-registers and displacements.
d. In most cases either the operands will contain invalid data or be out of range of the current region.

CASE STUDY

Using the first sample dump from Appendix E and the third sample program listing in Appendix D we will illustrate the above techniques.

First we will examine the symptom dump output:

```
IEA995I SYMPTOM DUMP OUTPUT

ABEND CODE SYSTEM=0C7  TIME=07.54.18 SEQ=00407 CPU=0000 ASID=0014

PSW AT TIME OF ERROR  078D0000   00006DEC  ILC 6  INTC 07

  ACTIVE LOAD MODULE=SAMPLE3   ADDRESS=00006CF8  OFFSET=000000F4

  DATA AT PSW  00006DE6 - FC74C13A  C13547F0  C05A4510

  GPR  0-3  00006E62  00006E62  00000040  009ECB24

  GPR  4-7  009ECB00  009FA8A8  009C8FF8  FD000000

  GPR  8-11 009D2DF8  809FAB88  00000000  009FA8A8

  GPR 12-15 40006D20  00006E08  40006D44  12C8B2FC

 END OF SYMPTOM DUMP
```

Noting that the offset to the instruction address is $F4_{16}$, we now proceed to that location within the assembly listing.

```
0000EE FC74 C13A C135 00162 0015D    83 PRODUCT  MP    RESULT,B

0000F4 47F0 C05A            00082    84          B     OUTPUT
```

On examining the instruction we see that it is indeed the instruction listed in the DATA AT PSW. However the context of the instruction does not necessarily reveal the cause of the problem. So we will now examine the contents of the operands. The operands may be located in the storage dump in one of two ways. We can add the displacements to the contents of the base register ($6D20_{16} + 13A_{16}$ and $6D20_{16} + 135_{16}$) or add the addresses contained in the assembly listing to the program load address ($162_{16} + 6CF8_{16}$ and $15D_{16} + 6CF8_{16}$). In either case we find the address of the first operand to be $6E5A_{16}$ and that of the second operand to be $6E55_{16}$. We now go to the DATA AREAS INDEX to locate the dump of the program module.

```
JOB SYST002A   STEP S1   TIME 075419   DATE 88225 ... PAGE 00000039

                          DUMP INDEX

                          ----------

DATA AREAS                                       PAGE NUMBER

-----------                                      -----------

 ENQ/DEQ CONTROL BLOCKS................          00000004
```

```
DATA MANAGEMENT CONTROL BLOCKS........  00000005
RTM CONTROL BLOCKS....................  00000006
PCLINK STACKS / SAVE AREAS............  00000009
INSTALLATION/SUBSYSTEM AREA...........  00000009
REGISTERS.............................  00000009
MODULES...............................  00000009
   AMDPRFMT...........................  00000017
   BLSQALLO...........................  00000019
   BLSQCFMT...........................  00000020
   BLSQIFMT...........................  00000023
   BLSQROUT...........................  00000018
   BLSQTIOF...........................  00000011
   BLSUPUTG...........................  00000016
   BLSUPUT2...........................  00000028
   IEAVTRF2...........................  00000012
   IEAVTRF4...........................  00000009
   IGG019AQ...........................  00000017
   IGG019DJ...........................  00000018
   IGG019DK...........................  00000019
   SAMPLE3 ...........................  00000009
USER SUBPOOLS.........................  00000030
TRACE TABLE...........................  00000032

END OF DUMP
```

We see that our program module (SAMPLE3) begins on page nine. We now go to that page to find the dump of the operands. While, for this particular case, the operands do indeed appear on the first page of the module dump; that is not necessarily the case. This location only indicates the beginning of our search.

```
00006E40 809FAB88 00000000 ... ...   ... 0F000000 010F0000 00000100   *...
00006E60 000C5C40 4040F1F0 ... ...   ... F1F04040 40404040 40404040   *...
```

We now see that the value of the operands are $000000000100000C_{16}$ and $000000010F_{16}$, respectively. These are perfectly valid packed decimal data operands. However, if we read the description of the multiply packed machine instruction we will see that for the instruction to be performed correctly the data in the first operand must contain at least as many bytes of leading zeros as the length of the second operand. Hence, our data exception and the result of the program ABEND. Corrective action will require either extending the length of the first operand or moving the data to a work area to perform the multiplication.

8

Bit Manipulation

In addition to the normal arithmetical operations performed on data another common class of computer operations are the Boolean operations of OR, AND, and EXCLUSIVE OR. These operations are named in honor of mathematician George Boole because they are based on the concepts he developed in his algebra of symbolic logic.

BOOLEAN OPERATIONS

These operations are defined by the following table:

A	B	A or B	A and B	A xor B
0	0	0	0	0
0	1	1	0	1
1	0	1	0	1
1	1	1	1	0

The system/370 instructions contain four instructions for each of these functions (RX, RR, SS, and SI instruction types). These are summarized as follows:

b. OR (O, OR, OC, and OI) the two operands are ORed together and the result replaces the first operand. The bits of each operand are processed, bit by bit, with the resulting bit being set to zero only if both of the corresponding operand bits are zero. Else, the bit is set to one.

b. AND (N, NR, NC, and NI) the two operands are ANDed together and the result replaces the first operand. The bits of each operand are processed, bit by bit, with the resulting bit being set to one only if both corresponding bits of each operand are one. Else, the bit is set to zero.

c. EXCLUSIVE OR (X, XR, XC, and XI) the two operands are EXCLUSIVE ORed together and the result replaces the first operand. The bits of each operand are processed, bit by bit, with the resulting bit being set to zero only if the corresponding bits are the same. Else, the bit is set to one. An equivalent definition is as follows: If the second operand bit is zero the resulting bit in the first operand is unchanged and, if the corresponding bit in the second operand is one, then the resulting bit in the first operand is reversed.

```
         NC     A,=X'F0A5'        RESULT IS X'C005'

         OC     B,=2C'0'          RESULT IS X'F2F4'

         XC     C,=X'3CC3'        RESULT IS X'9966'

         ...

A        DC     X'CF5F'           1100 1111 0101 1111

B        DC     X'1234'           0001 0010 0011 0100

C        DC     X'A5A5'           1010 0101 1010 0101

D        DC     X'F0FC'           1111 0000 1111 1100

E        DC     X'1234'           0001 0010 0011 0100

F        DC     X'9876'           1001 1000 0111 0110
```

Mini Exercise

What is the result of:

```
         XC     D,D

         XC     E,F

         XC     F,E

         XC     E,F
```

Prove your answer for any values. Hint: The Boolean instructions operate on their operands bit by bit.

SHIFT INSTRUCTIONS

The shift instructions move bits either left or right. These operations modify either a single register or an even-odd pair of registers. There are two general types of shifting—logical and arithmetical. In the first case the operand consists of 32 or 64 bits without regard to sign. In the later case the operands are 31 or 63 signed bits in length and the sign bit remains unchanged. The instructions are:

a. SLA (Shift Left Arithmetical) and SLDA (Shift Left Double Arithmetical) shifts the low order 31 and 63 bits, respectively, of the operand to the left for the specified number of bits. Bits shifted out of bit position 1 are lost. Zero bits replace the bits shifted out of the low order bit position. The sign bit (bit position 0) does not participate in this operation.
b. SLL (Shift Left Logical) and SLDL (Shift Left Double Logical) shifts the 32 and 64 bits, respectively, of the operand to the left for the specified number of bits. Bits shifted out of bit position 0 are lost. Zero bits replace the bits shifted out of the low order bit position.
c. SRA (Shift Right Arithmetical) and SRDA (Shift Right Double Arithmetical) shifts the low order 31 and 63 bits, respectively, of the operand to the right for the specified number of bits. Bits shifted out of the low order are lost. The value of the sign bit replaces the bits shifted out of bit position 1. The sign bit is unchanged by this operation.
d. SRL (Shift Right Logical) and SRDL (Shift Right Double Logical) shifts the 32 and 64 bits, respectively, of the operand to the right for the specified number of bits. Bits shifted out of the low order bit are lost. Zero bits replace the bits shifted out of bit position 0.

The following example reverses the bits within 'WORD'.

```
         LA    1,32             BITS PER WORD
         XR    0,0              CLEAR REGISTER FOR RESULT
         XR    4,4              INITIALIZE SHIFT COUNT
         L     3,WORD           LOAD VALUE
LOOP     XR    2,2              CLEAR WORK REGISTER
         SLDL  2,1              MOVE HI BIT OF R3 TO LOW OF R2
         SLL   2,0(4)           MOVE BIT 'I' POSITIONS LEFT
         OR    0,2              ACCUMULATE BIT TO RESULT
         LA    4,1(4)           I <== I + 1
         BCT   1,LOOP           CONTINUE
```

BIT TESTING

The Test Under Mask (TM) instruction uses a bit mask (second operand) to select bits of the first operand. The condition code is set to zero if all selected bits are zeros or if no bits were selected, to one if selected bits are mixed (zeros and ones), and to three if all selected bits are ones.

1)

```
            TM      OPTIONS,UPDATE+ADD
            BZ      NEITHER
            BO      BOTH
            BM      ADD_OR_U
NEITHER     ...
            ...
BOTH        ...
            ...
ADD_OR_U    ...
            ...
OPTIONS     DS      X
READ        EQU     X'80'
WRITE       EQU     X'40'
UPDATE      EQU     X'20'
ADD         EQU     X'10'
BROWSE      EQU     X'08'
OPENED      EQU     X'04'
BLOCKED     EQU     X'02'
VARIABLE    EQU     X'01'
```

2)

```
            STC     1,WORKBYTE          STORE LOW ORDER BYTE FROM R1
            TM      WORKBYTE,1          IS VALUE ODD?
            BO      R1ISODD             YES
            ...
WORKBYTE    DS      X
```

9

Loops and Indexing

Most programs involve the utilization of loops, which are simply repetitive or iterative processes. These iterations can be based on counts (e.g., tables), records from an input file, significance of computations (e.g., calculation of Pi to some number of digits), etc. For most traditional data processing the loops will be of some finite duration. Industrial applications (e.g., process monitoring) can continue indefinitely.

For example the first assignment involved a single loop—reading data records until the end of data was found.

Because of its brevity of definition the mathematical factorial (n!) is often used as an example of loops.

$$n! = n \times (n - 1) \times (n - 2) \times \ldots \times 3 \times 2 \times 1$$

Also by defining $0! = 1$ we can restate the above definition as:

$$n! = (n - 1)! \times n \; \{n > 0\}$$

This later definition will not be used here. Such a technique is called a recursive definition which leads to a programming technique called recursive programming.

One example of such a computational loop is:

```
         ZAP   FCTRL,=P'1'       INITIALIZE FACTORIAL
LOOP     MP    FCTRL,N           COMPUTE PRODUCT
         SP    N,=P'1'           DECREMENT VALUE
         CP    N,=P'1'           FINISHED?
```

```
         BH    LOOP              NO
               ...
N        DC    P'10'
FCTRL    DS    PL16
```

There are special instructions that are designed to facilitate loop control. These are explained below.

BRANCH ON COUNT

The Branch on Count (BCT) and Branch on Count Register (BCTR) instructions decrement the contents of the first (register) operand by 1. If the result is not zero, control is transferred to the address specified by the second operand (base-displacement or register, respectively). If the result is zero no transfer is performed. Also in the RR-form of this instruction, if the second operand specifies register 0, no transfer is performed.

Now we can demonstrate another form of the above example. This example computes the binary value n! using binary integers.

```
         LA    0,10              LOAD VALUE OF N
         LA    3,1               INITIALIZE VALUE OF N!
LOOP     MR    2,0               MULTIPLY BY N
         BCT   0,LOOP            N=N-1
```

Note the Multiply Register (MR) instruction computes the 64 bit product of the values contained in two 32 bit registers. The first operand is the ***even-odd*** pair of registers whose low order 32 bits contain the multiplicand—the high order register is ignored. The second operand is the register that contains the multiplier.

BRANCH ON INDEX LOW OR EQUAL AND BRANCH ON INDEX HIGH

The Branch on Index Low or Equal (BXLE) instruction adds the contents of R_3 to the first operand (R_1). If R_3 is an even numbered register this result is compared to the contents of register $R_3 + 1$. If R_3 is odd the result is compared to the value within R_3. If the comparison is low or equal, control is transferred to the address specified by the second operand (base + displacement).

The Branch on Index High (BXH) instruction performs in a like manner except that the branch occurs when the comparison is high.

In most cases the BXLE will be more convenient. In almost all cases an even register for R_3 will be chosen. For example, to compute the binary sum of a table of full word integers beginning at the location indicated by label 'BEGIN' and ending with the label 'END':

```
         LM    3,5,=A(BEGIN,4,END)
         XR    0,0                  CLEAR ACCUMULATOR
LOOP     A     0,0(3)               ADD ENTRY FROM TABLE
         BXLE  3,4,LOOP             POINT TO NEXT ENTRY
         ...
BEGIN    DC    F'1,2,5,10,-100,1000'
         ...
END      DC    F'100'
```

INDEX REGISTERS

When processing single arrays (as in the above BXLE example) a single register is sufficient to specify the address of the elements. For multiple arrays the use of the RX-type instruction's index register operand is often convenient. Such an example would be to add the elements of an array 'A' to the corresponding elements of an array 'B' and store the result in an array 'C'.

```
         LA    0,(ENDA-A)/4     LOAD NUMBER OF ENTRIES
         XR    1,1              CLEAR INDEX REGISTER
LOOP     L     2,A(1)           LOAD ELEMENT FROM A
         A     2,B(1)           ADD CORRESPONDING B ELEMENT
         ST    2,C(1)           STORE AS ELEMENT OF C
         LA    1,4(1)           INCREMENT INDEX REGISTER
         BCT   0,LOOP           CONTINUE FOR ALL ELEMENTS
         ...
A        DC    F'1,2,10,100,10000'
         DC    F' ... '
ENDA     DC    F'7'
B        DC    F' ...
C        DC    F' ...
```

Although the above is perhaps somewhat more straightforward the following BXLE example is often possible.

```
         LM    15,1,=A(A,4,ENDA)
LOOP     L     2,0(15)          LOAD ELEMENT FROM A
         A     2,B-A(15)        ADD CORRESPONDING B ELEMENT
         ST    2,C-A(15)        STORE AS ELEMENT OF C
         BXLE  15,0,LOOP        CONTINUE FOR NEXT ELEMENT
```

This last case required the knowledge that A is located prior to B and C and that the values of B-A and C-A be less than 4096 bytes (maximum displacement). Also, this technique requires that these relative addresses be known at assembly time—i.e., not be external or dynamic values such as subroutine parameters.

BRANCH VECTORS

Subroutines often return values (return codes) that are multiple of four. This is to facilitate ***branch vectors.*** Branch vectors are simply a table of consecutive unconditional branch instructions implemented as follows, by use of index register 15:

```
         B     *+4(15)          BRANCH VECTOR
FIRSTERR B     NOERROR          R15=0
         B     ERROR4           R15=4
         B     ERROR8           R15=8
         ...
LASTERR  B     ERROR4N          R15=4*N
```

Of course this example assumes that the programmer is sure that the register contains a value that is a multiple of 4 and that this multiple is between 0 and N. If not, a validation procedure such as the following could be utilized.

```
N        EQU   (LASTERR-FIRSTERR)/4
         LTR   15,15            IS R15 POSITIVE?
         BL    OTHERERR         NO
         CH    15,=AL2(4*N)     VALUE TOO LARGE?
         BH    OTHERERR         YES
```

```
LA     0,3                 SET 2 LOW BITS TO ONES
NR     0,15                IS VALUE A MULTIPLE OF 4?
BNZ    OTHERERR            NO
```

Note that the Load And Test Register (LTR) instruction loads the register specified by the first operand with the contents of the register specified by the second operand. This instruction also sets the condition code based on the value of the signed binary integer loaded into R_1.

10

Byte Manipulation

The Translate (TR) instruction is a very powerful ***instruction that replaces bytes*** of storage with values specified by a conversion table. It can also be used to *scatter or gather* bytes within storage.

To simplify the subsequent definition of the TR instruction consider the following:

```
        LA    2,L'OP1          LOAD LENGTH OF OPERAND 1
        XR    1,1              CLEAR REGISTER
LOOP    IC    1,OP1(2)         INSERT ITH BYTE OF OPERAND 1
        IC    1,TABLE(2)       INSERT CORRESPONDING ENTRY ENTRY
        STC   1,OP1(2)         REPLACE OPERAND BYTE WITH TABLE BYTE
        BCT   2,LOOP           CONTINUE FOR ALL BYTES
        ...
OP1     DC    X'0507030205'
TABLE   DC    C'0123456789'
```

This program will first load the byte to be converted ($OP1_5$, $OP1_4$, $OP1_3$, $OP1_2$, and then $OP1_1$) into register 1. Using this value as an index into TABLE we load the equivalent value into register 1. That is, for decimal values 0 to 9, we load the EBCDIC characters 0 to 9. Then we replace the original value with its equivalent EBCDIC value. Note that for this logic to perform correctly TABLE must have as many values as the maximum value stored in any byte of OP1. At the completion of this program OP1 would contain C'57325'.

The translate instruction duplicates the above function with the exception that the translate instruction processes the bytes from left to right and that registers 1 and 2 are not modified.

The translate instruction is of SS-format, with a single length operand. The first operand defines the starting address of the bytes to be translated. The second operand defines the translation table. The 8-bit values of the first operand (argument) bytes are used to select the corresponding (function) bytes from the second operand. These function bytes replace the argument bytes.

For example to translate ASCII data to EBCDIC:

```
         TR    ASCII,EBCDIC
         ...
ASCII    DS    CL256
EBCDIC   DC    128AL1(*-EBCDIC)                          0,1,2,...,255
         ORG   EBCDIC+4
         DC    X'372D2E2F160525'
         ORG   EBCDIC+20
         DC    X'3C3D32261819312722'
         ORG   EBCDIC+32
         DC    C'."#$%&&''()*+,-.0123456789:;,=.?@'
         DC    C'ABCDEFGHIJKLMNOPQRSTUVWXYZ[\]',X'FF',C'_\'
         ORG   EBCDIC+X'61'
         DC    9AL1(*-EBCDIC+X'81'-X'61')     LOWER CASE A-I
         DC    9AL1(*-EBCDIC+X'91'-X'6A')     LOWER CASE J-R
         DC    8AL1(*-EBCDIC+X'A3'-X'73')     LOWER CASE S-Z
         DC    C'{',X'6A',C'}~',X'07'
         ORG
```

Let's consider what the above DC instructions generate. The operand 128AL1(*—EBCDIC) generates 128 one byte address constants. For the first such constant the location counter ('*') is equal to EBCDIC, the second EBCDIC + 1, the third EBCDIC + 2, and so on. Hence the value of the expressions are 0, 1, 2, and so on.

Also note that the double quote and ampersand characters, when included in a character constant, each generate a single character.

Now let us consider the more complex expression AL1(*—EDCDIC +

X'81'−X'61'). Note that we had immediately previously defined the location counter to EBCDIC + X'61', hence this expression generates the nine equivalent expressions X'81',X'82', ..., X'89'. By referring to the Code Assignments: Code Tables section of the *IBM System/370 Extended Architecture: Reference Summary* we can find that the ASCII values of 'a', 'b', ..., 'i' is 61_{16}, 62_{16}, ..., 69_{16} while the EBCDIC values are 81_{16}, 82_{16}, ..., 89_{16}, respectively, as follows:

```
Dec. | Hex.| EBCDIC   ASCII|      ...
 97  |  61 | /          a    |
 98  |  62 |            b    |
 ...
129  |  81 | a               |
130  |  82 | b               |
```

Similar usage of this table yields all the other relationships generated in the above translate table.

The translate instruction, along with a properly chosen set of argument bytes, can be used to rearrange bytes in storage. For example:

```
          MVC    MM#DD#YY,=X'0304000506000102'
          TR     MM#DD#YY,SLASH     YIELDS 12/31/88
          MVC    MMDDYY,=X'000103040607'
          TR     MMDDYY,MM#DD#YY   YIELDS 123188
          ...
SLASH     DC     C'/'
YYMMDD    DC     C'881231'
MM#DD#YY DS      CL8
MMDDYY    DS     CL6
```

INSERT AND STORE CHARACTER INSTRUCTIONS

The following instructions are used to move individual bytes between registers and storage. Unlike the load instructions that we have previously examined, the insert instructions do not modify the unreferenced bytes within the register operands.

a. The Insert Character (IC) instruction inserts the byte referenced by the second operand into the low order byte position of the first (register) operand.

b. The Store Character (STC) instruction stores the low order byte within the register identified by the first operand into the storage location referenced by the second operand.
c. The Insert Characters Under Mask (ICM) instruction inserts consecutive bytes of storage from the storage address defined by the second operand into the register designated by the first operand. The location, within the specified register, is identified by the mask operand. The four bits of the mask, left to right, correspond to the four bytes, left to right, of the register. If the corresponding bit is a one, the corresponding byte of the register is replaced with the byte from the consecutive storage location. For example, if the mask is 1001_2, the high and low order bytes of the register are replaced with the first and second bytes from the storage location. If all inserted bits are zero, the condition code is set to zero. If the left most bit is a one, the condition code is set to one. If the left bit is zero but other bits are nonzero, the condition code is set to two.
d. The Store Characters Under Mask (STCM) instruction store bytes from the register specified by the first operand into consecutive bytes of storage at the address specified by the second operand. These bytes are identified by the mask operand in the same manner as defined by the above ICM instruction.

The ICM and STCM instructions were added to the architecture after the System/360 design. In cases where indexing is not used they can replace the IC and STC instructions, respectively, by specifying a mask of 0001_2. Likewise, by specifying a mask of 1111_2, the load (L) can be simulated. There are two considerations that might influence such selections. First, by replacing the load instruction with the ICM, the assembler does not diagnose storage operands that are not full word aligned. The second reason is that the ICM sets the condition code—which can be either advantageous or disadvantageous.

COMPARE UNDER MASK

The Compare Logical Characters Under Mask (CLM) instructions compares bytes from the register specified by the first operand to consecutive bytes in the storage address specified by the second operand. The bytes are identified by the mask operand as explained for the ICM and STCM instructions.

The ICM, CLM, and STCM instructions will be demonstrated in the String Manipulation section.

11

Execute and Linkage Instructions

These two categories of instructions are not related. They are grouped together only because their discussion does not require sufficient verbiage to justify separate treatment.

THE EXECUTE INSTRUCTION

The Execute (EX) instruction performs the operation located at the storage address specified by the second operand (target instruction). If not zero, the first operand specifies a general purpose register whose contents (low order byte) is ORed with the second byte of the target instruction. If the target instruction is a linkage instruction (see below), the linkage address will be the address following the execute instruction.

For example if register five contains the number of characters to be moved, register six contains the current location of the data (source or sending field), and register seven contains the address of the location where the characters are desired (sink or receiving field); the following performs the desired function:

```
         EX    5,MOVE6TO7
         ...
MOVE6TO7 MVC   0(*-*,7),0(6)
```

While the length sub-field could be specified as '0' or null; the expression '*—*', the difference of the address counter from itself, is used to emphasize that this field will be overridden by the value contained in the register specified by the execute instruction. This usage is a matter of taste and is not as common in current usage as in previous times.

Note that the storage containing the actual instruction at MOVE6TO7 is not altered. The ORed length is processed by the CPU only.

LINKAGE INSTRUCTIONS

The linkage instructions are branch instructions that also save the current instruction address. This allows the program to branch to some common routine (subroutine) and return to resume processing at the instruction following the branch.

There are three basic types of linkage instructions. The last two of these instructions were introduced mainly for XA and mixed (bimodal) addressing modes. These last two types will be discussed more fully in the XA and Bimodal Programming Techniques section.

a. Branch And Link (BAL) and Branch And Link Register (BALR) instructions branch to the address specified by the second operand and saves the current instruction address in the register specified by the first operand. As previously discussed, in loading base address registers, the special form of the RR-form of this instruction that specifies a zero in the second operand does not branch. In the 24-bit addressing mode the information loaded into the first operand is the instruction length code (ILC), the condition code (CC), the program mask bits, and the 24-bit instruction address. In the 31-bit addressing mode this information is the second half of the PSW which is the sign bit (always '1' when in 31-bit addressing mode) and the 31-bit instruction address. In either case, for most applications, the prime concern is the instruction address which will be used to return to the next location, be used as a base address register, etc.
b. The Branch And Save (BAS) and Branch And Save Register (BASR) instructions perform the same basic functions as the BAL and BALR instructions, respectively. The only difference is that, in 24-bit addressing mode, the first 8 bits of the first operand register is loaded with zeros. That is, the register is loaded with the second half of the PSW in either 24-bit or 31-bit modes.
c. The Branch And Save And Set Mask (BASSM) is an RR-type instruction that is used to set the addressing mode as well as establish a linkage address. The details of this instruction, along with the companion Branch and Set Mask (BSM), will be discussed fully in the XA and Bimodal Addressing section.

The *System/370 Extended Architecture: Principles of Operation* recommends that the BAS instructions be used instead of the BAL instructions. This recommendation is based on execution timing and problems that loading the additional high order bits into the first operand may cause. However, note that the BAS instructions are not available in the older architecture machines.

An example of the usage of linkage instructions follows.

```
         BAL  11,HEADPAGE       PRINT FIRST PAGE HEADING
         ...
         BAL  11,PRINT          PRINT REPORT LINE
         ...
         MVI  LINE,C'0'         FORCE DOUBLE SPACE
         BAL  11,DOUBLESP       ALLOW FOR DOUBLE SPACE
         BAL  11,PRINT          PRINT LINE AFTER DOUBLE SPACE
         ...
PRINT    PUT  PRINTER,LINE      PRINT LINE
         MVI  LINE,C' '         SET TO SINGLE SPACE
         MVC  LINE+1(132),LINE  CLEAR LINE TO BLANKS
DOUBLESP BCTR 10,11             DECREMENT LINE COUNT, RETURN
         SPACE
HEADPAGE AP   PAGES,=P'1'       INCREMENT PAGE COUNT
         MVC  PAGENO,PTTRN3     SET EDIT PATTERN
         ED   PAGENO,PAGES      FORMAT PAGE COUNT
         PUT  PRINTER,HEADING1  PRINT 1ST LINE OF HEADING
         ...
         MVI  LINE,C'0'         SET TO DOUBLE SPACE
         LA   10,56             SET LINES/PAGE
         BR   11                RETURN
         SPACE
PAGES    DC   PL2'0'
PTTRN3   DC   X'40202120'
HEADING1 DC   CL133'1HEADER LINE 1'
         ORG  HEADING1+L'HEADING1/2-4
```

```
TODAY    DS    CL8
         ORG   HEADING1+L'HEADING1-8
         DC    C'PAGE'
PAGENO   DS    CL4
         ORG
```

Note that the final ORG does not actually change the value of the address counter because it is already positioned at the end of HEADING1. However, this ORG without operands instructs the assembler that the 'redefining' process is complete. Without this final ORG the assembly process could be confused if another such ORG appears—which might be in a macro and not apparent to the programmer. Hence it is ***highly recommended*** that such a practice be a habit.

Also note that the value of LINE + 1(L'LINE−1),LINE for the operand of the MVC instruction used to clear the line to blanks would be preferred. The above is used for typographical reasons only.

12

String Manipulation

The Translate And Test (TRT) machine Instruction examines a string of consecutive argument bytes (first operand). This examination is based on a table of function bytes (second operand). The TRT is an SS-type instruction with a single length specification. The argument bytes are used to access the function bytes in the same manner as used by the Translate (TR) instruction but the argument bytes are not altered by the TRT instruction. Each byte of the first operand is examined until a non-zero function byte is found or until the entire operation is exhausted.

If a non-zero function byte is found it replaces the low order byte of general register 2 and the address of the corresponding argument byte (within the first operand) replaces the low order bits (24 or 31) of general register 1.

If no non-zero function byte is found, general registers 1 and 2 are unchanged and the condition code is set to zero.

If a non-zero function byte is found prior to the last byte of the first operand, the condition code is set to one. If only the last byte of the first operand results in a non-zero function byte the condition code is set to two.

EXAMPLES

1) Test for numerics. Note the MVN (Move Numerics) instruction is used. This instruction moves only the four low order bits of each byte. The MVZ (Move Zones) is a similar instruction that moves only the four high order bits of each byte. In either case up to 256 bytes can be processed.

```
         TRT     NUMBER,TABLE          IS FIELD NUMERIC?
         BZ      NUMERIC                YES
         BC      4,NONMERIC             NO
```

```
         CLI      NUMBER+L'NUMBER-1,X'A0' VALID SIGN?
         BL       NONMERIC               NO
         MVN      LASTBYTE,NUMBER+L'NUMBER-1 MOVE NUMERIC PART
         TRT      LASTBYTE,TABLE         IS LAST DIGIT VALID ZONED DEC?
         BNZ      NONMERIC               NO
NUMERIC  ...
         ...
NONMERIC ...
         ...
NUMBER   DS       ZL6
TABLE    DC       256X'FF'
         ORG      TABLE
HEADING  DC       CL133'1PAGE HEADING'
LASTBYTE DC       C'0'
         ORG      TABLE+C'0'
         DC       10X'0'
         ORG
```

Note that 'LASTBYTE' and 'HEADING' are contained within 'TABLE'. Since the TRT only needs binary non-zero values within the non-numeric function bytes, this technique is commonly used to conserve memory requirements.

2) Let a unit of text be defined as a substring of consecutive characters that do not contain '+', '−', '*', '/' or blank characters. First scan for the first character of the unit and then scan for the last character of the unit. Set registers 6 to point to the beginning of the unit (beginning with a non-specified character), register 7 to length-1 of the unit, and register 8 to the unprocessed remainder of the input stream.

```
         XR       1,1                    CLEAR REGISTER
         MVC      TABLE,TABLE-1          SET TO NON-ZERO
         MVI      TABLE+C' ',0           SET BLANK POSITION TO ZERO
         MVI      TABLE+C'+',0             " FOR PLUS
         MVI      TABLE+C'-',0             " FOR MINUS
```

```
         MVI   TABLE+C'*',0           " FOR ASTERISK
         MVI   TABLE+C'/',0           " FOR SLASH
         TRT   INPUT,TABLE           ANY NON-SPECIFIED CHARACTERS?
         BZ    NOSTRING               NO
         LR    6,1                   LOAD ADDRESS OF FIRST NON-SPEC
         XC    TABLE,TABLE           SET TO ZEROS
         MVI   TABLE+C' ',C' '       SET BLANK POSITION TO NON-ZERO
         MVI   TABLE+C'+',C'+'        " FOR PLUS
         MVI   TABLE+C'-',C'-'        " FOR MINUS
         MVI   TABLE+C'*',C'*'        " FOR ASTERISK
         MVI   TABLE+C'/',C'/'        " FOR SLASH
         LA    8,INPUT+L'INPUT-1     POINT TO LAST BYTE OF INPUT
         LA    1,INPUT+L'INPUT       SET DEFAULT UNIT END
         SR    8,6                   COMPUTE REMAINING LENGTH - 1
         EX    8,TRT                 FIND NEXT BLANK
         BCTR  1,0                   POINT TO LAST NON-SPECIFIED CHAR
         LR    7,1                   INITIALIZE REG WITH ABOVE ADDR
         SR    7,6                   COMPUTE LENGTH - 1 OF UNIT
         SR    8,7                   COMPUTE LENGTH OF
         BCTR  8,0                   .. REMAINING TEXT
         ...
NOSTRING ...
         ...
TRT      TRT   0(*-*,6),TABLE
         DC    X'FF'                 MUST IMMEDIATELY PRECEDE TABLE
TABLE    DS    CL256
```

The last example can be applied for processing character segments of input parameters, parsing symbolic expressions, etc. For example, to right and left justify segments and to convert numerical segments to packed decimal:

```
          ZAP   PACKED,=P'0'          INITIALIZE FOR NON NUMERIC
          MVC   TABLE,TABLE-1         SET TO NON-ZEROS
          XC    TABLE+C'0'(10),TABLE+C'0' CLEAR EBCDIC POS 0-9
          EX    7,TRT                 NUMERIC?
          BNZ   NONMERIC               NO
          CH    7,=AL2(L'PACKED-1)    IS SEGMENT TOO LONG?
          BH    NONMERIC               YES
          EX    7,PACK                PACK INPUT STRING
NONMERIC  MVC   LEFT(L'LEFT+L'RIGHT),BLANK INITIALIZE TO BLANKS
          LA    1,L'LEFT-1            SET MAXIMUM SIZE
          CR    1,7                   IS 'LEFT' < OR = STRING LEN?
          BNH   LEFTLE                 YES
          LR    1,7                   USE ACTUAL LENGTH
LEFTLE    EX    1,MOVELEFT            MOVE STRING LEFT JUSTIFIED
          LA    2,RIGHT               POINT TO START OF 'RIGHT'
          LA    1,L'RIGHT-1           SET MAXIMUM SIZE
          CR    1,7                   IS 'RIGHT' < OR = STRING LEN?
          BNH   RIGHTLE                YES
          LR    1,7                   USE ACTUAL LENGTH
          LA    2,RIGHT+L'RIGHT-1     POINT TO END OF 'RIGHT'
          SR    2,7                   POINT TO MOVE ADDRESS
RIGHTLE   EX    1,MOVERGHT            MOVE STRING, RIGHT JUSTIFIED
          ...
PACK      PACK  PACKED,0(*-*,6)
MOVELEFT  MVC   LEFT(*-*),0(6)
MOVERGHT  MVC   0(*-*,2),0(6)
BLANK     DC    C' '
LEFT      DS    CL5
```

```
RIGHT     DS     CL25

PACKED    DS     PL5
```

The Move Long (MVCL) instruction provides an alternate method for right justification.

WILD-CARD PATTERN MATCHING

It is often desirable to check only certain characters within a character string for specific values. Thus, the term 'wild card' is used to indicate those characters whose values are of no concern to the comparison. A convenient way to do this is to use the Insert Character Under Mask (ICM). Store Character Under Mask (STCM), and Compare Logical Characters Under Mask (CLM) instructions. These instructions were introduced in the Byte Manipulation section. For example, to check the first, second, and fourth characters of a character string for 'A', 'B', and 'D', respectively:

```
         ICM   1,X'F',STRING         LOAD 4 BYTES

         CLM   1,B'1101',=C'ABD'     BYTE 1=A, 2=B, 4=D?

         BNE   NOTAB#D                NO

         ...

NOTAB#D  ...

         ...

STRING   DS    CL4
```

A more complex example is to examine a pattern that specifies those characters to be examined and then compare other fields against that pattern. The following implements this technique. When a position within the pattern contains an asterisk, that position is ignored, otherwise the corresponding positions must match.

```
* DECODE PATTERN

         XR    1,1                   CLEAR REGISTER

         LA    0,8                   SET PATTERN BYTE LENGTH

         LA    2,PATTERN             POINT TO PATTERN

MASKLOOP SLL   1,1                   SHIFT PREVIOUS MASK BIT

         CLI   0(2),C'*'             WILD CARD INDICATOR?

         BE    WILDCARD               YES
```

```
         LA     1,1(1)            INSERT MASK BIT
WILDCARD LA     2,1(2)            POINT TO NEXT PATTERN BYTE
         BCT    0,MASKLOOP        CONTINUE FOR ALL BYTES
         STC    1,MASK2           STORE MASK BITS
         PACK   MASK1,MASK2       MOVE HI 4 BITS TO LOW 4 BITS
         NC     MASK1(2),=2X'F'   REMOVE 4 HI BITS OF MASK1 & 2
         L      1,FIRST4          LOAD FIRST 4 CHARACTERS
         IC     2,MASK1           LOAD MASK BITS
         EX     2,STCM1           STORE NON WILD CARD BYTES
         L      1,SECOND4         LOAD LAST 4 CHARACTERS
         IC     2,MASK2           LOAD MASK BITS
         EX     2,STCM2           STORE NON WILD CARD BYTES
         ...
* COMPARE NON-WILD CARD CHARACTERS
         L      1,STRING          LOAD FIRST 4 BYTES
         IC     2,MASK1           LOAD MASK BITS
         EX     2,CLM1            MATCH?
         BNE    NOMATCH            NO
         L      1,STRING+4        LOAD LAST 4 BYTES
         IC     2,MASK2           LOAD MASK BITS
         EX     2,CLM2            MATCH?
         BNE    NOMATCH            NO
         ...
STCM1    STCM   1,*-*,FIRST4
STCM2    STCM   1,*-*,SECOND4
CLM1     CLM    1,*-*,FIRST4
CLM2     CLM    1,*-*,SECOND4
         DS     0F
PATTERN  DS     0CL8
```

```
FIRST4    DS    CL4
SECOND4   DS    CL4
STRING    DS    CL8
MASK1     DS    X
MASK2     DS    X
```

Of course similar programming could process strings of any length. It should be noted, however, that comparisons must be made in 'chunks' of no more than four characters at a time.

13

Subroutines

The term *subroutine* is used to denote programming segments that are external to the main path of the program flow. Subroutines are normally used to perform generalized functions but can also be used to implement modular programming, etc. Subroutines are often grouped into two categories: internal and external. Internal subroutines are routines that are contained within a single assembly, for example the PRINT. SINGLESP, and HEADPAGE routines from the Execute and Linkage Instructions section. External subroutines are assembled as separate and independent modules. The remainder of this section will provide implementation considerations for external subroutines.

EXTERNAL ADDRESS CONSTANTS

The V-type address constant specifies a symbolic address that will be resolved at linkage time. The default length of such constants is four. Caution: While the assembler will permit the specification of other lengths the MVS linkage editor is not capable of processing such values.

Example:

```
          L      1,AEXTFNCT                LOAD ADDRESS OF 'EXTFNCT'
          ...
AEXTFNCT DC      V(EXTFNCT)
```

THE ENTRY ASSEMBLER INSTRUCTION

The ENTRY assembler instruction is used to define one or more external symbols within the object module produced by the assembler. These external symbols are used to resolve the above external address constants. Any label contained in the START assembler instruction also generates an external symbol.

Example:

```
TRIG     START 0
         ENTRY SINE,COSINE,TANGENT
         ...
SINE     ...
         ...
COSINE   ...
         ...
TANGENT  ...
         ...
         END
```

STANDARD LINKAGE

To provide a compatible interface between calling programs and subroutines the following convention is observed by the calling program.

a. Register 13 contains the address of an eighteen word area, within the calling program, for saving register contents, etc.
b. Register 14 contains the return address.
c. Register 15 contains the entry address of the subroutine.
d. Register 1 contains the address of a vector of parameter addresses. If the vector is of variable length, the sign bit of the last address is set to '1' or another parameter indicates the number of parameters.

The subroutine maintains the integrity of general registers contents with the exception that register 15 can be altered to provide a return code.

For example:

```
LA    13,SAVEAREA          POINT TO REGISTER SAVE AREA
...
LA    1,PARMLIST           POINT TO PARAMETER VECTOR
L     15,=V(SUM)           LOAD ADDRESS OF SUBROUTINE
```

```
         BALR  14,15              LINK TO SUBROUTINE
         ...
SAVEAREA DS    18F
PARMLIST DC    A(A,B,C)
         ORG   *-4                OPTIONAL LAST PARM INDICATOR
         DC    X'80'              NOTE: FOR 24 BIT ADDRESSES ONLY
         ORG
         ...
A        DC    F'50'
         ...
B        DC    ZL4'-100'
         ...
C        DS    PL5
         ...
         END
SUM      START 0
         USING SUM,15
         SAVE  (14,12)            SAVE REGISTERS
         LM    2,4,0(1)           LOAD ADDRESSES OF PARAMETERS
         L     2,0(2)             LOAD FIRST PARAMETER
         PACK  DOUBLE,0(4,3)      PACK SECOND PARAMETER
         CVB   3,DOUBLE           CONVERT TO BINARY
         AR    2,3                SUM PARAMETERS 1 & 2
         CVD   2,DOUBLE           CONVERT TO DECIMAL
         ZAP   0(5,4),DOUBLE      MOVE RESULT TO THIRD PARAMETER
         RETURN (14,12),RC=0      RESTORE REGISTERS/RETURN
DOUBLE   DS    D
         END   SUM
```

Note the special form of the RETURN macro. The parameter 'RC=0' loads register 15 with zero to indicate a successful completion. Any non-negative decimal value, up to 4095, can be coded. Another form, 'RC=(15)', can be used to return the current contents of register 15. Caution: 'RC=(*R*15)' or other symbolic representation is invalid.

Also note that it was unnecessary, ***in this particular subroutine,*** to save register 13 and to provide a register save area. Normally, however, such a convention is provided to ensure that any system resources (such as I/O, etc.) do not implicitly require such a facility.

THE CALL MACRO

To reduce the tedium of the above linkage a special macro, CALL, is provided which performs the housekeeping functions of loading the linkage registers, establishing the parameter vector, and branching to the subroutine.

For example:

```
         LA     13,SAVEAREA
         ...
         CALL   SUM,(A,B,C)
```

The first operand of the CALL macro is the name of the subroutine. The second operand, if present, provides the subroutine parameter(s). If more than one parameter is present, the list must be enclosed in parentheses.

The CALL macro is sometimes used by preloading register 1 with the address of the parameter vector and omitting the second operand. This usage is discouraged because the particular implementation of the CALL macro might clear register 1 in such cases. When such requirements are encountered it is suggested that the CALL macro not be used.

THE DUMMY CONTROL SECTION

While not used exclusively for subroutines the Dummy Control Section (DSECT) is often used when multifield parameters are present. The DSECT allows for the layout of storage definitions without actually reserving memory space.

For example:

```
         ...
         CALL   SUM,(A)               C=A+B
         ...
A        DC     F'50'
```

```
B        DC    ZL4'-100'
C        DC    PL5
         ...
         END
SUM      START 0
         SAVE  (14,12)            SAVE REGISTERS
         USING SUM,15             ESTABLISH ADDRESSABILITY
         USING DUMMY,1             " TO PARAMETER FIELDS
         L     1,0(1)             LOAD ADDRESS OF PARAMETER
```

14

COPY Instruction and Macro Facility

The COPY assembler instruction is used to insert predefined sections of source statements into the program. Such sequences must have been cataloged into the appropriate library prior to the assembly of the program containing the COPY statement.

The COPY statement contains a single operand—the name of the member to be copied. For example:

```
COPY   PAYMAST                        PAYROLL MASTER RECORD LAYOUT
```

The statements copied can contain other COPY statements. Such nested COPYs can be continued to any level but must not be recursive.

While all relative addressing has been discouraged, it is more important to observe this practice when referencing items within COPY and macro definitions. The reason for this is that such external definitions may be altered without regard to the programming techniques of individual programs.

MACROS

The macro facility is also used to insert sequences of source statements into programs. These sequences may also be contained within special libraries but, additionally, may be defined within an individual program. The sequence of statements generated by macro usage may vary by operand specifications and other factors.

Macros can be nested and this usage can be recursive.

The macro definition begins with the MACRO statement and ends with the MEND (Macro END) statement. These statements are sometimes referred to as the macro definition header and trailer, respectively.

```
MACRO
. . .
```

... macro definition statements ...

```
. . .
MEND
```

The first statement within the macro definition is called the macro prototype definition statement. This statement contains the name of the macro. If present, an entry in the name field specifies a parameter that is ***normally*** used as a label for ***some*** statement that ***may*** be generated by the macro. The identifiers in the name and operand fields must begin with an ampersand and are called symbolic parameters. The ampersand must be followed by an alphabetic character and that character may be followed by up to 61 (Assembler H) alphameric characters. For example:

```
&LABEL    MACNM &PARM1,&PARM2,&PARM3
```

Ordinary assembler instructions within the macro are called model statements. Model statements may contain fields composed of normal symbols and operation codes, symbolic parameters, or both.

The macro instruction statement is used to expand a specific macro. For example:

```
NAMEX     MACNM A,B,C+D
```

To illustrate the above concepts the macro 'SUM' which is designed to compute the sum of the first and second operand and place the result in the third operand. If a name field is present it is to be specified as the name field of the first generated instruction.

```
          MACRO
&NAME     SUM    &A,&B,&C
&NAME     ZAP    &C,&A
          AP     &C,&B
          MEND
```

When used in a macro instruction the symbolic operands in the model statements are replaced by the operands of the macro instruction. Unless suppressed by the 'PRINT NOGEN' option, the generated instructions will be printed with a preceding plus sign.

```
   X         SUM   ALPHA,BETA,GAMMA
+  X         ZAP   GAMMA,ALPHA
+            AP    GAMMA,BETA
```

KEYWORDS OPERANDS

The above description provided a description of the simplest form of macro instruction. The operands in that form are called positional operands. Like the machine instructions, their sequence within the operand field determines their identity. In more complex macros there may be many operands and this complexity may be compounded by the fact that not all operands are required. To simplify such specifications, keyword operands are introduced. Within the prototype statement keyword operands are identified by a terminal equal sign. Both positional and keyword operands may be specified with the restriction that the positional operands be specified prior to the keyword operands. For example:

```
         MACRO
&NAME    SUM   &A,&B,&RESULT=
&NAME    ZAP   &RESULT,&A
         AP    &RESULT,&B
         MEND
         ...
         SUM   ALPHA,BETA,RESULT=GAMMA
+        ZAP   GAMMA,ALPHA
+        AP    GAMMA,BETA
```

Additionally, default values may be specified:

```
         MACRO
&NAME    SUM   &A,&B,&RESULT=SUM
&NAME    ZAP   &RESULT,&A
         AP    &RESULT,&B
         MEND
         ...
         SUM   ALPHA,BETA,RESULT=GAMMA
+        ZAP   GAMMA,ALPHA
+        AP    GAMMA,BETA
         SUM   Z,=P'10'
+        ZAP   SUM,Z
+        AP    SUM,=P'10'
```

CONDITIONAL ASSEMBLY INSTRUCTIONS

While not specifically for use within macros the conditional assembly instruction are often used as a powerful tool for constructing complex macros. Conditional assembly instructions implement a sublanguage that directs the preassembly process. This sublanguage consists of:

a. Sequence symbols. These are special symbols that begin with a period and followed by an alphabetical character. Up to 61 additional alphanumeric characters may follow the first alphabetical character. These symbols are used as labels for conditional assembly branch instructions.

b. SET Symbols which define data during the preassembly process.
c. Attributes that are defined by the characteristics of data and macro operands.
d. Conditional assembly instructions. These instructions define SET symbols, assign values, and direct the flow of generated source statements.

ATTRIBUTES

Attributes of ordinary or variable symbols are specified by an identifier, a single quote mark, and the symbol (e.g., L'ALPHA). Available attributes are:

a. Defined (D'). The value of this attribute is one if the specified symbol has been previously defined. Else the value is zero.
b. Length (L'). The number of bytes of storage that a single replication of the data requires.
c. Scale (S'). The position of the decimal point within a decimal, fixed-point, or floating-point constant.
d. Integer (I'). A function of the length and scale attributes. This is an indication of the number of digits within the integer portion of the data. Specific formulae are defined for different data types.
e. Count (K'). Specifies the number of characters that are contained in macro operands or required to represent the character string of a SET or system variable symbol.
f. Number (N'). The number of suboperand entries in a macro operand sublist.
g. Type (T'). A character value that defines the data representation:

    1. C, X, B, F, H, E, D, L, P, Z, A, Y, S, V, and Q—see 'Summary of Constants' in Appendix A or IBM 370/Extended Architecture: Reference Summary.
    2. K—Floating-point constant with explicit length.
    3. R—An A-, S-, Q-, V-, or Y-type address constant with explicit length.
    4. @—Graphic (G) constant.
    5. I—Machine instruction.
    6. J—Control section (CSECT) name.
    7. M—Macro instruction.
    8. T—External symbol defined by an EXTRN instruction.
    9. $—External symbol defined by a WXTRN instruction.
    10. W—Channel Command Word (CCW, CCW0, or CCW1) instruction.
    11. N—Self-defining term or the value of a SETA or SETB variable symbol.
    12. O—Omitted macro operand.
    13. U—Undefined (i.e., none of the above).

SET SYMBOLS

SET symbols are variable symbols that can provide values at preassembly time. These values can be specified as constants, functions of expressions of attributes, etc. There are three types of SET symbols.

a. Arithmetic (SETA) can contain any signed 32-bit value.
b. Binary or Boolean (SETB) can contain the values '0' (false) or '1' (true).
c. Character (SETC) can contain a string of from 0 (null) to 255 characters.

SET symbols can have either local or global scope. When SET symbols are defined to have local scope they may be used in statements that are part of the same macro or open code. When the declaration is global their usage may also be in different macros. In either case the symbols must be declared in each part of the program in which they are used. For an example of global usage, see Example 'b' at the end of this section.

Declaration of SET symbols is by specifying the symbols as the operands in the following assembler instructions:

a. LCLA, LCLB, and LCLC instructions declare local SETA, SETB, and SETC symbols, respectively.
b. GBLA, GBLB, and GBLC instructions declare local SETA, SETB, and SETC symbols, respectively.

```
        GBLA   &GLOBALA,&I,&J
        LCLC   &X,&Y,&A
```

The initial values of SETA and SETB symbols are zero and SETC symbols are initialized to the null character string. Values are modified by the SETA, SETB, and SETC assembler instructions. The name field contains the variable symbol and the operand field contains a value or expression that is used as the assigned value. The allowed operands are:

a. The SETA instruction—an expression of one or more arithmetic terms, self-defining terms, or attributable references (L',S',I',K', or N' only). Expressions may contain '+' (addition), '—' (subtraction), '*' (multiplication), and '/' (division) operators—including both infix and unary plus and minus signs. Parentheses may be used. The expression must not contain blanks. If SETC symbols and &SYSPARM references are used, their values must be an unsigned self-defining term between zero and $2^{31}-1$. The value of the expression must be between -2^{31} and $2^{31}-1$.

```
&A          SETA  -100
&B          SETA  &A+10*((L'&X+10*K'&Y)/100)
```

b. For SETB instructions three distinct forms are allowed.

   a. A binary value ('0' or '1').
   2. A binary expression (see SETA) enclosed in parentheses. If the value is zero, the symbol is assigned the value '0'. Else, the symbol is assigned the value '1'.
   3. A logical expression enclosed in parentheses. If the expression is true the symbol is assigned the value '1'. Else, the value '0' is assigned. A logical expression can be either a logical term, an expression containing logical terms and/or logical expressions connected by the logical operators (OR, AND, OR NOT, and AND NOT), or comparands connected by relational operators. Relational operators are EQ (equal), NE (not equal), LE (less than or equal), LT (less than), GE (greater than or equal), GT (greater than). The comparands must be either both arithmetic or both character. All relational and logical operands must be proceeded and followed by at least one special character or blank.

```
&XB      SETB  0
&YB      SETB  (1+&A+L'&X)
&ZB      SETB  (&ZB AND (&A EQ 12) AND NOT &YB AND (T'&C EQ 'H'))
```

c. For SETC instructions four distinct forms are allowed. A duplication factor, enclosed in parentheses, may proceed the first three forms and may proceed each of the parts of the last form. The duplication factor may be any SETA expression.

   1. A type attribute (T').
   2. A character expression enclosed in single quote marks.
   3. A substring notation which is a character expression followed by two arithmetic expressions enclosed in parentheses and separated by a comma. The first expression designates the starting position within the character expression and the second arithmetic expression specifies the length of the substring.
   4. A concatenation of two or more character expressions and/or substring notations. When two quoted strings are concatenated together they must be separated by a period (the concatenation symbol).

```
&A       SETC  T'&X
&B       SETC  (3)'ABCD'                 ABCDABCDABCD
&C       SETC  '&B'(3,4)                 CDAB
&D       SETC  (2)&B(2,3).(3)'ABC'       DABDABABCABCABC
```

Provided a dimension had been specified in their declaration. SET symbols may be subscripted. Up to 5 subscript levels may be specified. Subscripts may be any arithmetic expression which results in a positive value and does not exceed the values of the corresponding dimension declaration. Subscripts are enclosed in parentheses and separated by commas.

```
            LCLA  &A(5,10),&I
            ...
&A(1,1)     SETA  1
&A(&I,3)    SETA  &I+&A(&I,2)
```

BRANCHING INSTRUCTIONS

These assembler branching instructions should not be confused with the branch machine instructions and extended mnemonic branch instructions. At preassembly time the conditional assembly branch instructions may ***bypass*** or ***repeat*** source statements depending on whether the branch location is below or above the branch instruction, respectively. Bypassed instructions are not assembled and repeated instructions are assembled multiple times. There are four conditional assembly branch instructions:

a. The AIF instruction is used for conditional branching. It can contain a sequence symbol ('.axxxx') in its name field. The operand field consists of a logical expression enclosed in parentheses and followed immediately (without intervening comma or blank) by a sequence symbol. If the logical expression is true the assembler branches to the source statement that contains the specified sequence symbol in its name field. If the expression is false no branch occurs.

```
.ONE      AIF   ('&ABC' NE 'XYZ').NOTXYZ
          ...
.NOTXYZ   ...
```

b. The AGO instruction performs an unconditional branch. It can contain a sequence symbol in its name field and its operand field contains a sequence symbol. The assembler branches to the source statement that contains the designated sequence field in its name field.

   An alternate form is the computed AGO instruction which branches to a source location depending on the value of an arithmetic expression and a list of sequence symbols. Its first operand consists of an arithmetic expression (SETA format) enclosed in parentheses and followed immediately by a sequence symbol. Additional operands, consisting of sequence symbols, may follow this operand. The arithmetic expression is evaluated and if its value (i) is between 1 and n (where n is the number of operands), the assembler branches to the sequence symbol identified by the ith operand. If the value is outside that range, no branch occurs.

```
AGO   .XYZ
...
```

```
AGO   (&I).ONE,.TWO,.THREE,.FOUR
```

c. The ANOP instruction is used to provide a reference point for AIF and AGO instructions. Its name field must contain a sequence symbol.

```
.NOTXYZ  ANOP
```

d. The ACTR instruction is used to specify a limit to the number of conditional branches. This protects against excessive (e.g., infinite) conditional assembly loops. Its name field may contain a sequence symbol and its operand consists of an arithmetic (SETA) expression.

```
ACTR  100
```

If no ACTR is present a default value (4096 for Assembler H) is provided.

Multiple ACTR instructions may be used to set the value for specific areas of source statements. The scope of this instruction is local; that is, a specific loop counter is assigned for open code and separate counters are assigned for each macro usage.

SUBLISTS AND &SYSLIST

Instead of using specific positional operand identifiers, from within the prototype statement, to reference the operands of a macro instruction the generic &SYSLIST operand is provided. The form &SYSLIST (x), where x is a SETA arithmetic expression, references the xth positional operand.

Sublists are operands that consist of multiple expressions, separated by commas and enclosed by parentheses. Sublist operands may also contain sublists.

```
MACK  A,(B,C),(D,(E,F,G,H))
```

Sublist operands may be referenced by multisubscripted &SYSLIST specifications. For example, &SYSLIST(3,2,4), provides the symbol 'H' in the above MACK macro instruction.

If the value of the expression x is zero, the &SYSLIST(x) specifies the name field entry of the macro instruction unless the name field contains a sequence symbol.

If &SYSLIST(n) refers to an omitted operand, or past the number of operands provided by the macro instruction, the null character string is substituted.

The normal attributes of &SYSLIST provide the equivalent attribute of the positional operand with the exception of the number (N'). The value of N'&SYSLIST is the number of operands specified in the macro instruction.

The term N'&SYSLIST(...) is the number of sublist entries for the particular operand.

```
         MACRO
 &NAME   MSUM   &A,&B,&C
         LCLA   &I
         AIF    (T'&NAME EQ 'O').LOOP
 &NAME   DS     OH
 .LOOP   AIF    (&I GE N'&B).END
 &I      SETA   &I+1
         ZAP    &SYSLIST(3,&I),&A
         AP     &SYSLIST(3,&I),&SYSLIST(2,&I)
         AGO    .LOOP
         MEND
         ...
 SUM     MSUM   ALPHA,(B1,B2,B3),(C1,C2,C3)
+SUM     DS     OH
+        ZAP    C1,ALPHA
+        AP     C1,B1
+        ZAP    C2,ALPHA
+        AP     C2,B2
+        ZAP    C3,ALPHA
+        AP     C3,B3
```

MEXIT AND MNOTE

The MEXIT (Macro EXIT) assembler instruction is used to exit from any point within a macro. It is equivalent to the MEND instruction except that the latter must appear as the last instruction within a macro definition. The MEXIT instruction may only be issued within a macro definition. It may contain a sequence symbol in its name field.

The MNOTE (Macro NOTE) assembler instruction is used to issue messages at assembly time. The MNOTE statement may be issued in open code as well as within macros. An MNOTE statement may contain a sequence symbol within its name field and must contain one or two operands. If only one operand is present, or if the first operand is an asterisk, the statement is used only to generate a message. Else, the first operand provides an assembler severity error level. For a null first operand (operand field beginning with a comma), a value of '1' is assumed. In all cases the last operand is a quoted character string.

```
        MACRO
&NAME   MSUM  &A,&B,&C
        LCLA  &I
        AIF   (N'&SYSLIST(2) EQ N'&SYSLIST(3)).OKAY
        MNOTE 2,'UNBALANCED NUMBER OF SUBARGUMENTS'
        MEXIT
.OKAY   AIF   (T'&NAME EQ 'O').LOOP
&NAME   DS    OH
```

```
.LOOP     AIF    (&I GE N'&B).END
&I        SETA   &I+1
          ZAP    &SYSLIST(3,&I),&A
          AP     &SYSLIST(3,&I),&SYSLIST(2,&I)
          AGO    .LOOP
          MEND
          ...
SUM       MSUM   ALPHA,(B1,B2B3),(C1,C2,C3)
+ 2,'UNBALANCED NUMBER OF SUBARGUMENTS'
```

MACRO EXAMPLES

a. To expand the date of the assembly into a textual representation. For the purposes of this example, a date of 10/02/88 is assumed.

```
          MACRO
&NAME     EXPDT &CENTURY=19
          LCLC  &M(12),&X,&Y,&Z
&M(1)     SETC  'JANUARY'
&M(2)     SETC  'FEBRUARY'
&M(3)     SETC  'MARCH'
&M(4)     SETC  'APRIL'
&M(5)     SETC  'MAY'
&M(6)     SETC  'JUNE'
&M(7)     SETC  'JULY'
&M(8)     SETC  'AUGUST'
&M(9)     SETC  'SEPTEMBER'
&M(10)    SETC  'OCTOBER'
&M(11)    SETC  'NOVEMBER'
&M(12)    SETC  'DECEMBER'
&X        SETC  '&SYSDATE'(1,2)
&Y        SETC  '&SYSDATE'(4,2)
&Z        SETC  '&SYSDATE'(7,2)
          AIF   ('&Y'(1,1) NE '0').AFTER9
&Y        SETC  '&Y'(2,1)
.AFTER9   ANOP
&NAME     DC    C'&M(&X) &Y, &CENTURY&Z'
          MEND
          ...
TODAY     EXPDT
+ TODAY   DC    C'OCTOBER 2, 1988'
          EXPDT CENTURY=20
+         DC    C'OCTOBER 2, 2088'
```

b. This macro generates instructions to compute the factorial value (n!). Note that it uses the recursive feature of macros. Also note the usage of the global SET symbol (&FIRST).

```
          MACRO
&NAME     NFACT &N,&NFACT
```

```
          GBLB  &FIRST
          LCLA  &X
          AIF   (&FIRST).NOT1ST
&FIRST    SETB  1
&NAME     ZAP   &NFACT,=P'1'
.NOT1ST   AIF   (&N LE 1).END
          MP    &NFACT,=P'&N'
&X        SETA  &N-1
          NFACT &X,&NFACT
          MEXIT
.END      ANOP
&FIRST    SETB  0
          MEND
          ...
NFACT     NFACT 5,DOUBLE
+ NFACT   ZAP   DOUBLE,=P'1'
+         MP    DOUBLE,=P'5'
+         MP    DOUBLE,=P'4'
+         MP    DOUBLE,=P'3'
+         MP    DOUBLE,=P'2'
```

c. This macro moves the contents of the field specified by the first operand to the field specified by the second operand. The instructions generated are based on the field types. Note that the order of the operands are not the same as most machine instructions—to retain the machine instruction convention it would be necessary to reverse the two positional operands in the macro prototype instruction and it would be desirable to modify the comments within the macro. Also note comments within a macro, that are not intended to print upon macro expansion, begin with '•★'. The instructions generated are summarized in the decision table within the comments.

More complex examples that provide arithmetical operations are common but the casual usage of such facilities can generate inefficient programs and is discouraged. That is, the data types are transparent to the programmer and this often results in the same disregard for design and programming practices that are found in many 'high level' language programs.

```
          MACRO
&NAME     MOVE  &A,&B,&D=DOUBLE,&R=0
.* THIS MACRO MOVES THE CONTENTS OF THE FIRST OPERAND TO THE SECOND
.* OPERAND.  THE KEYWORD '&D' IS USED TO SPECIFY A DOUBLE WORD WORK
.* AREA AND '&R' IS USED TO SPECIFY A WORK REGISTER.  THE DATA TYPES
.* OF THE FIRST TWO OPERANDS ARE EXAMINED TO GENERATE THE PROPER
.* INSTRUCTIONS BASED ON THE DECISION TABLE GIVEN BELOW.  DATA TYPES
.* ARE RESTRICTED TO FULL WORDS, HALF WORDS, ZONED DECIMAL, AND PACKED
.* DECIMAL.
.*
.*
```

```
.* T'&A| T'&B='F'      | T'&B='H'      | T'&B='Z'      | T'&B='P'      |
.*-----+---------------+---------------+---------------+---------------|
.* 'F' | MVC   &B,&A   | MVC   &B,&A+2 | L     &R,&A   | L       $R,&A |
.*     |               |               | CVD   &R,&D   | CVD     &R,&D |
.*     |               |               | UNPK  &B,&D   | ZAP     &B,&D |
.*-----+---------------+---------------+---------------+---------------|
.* 'H' | LH    &R,&A   | MVC   &B,&A   | LH    &R,&A   | LH      &R,&A |
.*     | ST    &R,&B   |               | CVD   &R,&D   | CVD     &R,&D |
.*     |               |               | UNPK  &B,&D   | ZAP     &B,&D |
.*-----+---------------+---------------+---------------+---------------|
.* 'Z' | PACK  &D,&A   | PACK  &D,&A   | PACK  &D,&A   | PACK &B,&A    |
.*     | CVB   &R,&D   | PACK  &R,&D   | UNPK  &B,&D   |               |
.*     | ST    &R,&B   | STH   &R,&B   |               |               |
.*-----+---------------+---------------+---------------+---------------|
.* 'P' | ZAP   &D,&A   | ZAP     &D,&A | UNPK  &B,&A   | ZAP  &B,&A    |
.*     | CVB   &R,&D   | PACK  &R,&D   |               |               |
.*     | ST    &R,&B   | STH   &R,&B   |               |               |
.*-----+---------------+---------------+---------------+---------------|
.*
         LCLC  &OP1,&OP2
         AIF   (T'&A NE 'F').ANOTF
         AIF   (T'&B EQ 'F').FF
         AIF   (T'&B EQ 'H').FH
&OP1     SETC  'L'
&OP2     SETC  'UNPK'
         AIF   (T'&B EQ 'Z').FZP
&OP2     SETC  'ZAP'
         AIF   (T'&B EQ 'P').FZP
.ERROR   MNOTE 2,'INVALID DATA TYPE'
         MEXIT
.FF      ANOP
&NAME    MVC   &B,&A
         MEXIT
.FH      ANOP
&NAME    MVC   &B,&A+2
         MEXIT
.FZP     ANOP
&NAME    &OP1  &R,&A
         CVD   &R,&D
         &OP2  &B,&D
         MEXIT
.ANOTF   AIF   (T'&A NE 'H').ANOTH
         AIF   (T'&B EQ 'F').HF
         AIF   (T'&B EQ 'H').FF
&OP1     SETC  'LH'
&OP2     SETC  'UNPK'
         AIF   (T'&B EQ 'Z').FZP
&OP2     SETC  'ZAP'
         AIF   (T'&B EQ 'P').FZP
         AGO   .ERROR
.HF      ANOP
&NAME    LH    &R,&A
```

```
         ST    &R,&B
         MEXIT
.ANOTH   AIF   (T'&A NE 'Z').ANOTZ
&OP1     SETC  'PACK'
&OP2     SETC  'ST'
         AIF   (T'&B EQ 'F').ZFH
&OP2     SETC  'STH'
         AIF   (T'&B EQ 'H').ZFH
         AIF   (T'&B EQ 'Z').ZZ
         AIF   (T'&B EQ 'P').ZP
         AGO   .ERROR
.ZFH     ANOP
&NAME    &OP1  &D,&A
         CVB   &R,&D
         &OP2  &R,&B
         MEXIT
.ZZ      ANOP
&NAME    PACK  &D,&A
         UNPK  &B,&D
         MEXIT
.ZP      ANOP
&NAME    PACK  &B,&A
         MEXIT
.ANOTZ   AIF   (T'&A NE 'P').ERROR
&OP1     SETC  'PACK'
&OP2     SETC  'ST'
         AIF   (T'&B EQ 'F').ZFH
&OP2     SETC  'STH'
         AIF   (T'&B EQ 'H').ZFH
         AIF   (T'&B EQ 'Z').PZ
         AIF   (T'&B NE 'P').ERROR
&NAME    ZAP   &B,&A
         MEXIT
.PZ      UNPK  &B,&A
         MEND
         ...
         MOVE  FULL,HALF
+        MVC   HALF,FULL+2
         MOVE  HALF,PACKED
+        LH    0,HALF
+        CVD   0,DOUBLE
+        ZAP   PACKED,DOUBLE
         MOVE  ZONED,FULL
+        PACK  DOUBLE,ZONED
+        CVB   0,DOUBLE
+        ST    0,FULL
         MOVE  PACKED,ZONED
+        UNPK  ZONED,PACKED
         ..
FULL     DS    F
HALF     DS    H.
PACKED   DS    PL5
```

```
ZONED    DS    ZL8
         AIF   (D'DOUBLE EQ 1).END
DOUBLE   DS    D
.END     END
```

MACRO HELP FACILITY

Because of the complexity of the above options it is sometimes difficult to find errors created by improper macro specifications or usages. The Macro Help (MHELP) instruction provides various traces and dumps of the expansion process of the assembler. This assembler instruction has a single arithmetic (SETA) operand that specifies the desired option(s). These arguments and their corresponding actions are listed below.

a. When the value of the operand is "1" a trace of all macro calls is provided.
b. When the value of the operand is "2" a trace of all assembler branch instructions is provided. This includes all AGO statements and those AIF statements that result in branches.
c. When the value of the operand is "4" a trace of all AIF usage is provided.
d. When the value of the operand is "8" a dump of values at macro exits (MEXIT and MEND statements) is provided.
e. When the value of the operand is "16" a dump of values at macro entries is provided.
f. When the value of the operand is "64" a hexadecimal and EBCDIC dump of all variable symbols is provided if either the AIF, exit, or entry trace(s) are specified. Only the EBCDIC values of system variables are provided.

The above values may be added together to specify multiple HELP options. In the following examples the operand is specified in binary to better distinguish the above options.

```
MHELP B'1'                MACRO CALL TRACE
MHELP B'10'               MACRO BRANCH TRACE
MHELP B'100'              MACRO AIF TRACE
MHELP B'1000'             MACRO EXIT TRACE
MHELP B'10000'            MACRO ENTRY TRACE
MHELP B'1000100'          MACRO HEX DUMP W/ AIF TRACE
MHELP B'1001000'          MACRO HEX DUMP W/ EXIT TRACE
MHELP B'1010000'          MACRO HEX DUMP W/ ENTRY TRACE
MHELP B'1011111'          ALL MACRO TRACE & DUMP OPTIONS
```

For detailed examples of the above debugging options, see Appendix D.

15

Dump Analysis—CICS Applications

The analysis of CICS transaction dumps is quite similar to the analysis of batch dumps. The main difference is that many components of CICS, that are unrelated to the failing transaction, resides in the specific address space. In the typical batch application all components are related to that application. While the transaction dump is primarily limited to those components of the failing transaction, the order and format of the listing is necessarily somewhat different from the batch environment. One major difference is that the actual memory addresses appear on the right column—the left column is an address that is relative to the beginning of the particular storage area.

Because of the above differences it will probably help to have some basic understanding of the major structure of the CICS environment.

a. The Common System Area (CSA) is a collection of address pointers, system values, etc. that provide a common reference for all of the CICS system modules.
b. The Task Control Area (TCA) is created at the initiation of each task (transaction). The TCA contains information similar to the CSA but is related to the particular task. The TCA can have four major components.

    1. System Area.
    2. User Area.
    3. Transaction Work Area (TWA).
    4. Last in, first out (LIFO) stack.

c. Trace Table. Contains an entry for each CICS system request.
d. Transaction Storage Areas. These are areas of storage that are dynam-

ically obtained and deleted by, or for, the transaction. For example, for storage of data records, registers, etc.

e. Terminal Storage is simply a special form of transaction storage.
f. Program Storage is the storage obtained in CICS to contain programs.

Now let us consider the parts of the dump that will be used for problem determination.

a. CODE = xxxx, indicates a four character code, printed at the top of each page, that identifies the reason for the dump. These dumps may be issued by CICS, by the application, or perhaps by a subsystem component.
b. TASK = xxxx, provides the transaction identifier of the task. This datum also appears in the page headings.
c. PSW, at the top of the first page.
d. Registers. *Be careful*—for CODE = ASRA and CODE = ASRB the register contents displayed at the top of the first page are not the values of the register contents at the time of the abort. The proper values are listed as 'REGS 0 THRU 15' which normally appears immediately before the dump of the CSA—generally on page 2 or 3.
e. The TCA. the user area is the first storage area dumped. This is followed, within the same area, by the TWA (at relative location 100_{16}, if present) and the LIFO stack.
f. The task number (a packed decimal value, sequentially assigned to each task) is contained in bytes $11_{16}-13_{16}$ of the TCA systems area.
g. The CSA is rarely needed for problem determination of a transaction dump.
h. The trace table follows the CSA and provides an entry for each CICS resource request. The complete trace appears; that is, for all transactions. Normally the task number of the entries are examined to determine if the entry is related to the particular transaction.
i. Transaction storage areas owned by the transaction at the time of the failure.
k. Program storage area(s). If more than one program module is present (via LINKs), the storage areas are normally in reverse order of acquisition sequence (i.e., the currently executing program normally appears fist). This is sometimes not necessarily the case if programs are used recursively or when program control is not processed by normal CICS requests.

SAMPLE CASE

The following description uses the sample CICS dump provided in Appendix E. This sample consists of selected pages from an 'ASRA' dump. In the 'ASRA' dump, as in the batch environment, a good place to start is with the failing instruction. Again, the PSW is used to obtain the address of that instruction.

From page 1 (of the sample dump):

```
PSW                    078D1000    003BF0C0    00060007    00000000
```

The second word of the PSW, as we have previously learned, contains the instruction address ($3BF0C0_{16}$). The following word (not really part of the PSW) contains the instruction length (6) in its first half and the program interrupt code (7) in its second half. From Appendix A, page 1, we can determine that a program interrupt code of 7 results from a data exception.

Now go to page 35 of the sample dump and locate the six byte instruction at location $3BF0BA_{16}$ (3BF0C0 − 6).

```
000020A0   F0125810 ... F274D208  E131F922 D20DC4D0 58F0C2C8 ...   003BF0A8
```

By examining the operation code ($F9_{16}$) it is determined that the instruction is a COMPARE PACKED and we can write it as:

```
CP     20D16(3,13),4D016(3,12)
```

Using the relative location (left hand column) we can determine that this instruction is at relative location $20B2_{16}$ and by the 'SYMPTOMS = ' line of page 1 we find that the failing program is KA255OC.

From page 2 we find the contents of the general registers:

```
      REGS  0 THRU 15          ADDRESS 0068FC70 TO 0068FCAF     LENGTH 000040

00000000   003BFD86 003BF064 003BF0B0 00000005  0027E0E3 503C047C 003BD0A8 ...

00000020   003BD448 003C0432 003BD008 003BD008  003BD5A0 0027D870 001B280C ...
```

We note that registers 12 and 13 contained $3BD5A0_{16}$ and $27D870_{16}$ respectively. Hence the absolute addresses of the operands of the above instruction is $27DA7D_{16}$ (27D870 + 20D) and $3BDA70_{16}$ (3BD5A0 + 4D0), respectively.

From page 24, the first operand is found at relative location $21D_{16}$ of the first 'TRANSACTION STORAGE -USER' area and that its value is "$C9699F_{16}$" which is clearly not a valid packed decimal value. From page 31, the second operand may be found at relative location $A68_{16}$ of 'PROGRAM STORAGE' and its value is '$79697C_{16}$—a valid packed number.

The cause of the abort is now apparent. We must now establish the source of the invalid value. One possible approach is to obtain a listing from the compiled program and examine the statement that generates the instruction at relative location $20B2_{16}$. However, by a deduction, we may expect that—because of the format of the invalid data—that it was obtained by packing a partially invalid value which ended with the characters '699'. Since the most common occurrence of such invalid data is from terminal input we examine the terminal input area. The dump of this area is on page 30 and is identified as 'TERMINAL STORAGE'. As you will see there are two terminal input/output areas. One contains the input from the terminal and the other is probably an area that was obtained as an output area. By examining the input area the expected characters are found at relative location 90_{16}. The contents of that location are C'*9699' = X'5CF9F6F9F9' which, when packed, becomes $C9699F_{16}$—the value that caused the abend. As will be explained in the IBM 3270 Data Streams section the three bytes preceding this value ($11D4D2_{16}$) specifies the buffer address (i.e., the location on the terminals screen) of the input field. This location can be determined to be row 17, column 19. With this information, it is expected that the operator keyed in this value and the program did not validate the format of the data.

Thus, without any knowledge of the failing program, the transaction dump was used to determine the cause of the failure. In some cases problem determination is not as direct. In such cases it might be necessary to refer to the program source. Another approach is to analyze the trace table.

TRACE TABLE ANALYSIS

The trace table provides a trail of all CICS requests and responses. Because it does not exclude entries from other transactions it is necessary to select only those that are the result of the failing transaction—although some very rare instances, the other entries may also be relevant. The entire trace table is printed, which—depending on the time used by the particular transaction—may provide excessive or insufficient data. The size of the trace is fixed by the amount of main storage that was defined at system initiation.

The trace table is an array, in main memory, of 32 byte entries. The entries are added until the end of the table is reached and then the entries "wrap around" to the top of the table and overlay the oldest entry. The first line of the trace table data provides the memory addresses for the current entry, first entry, and last entry, respectively, of the trace table. For a formatted dump, such as a transaction dump, these values are of little interest.

The following description summaries the parts of each trace table entry and relates those to the formatted, or interpreted, entries.

a. The Trace ID is the first byte (byte 0) of the entry. It is a code that indicates the type of entry. See column ID of the formatted trace.
b. The first 8 bits of the type of request is stored in the second byte (byte 1) and the last 4 bits are stored in the first 4 bits of the third byte (byte 2, bits 0–3). The last 4 bits of the third byte (byte 2, bits 4–7) contain the entry type. These two bytes are displayed under the column REQD.
c. The next two bytes (bytes 3 and 4) are not used.
d. The packed decimal task number is placed in bytes 5–7.
e. The fields in bytes 8–11 and 12–15 are called Field A and Field B,

respectively, and contain data specific to the type of entry. The formatted entries provide hexadecimal and character displays of these data.

f. The Resource Name is stored in the 8 byte field located at bytes 16–23. This data is also dependent on the type of entry and may contain such information as the identifiers for files, programs, temporary storage, etc.
g. Register 14 is stored in bytes 24–27. This entry can often be used to determine the location from which the request was made.
h. The Time of Day is stored in bytes 28–31 of the entry. This is a binary value, initialized at midnight and incremented by one every 32 microseconds.

For more detailed information on these entries see CICS Programming Debugging Reference Summary (IBM Form Number SX33-6010).

The actual format of these entries are not necessary for transaction dump analysis. These values are formatted and printed, along with a description of the entry, etc.

The first step in selecting the relevant trace entries is to determine the task number of the particular transaction. Above, we find that this value is located in relative positions 11_{16} to 13_{16} of the system area of the TCA. From page two of the sample dump we find the 'TASK CONTROL AREA (SYSTEM AREA)' and determine that the task number is 56079.

Listed below are those entries that refer to task number 56079. For typographical reasons this task number and the hours:minutes:seconds (14:08:02.) portion of the time, and the interval between entries have been removed. Also, to maintain a single print line per entry, some of the TRACE TYPEs were moved into the RESOURCE column. The fractional seconds may be used to locate the entry in the dump in Appendix E.

```
TRACE TABLE                    ADDRESS 00696A20 TO 0069EA1F     LENGTH 008000

TRACE HDR            00699B80    00696A20    0069EA00    00000000

TIME    ID  REG 14   REQD  FIELD A   FIELD B   CHARS     RESOURCE TRACE TYPE

193760 D0 50EB57C0 0604  C1E3C3E5 C1F0F1F0 ATCVA010              KCP CREATE

193792 EA 40EB4E08 0003 *0C000100 006CFA88 ........ A010        TMP PCT TRANSFER

193824 EA 40E7F114 0025 *0C000100 00000000 ........              TMP RETN NORMAL

193824 FC 40E5D104 1125 *0C000100 00000000 ........              ZCP RETN ZATT ATH

193856 F0 40E5B1E0 4004 *40000000 0073CE38  .......              KCP WAIT DCI=LIST

193888 D5 00EB4026 0104 *E7D2C3D9 C5D84040 XKCREQ    TIXKCREQ  OH BEFORE
```

```
193888 D5 00EB4026 0204 *00000000 001A39A0 ........ TIXKCREQ  UEH AFTER
193920 FC 05E5D6E8 0503  00200001 006ED8A0 ......Q.       ZCP ZSUP START UP TASK
193984 E7 00E5DF1C 0504  00000000 00000000 ........              ERM ENTRY
193984 E7 00E5DF1C 0504  00000000 000000FF ........            ERM RESPONSE
194016 F2 50E5DF4E 8804  00000000 00000000 ........ KA0100C PCP XCTL-CONDITIONAL
194016 EA 40E906F6 0003  01000300 002799C4 .......D KA0100C TMP PPT LOCATE
194048 EA 40E7F114 0005  01000300 006BB2C8 ......,.H          TMP RETN NORMAL
194656 F1 60E913B6 8C04  00000408 016ED8A0 ......Q.           SCP GETMAIN
194688 C8 50E89802 0004  0027A040 8C000418 ... ....  SCP ACQUIRED USER STORAGE
194752 F7 50E91754 8003  C1E3C3E5 40404040 ATCV              TSP APPL REQ GET
195328 F0 50E7898C C004  43000000 005993BC ........          KCP WAIT+CANCADDR
195328 D5 00EB4026 0104  E7D2C3D9 C5D84040 XKCREQ  TIXKCREQ UEH BEFORE
195360 D5 00EB4026 0204  00000000 001A39A0 ........TIXKCREQ UEH AFTER
211616 F1 40E757FC AE04  00270738 016ED8A0 ......Q.       SCP GETMAIN CONDITIONAL
211648 C8 50E89802 0004  0027A460 8E270748 ...-....       SCP ACQUIRED TEMPSTRG
211712 F7 40E75D68 0005  0027A460 8E270748 ...-....   TSP RETN APPL RESP NORMAL
211776 F7 50E91754 8003  C1E3C3E5 C9D5E2D9 ATCVINSR            TSP APPL REQ GET
212896 F0 50E7898C C004  43000000 005993BC ........  KCP WAIT+CANCADDR DCI=
212928 D5 00EB4026 0104  E7D2C3D9 C5D84040 XKCREQ   TIXKCREQ  UEH BEFORE
212960 D5 00EB4026 0204  00000000 001A39A0 ........ TIXKCREQ  UEH AFTER
228064 F1 40E757FC AE04  00270DCB 016ED8A0 ......Q.  SCP GETMAIN CONDITIONAL
228224 C8 50E89802 0004  0027ABB0 8E270DD8 .......Q  SCP ACQUIRED TEMPSTRG
228320 F7 40E75D68 0005  0027ABB0 8E270DD8 .......Q  TSP RETN APPL RESP NORMAL
228352 F7 50E91754 8003  C1E3C3E5 C1C4E340 ATCVADT             TSP APPL REQ GET
228416 F1 40E757FC AE04  002701CD 016ED8A0 ......Q.  SCP GETMAIN CONDITIONAL
228448 C8 50E89802 0004  0027B990 8E2701D8 .......Q  SCP ACQUIRED TEMPSTRG
228480 F7 40E75D68 0005  0027B990 8E2701D8 .......Q  TSP RETN APPL RESP NORMAL
228544 FA 50E91754 0003  00000525 00000000 ........  BMS MAP MAPSET SAVE
228544 F1 40EA9188 CC04  000002FC 016ED8A0 ......Q.  SCP GETMAIN INITIMG
```

```
228576 C8 50E89802 0004  0027BB70 8C000308 ........  SCP ACQUIRED USER STORAGE
228640 F1 60DD79DC CC04  000000A4 016ED8A0 ......Q.   SCP GETMAIN INITIMG
228640 C8 50E89802 0004  0027BE80 8C0000B8 ........  SCP ACQUIRED USER STORAGE
228672 F2 40EAA3B2 8404  00000000 00000000 ........ KAEP1PCM  PCPL
228704 EA 40E906F6 0003  01000300 002799C4 .......D KAEP1PCM  TMP PPT LOCATE
228736 EA 40E7F114 0405  01000304 00000000 ........           TMP RETN NOT FOUND
228768 F2 40EAA3F4 0404  00000000 00000000 ........ KAEP1PC   PCP LOAD
228768 EA 40E906F6 0003  01000300 002799C4 .......D KAEP1PC   TMP PPT LOCATE
228800 EA 40E7F114 0005  01000300 006BB024 .....,..           TMP RETN NORMAL
228864 F1 60E96D0A C504  000002B4 016ED8A0 ......Q.  SCP GETMAIN INITIMG
228896 C8 50E89802 0004  001B3B40 850002C8 ... ...H  SCP ACQUIRED TERMINAL
229056 FA 40EA9F78 0005  00000000 00000000 ........           BMS RETN
229088 F2 50E91754 0104  00000000 00000000 ........ KA0250C   PCP LINK
229120 EA 40E906F6 0003  01000300 002799C4 .......D KA0250C   TMP PPT LOCATE
229152 EA 40E7F114 0005  01000300 006BB330 .....,..           TMP RETN NORMAL
229152 F1 40E90306 8904  001B0050 016ED8A0 ...&..Q.           SCP GETMAIN
229184 C8 50E89802 0004  0027BF40 891B0058 ... ....  SCP ACQUIRED ACE STORAGE
229216 F1 60E913B6 8C04  002702F8 016ED8A0 ...8..Q.           SCP GETMAIN
229344 C8 50E89802 0004  0027BFA0 8C270308 ........  SCP ACQUIRED USER STORAGE
229376 F1 50E91754 CC04  00000064 016ED8A0 ......Q.  SCP GETMAIN INITIMG
229408 C8 50E89802 0004  0027C2B0 8C000078 ..B.....  SCP ACQUIRED USER STORAGE
229440 F2 50E91754 0104  00000000 00000000 ........ KUPFA0C   PCP LINK
229440 EA 40E906F6 0003  01000300 002799C4 .......D KUPFA0C   TMP PPT LOCATE
229504 EA 40E7F114 0005  01000300 006BEDC8 .....,.H           TMP RETN NORMAL
229504 F1 40E90306 8904  00270050 016ED8A0 ...&..Q.           SCP GETMAIN
229536 C8 50E89802 0004  0027C330 89270058 ..C.....  SCP ACQUIRED ACE STORAG
229536 F1 60E913B6 8C04  00270260 016ED8A0 ...-..Q.           SCP GETMAIN
229568 C8 50E89802 0004  0027C390 8C270268 ..C.....  SCP ACQUIRED USER STORAGE
229600 F1 50E91754 CC04  00000064 016ED8A0 ......Q.           SCP GETMAIN IGNITE
```

```
229632 C8 50E89802 0004  0027C600 8C000078 ..F.....  SCP ACQUIRED USER STORAGE
229664 F7 50E91754 8003  00C1D7E3 C4C5D4D6 .APTDEMO            TSP APPL REQ GET
230208 F0 50E7898C C004  43000000 005993BC ........ KCP WAIT+CANCADDR
230240 D5 00EB4026 0104  E7D2C3D9 C5D84040 XKCREQ   TIXKCREQ  UEH BEFORE
230240 D5 00EB4026 0204  00000000 001A39A0 ........ TIXKCREQ  UEH AFTER
250720 F1 40E757FC AE04  00270E04 016ED8A0 ......Q.  SCP GETMAIN CONDITIONAL
250752 C8 50E89802 0004  0027C680 8E270E18 ..F.....  SCP ACQUIRED TEMPSTRG
250848 F7 40E75D68 0005  0027C680 8E270E18 ..F.....  TSP RETN APPL RESP NORMAL
250880 F1 50E91754 4004  0027C600 016ED8A0 ..F...Q.            SCP FREEMAIN
250912 C9 50E89882 0004  0027C600 8C000078 ..F.....  SCP RELEASED USER STORAGE
250912 F2 50E91754 1004  00000000 00000000 ........ KUPFAOC   PCP RETURN
250944 F1 60E90A4E 4004  0027C390 016ED8A0 ..C...Q.            SCP FREEMAIN
250944 C9 50E89882 0004  0027C390 8C270268 ..C.....  SCP RELEASED USER STORAGE
250976 F1 60E9075E 4004  0027C330 016ED8A0 ..C...Q.            SCP FREEMAIN
251008 C9 50E89882 0004  0027C330 89270058 ..C.....  SCP RELEASED RSA STORAGE
251104 F2 50E91754 0104  00000000 00000000 ........ KUPFAOC   PCP LINK
251104 EA 40E906F6 0003  01000300 002799C4 .......D KUPFAOC   TMP PPT LOCATE
251168 EA 40E7F114 0005  01000300 006BEDC8 ......,.H          TMP RETN NORMAL
251168 F1 40E90306 8904  00270050 016ED8A0 ...&..Q.            SCP GETMAIN
251200 C8 50E89802 0004  0027D4A0 89270058 ..M.....  SCP ACQUIRED RSA STORAGE
251328 F1 60E913B6 8C04  00270260 016ED8A0 ...-..Q.            SCP GETMAIN
251360 C8 50E89802 0004  0027D500 8C270268 ..N.....  SCP ACQUIRED USER STORAGE
251392 F1 50E91754 CC04  00000064 016ED8A0 ......Q.  SCP GETMAIN INITIMG
251424 C8 50E89802 0004  0027D770 8C000078 ..P.....            SCP ACQUIRED USER
251424 F7 50E91754 8003  00C1D7E3 C5D4D740 .APTEMP             TSP APPL REQ GET
251968 F0 50E7898C C004  43000000 005993BC ........            KCP WAIT+CANCADDR
252000 D5 00EB4026 0104  E7D2C3D9 C5D84040 XKCREQ   TIXKCREQ  UEH BEFORE
252032 D5 00EB4026 0204  00000000 001A39A0 ........ TIXKCREQ  UEH AFTER
264128 F1 40E757FC AE04  002700D0 016ED8A0 ......Q.            SCP GETMAIN COND
```

```
264192 C8 50E89802 0004  0027D7F0 8E2700D8 ..PO...Q           SCP ACQUIRED TEMP
264224 F7 40E75D68 0005  0027D7F0 8E2700D8 ..PO...Q    TSP RETN APPL RESP NORMAL
264256 F1 50E91754 4004  0027D770 016ED8A0 ..P...Q.           SCP FREEMAIN
264288 C9 50E89882 0004  0027D770 8C000078 ..P.....   SCP RELEASED USER STORAGE
264288 F2 50E91754 1004  00000000 00000000 ........ KUPFA0C   PCP RETURN
264320 F1 60E90A4E 4004  0027D500 016ED8A0 ..N...Q.   SCP FREEMAIN
264320 C9 50E89882 0004  0027D500 8C270268 ..N.....   SCP RELEASED USER STORAGE
264352 F1 60E9075E 4004  0027D4A0 016ED8A0 ..M...Q.           SCP FREEMAIN
264384 C9 50E89882 0004  0027D4A0 89270058 ..M.....   SCP RELEASED RSA STORAGE
264512 F1 50E91754 4004  0027C680 016ED8A0 ..F...Q.           SCP FREEMAIN
264512 C9 50E89882 0004  0027C680 8E270E18 ..F.....   SCP RELEASED TEMPSTRG
264640 F1 50E91754 4004  0027D7F0 016ED8A0 ..PO..Q.           SCP FREEMAIN
264672 C9 50E89882 0004  0027D7F0 8E2700D8 ..PO...Q   SCP RELEASED TEMPSTRG
264800 F1 50E91754 4004  0027C2B0 016ED8A0 ..B...Q.           SCP FREEMAIN
264800 C9 50E89882 0004  0027C2B0 8C000078 ..B.....   SCP RELEASED USER STORAGE
264832 F2 50E91754 1004  00000000 00000000 ........ KA0250C   PCP RETURN
264832 F1 60E90A4E 4004  0027BFA0 016ED8A0 ......Q.           SCP FREEMAIN
264864 C9 50E89882 0004  0027BFA0 8C270308 ........   SCP RELEASED USER STORAGE
264928 F1 60E9075E 4004  0027BF40 016ED8A0 ... ..Q.           SCP FREEMAIN
264960 C9 50E89882 0004  0027BF40 891B0058 ... ....   SCP RELEASED RSA STORAGE
264992 FA 50E91754 0003  00000525 00000000 ........   BMS MAP MAPSET SAVE MAP
265056 F1 60E96D0A C504  000001FE 016ED8A0 ......Q.   SCP GETMAIN INITIMG
265088 C8 50E89802 0004  001B2800 85000218 ........   SCP ACQUIRED TERMINAL
265312 FA 40EA9F78 0005  00000000 00000000 ........           BMS RETN
265344 F2 50E91754 0104  00000000 00000000 ........ KA2250C   PCP LINK
265376 EA 40E906F6 0003  01000300 002799C4 .......D KA2250C   TMP PPT LOCATE
265408 EA 40E7F114 0005  01000300 006BBB1C .....,..           TMP RETN NORMAL
265440 F1 40E90306 8904  001B0050 016ED8A0 ...&..Q.           SCP GETMAIN
265568 C8 50E89802 0004  0027D800 891B0058 ..Q.....   SCP ACQUIRED RSA STORAGE
```

```
265600 F1 60E913B6 8C04  00270368 016ED8A0 ......Q.               SCP GETMAIN
265632 C8 50E89802 0004  0027D860 8C270378 ..Q-....     SCP ACQUIRED USER STORAGE
265664 F1 50E91754 CC04  00000096 016ED8A0 ......Q.     SCP GETMAIN INITIMG
265696 C8 50E89802 0004  0027DBE0 8C0000A8 ........     SCP ACQUIRED USER STORAGE
265696 F2 50E91754 0104  00000000 00000000 ........ KUPFAOC   PCP LINK
265728 EA 40E906F6 0003  01000300 002799C4 .......D KUPFAOC   TMP PPT LOCATE
265760 EA 40E7F114 0005  01000300 006BEDC8 .....,.H           TMP RETN NORMAL
265792 F1 40E90306 8904  00270050 016ED8A0 ...&..Q.           SCP GETMAIN
265792 C8 50E89802 0004  0027DC90 89270058 ........     SCP ACQUIRED RSA STORAGE
265824 F1 60E913B6 8C04  00270260 016ED8A0 ...-..Q.           SCP GETMAIN
265856 C8 50E89802 0004  0027DCF0 8C270268 ...0....     SCP ACQUIRED USER STORAGE
265888 F1 50E91754 CC04  00000064 016ED8A0 ......Q.     SCP GETMAIN INITIMG
265888 C8 50E89802 0004  0027DF60 8C000078 ...-....     SCP ACQUIRED USER STORAGE
265920 F7 50E91754 8003  00C1D7E3 C4C5E2C3 .APTDESC           TSP APPL REQ GET
266496 F0 50E7898C C004  43000000 005993BC ........     KCP WAIT+CANCADDR DCI=
266496 D5 00EB4026 0104  E7D2C3D9 C5D84040 XKCREQ   TIXKCREQ  UEH BEFORE
266528 D5 00EB4026 0204  00000000 001A39A0 ........ TIXKCREQ  UEH AFTER
273344 F1 40E757FC AE04  00270922 016ED8A0 ......Q.           SCP GETMAIN COND
273504 C8 50E89802 0004  0027DFE0 8E270938 ........     SCP ACQUIRED TEMPSTRG
273568 F7 40E75D68 0005  0027DFE0 8E270938 ........     TSP RETN APPL RESP NORMAL
273600 F1 50E91754 4004  0027DF60 016ED8A0 ...-..Q.           SCP FREEMAIN
273600 C9 50E89882 0004  0027DF60 8C000078 ...-....     SCP RELEASED USER STORAGE
273632 F2 50E91754 1004  00000000 00000000 ........ KUPFAOC   PCP RETURN
273664 F1 60E90A4E 4004  0027DCF0 016ED8A0 ...0..Q.           SCP FREEMAIN
273664 C9 50E89882 0004  0027DCF0 8C270268 ...0....     SCP RELEASED USER STORAGE
273696 F1 60E9075E 4004  0027DC90 016ED8A0 ......Q.           SCP FREEMAIN
273696 C9 50E89882 0004  0027DC90 89270058 ........     SCP RELEASED RSA STORAGE
273792 F2 50E91754 0104  00000000 00000000 ........ KUDATOA   PCP LINK
273824 EA 40E906F6 0003  01000300 002799C4 .......D KUDATOA   TMP PPT LOCATE
```

```
273856 EA 40E7F114 0005  01000300 006BECB0 .....,..              TMP RETN NORMAL
273888 F1 40E90306 8904  00270050 016ED8A0 ...&..Q.              SCP GETMAIN
273888 C8 50E89802 0004  0027E920 89270058 ..Z.....        SCP ACQUIRED RSA STORAGE
273920 F1 50528DCC CC04  00000032 016ED8A0 ......Q.        SCP GETMAIN INITIMG
273952 C8 50E89802 0004  0027E980 8C000048 ..Z.....        SCP ACQUIRED USER STORAGE
273984 F1 60528E0E 4004  0027E980 016ED8A0 ..Z...Q.              SCP FREEMAIN
273984 C9 50E89882 0004  0027E980 8C000048 ..Z.....        SCP RELEASED USER STORAGE
274016 F2 50528E1C 1004  00000000 00000000 ........ KUDATOA  PCP RETURN
274016 F1 60E9075E 4004  0027E920 016ED8A0 ..Z...Q.        SCP FREEMAIN
274048 C9 50E89882 0004  0027E920 89270058 ..Z.....        SCP RELEASED RSA STORAGE
274080 F2 50E91754 0104  00000000 00000000 ........ KUDATOA  PCP LINK
274080 EA 40E906F6 0003  01000300 002799C4 .......D KUDATOA  TMP PPT LOCATE
274144 EA 40E7F114 0005  01000300 006BECB0 .....,..              TMP RETN NORMAL
274144 F1 40E90306 8904  00270050 016ED8A0 ...&..Q.              SCP GETMAIN
274176 C8 50E89802 0004  0027E9D0 89270058 ..Z.....        SCP ACQUIRED RSA STORAGE
274176 F1 50528DCC CC04  00000032 016ED8A0 ......Q.        SCP GETMAIN INITIMG
274208 C8 50E89802 0004  0027EA30 8C000048 ........        SCP ACQUIRED USER STORAGE
274240 F1 60528E0E 4004  0027EA30 016ED8A0 ......Q.              SCP FREEMAIN
274240 C9 50E89882 0004  0027EA30 8C000048 ........        SCP RELEASED USER STORAGE
274272 F2 50528E1C 1004  00000000 00000000 ........ KUDATOA  PCP RETURN
274272 F1 60E9075E 4004  0027E9D0 016ED8A0 ..Z...Q.        SCP FREEMAIN
274304 C9 50E89882 0004  0027E9D0 89270058 ..Z.....        SCP RELEASED RSA STORAGE
274400 F1 50E91754 4004  0027DFE0 016ED8A0 ......Q.              SCP FREEMAIN
274432 C9 50E89882 0004  0027DFE0 8E270938 ........        SCP RELEASED TEMPSTRG
274592 F2 50E91754 0104  00000000 00000000 ........ KUPFA0C  PCP LINK
274592 EA 40E906F6 0003  01000300 002799C4 .......D KUPFA0C  TMP PPT LOCATE
274656 EA 40E7F114 0005  01000300 006BEDC8 .....,.H              TMP RETN NORMAL
274656 F1 40E90306 8904  00270050 016ED8A0 ...&..Q.              SCP GETMAIN
274784 C8 50E89802 0004  0027F000 89270058 ..0.....        SCP ACQUIRED RSA STORAGE
```

```
274816 F1 60E913B6 8C04  00270260 016ED8A0 ...-..Q.           SCP GETMAIN
274848 C8 50E89802 0004  0027F060 8C270268 ..0-....      SCP ACQUIRED USER STORAGE
274880 F1 50E91754 CC04  00000064 016ED8A0 ......Q.      SCP GETMAIN INITIMG
274880 C8 50E89802 0004  0027F2D0 8C000078 ..2.....      SCP ACQUIRED USER STORAGE
274912 F7 50E91754 8003  00C1D7C4 D6C34040 .APDOC             TSP APPL REQ GET
275456 F0 50E7898C C004  43000000 005993BC ........      KCP WAIT+CANCADDR DCI=
275488 D5 00EB4026 0104  E7D2C3D9 C5D84040 XKCREQ   TIXKCREQ  UEH BEFORE
275488 D5 00EB4026 0204  00000000 001A39A0 ........ TIXKCREQ  UEH AFTER
283712 F1 40E757FC AE04  00270645 016ED8A0 ......Q.      SCP GETMAIN CONDITIONAL
283776 C8 50E89802 0004  0027F350 8E270658 ..3&....      SCP ACQUIRED TEMPSTRG
283840 F7 40E75D68 0005  0027F350 8E270658 ..3&....      TSP RETN APPL RESP NORMAL
283872 F1 50E91754 4004  0027F2D0 016ED8A0 ..2...Q.           SCP FREEMAIN
283872 C9 50E89882 0004  0027F2D0 8C000078 ..2.....      SCP RELEASED USER STORAGE
283904 F2 50E91754 1004  00000000 00000000 ........ KUPFAOC   PCP RETURN
283936 F1 60E90A4E 4004  0027F060 016ED8A0 ..0-..Q.           SCP FREEMAIN
283936 C9 50E89882 0004  0027F060 8C270268 ..0-....      SCP RELEASED USER STORAGE
283968 F1 60E9075E 4004  0027F000 016ED8A0 ..0...Q.           SCP FREEMAIN
283968 C9 50E89882 0004  0027F000 89270058 ..0.....      SCP RELEASED RSA STORAGE
284288 F2 80E8B6E0 6004  C1E2D9C1 00000000 ASRA....           PCP ABEND
284320 F1 40E8F80A CC04  000000A0 016ED8A0 ......Q.      SCP GETMAIN INITIMG
284352 C8 50E89802 0004  0027F9B0 8C0000A8 ..9.....      SCP ACQUIRED USER STORAGE
284352 F4 50E8F9E2 FE04  00000000 C1E2D9C1 ....ASRA           DCP TRANSACTION
297920 F0 40F1506C 4004  80000000 0068FD5C .......*      KCP WAIT DCI=SINGLE
297952 D5 00EB4026 0104  E7D2C3D9 C5D84040 XKCREQ   TIXKCREQ  UEH BEFORE
297952 D5 00EB4026 0204  00000000 001A39A0 ........ TIXKCREQ  UEH AFTER
```

AUXILIARY TRACES

While, strictly speaking, auxiliary traces are not in the realm of CICS dumps, that facility may be used for debugging transactions that do not fail with a transaction dump. They are mentioned here in this context and because the format of their entries are the same as those of the above trace table.

To use the auxiliary dump the facility must be defined to CICS, the dataset must be opened, and the auxiliary trace started. These last two actions may be performed by the special CSMT or CEMT transactions. Once the facility is started the trace table entries are written to the defined dataset until it is filled or until the auxiliary trace is stopped.

A utility program is provided that will display this trace in the same format as described above. Further, selection criteria (time range, task number, terminal identifier, and/or transaction identifier) may be specified to select specific entries.

16

Input/Output Channel Programming

The basic hardware components of the input/output (I/O) system consists of the following machines.

a. I/O Devices. The machine—such as printers, disk and tape drives, etc.—that perform the process of transferring data to, or from, a particular medium.
b. I/O Control Units. A machine that provides the attachment of similar I/O devices. These provide common circuitry that would otherwise need to be included in each I/O device. Normally a control unit can be attached to a maximum of 16 devices but there are exceptions such as the 3380 DASD in which each actuator is considered a device and 64 such devices are allowed.
c. I/O Channels. A machine that moves data between the control units and main memory. Once started, by a CPU instruction, the channel transfers data without dependence upon the CPU—thus, allowing the CPU to perform other tasks. Multiple control units can be attached to a single channel and multiple channels can be attached to a single control unit.

The I/O subsystems differ significantly between the IBM 370 (non-XA) and 370-XA modes. Besides the ability to use 31-bit addresses this is the major difference between the two architectures. In the 370 mode, the architecture uses multiple channels with attached control units and devices. Within the 370-XA mode, the architecture provides a single channel subsystem with multiple subchannels. This later concept provides more flexibility and efficiency by assigning a specific device, in a one-to-one relationship, to a unique sub-channel. Thus, XA may allow multiple paths to a specific device without programming considerations.

I/O operations may operate in two modes:

a. Burst mode monopolizes the channel path for the duration of the operation. This mode of operation is normally used for high speed I/O devices.
b. Byte-multiplex mode allows the sharing of the path with other I/O devices. This mode is normally used for slow speed I/O devices.

The above modes are normally of no programming consequence.

CHANNEL COMMAND WORDS

Much as the CPU executes instructions to perform specific functions, the channel executes channel command words (CCWs) to instruct the channel to perform such functions as transfer data between main memory and I/O control units, etc. A channel program consists of one or more CCWs. If the channel program contains more than one CCW they may be in contiguous memory locations or, if a transfer-in-channel command is used, in non-contiguous memory locations. The program ends when no chain-data or chain-command fields or transfer-in-channel commands are present within the last CCW processed, or when the suspend flag is present in the next CCW. The transfer-in-channel command, chain fields, and the suspend flag are described below.

CCWs are 64 bits in length, begin on double word boundaries, and contain the following fields:

a. Command Code, a one byte code that specifies the desired function (similar to an operation code in a machine instruction). For specific codes see 'I/O Command Codes' in IBM System/370 Reference Summary or documentation for the specific I/O device.
b. Data Address, a 24 or 31 bit field that specifies an absolute memory address.
c. Chain-Data Flag (CD), a single bit field that, if on, causes the storage area designated by the next CCW to be used with the current I/O operation and causes the chain-command and suppress-length-indication (below) to be ignored.
d. Chain-Command Flag (CC), a single bit field that indicates whether command chaining is to be performed. That is; if the chain-command, the chain-data, and suspend (below) flags are on; the next CCW is performed when the operation of the current CCW is completed.
e. Suppress-Length-Indication Flag (SLI), is a single bit field that controls whether an indication is to be made to the program when an incorrect length specification is encountered.
f. Skip Flag (SKIP) suppresses transfer of information to main storage during a read or sense operation.
g. Program-Controlled-Instruction Flag (PCI), is a single bit field that, if

on, causes an intermediate interruption to be generated at the completion of the CCW.

h. Indirect-Data-Address Flag (IDA), is a single bit field that, if on, causes the data addressing to be indirect (i.e., the value of the actual address is obtained from the memory location specified at the data address—which is not the address of the data to be transferred).
i. Suspend Flag (S) is a single bit field that, if on, causes the channel program to be suspended before the execution of the CCW containing this flag.
j. Count, a 16 bit field that specifies the size—in bytes—of the data area that begins with the specified data address.

There are two formats of the CCW:

a. Format-0, which must be located in the first 2^{24} bytes of memory:

   1. Bits 1–7 specifies the command code.
   2. Bits 8–31 specifies the data address.
   3. Bits 32–38 specifies the CD, CC, SLI, SKIP, PCI, IDA, and S flags; respectively.
   4. Bit 39 must contain zero.
   5. Bits 40–47 is unused.
   6. Bits 48–63 contains the count field.

b. Format-1, which may be located at any memory location:

   1. Bits 1–7 specifies the command code.
   2. Bits 8–14 specifies the CD, CC, SLI, SKIP, PCI, IDA, and S flags; respectively.
   3. Bit 15 must contain zero.
   4. Bits 16–31 contains the count field.
   5. Bit 32 must contain zero.
   6. Bits 33–63 specifies the data address.

Assembler H provides mnemonics CCW and CCW0 to generate format-0 CCWs and CCW1 to generate format-1 CCWs. There are no differences in the object code generated by CCW and CCW0 but, if there is a possibility that the program will be assembled with a pre-XA assembler, CCW is recommended. On the other hand, to emphasize that a format-0 CCW is intended, the CCW0 usage might be more meaningful. In all cases the operands are, respectively:

a. Command code.
b. Data address.
c. Flags. this operand contains the trailing zero bit—i.e., the full byte containing the flags is generated by this operand and can, therefore, not contain a low order bit.

d. Count.

For example:

```
READ     EQU   2                     READ COMMAND CODE
WRITE    EQU   1                     WRITE COMMAND CODE
TIC      EQU   8                     TRANSFER-IN-CHANNEL COMMAND CODE
CD       EQU   X'80'                 DATA CHAINING FLAG
CC       EQU   X'40'                 COMMAND CHAINING FLAG
SLI      EQU   X'20'                 SUPPRESS LENGTH INDICATOR FLAG
SKIP     EQU   X'10'                 SKIP FLAG
PCI      EQU   X'08'                 PROGRAM CONTROLLED INTERRUPT FLAG
IDA      EQU   X'04'                 INDIRECT ADDRESS FLAG
S        EQU   X'02'                 SUSPEND FLAG
         ...
WRITEX   CCW   1,OUTAREA,X'48',132
WRITE0   CCW0  WRITE,OUTAREA,CC+IDA,L'OUTAREA
WRITE1   CCW1  WRITE,OUTAREA,CC+IDA,L'OUTAREA
         ...
OUTAREA  DS    CL128
```

The first two CCWs will each generate 01xxxxxx 48000084_{16} and the third CCW would generate 01480084 $xxxxxxxx_{16}$, where x...x is the address (hexadecimal) of 'OUTAREA'.

I/O MACROS

While the execution of a channel program is initiated by machine instructions, the operating system environment requires very specific controls. These controls usually prohibit the execution of such privileged instructions. Various macros are provided that permit the general user access to the channel programming facilities but enforce the controls necessary to protect the overall environment.

The EXCP (Execute Channel Program) is one such macro. This macro generates a Supervisor Call (SVC) that passes control to the I/O supervisor. The EXCP provides the following services:

a. Schedules I/O requests for the specific device.
b. Initiates the specific channel program.
c. Handles interrupts.
d. Processes error recover directly or by user procedures.
e. Provides status information.

Restrictions to EXCP usage:

a. SYSIN and SYSOUT data sets are prohibited.
b. Format-1 CCWs are not permitted.
c. All areas related to the I/O operation must be contained in the first 2^{24} bytes of virtual memory. The program issuing the EXCP may, however, be executing in either the 24 or 31-bit mode.
d. Control to all user exit (appendages) routines is in 24-bit addressing mode and the return must be made in that mode.
e. Channel programs that modify themselves are not supported.

Requirements for the EXCP are:

a. The Input/Output Block (EBB) address is the only parameter specified in the macro instruction. The IOB contains the addresses of other control blocks and maintains information and status data. For unit record and magnetic tape devices the IOB is 32 bytes in length. For most other devices 40 bytes must be provided. A DSECT macro, IEZIOB, may be used to specify the fields of the IOB.
b. The Event Control Block (ECB) provides an area to store the status (completion code) of the I/O operation. The ECB occupies four bytes and begins on a full word boundary. The first bit (wait bit) is one if a WAIT has been issued but the I/O operation has not completed. The second bit (completion bit) is zero if the operation is incomplete, else it is set to one. After completion of the I/O, the remaining thirty bits contains a code specifying the condition of the I/O, as follows:

   1. $3F000000_{16}$ indicates no detected errors.
   2. 01000000_{16} indicates that a permanent error was detected.
   3. 02000000_{16} indicates that a DASD extent violation occurred.
   4. 04000000_{16} indicates that a device end occurred.
   5. 08000000_{16} indicates that RQE is available after purge.
   6. $0B000000_{16}$ indicates either an unexpected load point was found or that a CSW command address is zero within the IOB.
   7. $0F000000_{16}$ indicates a direct access error.

The address of the ECB must be contained in bytes 5–7 of the specified IOB.

c. The Data Control Block defines the characteristics of the specified data set. The DCB is defined by the same macro (DCB) that has been used in earlier data sets. The operand MACRF = (E) indicates that EXCP macro instructions are to be used. The MACRF and DDNAME operands are required. The address of the DCB is contained in bytes 21 – 23 of the IOB.

d. The Data Extent Block (DEB) contains one or more extent entries for the specified data set. These entries specify the boundaries of the data set and contain the address(es) of Unit Control Blocks (UCBs) that identify the type and location of the associated I/O device(s). The DEB is created by the system when the data set is OPENed.

Upon execution of the EXCP the operation of the channel program begins and control is given back to the issuing program. When the program is ready to use input data or delete output data (i.e., to determine if the I/O operation is complete), the WAIT macro is provided.

```
          OPEN   (TAPEDCB,OUTPUT)        OPEN DATA SET
          ...
          EXCP   WTAPEIOB                BEGIN CHANNEL PROGRAM
          ...
          WAIT   ECB=WTAPEECB            WAIT FOR I/O TO COMPLETE
          ...
          CLOSE  (TAPEDCB)               CLOSE DATA SET
          ...
WTAPEECB  DC     F'0'
WTAPEIOB  DC     4X'0'
          DC     A(WTAPEECB)
WTAPECSW  DC     2F'0'
WTCCWAD   DC     A(WTAPECCW)
          DC     A(TAPEDCB)
          DC     F'0'
WTAPEINC  DC     6H'0'
          ...
WTAPECCW  CCW    1,OUTAREA,0,L'OUTAREA
          ...
```

```
TAPEDCB  DCB   DDNAME=OUTPUT,MACRF=(E),DSORG=PS

         ...

OUTAREA  DS    300C
```

The above example suffices for sequential devices such as tape drives and printers.

However, for DASD, a somewhat more complex channel program is required. Such channel programs also, because of the necessity to specify physical locations, are more dependent on specific device types. Because of these difficulties special macros and system routines are provided.

Before examining the facilities to aid in the development of direct access I/O programming let us first discuss the attributes of such devices. This discussion will be limited to count-key-data (CKD) device architecture. In this architecture each physical block is recorded as either two or three separate units, separated by gaps in the recording medium. These units are:

a. Count, a block identifier that allows the device to recognize and (verify) the presence of a specific block. The information contained in this unit includes the cylinder number, track (or head), block number, and lengths of the key and data areas.
b. Key, this is a special area that may be used to implement special searches. This area is optional. If present the key length in the above count area will be positive, else zero.
c. Data, the information part of the block. In a very special case this information is also omitted. This special case defines the end-of-life (EOF) indicator.

Each track begins with a special mark (index point) followed by the track's home address. These physical characteristics are pre-recorded within the media and are only altered in the very special case in which alternate tracks are assigned. These items are used by the hardware and the only programming consideration is that an indicator is returned when an index point is encountered and this information may be used to determine the end of a track.

The home address is followed by a special record (record zero or R_0). The medium is also prerecorded with this record but its contents may be read or altered by special read and write CCW operations. In most cases, however, R_0 is not used in application programming. R_0 is also referred to as the ***track descriptor record.*** If the track is flagged as defective (by an indicator in the home address area), the count area of R_0 must contain the address of the alternate track.

Once records are created on a specific track they may be updated as long as their lengths (key and data) do not change. However if the length(s) are altered the entire track (after that block) must be rewritten.

Now that we have a better understanding of the CKD architecture we will consider those facilities to simplify channel programming and that ease device dependencies. The first such facility is the XDAP (Execute Direct Access Program) macro which generates the ECB, IOB, and channel program and executes that channel program. The XDAP macro has the following positional operands:

a. ecb-symbol, the symbolic name of the XDAP event control block (ECB). For MF = E (see below), this operand may specify general purpose register (2–12) enclosed by parentheses.
b. type, specifies the type of operation and, if specified, must be either RI, RK, WI, WK, VI, VR. These codes indicate:

    1. R, read a block.
    2. W, update a block.
    3. V, verify that the device is able to read a block but do not transfer data.
    4. I, locate a block by identification (count area). The generated channel program will read, update, or verify the key (if present) and data areas.
    5. K, locate a block by key. The generated channel program will read, update, or verify only the data area. If this option is specified, the key-addr and keylength-value operands (below) must be specified.

c. dcb-addr, the address of the data control block (DCB) for the data set. If present, this operand must be a symbolic address or a general register (2–12) enclosed in parentheses.
d. area-addr, the address of the input or output area. If present, this operand must be a symbolic address or a general register (2–12) enclosed in parentheses.
e. length-value, the number of bytes to be transferred. This operand, if present, must specify an absolute value or a general purpose register (2–12) enclosed in parentheses. The maximum value that may be specified is 32,768.
f. key-addr, the address of a virtual storage area that contains the key of the block. If present it must contain the symbolic address or a general purpose register (2–12) enclosed in parentheses.
g. keylength-value, the length of the key. If present, this operand must be an absolute value or a general register (2–12) enclosed in parentheses. The maximum value that may be specified is 256.
h. blkref-addr, the address of a virtual storage area that contains the actual DASD address of the block in the form MBBCCHHR. M is the one byte indicator of the extent entry of the DCB, BB contains two bytes of binary zeros, CC is the two byte cylinder number, HH is the two byte head number, and R is the one byte record number.
i. sector-addr, is the virtual address of a single byte sector value. This parameter is used only for rotational position sensing (RPS) devices. This discussion will not consider the RPS facility whose usage is not

necessary but should be investigated if large numbers of DASD I/O operations are to be performed. If present, this operand must be a symbolic address or a general register (2-12) enclosed in parentheses.

Additionally, a key-word operand is provided to specify if the specification is for the execution or list form of the macro. The execution form generates the instructions necessary to execute the channel program. The list form generates the necessary control blocks and channel program. The value of this parameter is limited to MF = E and MF = L, respectively.

```
         OPEN  (DASDIN)                  OPEN FILE
         ...
         XDAP  DASDECB,MF=E              EXECUTE CHANNEL PROGRAM
         ...
         WAIT  ECB=DASDECB               WAIT FOR READ TO COMPLETE
         ...
EOF      CLOSE (DASDIN)                  CLOSE FILE
         ...
INAREA   DS    CL500                     I/O AREA
DASDIN   DCB   DDNAME=INPUT,DSORG=PS,MACRF=(E),DEVDA=DA,EODAD=EOF
MBBCCHHR DS    OD
         DC    AL1(0)                    EXTENT
         DC    XL2(0)                    UNUSED
         DC    AL2(100)                  CYLINDER
         DC    AL2(5)                    TRACK
         DC    AL1(10)                   RECORD
         XDAP  DASDECB,RI,DASDIN,INAREA,L'INAREA,,,MBBCCHHR,MF=L
         END
```

The XDAP macro requires the absolute DASD address. Normally this address is not known at programming time and, in fact, often changes. To simplify the programming there are system routines that convert between absolute and relative DASD addresses. These two routines, IECPCNVT and IECPRLTV, convert relative track address to actual track address and actual track address to relative track address, respectively. Unlike normal subroutines, these routines are not CALLed—their locations are stored in the

Communications Vector Table (CVT) at symbolic locations CVTPCNVT and CVTPELTV, respectively. The location of the CVT is contained in the full word beginning at location 16 (10_{16}). The macro CVT provides a DSECT of the CVT which may be used to determine the relative positions of the above symbolic locations.

To convert a relative address to an actual address (IECPCNVT):

a. Load the four byte value TTRN into register 0. TT is the two byte track address (relative to the beginning of the data set), R is the one byte record number on the track, and N (normally zero) is the concatenation number of the data set.
b. Load register 1 with the address of the data extent block (DEB) of the data set.
c. Load register 2 with the address of an eight byte field where the actual address will be returned (MBBCCHHR).
d. Load register 14 with the return address.
e. Load register 15 with the address of the conversion routine. Upon return this register will contain a return code: zero if successful, four if the relative address exceeds the data set extents.

To convert an actual address to a relative address (IECPRLTV):

a. On return register 0 will contain the resulting TTRN as defined above.
b. Load register 1 with the address of the data extent block (DEB) of the data set.
c. Load register 2 with the address of an eight byte field that contains the actual address (MBBCCHHR).
d. Load register 14 with the return address.
e. Load register 15 with the address of the conversion routine.

Another difference between the usage of these routines and CALLed subroutines is that they *modify* but do not restore general registers 9–13. Special care must be used if these registers contain base register(s) of the application program—see SAMPLE7, in Appendix D for such usage (remember that, if the base register(s) are modified, addressability to any register save area is lost).

```
L      1,16                      LOAD ADDRESS OF CVT

USING CVT,1                      ESTABLISH ADDRESSABILITY

L      15,CVTPCNVT               GET ADDRESS OF ICEPCNVT

DROP   1                         DROP CVT ADDRESSABILITY

L      0,TTRN                    LOAD RELATIVE ADDRESS

L      1,DASDIN+DCBDEBAD-DCBRELAD ADDR OF DEB FROM DCB
```

```
         LA     2,MBBCCHHR              LOAD ADDRESS OF RESULT
         BALR   14,15                   CONVERT TO ACTUAL ADDRESS
         LTR    15,15                   RELATIVE ADDRESS IN DATA SET?
         BNZ    EXTERROR                 NO
         ...
         L      1,16                    LOAD ADDRESS OF CVT
         USING  CVT,1                   ESTABLISH ADDRESSABILITY
         L      15,CVTPCNVT             GET ADDRESS OF ICEPCNVT
         DROP   1                       DROP CVT ADDRESSABILITY
         L      1,DASDIN+DCBDEBAD-DCBRELAD ADDR OF DEB FROM DCB
         LA     2,MBBCCHHR              LOAD ADDRESS OF RESULT
         BALR   14,15                   CONVERT TO ACTUAL ADDRESS
         ST     0,TTRN                  STORE RELATIVE DASD ADDRESS
         ...
TTRN     DC     F'0'
MBBCCHHR DS     XL8
DASDIN   DCB    DDNAME=...
         DCBD   DEVD=DA                 DATA CONTROL BLOCK DSECT
         CVT    DSECT=YES               COMMUNICATIONS VECTOR TABLE DSECT
         IEZIOB DSECT=YES               INPUT/OUTPUT BLOCK DSECT
```

If the program is intended to be used with multiple (or changing) DASD device types it may be necessary to dynamically determine the specifications of the device. The most common such requirement is the number of tracks per cylinder. The macro DEVTYPE provides such information. This macro has other usages as well but we will consider only the following:

DEVTYPE *ddloc-addr,area-addr,*DEVTAB

Where:

a. ddloc-addr is the symbolic address of an eight byte field that contains the DD name to which the device is assigned. This field is left justified and blank filled.

b. area-addr is the symbolic address where the device information is to be placed. For DASD, this information consists of five words:

   1. Word 0 describes the device as defined by the UCBTYP field of the Unit Control Block (UCB).
   2. Word 1 contains the maximum block size.
   3. Bytes 0–1 of word 2 contains the number of physical cylinders on the device.
   4. Bytes 2–3 of word 2 contains the number of tracks per cylinder.
   5. Words 4 and 5 contain information concerning more complex aspects of the device and will not be discussed here.

```
         DEVTYPE DDNAME,DASDINFO,DEVTAB

         ...

DDNAME   DC      CL8'DASDIN'

DASDINFO DS      2F

CYLS     DS      H

HEADS    DS      H

         DS      2F
```

17

Stacks

Stacks are similar to queues. Each are collections of items arranged in sequential order with the difference being the order in which items are removed from the collection. Stacks are last in, first our (LIFO) collections and queues are first in, first out (FIFO) collections. Examples of a stack are the vertical storage bins for trays found at a cafeteria line, the placement of cartridges in an ammunition clip, etc. Examples of queues are checkout lines at a market, buffering of records from an I/O device, etc.

While queues are common in computer applications, their use is normally apparent to the casual user and will not be dealt with in any further detail. On the other hand stacks have been used in some rather novel ways which led to the inclusion of this topic.

Stacks are normally processed by maintaining an array of memory for storing their items. Items are placed (pushed) and removed (popped) from this array. In the IBM System/370 there are no instructions to specifically process stacks—although in other machines, especially microprocessors, such instructions are common. There are two assembler instructions (PUSH and POP) that allow for saving and restoring the operands of the PRINT and USING assembler instructions.

A sample program to push the contents of register 2 onto a stack and to pop entries from that stack is:

```
PUSH     L     1,STACKPTR           LOAD PREVIOUS STACK POINTER
         LA    1,4(1)               POINT TO NEXT POSITION
         C     1,=A(STACKEND)       STACK CAPACITY EXCEEDED?
         BH    STKFULL               YES
         ST    1,STACKPTR           SAVE UPDATED POINTER
```

```
         ST    2,0(1)               PUSH CONTENTS OF REGISTER 2
         ...
POP      L     1,STACKPTR           LOAD CURRENT STACK POINTER
         C     1,=A(STACK)          IS STACK EMPTY?
         BL    STKEMPTY              YES
         L     2,0(1)               POP STACKED VALUE INTO REGISTER 2
         SH    2,=H'4'              POINT TO PREVIOUS ITEM
         ST    1,STACKPTR           MAKE PREVIOUS ENTRY CURRENT
         ...
STACKPTR DC    A(STACK-4)
STACK    DC    99F
STACKEND DC    F
```

Examination of the above procedure will reveal that it is a simple implementation of a single dimensional array that is indexed by 'STACKPTR'.

Some of the most common usage of stacks are:

a. Recursive processing. Consider the case where a subroutine calls itself. Using the standard subroutine linkage the calling program provides a register save area within the calling program. However, in such recursive usage, a single save area would be destroyed on each successive CALL. A normal procedure for providing protection from such destruction is to employ a technique similar to the above. On each call the registers to be saved would be PUSHed onto a stack and on each return the registers would be POPed from the stack. Of course, if register 13 must be saved in the CALLed routine, a similar procedure must also be provided for the return logic.

   The above procedure requires that the size of the stack would need to be sufficient to account for the maximum depth of the recursion. An alternate implementation, which eliminates the restriction of the fixed array stack, would use the GETMAIN and FREEMAIN macros to dynamically acquire and release storage for stack entries.

b. Processing of interrupts. External events, such as the completion of an I/O request, results in an interrupt of the normal instruction flow. Because, under normal operation, additional interrupts may occur while processing a previous interrupt; the interrupt processing is inherently recursive. The customary method for processing these secondary interrupts is to stack such information as the PSW, registers, and status information at the time of interruption and either process or queue the latest interrupt—depending on priority of the event.

c. Parsing algebraic expressions. One of the more complex parts of earlier compiler construction was the analysis (parsing) of the syntax of statements. This chore has been eased by employing the work of Polish mathematician J. Lukasiewicz. This particular work, known as Polish notation, allows the transformation of a parenthesized algebraic expression into an expression without parentheses. The mechanization of this procedure is ideally suited to stack techniques and will comprise the remainder of this section.

POLISH NOTATION

In normal (infix) algebraic notation, the order of calculation is specified by the hierarchy of mathematical operations and by the use of parentheses when necessary. For example the expression:

$$a + b \times c - (d - e) / f$$

implies that the product of b and c is added to the quantity a, the difference of d and e is divided by f, and that quotient is subtracted from the above sum. This implication is based on the following rules:

a. The operation with the highest hierarchy is performed first. The hierarchical relationships, from high to low are:

   1. Exponentiation.
   2. Multiplication and division.
   3. Addition and subtraction.

b. Expressions enclosed in parentheses are computed prior to applying the normal hierarchical relationships.

In Polish notation the operation symbols are removed from between the operands and placed after the operands. (E.g., 'a + b' becomes 'a b +'). The decision to place the operator after the operands is arbitrary but proves to be the most convenient location for mechanization reasons. This postfix or suffix notation is termed reverse Polish notation.

The above technique can be continued for multiple operators of the same hierarchy by repeated application of the rule. For example, consider the expression x × y / z. We first process the subexpression x × y and obtain x y ×. Now, for clarity, let θ = x y × which transforms the original expression into θ / z which yields θ z / or x y × z /.

Now consider the expression a + b × c. Because, by normal algebraic rules the value of b × c must be determined first, we determine the intermediate conversion θ = 'b c ×'. By substitution we now have the expression 'a + θ' which converts to 'a θ +' = 'a b c × +'.

When the hierarchy of operations is reversed, as in 'a × b + c' we proceed by transforming 'a × b' into 'a b x' and substituting θ = 'a b ×' which yields 'θ + c' = 'θ c +' = 'a b × c +'.

By examining the above it is apparent that all operands of the original expression are unchanged in reverse Polish notation. When considering the placement of the operations it is convenient to define the arguments of the operations to be either an operand or reverse Polish string of operands and operations. From the above, it is apparent that each operation symbol is preceded by its two arguments. Hence the mechanization of the evaluation of expressions in reverse Polish notation is trivial: Simply scan the string for an operation symbol and apply the indicated operation to the two preceding arguments. For example:

$$3\ 5 \times 10 + 8 - \ = 15\ 10 + 8 - \ = 25\ 8 - \ = 17$$

It is now clear that, if a technique can be developed to easily convert expressions from the normal algebraic notation to reverse Polish notation, the task of automating their evaluation is greatly simplified. Such a technique has been developed and may be defined as follows:

a. Associate ascending hierarchical values to the operations that are defined for a particular algebra. For example let the hierarchical value of addition and subtraction be 2, for multiplication and division the value is 3, and for exponentiation the value is 4. The reason for the choice of the beginning value will be shown in the explanation of processing parentheses, below.
b. Create a null string which will be used to build the reverse Polish notation (target) expression.
c. Create an empty stack which will be used to process operation codes.
d. Scan the original (source) expression from left to right.
e. If the end of the source string is found, go to step 'i'.
f. If an operand is found, copy it to the right end of the target string created in step 'b' and go to step 'd'.
g. If an operation symbol is found compare it to the top entry in the stack created in step 'c'.

    1. If the stack is empty, or if the hierarchical value of the operation is greater than the hierarchical value of the operation at the top of the string, push the current operation onto the stack and go to step 'd'.
    2. If the hierarchical value of the operation is less than or equal to that of the top of the stack, pop the operation symbol from the top of the stack and add it to the right end of the target string. Repeat step 'g'.

h. A syntax error appears in the source expression if none of the above conditions were found. That is, this step should not be reached.
i. If the stack is empty the translation is complete. Else, pop each

operation symbol off the stack and place it at the right end of the target string.

The above technique will process all valid expressions that do not contain parentheses. Parentheses are dealt with as a slightly special case. The open parentheses is defined to have a hierarchical value of zero but is always pushed onto the stack (in violation of rule 'g-2'). The closed parenthesis is assigned the hierarchical value of one which will cause the above algorithm to properly pop the symbols from the stack. Neither of the parentheses are moved to the target string—they are simply discarded and processing continues at step 'd' when the matching open parenthesis is found. The above logic is added after step 'd' of the original algorithm.

For example, to convert the string:

$$a + b \times c - (d - e) / f$$

The individual steps of the algorithm are illustrated as:

Scanned input	Stack	Target
a	Empty	a
a +	+	a
a + b	+	a b
a + b ×	+ , ×	a b
a + b × c	+ , ×	a b c
a + b × c-	-	a b c × +
a + b × c-(	-,(	a b c × +
a + b × c-(d	-,(	a b c × + d
a + b × c-(d-	-,(,-	a b c × + d
a + b × c-(d-e	-,(,-	a b c × + d e
a + b × c-(d-e)	-	a b c × + d e -
a + b × c-(d-e)/	-,/	a b c × + d e -
a + b × c-(d-e)/f	-,/	a b c × + d e - f
	Empty	a b c × + d e - f / -

A full implementation of the above techniques are included, as SAMPLE8, in Appendix D. While the above explanation is limited to simple algebraic equations it may be expanded to much more complex expressions—it is at least theoretically possible to parse a complete program as a single unit. To expand the capabilities of the above algorithm to more complex expressions it is only necessary to adjust or expand the hierarchical levels and analyze the syntax for possible special processing needs. For example the above procedure does not support unary plus and minus signs. Extensions could be made by artificially introducing a preceding zero or by converting the unary signs to different operation codes. Other examples would be the extension of expressions to include logical operators, assignment symbols (e.g., '=' in FORTRAN), if-then-else clauses, etc.

The first utilization of Polish notation for mechanization of compiler statement decomposition occurred in the implementation of the ALGOL compiler for the Burroughs B5000 computer.

18

Redundancy and Error-Correction Techniques

Because of the vast quantities of data processed by a computer it is essential that there be practically no question as to whether undetected errors may occur. Unlike manual processes, where a single error in a million samples would be considered an impossible achievement, such an error rate would render computer processing useless—even for relative slow processors, ***an error would occur approximately every second***!

Fortunately the components of contemporary processors are extremely reliable and very few errors are introduced. Still, with the requirements of such great accuracy, whenever errors occur they must at least be detected. Such requirements led to the development of techniques to address the problems of data integrity and many of these techniques have been implemented in the hardware and firmware of computers. Despite these implementations there are still rare instances—such as in the interfacing of non-standard devices and in situations where error detection alone is insufficient—that the programmer still might need to be familiar with such techniques.

PARITY BITS

One of the simplest error detection techniques for binary data is to introduce an additional bit that causes the sum of all bits to be an odd value. Whenever the data is accessed the bits are summed and verified to be odd. In some cases an even parity is used but this is normally undesirable because all bits would be off for a zero value and, for technical reasons, this is inconvenient.

The use of parity bits will provide detection of all single bit errors. Normally each byte of memory contains a parity bit which is generated when the value is stored and verified each time the byte is fetched—all transparent to programming. In a similar manner a parity bit is included for each value stored on magnetic tape but, additionally, a special byte is written after each physical block of data. This trailing value is simply a group of bits which are the parity values of the corresponding bits of each byte (or frame) along the length of the block. The parity bit for each byte is called the horizontal redundancy check (HRC) and that for the block is called the vertical redundancy check (VRC). For example:

```
10101010 1 <—HRC

00000011 0

11111011 0


10101101 0 <—VRC
```

The addition of the VRC greatly increases the probability of detecting multiple bit errors and provides the ability to correct a single bit error within a block. This correction is possible because the HRC identifies the byte that is in error and the VRC identifies the bit that is in error.

For standard 9-track tapes, the tracks are arranged with the parity bit in the center of the tape and the data bits alternating around this track, with the high order bits closest to the center. Since data loss is most probable near the edges of the tape, this technique increases the probability that any loss will be least significant bits. The designers of this arrangement considered the parity bit to be the most important while this writer thinks otherwise but does concur with the reasoning for arranging the actual data bits.

Thus, for binary values, the data might still be usable where it is impractical to recover such loss and the exact values are not essential. An application of this property might be the analysis of geophysical data where the values represent measurements of amplitudes, that would be extremely difficult and expensive to recreate, while the processing is minimally dependent on the accuracy of all samples—(i.e., statistically of little significance). Such usage is inappropriate for applications where exact values are required; (e.g., accounting records, programs, text, etc). In this later case the data must either be corrected or recreated.

CHECK SUMS

Another method that is sometimes used to verify the validity of data is to compute a binary sum of the data and use this value for verification. Because of the properties of such binary sums they are often computed by logical addition (see the ADD LOGICAL instruction in the IBM System/370 Principles of Operation) instead of with the arithmetical addition instructions.

A previous exercise introduced the concept of "modulus 10 self-checking digits." This concept is a special case of checksum but is used to validate the accuracy of manual input rather than the validity of electronic storage.

Another type of checksum is also used in addition to the VRC and HRC for magnetic tape as well as other magnetic media recordings. This sum is a cyclic redundancy check (CRC) which is defined by a complex polynomial algorithm. The CRC is normally included after the VRC for each physical block of data. As defined for this standard format, the CRC is a sixteen bit value.

HAMMING CODES

Much of the above discussion has been related to the detection of errors. For normal processing this is sufficient because it is normally easier and more efficient to recreate erroneous data than bother with elaborate correction schemes that would rarely be used. Such recreation is normally available by retaining "backup" copies of major data files and from re-applying updates to previous generations of such files.

In some cases, however, it is impractical or impossible to recreate data or maintain redundant copies. In these cases, an alternate technique is to increase the number of parity bits in such a way that multiple bits can be corrected. A class of such techniques is called Hamming Codes in honor of R. W. Hamming for his work in developing rules for such codes.

Hamming's technique is to arrange the parity bits, interspersed among the data bits, in such a way that the sum of the positions of invalid parity bits will identify the bits in error. To illustrate consider the bit pattern $p_1p_2d_3p_4d_5d_6d_7$ where $d_3d_5d_6d_7$ is a 4-bit data value and p_1, p_2, and p_4 are parity bits. These parity bits are generated so that the following groups have odd parity:

$$p_1d_3d_5d_7$$

$$p_2d_3d_6d_7$$

$$p_4d_5d_6d_7$$

Now when any of these groups' parity is invalid the bit that is in error can be identified as that bit position that is the sum of the subscripts of the parity bits that are invalid. That is, if only a single group has a parity error, then only the parity bit is in error and all data bits are correct. If groups beginning with p_1 and p_2 are in error, then bit d_3 is incorrect; errors in groups beginning with p_1 and p_4 indicate that d_5 is erroneous; errors in groups beginning with p_2 and p_4 indicate that d_6 is erroneous; and if all groups are in error, then d_7 is the erroneous bit.

The above example will correct a single bit error but is not every efficient because it requires three parity bits for four data bits. As the number of bits in such a string increases the efficiency also increases. Consider the string

$$p_1p_2d_3p_4d_5d_6d_7p_8d_9d_{10}d_{11}d_{12}d_{13}d_{14}d_{15}$$

and the parity groups:

$p_1d_3d_5d_7d_9d_{11}d_{13}d_{15}$

$p_2d_3d_6d_7d_{11}d_{12}d_{14}d_{15}$

$p_4d_5d_6d_7d_{12}d_{13}d_{14}d_{15}$

$p_8d_9d_{10}d_{11}d_{12}d_{13}d_{14}d_{15}$

This set of groups provide the same protection as the first case but is more efficient—four parity bits allow correction for eleven data bits. This same technique can be extended to any length. As the number of parity bits is increased by one the number of data bits may be increased by one less than the next power of 2. Depending on the processor architecture this efficiency of storage might, however, be at the expense of computational complexity—(e.g., since the above codes are contained in seven bits, they may be analyzed by use of the translate instruction while multibyte data will require a different approach).

To develop Hamming patterns for any number of digits it is only necessary to observe that the powers of two yield the positions of the parity bits. The parity groups are determined by producing the positions that are the sums of all possible combinations of the parity bit positions.

The above procedure provides a technique to correct all single bit errors. By adding additional bits, multiple bit errors can be corrected.

OTHER CONSIDERATIONS

For normal applications all practical care should be exercised to enable the detection of data errors. The techniques and efforts of correction such errors will be dependent on the type of data, the availability of redundancies, and the type of processing. The extent of such detection and correction techniques will depend on the relative importance of that data. For example, the accuracy of inputs to a recreational game would not justify any significant concern while that involving human life—(e.g., manned space flight)—would justify extreme concern. In cases where accuracy is of considerable importance redundancy often leads to the implementation of such techniques as multiple storage facilities, processors, entire redundant facilities, etc.

19

XA and Bimodal Programming

The introduction of 31-bit addressing within the IBM System/370 architecture required certain programming considerations. The previous architecture, that we have been studying, permitted only 24-bit addressing. This older addressing ignored the first eight bits of registers used in addressing and, therefore, existing programs could not be expected to be concerned with the contents of these bits—in fact many programmers intentionally used those bits for other purposes. In order to preserve the enormous existing software assets it was mandatory that a technique be developed to preserve the function of such programming while extending the architecture to a larger addressable memory space. This section will explore how these requirements were met.

First, by increasing the addressing range from 24 bits to 31 bits the amount of addressable memory could be increased by a factor of 2^7 (from 16,777.216 to 2,147,483,648 bytes—16 megabytes to 2 gigabytes) which would relieve the constraints of the older architecture. The needs for this expanded memory grew primarily from large networks of terminals which were not envisioned when the IBM System/360 was designed—to replace computers which had a memory size from 4000 characters to 32,768 36-bit words.

Next, to accommodate the desired compatibility with existing software, the new architecture was designed to operate in both 31-bit and 24-bit addressing modes. This was done by altering the contents of the program status word (PSW) to contain a bit (bit 32) that would indicate which addressing mode is to be used. To accommodate this bit, and the need to use bits 33–39 for the extended instruction address, it was necessary to remove the previous contents (instruction length code, condition code, and program mask) from the PSW. Bit 32 is called the addressing mode or AMODE bit.

MODE-SENSITIVE INSTRUCTIONS

While the above discussion explained the addressing consequences of the extended architecture; there are some instructions that, by the nature of their operation, perform slightly differently in 32-bit and 24-bit modes. These instructions are called *mode sensitive instructions* and include the BAL (Branch and Link), BALR (Branch and Link Register), LA (Load Address), and LRA (Load Real Address). As explained in the Execute and Linkage section it is noted that there is a recommendation that the BAL and BALR instructions be replaced by the branch and save (BAS and BASR) instructions but also note the caveat to this recommendation.

AMODE AND RMODE ASSEMBLER INSTRUCTIONS

The assembler may be informed of the intended addressing mode by the AMODE assembler instruction. This instruction requires a single operand and must be either '24', '31', or 'ANY' to indicate that it expects control in 24-bit, 31-bit, or either mode; respectively. This mode, or attribute, is communicated to the loader.

In addition to the addressing mode used by a program it may also be important where the program is loaded—either above the 24-bit addressable memory (sometimes called 'the 16-meg line'). This is specified by the RMODE (residency mode) assembler language instruction. Its operand is either '24' to indicate that it must be loaded into the 24-bit addressable memory or 'ANY' to indicate that placement is not important. In this later case, the operating system would load it above the 24-bit space unless there was insufficient room in that area.

There may be multiple AMODE and RMODE instructions within a program but, if so, each must have different name fields (although an AMODE may have the same name field as an RMODE which specify the control section (CSECT) name. These instructions may be placed anywhere within the program. In addition to using these instructions, the loader can be informed of the attributes within special control cards.

SWITCHING MODES

As indicated above, bit 32 of the PSW controls the addressing mode ('0' indicates 24-bit addressing and '1' indicates 31-bit addressing. This bit, and thus the addressing mode, can be conveniently changed by the use of two instructions.

The Branch And Save and Set Mode (BASSM) instruction contains two register operands. Bits 32–63 of the current PSW (AMODE bit and instruction address) replaces the contents of the general register specified by the first operand. Thus, the contents of this register can be used as a linkage return address but also contains the addressing mode bit. If the second operand is not zero, the AMODE bit and instruction address (bits 32–63 of the current PSW) are replaced by the value contained in the indicated register.

The Branch and Set Mode (BSM) instruction contains two register operands. If the first operand is not zero, bit 32 of the current PSW (AMODE bit) replaces bit 0 of the general register specified by that operand (bits 1–31 are not changed). If the second operand is not zero, the AMODE bit and instruction address (bits 32–63 of the current PSW) are replaced by the value contained in the indicated register.

```
         L     5,ADDRESS              LOAD AMODE & ADDRESS

         BASSM 6,5                    SET AMODE AND BRANCH

         ...

ADDRESS  DC    A(X'80000000'+ENTRY)   AMODE + ADDRESS

         ...

         USING ENTRY,5                ESTABLISH ADDRESSABILITY

ENTRY    ...

         ...

         BSM   0,6                    RESET AMODE AND RETURN
```

The above load (L) instruction loads the address of the instruction specified by label ENTRY into register 5 and also sets bit 0 of register 5 to "1" (note how the address constant is specified).

The following BASSM instruction loads the current addressing mode into bit 0 of general register six, loads bits 1–31 of that register with the current instruction address, sets the addressing mode to 31-bit addressing (from bit 0 of register five), and branches to the location specified by ENTRY.

The code beginning at ENTRY performs some function (in 31-bit addressing mode) and should either leave register six unchanged or restore its contents to the value that was present from the above BASSM execution.

The BSM instruction resets the addressing mode from bit 0 of register six and returns to the address specified by bits 1–31 of register six. Note that, because the first operand is zero, the addressing mode at the time of the return is not saved in register zero. If the previous AMODE value is needed, the first operand must specify a register from 1 to 15.

Reference

MVS/Extended Architecture Systems Programming Library: 31-Bit Addressing (IBM Form Number GC28-1158).

20

Floating-Point Instructions

Up until now, all arithmetic instructions that have been discussed were fixed-point operations. Fixed-point arithmetic requires that the program allow for any fractions (decimal or binary) and the arithmetic is actually integer arithmetic. Commercial data, such as monetary values, are conveniently represented and processed by such techniques. Processing of scientific and engineering data by these techniques, however, results in a tedious process of scaling values to assure that fixed magnitudes are not exceeded, proper precision is retained, etc.

DATA REPRESENTATION

Floating-point arithmetic instructions, as was mentioned briefly in Basic Architecture, performs operations on data that consists of a pair of values. The first part of a floating-point operation consists of an exponent (characteristic) and the second part represents the fraction (mantissa). Actually there is a third component, the sign, but it is considered to be part of the fraction—although distinct in that the fraction is not in 2's complement notation but is represented by a single bit (bit 0).

First, let us consider the following decimal representation:

$$1234.567 = .1234567 \times 10^4.$$

In this case the fraction is .1234567 and the characteristic is 4. This value is said to be in normal form, or normalized, when the absolute value of the fraction is less than one and not less than one tenth ($1/10 \leq x < 1$, where x is the absolute value of the fraction). Now consider:

$$-1034_{10} = -40A_{16} = -.40A_{16} \times 16^3.$$

Which, of course, provides us a similar definition for a normalized hexadecimal value. In this later case the characteristic is the power of ***sixteen*** which provides a fraction whose absolute value is less than one and not less than one sixteenth ($1/16 \leq x < 1$). In the case of a pure zero, both the characteristic and fraction have the value zero.

In the IBM System/370 architecture the characteristic of floating-point values are represented by bits 1–7. Since it was considered undesirable to maintain a sign bit for the characteristic the range of exponent values from 0 to 63 is represented by the values from 64 to 127 and the values from −64 to −1 is represented by the values from 0 to 63. This technique is called "excess 64" notation to indicate that the actual exponent values are increased by 64.

In fixed-point binary arithmetic we can use either full words or half words depending on the magnitude of the values, the constraints on memory sizes, etc. In a like manner there are three floating-point formats that can be selected depending on the precision needed (since the size of the characteristic is the same, the magnitude does not change). These formats are:

a. Short; where the sign is represented by bit 0, the characteristic by bits 1–7, and the mantissa by bits 8–31.
b. Long; where the sign is represented by bit 0, the characteristic by bits 1–7, and the mantissa by bits 8–63.
c. Extended; where the sign is represented by bit 0, the characteristic by bits 1–7, and the mantissa by bits 8–63 and bits 72–127. Bits 64–71 are called the low-order characteristic but are ignored in all computations.

While representation of integers maintain the same decimal to binary relationships that we are accustomed to from fixed-point binary, the representation of fractions might be somewhat confusing. To understand this representation it is necessary to recognize that the digits of decimal fraction representations (such as .123) specify the fractions of powers of ten (such as $1/10 + 2/100 + 3/1000$) while those of hexadecimal fractions specify the fractions of powers of sixteen ($.1A4_{16} = 1/16 + 10/256 + 4/4096$). Thus:

$$
\begin{aligned}
&5_{10} = 8/16 = .8_{16} \\
&.25_{10} = 4/16 = .4_{16} \\
&.125_{10} = 2/16 = .2_{16} \\
&.0625_{10} = 1/16 = .1_{16} \\
&1034.5 = 1034 + .5 = 40A.8_{16}
\end{aligned}
$$

Hence, by using the above representation, the hexadecimal value of −1034.5 can be represented as a short form floating-point representation as:

$$C340A800_{16} = 1\ 1000011\ 0100\ 0000\ 1010\ 1000\ 0000\ 0000_2$$

Where bit 0 is one to indicate a negative value, bits 1–7 contain 43_{16}

($67_{10} = 64_{10} + 3$) to represent an exponent of three, and bits 8–31 contain the hexadecimal fraction (.40A8000).

As mentioned earlier this form is normalized. In some special cases unnormalized representations are desirable. As an example of unnormalized representations, all of the following represent the value of 2^{31} ($= 1/2 \times 2^{32} = .8_{16} \times 16^8$).

```
48800000

49080000

4A008000

4B000800

4C000080

4D000008
```

The reason that each of the above forms represent the same value is that there is only one bit of precision in the fraction. If the normalized value had been, for example, 48812345_{16} then unnormalization by a single hexadecimal digit would yield 48081234_{16}. This later value would differ from the original value by five.

FLOATING-POINT REGISTERS AND INSTRUCTIONS

The hardware facilities to process floating-point data consists of special floating-point registers and floating-point machine instructions. There are four 64-bit floating-point registers—numbered 0, 2, 4, and 6. Short and long floating-point values can be contained in a single register while two registers are required for extended floating-point values.

The floating-point instructions provide the normal arithmetic, comparison, and manipulation operations that are similar to their fixed-point counterparts. Register operands of these instructions refer to the floating-point registers and must be those *even* values specified above and instructions for extended format are restricted to the register pair specified by 0 or 4. While register-storage instructions are provided for long and short data formats only register-register instruction types are provided for extended data formats.

The floating-point instructions (for short, long, and—if available—extended data formats) are:

a. Add Normalized (AE and AD). These RX-type instructions add the contents of storage specified by the address of the second operand to the contents of the floating-point register specified by the first operand.
b. Add Normalized-Register (AER, ADR, and AXR). These instructions add the contents of the floating-point register specified by the second operand to that specified by the first operand.

c. Add Unnormalized (AU and AW). These RX-type instructions add the contents of storage specified by the address of the second operand to the contents of the floating-point register specified by the first operand. The result is unnormalized (i.e., the leading zeros in the resulting fraction remain).
d. Add Unnormalized-Register (AUR and AWR). These instructions add the contents of the floating-point register specified by the second operand to that specified by the first operand. The result is unnormalized.
e. Compare (CE and CD). These RX-type instructions arithmetically compare the contents of the floating-point register specified by the first operand to the contents of storage specified by the address of the second operand. If the values are equal the condition code is set to zero, if the value of the first operand is smaller than the second operand the condition code is set to one, otherwise the condition code is set to two.
f. Divide (DE and DD). These RX-type instructions divide the contents of the floating-point register specified by the first operand by the contents of storage specified by the second operand.
g. Divide-Register (DER, DDR, and DXR). These instructions divide the contents of the floating-point register specified by the first operand by that specified by the second operand. The extended form of this instruction is an RRE-type instruction and is only available on XA models.
h. Halve-Register (HER and HDR). The contents of the value contained in the floating register specified by the second operand is divided by two and the result is placed in the floating-point register specified by the first operand.
i. Load (LE and LD). The value specified by the second operand address is placed in the floating-point register specified by the first operand.
j. Load-Register (LER and LDR). The contents of the floating-point register specified by the second operand replaces the contents of the floating-point register specified by the first operand.
k. Load and Test-Register (LTER and LTDR). The contents of the floating-point register specified by the second operand replaces the contents of the floating-point register specified by the first operand. The condition code is set to 0, 1, or 2 depending on whether the fraction is zero, less than zero, or greater than; respectively.
l. Load Complement-Register (LCER and LCDR). The contents of the floating-point register specified by the second operand is placed in the floating-point register specified by the first operand and the sign of the later register is reversed. The condition code is set to 0, 1, or 2 depending on whether the fraction of the result is zero, less than zero, or greater than zero; respectively.
m. Load Negative-Register (LNER and LNDR). The contents of the floating-point register specified by the second operand is placed in

the floating-point register specified by the first operand and the sign of the later register is forced negative. The condition code is set to 0 or 1 depending on whether the fraction of the result is zero or less than zero, respectively.

n. Load Positive-Register (LPER and LPDR). The contents of the floating-point register specified by the second operand is placed in the floating-point register specified by the first operand and the sign of the later register is forced positive. The condition code is set to 0 or 2 depending on whether the fraction of the result is zero or greater than zero, respectively.
o. Load Rounded-Register (LRDR and LRER). The contents of the floating-point register specified by the second operand is placed in the floating-point register specified by the first operand. The result is rounded to the next shorter form (long to short and extended to long, respectively).
p. Multiply (ME and MD). These RX-type instructions multiplies the contents of the floating-point register specified by the first operand by the contents of storage specified by the second operand. The product replaces the contents of the floating-point register specified by the first operand. The short form (ME) produces a long result. There is also a special form, MXD, which produces an extended form result from long form operands.
q. Multiply-Register (DER, DDR, and DXR). These instructions multiplies the contents of the floating-point register specified by the first operand by that specified by the second operand. The extended form of this instruction is an RRE-type instruction. The product replaces the contents of the register specified by the first operand. The short form (MER) produces a long result. There is also a special form, MXDR, which produces an extended form result from long form operands.
r. Store (STE and STD). The contents of the floating-point register specified by the first operand is placed in memory at the address specified by the second operand.
s. Subtract Normalized (SE and SD). These RX-type instructions subtract the contents of storage specified by the address of the second operand to the contents of the floating-point register specified by the first operand.
t. Subtract Normalized-Register (SER, SDR, and SXR). These instructions subtract the contents of the floating-point register specified by the second operand to that specified by the first operand.
u. Subtract Unnormalized (SU and SW). These RX-type instructions subtract the contents of storage specified by the address of the second operand to the contents of the floating-point register specified by the first operand. The result is unnormalized.
v. Subtract Unnormalized-Register (SUR and SWR). These instructions subtract the contents of the floating-point register specified by the

second operand to that specified by the first operand. The result is unnormalized.

Example:

```
         LD    0,DIAMETER        GET DIAMETER OF A CIRCLE
         HDR   0,0               COMPUTE RADIUS=DIAMETER/2
         MDR   0,0               RADIUS**2
         MD    0,PI              PI*RADIUS**2
         STD   0,AREA            AREA=PI*RADIUS**2
         ...
PI       DC    D'3.1415927'
DIAMETER DS    D
AREA     DS    D
```

Note that the definition of short, long, and extended format floating-point data constants are denoted by the modifiers 'E', 'D', and 'L'; respectively. The selection of these characters might seem a bit confusing but resulted from the fact that the extended format was not part of the original architecture. We have used the modifier "D" to force double word alignment and define storage for eight bytes but, until now, such usage was only to define storage and not to define constants.

DATA CONVERSION

To convert from fixed-point binary to floating-point assume that fixed-value is a representation of a full word (31 bits) positive binary integer. Such a value can be represented as

$$.\text{fixed-value}_2 \times 2^{31} = .0\text{fixed-value}_2 \times 2_{32} = .0\text{fixed-value}_2 \times 16^8$$

which would result in the floating-point value (not necessarily normalized—it would be normalized if, and only if, its value is at least 2^{24}).

0 1001000 0fixed-value

Thus, for positive values, conversion from fixed-point to floating-point can be accomplished by concatenating a characteristic of 48_{16} prior to the fixed-point binary value. For example, the value $256_{10} = 100_{16}$ would become $48000001\ 00000000_{16}$ in (long-form, unnormalized) floating point and, when normalized would be $43100000\ 00000000_{16}$.

Since negative fixed-point binary values are stored in 2's complement form and floating numbers are stored in signed-magnitude form the negative value must first be complemented. Thus, $-256_{10} = FFFFFF00_{16}$ and the floating-point representation would be:

$$C80000001\ 00000000_{16} = C31000000\ 00000000_{16}.$$

A simple method of affecting the above is:

```
         MVC   X48+1(4),FIXED          MOVE FIXED-POINT BINARY
         XI    X48+1,X'80'             REVERSE SIGN BIT
         LD    0,X48                   LOAD FLOATING POINT VALUE
         SD    0,D2X31                 ADD 2**31
         STD   0,FLOAT                 SAVE CONVERTED VALUE
         ...
FLOAT    DS    D
D2X31    DC    X'4880',6X'0'
X48      DC    X'48',4X'0',3X'0'
FIXED    DS    F
```

The MVC instructions appends the fixed-point value to the characteristic in the manner that we described above. Reversal of bit 8 (bit 0 of the fixed-point quantity) adds 2^{31} to the fixed-point value. This value is loaded into *floating*-point register 0 and the value of 2^{31} is subtracted from the floating-point value. This subtraction will result in a negative floating-point value if the fixed-point value was negative. The above procedure provides conversion for both positive and negative values. If it is known that all values will be positive, the unnormalized value resulting from the MVC instruction suffices.

To convert from floating-point to fixed-point the above procedure is reversed. For example:

```
         LD    0,FLOAT                 LOAD FLOATING-POINT VALUE
         SD    0,D2X31Z                SUBTRACT 2**31
         AW    0,D2X32                 ADD 2**32 (UNNORMALIZED)
         STD   0,WORKAREA              SAVE RESULT
         MVC   FIXED,WORKAREA+2        MOVE TO FIXED POINT RESULT
         XI    FIXED,X'80'             REVERSE BIT 0
         ...
```

```
WORKAREA DS     D
D2X32    DC     X'4A01',6X'0'
D2X31Z   DC     X'4B0008',5X'0'
```

In this case we subtract 2^{31} and add 2^{32}. Mathematically, this results in the net difference of 2^{31}, but the fixed-point value is obtained from bits 16–47 of the resulting (unnormalized) result—which provides the necessary allowance for this computation.

The following demonstrate the individual steps of the above techniques. On the line following each instruction are two values. These values are in hexadecimal and indicate the results of beginning positive and negative values of 256_{10} respectively.

```
         MVC   X48+1(4),BINARY       MOVE FIXED-POINT BINARY
X48:  4800000100000000, 48FFFFFF00000000
         XI    X48+1,X'80'           REVERSE SIGN BIT
X48:  4880000100000000, 48EFFFFF00000000
         LD    0,X48                 LOAD FLOATING POINT VALUE
R0:   4880000100000000, 48EFFFFE00000000
         SD    0,D2X31               ADD 2**31
R0:   4310000000000000, C310000000000000
         STD   0,FLOAT               SAVE CONVERTED VALUE
-------------------------------------------
         LD    0,FLOAT               LOAD FLOATING-POINT VALUE
R0:   4310000000000000, C310000000000000
         SD    0,D2X31Z              SUBTRACT 2**31
R0:   C87FFFFF00000000, C880000100000000
         AW    0,D2X32               ADD 2**32 (UNNORMALIZED)
R0:   4A00800001000000, 4A007FFFFF000000
         STD   0,WORKAREA            SAVE RESULT
         MVC   FIXED,WORKAREA+2      MOVE TO FIXED POINT RESULT
FIXED:    80000100,         7FFFFF00
         XI    FIXED,X'80'           REVERSE BIT 0
FIXED:    00000100,         FFFFFF00
```

SCALING AND PRECISION

The above conversions treat the values as integers. In fixed-point arithmetic the program's logic accounts for any decimal or binary points (fractions). This could be done in floating-point as well but in most cases it is more convenient to maintain the actual values and remove any such considerations from the program. For this reason it is normally necessary to adjust the floating-point value after conversion from fixed-point and, again, prior to conversion to fixed-point. Also, it is normally appropriate to round the value before converting it to fixed-point. For example, suppose PERSHARE contains the price/share of stock (expressed in 32nds of a dollar, i.e., five binary points) and this value is to be converted to floating point and used to compute TOTAL$ (expressed in dollars and cents, i.e., two decimal points).

```
         ...   Convert 'PERSHARE' to floating-point.
         DD    0,=D'32'               CONVERT FROM 32NDS
         ...   Compute result
         MD    0,=D'100'              CONVERT TO CENTS
         NI    ONEHALF,X'7F'          SET SIGN POSITIVE
         LTDR  0,0                    IS VALUE NEGATIVE?
         BNM   POSITIVE                NO
         OI    ONEHALF,X'80'          SET SIGN NEGATIVE
POSITIVE AD    0,ONEHALF              ROUND VALUE
         ...   Convert to fixed-point and store in TOTAL$
         ...
ONEHALF  DC    D'.5'
PERSHARE DC    F
TOTAL$   DC    F
```

The above is a procedure that scales the value based on the implicit fractional values (32nds and 100ths of a dollar). Another situation often arises in scientific and engineering computation. In this situation the analyst wants to obtain a certain number of digits of precision regardless of the magnitude of the value. For instance, to provide nine decimal digits of precision:

```
      ZAP   EXPONENT,=P'0'        INITIALIZE EXPONENT
      MVI   SIGN,0                INITIALIZE SIGN FLAG
      LTDR  0,0                   WHAT IS SIGN?
```

```
         BZ    ZERO                  ZERO
         BP    POSITIVE              POSITIVE
         MVI   SIGN,1               INDICATE NEGATIVE
         LPDR  0,0                  FORCE POSITIVE
POSITIVE CD    0,=D'10'             IS VALUE TOO LARGE?
         BH    TOOBIG                YES
         CD    0,=D'1'              IS VALUE TOO SMALL?
         BNL   JUSTRITE              NO
         MD    0,=D'10'             INCREASE MAGNITUDE
         SP    EXPONENT,=P'1'       DECREASE EXPONENT
         B     POSITIVE             GO REPEAT TEST
TOOBIG   DD    0,=D'10'             DECREASE MAGNITUDE
         AP    EXPONENT,=P'1'       INCREASE EXPONENT
         B     POSITIVE             GO REPEAT TEST
JUSTRITE MD    0,=D'1E+8'           MULTIPLY BY 10**7
         AD    0,=D'.5'             ROUND TO NEAREST INTEGER
         CD    0,=D'1E+9'           TRUNCATION FROM DIVISION?
         BL    NOTRUNC               NO
         DD    0,=D'10'             REDUCE BY A FACTOR OF 10
         AP    EXPONENT,=P'1'       INCREASE EXPONENT LIKE AMT
NOTRUNC  TM    SIGN,1               WAS VALUE POSITIVE?
         BZ    ZERO                  YES
         LDNR  0,0                  REVERSE SIGN
ZERO     ...   Convert to fixed-point and place in FIXED
         L     0,FIXED              LOAD FIXED-POINT RESULT
         CVD   0,DOUBLE             CONVERT TO DECIMAL
         MVC   OUTPUT+13(5),PAT1    SET EDIT PATTERN
         ED    OUTPUT+13(5),EXPONENT FORMAT EXPONENT
         MVC   OUTPUT(14),PAT2      SET EDIT PATTERN
```

```
         ED    OUTPUT(14),DOUBLE+2     FORMAT X.XXXXXXX-
         MVC   OUTPUT+2(1),OUTPUT+13   MOVE SIGN TO PREFIX POSITION
         MVI   OUTPUT+13,C'E'          INDICATE EXPONENT
         MVC   OUTPUT+14(1),OUTPUT+17  MOVE EXP SIGN TO PREFIX POS
         MVI   OUTPUT+17,C' '          OVERLAY POSTFIX SIGN POSITION
         ...
FIXED    DS    F
DOUBLE   DS    D
PAT1     DC    X'4021202060'
PAT2     DC    C' ',X'202120',C'.',7X'20',C'-'
SIGN     DS    C
OUTPUT   DS    CL18
EXPONENT DS    PL3
```

Such scaling might also be needed prior to the normal conversion from floating-point to fixed-point values because our technique is valid only for values whose magnitude is less than 2^{31}. For clarity, this caution was not mentioned at the time of that conversion example.

It is important to realize that whenever fractions are used, computations may not result in exact values. In decimal arithmetic that preserves two decimal points of precision the value 1/3 is represented by 0.33, hence if this value is multiplied by 3 the result is 0.99. When using binary arithmetic a similar situation occurs for values that could represent precisely in a fixed number of decimal places—for instance 1/10 is .1 in decimal but .1999... in hexadecimal. Thus, $A_{16}(1/A_{16}) = A_{16} \times .199_{16} = .FFA_{16}$ with three hexadecimal digits of precision and, when rounded (by adding $.008_{16}$), becomes 1.004_{16}. This is why the truncation test was necessary in the above example—after the rounding constant had been added the magnitude increased.

The magnitude of the smallest absolute value that can be represented in floating-point format is approximately 5.4×10^{-79} while the largest is approximately 7.2×10^{75}. The maximum precision for the short, long, and extended formats are approximately 7, 21, and 43 digits; respectively.

21

Cross Memory and ESA/370 Instructions

The IBM MVS (Multiple Virtual Storage) system is divided into regions called address spaces. While different address spaces share some common areas, the area used exclusively by the owner of an address space (the private area) cannot normally be accessed by other address spaces. One reason for this restriction is to provide security and protection from other address spaces. Another reason is that all private areas contain the same range of virtual addresses and, therefore cannot be addressed directly.

The IBM ESA/370 (Enterprise Systems Architecture) environment extends this concept by allowing address spaces the ability to create and delete data spaces. The data space allows an extension of the previously 2-gigabyte main storage addressability limit that is available with the 370-XA facilities.

CROSS MEMORY SERVICES

While the above mentioned restrictions of inter-address space access provides benefits it also poses drawbacks. Many of the utilities that are normally thought of as part of the operating system are implemented within their own address spaces. These components include such facilities as JES (Job Entry Subsystem), VTAM (Virtual Telecommunications Access Method), etc. It is necessary for these facilities to serve the other address spaces and, therefore, it is necessary to communicate with these other address spaces. Such communication is implemented by use of the common areas, cross memory service facilities, or a combination of the two approaches.

For a complete description of Cross Memory Services see the IBM Publication that are referenced below. Cross Memory Services facilities are complex and improper usage can cause system performance degradation or more serious problems. For these reasons and because they may be amplified by the inevitable changing and extensions of the software interfaces, our discussion is concerned only with the instructions that permit direct communications between different address spaces once such communication has been established. These semi-privileged instructions are:

1. Extract Primary ASN-Register (EPAR). The 16-bit primary address space number is placed in bits 16–31 of the register specified by the single register operand. Bits 0–15 of that general register is cleared to binary zeros. The value is obtained from bits 16–31 of control register 4.
2. Extract Secondary ASN-Register (ESAR). The 16-bit secondary address space number is placed in bits 16–31 of the register specified by the single register operand. Bits 0–15 of that general register is cleared to binary zeros. The value is obtained from bits 16–31 of control register 3.
3. Insert Address Space Control (IAC). Bit 16 of the current PSW, the address space control bit, is placed in bit 23 of the single register operand. Bits 16–22 of that register is set to zeros and the remainder of the register is unchanged.
4. Insert Virtual Storage Key (IVSK). The storage key of the address contained in the second register operand is placed in the first register operand.
5. Set Address Space Control (SAC). Bits 20–23 of the operand address replaces the address-space-control bit in the PSW. Bits 20–22 must contain zeros. This address is not used to indicate a memory address but its value is used in the same manner as used by shift instructions —to calculate an effective value—and this value can be specified only by the displacement or modified by a base register.
6. Set PSW Key from Address (SPKA). Bits 24–27 of the operand address replaces bits 8–11 of the current PSW, the PSW key. This value is obtained in the same manner as that of the SAC instruction.
7. Move Characters to Primary (MVCP). The contents of the second operand is moved to the first operand. The first operand is designated as displacement(register,base) where "register" is a general purpose register that contains the true length of the operands. If the value contained in this register is greater than 256, then the effective length is 256. If the value is zero then no movement occurs. A third register operand specifies, in bits 24–27, secondary-space access key.
8. Move Characters to Secondary (MVCS). The contents of the second operand is moved to the first operand. The operands are the same as for the above MVCP but movement is from the primary address space to the secondary address space.
9. Move Characters with Key (MVCK). The contents of the second operand is moved to the first operand. The operands are the same as for the above move instructions but movement is from the address space specified by the key contained in the third operand to the address space specified by the key within the PSW.

The above are the more common instructions used for Cross Memory Service applications. For a more detailed discussion of these instructions and for other instructions that might be useful see 'Control Instructions' in the IBM System/370 Principles of Operation manuals. Such instructions include the Program Call (PC) and Program Transfer (PT) which are too complex to discuss in this introduction.

Note that the above move instructions could be used to replace other move instructions but, because of efficiency, should be avoided for intra-address space moves.

ENTERPRISE SYSTEMS ARCHITECTURE INSTRUCTIONS

ESA/370 is the latest enhancement to the MVS operating system. It allows for each address space to access up to 15 two-gigabyte data or address spaces. Facilities are available to create, delete, and share data spaces.

While ESA offers capabilities similar to CMS the implementation is completely different. ESA addressing is implemented by means of a set of access or 'shadow' registers. The CMS instructions provided means to access data in a primary and secondary address space and this specific facility is called Address Space Control (ASC). ESA's access register mode is another ASC mode and is referred to as the AR mode.

In primary and secondary ASC modes the processor ignores access register modes. In AR mode access to other address and data spaces is given to the common machine instructions. In this mode the base registers of instructions refer to the special access registers instead of the general purpose registers that would be in effect during normal operation. Thus the instruction:

```
L        1,100(2,3)
```

would load the data at the location that is computed by adding the value of 100 to the sum of the contents of general register 2 and access register 3. Note that it is important to note that the access register is specified as the base register field(s) of the instruction. In non-AR mode indexed instructions can specify the base as an index or base register. For example:

```
L        1,0(2)

L        1,0(,2)
```

results in the same operation in non-AR mode but differ in AR mode. That is, in normal mode, either form results in the contents of general register 1 being replaced by the data stored at the virtual memory location whose address is specified by general register 2. But in AR mode the second form results in replacement by the data whose address is specified by access register 2.

References

IBM Publication GC28-1823, Introduction to MVS.
IBM Publication GG22-9201, Introduction to Cross Memory Services.
IBM Publication GG22-9231, Cross Memory Services User's Guide.
IBM Publication GC28-1359, MVS/ESA General Information Manual for System Product Version 3.
IBM Publication GC28-1821, MVS/ESA Application Development Guide.
IBM Publication GC28-1822, MVS/ESA Application Development Reference.
IBM Publication GC28-1820, MVS/ESA System Programming Library: Application Development 31-Bit Addressing.
IBM Publication GC28-1854, MVS/ESA System Programming Library: Application Development—Addressability.
IBM Publication GC28-1857, MVS/ESA System Programming Library: Application Development Macro Reference.

22

IBM 3270 Data Streams

While the IBM 3270 architecture is not a part of the IBM System/370 architecture, it is included here because the knowledge of this device is often helpful to the assembler programmer. Although newer terminals are now common they are normally members of the IBM 3270 Information Display System family and are compatible with this discussion. Although the input/output commands from the Channel Programming section apply to IBM 3270 the data transmitted can also contain special control information that directs the placement of the displayed information on the video screen or, on input, indicates the location of the fields from which the data was obtained. The control unit identifies this control information by the values contained within the data that is transmitted to the device. Actually the control information and the data stream are transmitted to and from a buffer in the control unit which in turn controls the display but, for now, we will consider this I/O to communicate with the terminal device itself.

DATA STREAM ORDERS

The primary control is the data stream order which either defines a specific function or notifies the control unit that additional bytes of control information will follow. The valid orders and their values are:

a. The Start Field (SF) order indicates that the next byte of data will define the characteristics of the field to be written to the screen (e.g., non-displayable, bright, protected, etc.). These field characteristics are called attributes and are discussed below. The value of the start field is $1D_{16}$ for either EBCDIC or ASCII.
b. The Set Buffer Address (SBA) order indicates that the next two bytes

of data will specify the location on the screen. The value of the SBA is 11_{16} for both ASCII and EBCDIC.

c. The Insert Cursor (IC) order places the cursor at the current screen location. The value of the IC order is 13_{16} for both EBCDIC and ASCII.
d. The Program Tab (PT) order advances the cursor to the first position of the next unprotected field. The value for the PT order is 05_{16} for EBCDIC and is 09_{16} for ASCII.
e. The Repeat to Address (RA) order indicates that the character following this order will be replicated from the current buffer location to the address defined by the two bytes immediately following the order. The value of the RA order is $3C_{16}$ in EBCDIC and 14_{16} in ASCII.
f. The Start Field Extended (SFE) order indicates that an extended attribute follows this character. The byte following the order specifies the number of attribute type/value pairs and this byte is followed by the sequence of type/value pairs (see Extended Field Attributes below). I.e., Color/Red, Highlight/Normal, etc. The value of the SFE order is 29_{16} in EBCDIC and is not defined for ASCII.
g. The Erase Unprotected to Address (EUA) order causes all unprotected fields to be erased from the current position to the address defined by the two bytes following this order. The value of the EUA is 12_{16} for both EBCDIC and ASCII.
h. The Modify Field (MF) order modifies the field attributes at the current buffer position. The format of the bytes following this order is the same as those for the SFE, above. The value of the MF order is $2C_{16}$ in EBCDIC and is not defined for ASCII.
i. The Set Attribute (SA) order specifies character attributes and it is followed by an attribute type and value pair (see Extended Character Attributes below). The value of the SA order is 28_{16} in EBCDIC and is not defined for ASCII.

FIELD ATTRIBUTES

The field attribute defines the start of a field and specifies its characteristics. The field attribute occupies a one character space on the screen (in the buffer). The characteristics are defined by the six low order bits of the byte following the start field order as follows:

a. If bit 2 is off the field is unprotected (i.e., the field is available for keyboard input), else the field is protected.
b. If bit 3 is off the field is alphameric, else the field is numeric. In numeric mode only input of characters 0–9, plus, minus, decimal point, and commas are allowed.
c. Bits 4 and 5 define a two-bit value with the following meaning:

    1. If '00', the field is displayable and not selector pen detectable.
    2. If '01', the field is displayable and selector pen detectable.

3. If '10', the field is highlighted and selector pen detectable.
4. If '11', the field is not displayable (DARK) and not selector pen detectable.

d. Bit 6 must be zero.
e. Bit 7 is the Modified Data Tag (MDT). If on, the field is input during Read Modified operations. It can be set by the data stream or when the field is modified by use of the keyboard.

If both bits 2 and 3 are on an automatic skip (AUTOSKIP) of the field is made whenever the cursor reaches that position.

Bits 0 and 1 are set to assure a proper EBCDIC or ASCII value.

EXTENDED FIELD ATTRIBUTES

Extended field attributes are defined by the start field extended field (SFE) or modify field (MF) orders, as discussed above. These attributes are composed of an attribute type and value pair. No screen (buffer) space is occupied by these attributes.

Extended field attribute types and their associated values are:

a. Extended Highlighting (41_{16}).

1. Default (00_{16}).
2. Normal, as specified by field attribute (FO_{16}).
3. Blinking ($F2_{16}$).
4. Reverse video ($F2_{16}$).
5. Underscore ($F3_{16}$).

b. Foreground Color (42_{16}).

1. Default (00_{16}).
2. Neutral ($F7_{16}$),
3. Blue ($F1_{16}$)
4. Red ($F2_{16}$)
5. Pink ($F3_{16}$ = blue + red),
6. Green ($F4_{16}$).
7. Turquoise ($F5_{16}$ = blue + green).
8. Yellow ($F6_{16}$ = blue + red).

c. Background Color (45_{16}, values as above).
d. Character Sets (43_{16}, see specific hardware manuals for full description).

1. Default (00_{16}).
2. Loadable character sets (40_{16}-EF_{16}).

3. Nonloadable character sets ($F0_{16}$-$F7_{16}$, $F1_{16}$ is normally the APL character set
4. Two-byte coded character sets ($F8_{16}$-FE_{16}). These sets are also referred to as Double-Byte Character Sets (DBCS).

e. Field Outlining ($C2_{16}$).

1. No outlining (00_{16}).
2. Underlining (01_{16}).
3. Vertical line at right of field (02_{16}).
4. Overline (04_{16}).
5. Vertical line at left of field (08_{16}).
6. Combinations. The sum of the above values may be used to yield multiple combinations of outlining. For example, $0F_{16}$ outlines the field in a rectangle.

f. Transparency (46_{16}). This feature provides the ability for the background of a field to be transparent or opaque to the viewer.

1. Default (00_{16}).
2. Background transparent with the pixels being ORed ($F0_{16}$).
3. Background transparent with the pixels being exclusively ORed ($F1_{16}$).
4. Background is opaque (FF_{16}).

g. Field Validation ($C1_{16}$).

1. Trigger (00_{16}) causes transmission when each field is filled.
2. Mandatory entry (02_{16}) requires that the field be entered by the operator.
3. Mandatory fill (04_{16}) requires that, if an entry is made in the field, that it be completely filled.
4. Combinations. Multiple combinations of the above may be specified by summing their corresponding values.

EXTENDED CHARACTER ATTRIBUTES

Extended character attributes are very similar to the extended field attributes except that they specify attributes for individual characters or character strings within a field. They are preceded by the set attribute order. Valid character attributes are:

a. All character attributes. This attribute resets all character attribute types to their default values. Both the attribute type and value is zero.
b. Extended highlighting, foreground and background color, character set, and transparency character attributes are permitted. Their attri-

bute type and values are the same as for the corresponding extended field attributes.

Many of the above attributes refer to specific members of the IBM 3270 family. For example, extended colors are not supported for monochrome devices, etc. Therefore programming must consider the specific device to be supported. Multiple types can be provided for at assembly time by using conditional assembly statements or dynamic support can be provided by examining characteristics and building data streams based on the results of that examination.

BUFFER ADDRESS CODES

As mentioned above, data is transmitted to and from a buffer in the control unit. This buffer is addressed sequentially, beginning with zero, just as main System/370 memory is addressed. However screen positions and addresses are addressed by row (horizontal) and column (vertical) position. This is further complicated by the fact that screen sizes can have 40 (rare in contemporary facilities), 80, or 132 columns. Also there can be 12, 24, 32, 43, and 27 rows. The number of rows are of lesser complication but must still be considered.

The buffer position that corresponds to a specific "row" and "column" of a device with a column width of "width" can be computed as follows:

$$\text{buffer position} = \text{width} \times (\text{row}-1) + \text{column} - 1$$

In a like manner the converse is:

$$\text{row} = (\text{buffer position})/\text{width} + 1$$

and

$$\text{column} = [\text{buffer position} - (\text{row} - 1) \times \text{width}] + 1$$

To compute the screen addresses used in the SBA, RA, and EUA data stream orders it is necessary to realize that such addresses are actually two 6-bit values stored in consecutive 8-bit bytes. The two high order bits of each byte are set to provide a valid EBCDIC or ASCII graphic character. These 12 bits are the buffer address. The corresponding values can be obtained from tables in such documents as IBM 3270 Information Display System: Reference summary (IBM Form Number GX20-1878), computed directly, or generated by macros (see Appendix D for implementation of such macros). Such conversion can be done as follows:

a. Divide the buffer address by 64 (2^6). The quotient provides the first six bytes and the remainder provides the second six bytes.

b. Convert each quantity to an EBCDIC value as follows (a similar technique would yield the proper value for ASCII data streams) where all values are in hexadecimal:

   1. 00 converts to 40.
   2. 01–09 converts to C1–C9.
   3. 0A–10 converts to 4A–50.
   4. 11–19 converts to D1–D9.
   5. 1A–21 converts to 5A–61.
   6. 22–29 converts to E2–E9.
   7. 2A–2F converts to 6A–6F.
   8. 30–39 converts to F0–F9.
   9. 3A–3F converts to 7A–7F.

WRITE CONTROL AND COPY CONTROL CHARACTERS

When data is sent to the display station it is preceded by a Write Control Character (WCC). The WCC is a single byte specified as follows:

a. Bit 0 is set to assure a proper EBCDIC or ASCII graphic character.
b. Bit 1 is a reset bit and is used for partioned data streams which is not included in this discussion.
c. Bits 2 and 3 comprise a two-bit value that controls printer operations as follows:

   1. The value 00_2 indicates that embedded NL (New Line), CR (Carriage Return) and EM (End of Message) characters within the data stream provides the length of print lines. If such characters are not present within intervals of 132 characters, a 132 character print line is provided.
   2. The value 01_2 specifies a 40-character print line.
   3. The value 10_2 specifies a 64-character print line.
   4. The value 11_2 specifies an 80-character print line.

d. Bit 4, if on and the data stream is directed to a printer device, activates the printer at the completion of the receipt of the data stream.
e. Bit 5, if on, sounds the alarm of devices that have audible alarms.
f. Bit 6, if on, unlocks the keyboard.
g. Bit 7, if on, resets the MDT flags of all fields. The following data stream, however, might contain attributes that will set MDT flags.

The above WCC controls the result of data streams that are written from main memory to the device buffer. When two devices are attached to the same control unit a copy command can be issued to copy the contents of one device's buffer to the buffer of the other device. Such copying is directed by a Copy Control Character in a manner very similar to the role of the WCC in write operations. The values of the bits within the CCC are as follows:

a. Bits 0–5 are the same as specified for the WCC.
b. Bits 6–7 define a two-bit field as follows:

1. The value 00_2 results in copying only attribute information.
2. The value 01_2 results in the copying of attributes and unprotected alphameric fields. Alphameric characters within protected fields result in movement of nulls to their corresponding position. Nulls within unprotected fields are copied.
3. The value 10_2 results in the copying of attributes and unprotected alphameric fields. Alphameric characters within unprotected fields result in movement of nulls to their corresponding position. Nulls within protected fields are copied.
4. The entire buffer is copied. That is all attribute characters, protected and unprotected fields, and nulls.

The above discussion is intended to provide an introduction to IBM 3270 data streams. It provides the basic information of the most common features of these devices. There are, however, features that are currently available that are not considered. Also, new features will probably be added to these devices. For such additional information please see the appropriate manuals. It is hoped, however, that the above introduction will provide the necessary background to easily process such additional information.

Appendix A

System/370 Reference Summary Examples

This appendix consist of pages reproduced from IBM Form GX20-0157, System/370 Extended Architecture Reference Summary. It is intended as an introductory guide to the use of that publication.

Item	Description	GX20-0157-2 Page Nos.	Appendix Page Nos.
1.	Machine Instruction Formats	2–3	137–138
2.	Machine Instructions by Mnemonic	4–11	139–146
3.	Machine Instructions by Operation Code	12–13	147–148
4.	Assembler Instructions	18	149
5.	Extended Mnemonic Instructions	19	150
6.	CNOP Alignment	19	150
7.	Summary of Constants	19	150
8.	Program Status Word	22	151
9.	External-Interruption Codes	22	151
10.	Program-Interruption Codes	23	152
11.	Exception-Extension Code	23	152
12.	Fixed Storage Locations	20	153
13.	Operation-Request Block	28	154
14.	Channel Command Word	28	154
15.	I/O Command Codes	34–39	155–160
16.	Code Assignments	40–43	161–164
17.	Hexadecimal and Decimal Conversion	45–46	165–166

MACHINE INSTRUCTION FORMATS

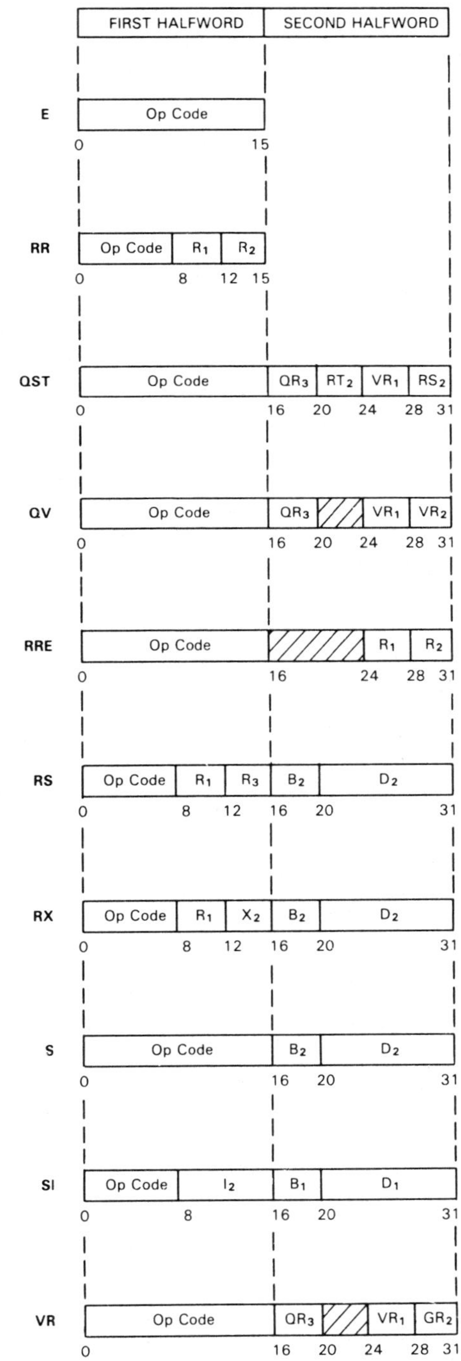

MACHINE INSTRUCTION FORMATS (Cont'd)

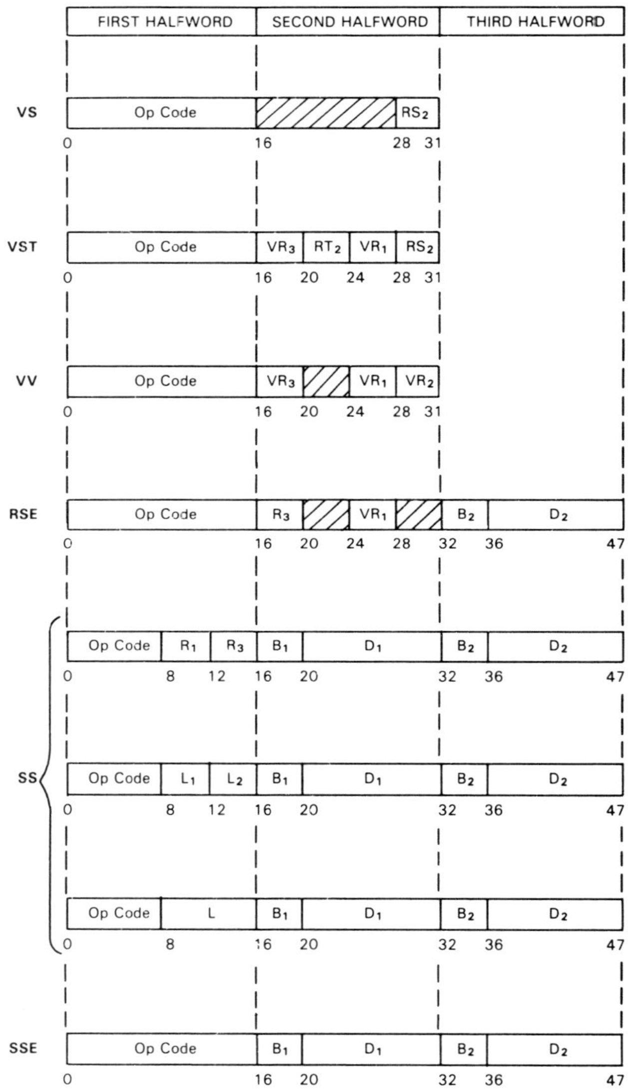

1, 2, 3: Denotes association with first, second, or third operand
B_1, B_2: Base register designation field
D_1, D_2: Displacement field
GR_2: Register designation field (general register)
I_2: Immediate operand field
L, L_1, L_2: Length field
QR_3: Register designation field (equivalent to GR_3 if general register, or FR_3 if floating-point register)
R_1, R_2, R_3: Register designation field
RS_2: Register designation field (starting address of vector)
RT_2: Register designation field (stride of vector)
VR_1, VR_2, VR_3: Register designation field (vector register)
X_2: Index register designation field

MACHINE INSTRUCTIONS

By Mnemonic

Mnemonic	Operands	Name	Format	Op Code	Class & Notes
A	$R_1,D_2(X_2,B_2)$	Add	RX	5A	c
AD	$R_1,D_2(X_2,B_2)$	Add Normalized (L)	RX	6A	c
ADR	R_1,R_2	Add Normalized (L)	RR	2A	c
AE	$R_1,D_2(X_2,B_2)$	Add Normalized (S)	RX	7A	c
AER	R_1,R_2	Add Normalized (S)	RR	3A	c
AH	$R_1,D_2(X_2,B_2)$	Add Halfword	RX	4A	c
AL	$R_1,D_2(X_2,B_2)$	Add Logical	RX	5E	c
ALR	R_1,R_2	Add Logical	RR	1E	c
AP	$D_1(L_1,B_1),D_2(L_2,B_2)$	Add Decimal	SS	FA	c
AR	R_1,R_2	Add	RR	1A	c
AU	$R_1,D_2(X_2,B_2)$	Add Unnormalized (S)	RX	7E	c
AUR	R_1,R_2	Add Unnormalized (S)	RR	3E	c
AW	$R_1,D_2(X_2,B_2)$	Add Unnormalized (L)	RX	6E	c
AWR	R_1,R_2	Add Unnormalized (L)	RR	2E	c
AXR	R_1,R_2	Add Normalized (E)	RR	36	c
BAL	$R_1,D_2(X_2,B_2)$	Branch and Link	RX	45	
BALR	R_1,R_2	Branch and Link	RR	05	
BAS	$R_1,D_2(X_2,B_2)$	Branch and Save	RX	4D	
BASR	R_1,R_2	Branch and Save	RR	0D	
BASSM	R_1,R_2	Branch and Save and Set Mode	RR	0C	
BC	$M_1,D_2(X_2,B_2)$	Branch on Condition	RX	47	
BCR	M_1,R_2	Branch on Condition	RR	07	
BCT	$R_1,D_2(X_2,B_2)$	Branch on Count	RX	46	
BCTR	R_1,R_2	Branch on Count	RR	06	
BSM	R_1,R_2	Branch and Set Mode	RR	0B	
BXH	$R_1,R_3,D_2(B_2)$	Branch on Index High	RS	86	
BXLE	$R_1,R_3,D_2(B_2)$	Branch on Index Low or Equal	RS	87	
C	$R_1,D_2(X_2,B_2)$	Compare	RX	59	c
CD	$R_1,D_2(X_2,B_2)$	Compare (L)	RX	69	c
CDR	R_1,R_2	Compare (L)	RR	29	c
CDS	$R_1,R_3,D_2(B_2)$	Compare Double and Swap	RS	BB	c
CE	$R_1,D_2(X_2,B_2)$	Compare (S)	RX	79	c
CER	R_1,R_2	Compare (S)	RR	39	c
CFC	$D_2(B_2)$	Compare and Form Codeword	S	B21A	i c
CH	$R_1,D_2(X_2,B_2)$	Compare Halfword	RX	49	c
CL	$R_1,D_2(X_2,B_2)$	Compare Logical	RX	55	c
CLC	$D_1(L,B_1),D_2(B_2)$	Compare Logical	SS	D5	c
CLCL	R_1,R_2	Compare Logical Long	RR	0F	i c
CLI	$D_1(B_1),I_2$	Compare Logical	SI	95	c
CLM	$R_1,M_3,D_2(B_2)$	Compare Logical Characters under Mask	RS	BD	c
CLR	R_1,R_2	Compare Logical	RR	15	c
CP	$D_1(L_1,B_1),D_2(L_2,B_2)$	Compare Decimal	SS	F9	c
CR	R_1,R_2	Compare	RR	19	c
CS	$R_1,R_3,D_2(B_2)$	Compare and Swap	RS	BA	c
CSCH		Clear Subchannel	S	B230	pc
CVB	$R_1,D_2(X_2,B_2)$	Convert to Binary	RX	4F	
CVD	$R_1,D_2(X_2,B_2)$	Convert to Decimal	RX	4E	
D	$R_1,D_2(X_2,B_2)$	Divide	RX	5D	
DD	$R_1,D_2(X_2,B_2)$	Divide (L)	RX	6D	
DDR	R_1,R_2	Divide (L)	RR	2D	
DE	$R_1,D_2(X_2,B_2)$	Divide (S)	RX	7D	
DER	R_1,R_2	Divide (S)	RR	3D	
DP	$D_1(L_1,B_1),D_2(L_2,B_2)$	Divide Decimal	SS	FD	
DR	R_1,R_2	Divide	RR	1D	
DXR	R_1,R_2	Divide (E)	RRE	B22D	
ED	$D_1(L,B_1),D_2(B_2)$	Edit	SS	DE	c
EDMK	$D_1(L,B_1),D_2(B_2)$	Edit and Mark	SS	DF	c
EPAR	R_1	Extract Primary ASN	RRE	B226	q
ESAR	R_1	Extract Secondary ASN	RRE	B227	q
EX	$R_1,D_2(X_2,B_2)$	Execute	RX	44	
HDR	R_1,R_2	Halve (L)	RR	24	
HER	R_1,R_2	Halve (S)	RR	34	
HSCH		Halt Subchannel	S	B231	pc

MACHINE INSTRUCTIONS (Cont'd)

By Mnemonic (Cont'd)

Mne-monic	Operands	Name	For-mat	Op Code	Class & Notes
IAC	R_1	Insert Address Space Control	RRE	B224	qc
IC	$R_1,D_2(X_2,B_2)$	Insert Character	RX	43	
ICM	$R_1,M_3,D_2(B_2)$	Insert Characters under Mask	RS	BF	c
IPK		Insert PSW Key	S	B20B	q
IPM	R_1	Insert Program Mask	RRE	B222	
IPTE	R_1,R_2	Invalidate Page Table Entry	RRE	B221	p
ISKE	R_1,R_2	Insert Storage Key Extended	RRE	B229	p
IVSK	R_1,R_2	Insert Virtual Storage Key	RRE	B223	q
L	$R_1,D_2(X_2,B_2)$	Load	RX	58	
LA	$R_1,D_2(X_2,B_2)$	Load Address	RX	41	
LASP	$D_1(B_1),D_2(B_2)$	Load Address Space Parameters	SSE	E500	pc
LCDR	R_1,R_2	Load Complement (L)	RR	23	c
LCER	R_1,R_2	Load Complement (S)	RR	33	c
LCR	R_1,R_2	Load Complement	RR	13	c
LCTL	$R_1,R_3,D_2(B_2)$	Load Control	RS	B7	p
LD	$R_1,D_2(X_2,B_2)$	Load (L)	RX	68	
LDR	R_1,R_2	Load (L)	RR	28	
LE	$R_1,D_2(X_2,B_2)$	Load (S)	RX	78	
LER	R_1,R_2	Load (S)	RR	38	
LH	$R_1,D_2(X_2,B_2)$	Load Halfword	RX	48	
LM	$R_1,R_3,D_2(B_2)$	Load Multiple	RS	98	
LNDR	R_1,R_2	Load Negative (L)	RR	21	c
LNER	R_1,R_2	Load Negative (S)	RR	31	c
LNR	R_1,R_2	Load Negative	RR	11	c
LPDR	R_1,R_2	Load Positive (L)	RR	20	c
LPER	R_1,R_2	Load Positive (S)	RR	30	c
LPR	R_1,R_2	Load Positive	RR	10	c
LPSW	$D_2(B_2)$	Load PSW	S	82	pn
LR	R_1,R_2	Load	RR	18	
LRA	$R_1,D_2(X_2,B_2)$	Load Real Address	RX	B1	pc
LRDR	R_1,R_2	Load Rounded (E/L)	RR	25	
LRER	R_1,R_2	Load Rounded (L/S)	RR	35	
LTDR	R_1,R_2	Load and Test (L)	RR	22	c
LTER	R_1,R_2	Load and Test (S)	RR	32	c
LTR	R_1,R_2	Load and Test	RR	12	c
M	$R_1,D_2(X_2,B_2)$	Multiply	RX	5C	
MC	$D_1(B_1),I_2$	Monitor Call	SI	AF	
MD	$R_1,D_2(X_2,B_2)$	Multiply (L)	RX	6C	
MDR	R_1,R_2	Multiply (L)	RR	2C	
ME	$R_1,D_2(X_2,B_2)$	Multiply (S/L)	RX	7C	
MER	R_1,R_2	Multiply (S/L)	RR	3C	
MH	$R_1,D_2(X_2,B_2)$	Multiply Halfword	RX	4C	

Floating-point operand lengths:

- (E) Extended source and result.
- (E/L) Extended source, long result.
- (L/E) Long source, extended result.
- (L) Long source and result.
- (L/S) Long source, short result.
- (S/L) Short source, long result.
- (S) Short source and result.

Notes:

- c. Condition code set.
- i. Interruptible instruction.
- n. New condition code loaded.
- p. Privileged instruction.
- q. Semiprivileged instruction.
- x. Execution in problem state and supervisor state differs.
- y. Condition code may be set.

Class (for instructions subject to vector-control bit, CR 0 bit 14)

- IC: Interruptible; (VCT − VIX) elements processed.
- IG: Interruptible; either (bit count in a general register) elements or (section-size − VIX) elements processed, whichever is fewer.
- IM: Interruptible; (VCT − VIX) elements processed, vector-mask mode.
- IP: Interruptible; (partial-sum-number − VIX) elements processed.
- IZ: Interruptible; (section-size) elements processed.
- NC: Not interruptible; (VCT) elements processed.
- NZ: Not interruptible; (section-size) elements processed.
- N0: Not interruptible; no elements processed (VSR/VAC housekeeping).
- N1: Not interruptible; one element processed.

MACHINE INSTRUCTIONS (Cont'd)

By Mnemonic (Cont'd)

Mne-monic	Operands	Name	For-mat	Op Code	Class & Notes
MP	$D_1(L_1,B_1),D_2(L_2,B_2)$	Multiply Decimal	SS	FC	
MR	R_1,R_2	Multiply	RR	1C	
MSCH	$D_2(B_2)$	Modify Subchannel	S	B232	pc
MVC	$D_1(L,B_1),D_2(B_2)$	Move	SS	D2	
MVCIN	$D_1(L,B_1),D_2(B_2)$	Move Inverse	SS	E8	
MVCK	$D_1(R_1,B_1),D_2(B_2),R_3$	Move with Key	SS	D9	qc
MVCL	R_1,R_2	Move Long	RR	0E	i c
MVCP	$D_1(R_1,B_1),D_2(B_2),R_3$	Move to Primary	SS	DA	qc
MVCS	$D_1(R_1,B_1),D_2(B_2),R_3$	Move to Secondary	SS	DB	qc
MVI	$D_1(B_1),I_2$	Move	SI	92	
MVN	$D_1(L,B_1),D_2(B_2)$	Move Numerics	SS	D1	
MVO	$D_1(L_1,B_1),D_2(L_2,B_2)$	Move with Offset	SS	F1	
MVZ	$D_1(L,B_1),D_2(B_2)$	Move Zones	SS	D3	
MXD	$R_1,D_2(X_2,B_2)$	Multiply (L/E)	RX	67	
MXDR	R_1,R_2	Multiply (L/E)	RR	27	
MXR	R_1,R_2	Multiply (E)	RR	26	
N	$R_1,D_2(X_2,B_2)$	AND	RX	54	c
NC	$D_1(L,B_1),D_2(B_2)$	AND	SS	D4	c
NI	$D_1(B_1),I_2$	AND	SI	94	c
NR	R_1,R_2	AND	RR	14	c
O	$R_1,D_2(X_2,B_2)$	OR	RX	56	c
OC	$D_1(L,B_1),D_2(B_2)$	OR	SS	D6	c
OI	$D_1(B_1),I_2$	OR	SI	96	c
OR	R_1,R_2	OR	RR	16	c
PACK	$D_1(L_1,B_1),D_2(L_2,B_2)$	Pack	SS	F2	
PC	$D_2(B_2)$	Program Call	S	B218	q
PT	R_1,R_2	Program Transfer	RRE	B228	q
PTLB		Purge TLB	S	B20D	p
RCHP		Reset Channel Path	S	B23B	pc
RRBE	R_1,R_2	Reset Reference Bit Extended	RRE	B22A	pc
RSCH		Resume Subchannel	S	B238	pc
S	$R_1,D_2(X_2,B_2)$	Subtract	RX	5B	c
SAC	$D_2(B_2)$	Set Address Space Control	S	B219	q
SAL		Set Address Limit	S	B237	p
SCHM		Set Channel Monitor	S	B23C	p
SCK	$D_2(B_2)$	Set Clock	S	B204	pc
SCKC	$D_2(B_2)$	Set Clock Comparator	S	B206	p
SD	$R_1,D_2(X_2,B_2)$	Subtract Normalized (L)	RX	6B	c
SDR	R_1,R_2	Subtract Normalized (L)	RR	2B	c
SE	$R_1,D_2(X_2,B_2)$	Subtract Normalized (S)	RX	7B	c
SER	R_1,R_2	Subtract Normalized (S)	RR	3B	c
SH	$R_1,D_2(X_2,B_2)$	Subtract Halfword	RX	4B	c
SIE	$D_2(B_2)$	Start Interpretive Execution	S	B214	ip
SIGP	$R_1,R_3,D_2(B_2)$	Signal Processor	RS	AE	pc
SL	$R_1,D_2(X_2,B_2)$	Subtract Logical	RX	5F	c
SLA	$R_1,D_2(B_2)$	Shift Left Single	RS	8B	c
SLDA	$R_1,D_2(B_2)$	Shift Left Double	RS	8F	c
SLDL	$R_1,D_2(B_2)$	Shift Left Double Logical	RS	8D	
SLL	$R_1,D_2(B_2)$	Shift Left Single Logical	RS	89	
SLR	R_1,R_2	Subtract Logical	RR	1F	c
SP	$D_1(L_1,B_1),D_2(L_2,B_2)$	Subtract Decimal	SS	FB	c
SPKA	$D_2(B_2)$	Set PSW Key from Address	S	B20A	q
SPM	R_1	Set Program Mask	RR	04	n
SPT	$D_2(B_2)$	Set CPU Timer	S	B208	p
SPX	$D_2(B_2)$	Set Prefix	S	B210	p
SR	R_1,R_2	Subtract	RR	1B	c
SRA	$R_1,D_2(B_2)$	Shift Right Single	RS	8A	c
SRDA	$R_1,D_2(B_2)$	Shift Right Double	RS	8E	c
SRDL	$R_1,D_2(B_2)$	Shift Right Double Logical	RS	8C	
SRL	$R_1,D_2(B_2)$	Shift Right Single Logical	RS	88	
SRP	$D_1(L_1,B_1),D_2(B_2),I_3$	Shift and Round Decimal	SS	F0	c
SSAR	R_1	Set Secondary ASN	RRE	B225	q
SSCH	$D_2(B_2)$	Start Subchannel	S	B233	pc
SSKE	R_1,R_2	Set Storage Key Extended	RRE	B22B	p

MACHINE INSTRUCTIONS (Cont'd)

By Mnemonic (Cont'd)

Mne-monic	Operands	Name	For-mat	Op Code	Class & Notes
SSM	$D_2(B_2)$	Set System Mask	S	80	p
ST	$R_1,D_2(X_2,B_2)$	Store	RX	50	
STAP	$D_2(B_2)$	Store CPU Address	S	B212	p
STC	$R_1,D_2(X_2,B_2)$	Store Character	RX	42	
STCK	$D_2(B_2)$	Store Clock	S	B205	c
STCKC	$D_2(B_2)$	Store Clock Comparator	S	B207	p
STCM	$R_1,M_3,D_2(B_2)$	Store Characters under Mask	RS	BE	
STCPS	$D_2(B_2)$	Store Channel Path Status	S	B23A	p
STCRW	$D_2(B_2)$	Store Channel Report Word	S	B239	pc
STCTL	$R_1,R_3,D_2(B_2)$	Store Control	RS	B6	p
STD	$R_1,D_2(X_2,B_2)$	Store (L)	RX	60	
STE	$R_1,D_2(X_2,B_2)$	Store (S)	RX	70	
STH	$R_1,D_2(X_2,B_2)$	Store Halfword	RX	40	
STIDP	$D_2(B_2)$	Store CPU ID	S	B202	p
STM	$R_1,R_3,D_2(B_2)$	Store Multiple	RS	90	
STNSM	$D_1(B_1),I_2$	Store Then AND System Mask	SI	AC	p
STOSM	$D_1(B_1),I_2$	Store Then OR System Mask	SI	AD	p
STPT	$D_2(B_2)$	Store CPU Timer	S	B209	p
STPX	$D_2(B_2)$	Store Prefix	S	B211	p
STSCH	$D_2(B_2)$	Store Subchannel	S	B234	pc
SU	$R_1,D_2(X_2,B_2)$	Subtract Unnormalized (S)	RX	7F	c
SUR	R_1,R_2	Subtract Unnormalized (S)	RR	3F	c
SVC	I	Supervisor Call	RR	0A	
SW	$R_1,D_2(X_2,B_2)$	Subtract Unnormalized (L)	RX	6F	c
SWR	R_1,R_2	Subtract Unnormalized (L)	RR	2F	c
SXR	R_1,R_2	Subtract Normalized (E)	RR	37	c
TB	R_1,R_2	Test Block	RRE	B22C	ipc
TM	$D_1(B_1),I_2$	Test under Mask	SI	91	c
TPI	$D_2(B_2)$	Test Pending Interruption	S	B236	pc
TPROT	$D_1(B_1),D_2(B_2)$	Test Protection	SSE	E501	pc
TR	$D_1(L,B_1),D_2(B_2)$	Translate	SS	DC	
TRACE	$R_1,R_3,D_2(B_2)$	Trace	RS	99	p
TRT	$D_1(L,B_1),D_2(B_2)$	Translate and Test	SS	DD	c
TS	$D_2(B_2)$	Test and Set	S	93	c
TSCH	$D_2(B_2)$	Test Subchannel	S	B235	pc
UNPK	$D_1(L_1,B_1),D_2(L_2,B_2)$	Unpack	SS	F3	
UPT		Update Tree	E	0102	i c
VA	$VR_1,VR_3,RS_2(RT_2)$	Add	VST	A420	IM
VACD	$VR_1,RS_2(RT_2)$	Accumulate (L)	VST	A417	IM
VACDR	VR_1,VR_2	Accumulate (L)	VV	A517	IM
VACE	$VR_1,RS_2(RT_2)$	Accumulate (S/L)	VST	A407	IM
VACER	VR_1,VR_2	Accumulate (S/L)	VV	A507	IM
VACRS	$D_2(B_2)$	Restore VAC	S	A6CB	NC p

Floating-point operand lengths:

- (E) Extended source and result.
- (E/L) Extended source, long result.
- (L/E) Long source, extended result.
- (L) Long source and result.
- (L/S) Long source, short result.
- (S/L) Short source, long result.
- (S) Short source and result.

Notes:

- c. Condition code set.
- i. Interruptible instruction.
- n. New condition code loaded.
- p. Privileged instruction.
- q. Semiprivileged instruction.
- x. Execution in problem state and supervisor state differs.
- y. Condition code may be set.

Class (for instructions subject to vector-control bit, CR 0 bit 14)

- IC: Interruptible; (VCT − VIX) elements processed.
- IG: Interruptible; either (bit count in a general register) elements or (section-size − VIX) elements processed, whichever is fewer.
- IM: Interruptible; (VCT − VIX) elements processed, vector-mask mode.
- IP: Interruptible; (partial-sum-number − VIX) elements processed.
- IZ: Interruptible; (section-size) elements processed.
- NC: Not interruptible; (VCT) elements processed.
- NZ: Not interruptible; (section-size) elements processed.
- N0: Not interruptible; no elements processed (VSR/VAC housekeeping).
- N1: Not interruptible; one element processed.

MACHINE INSTRUCTIONS (Cont'd)

By Mnemonic (Cont'd)

Mnemonic	Operands	Name	Format	Op Code	Class & Notes
VACSV	$D_2(B_2$	Save VAC	S	A6CA	NO p
VAD	$VR_1,VR_3,RS_2(RT_2)$	Add (L)	VST	A410	IM
VADQ	VR_1,FR_3,VR_2	Add (L)	QV	A590	IM
VADR	VR_1,VR_3,VR_2	Add (L)	VV	A510	IM
VADS	$VR_1,FR_3,RS_2(RT_2)$	Add (L)	QST	A490	IM
VAE	$VR_1,VR_3,RS_2(RT_2)$	Add (S)	VST	A400	IM
VAEQ	VR_1,FR_3,VR_2	Add (S)	QV	A580	IM
VAER	VR_1,VR_3,VR_2	Add (S)	VV	A500	IM
VAES	$VR_1,FR_3,RS_2(RT_2)$	Add (S)	QST	A480	IM
VAQ	VR_1,GR_3,VR_2	Add	QV	A5A0	IM
VAR	VR_1,VR_3,VR_2	Add	VV	A520	IM
VAS	$VR_1,GR_3,RS_2(RT_2)$	Add	QST	A4A0	IM
VC	$M_1,VF_3,RS_2(RT_2)$	Compare	VST	A428	IC
VCD	$M_1,VF_3,RS_2(RT_2)$	Compare (L)	VST	A418	IC
VCDQ	M_1,FR_3,VR_2	Compare (L)	QV	A598	IC
VCDR	M_1,VF_3,VR_2	Compare (L)	VV	A518	IC
VCDS	$M_1,FR_3,RS_2(RT_2)$	Compare (L)	QST	A498	IC
VCE	$M_1,VF_3,RS_2(RT_2)$	Compare (S)	VST	A408	IC
VCEQ	M_1,FR_3,VR_2	Compare (S)	QV	A588	IC
VCER	M_1,VR_3,VR_2	Compare (S)	VV	A508	IC
VCES	$M_1,FR_3,RS_2(RT_2)$	Compare (S)	QST	A488	IC
VCOVM	GR_1	Count Ones in VMR	RRE	A643	NC c
VCQ	M_1,GR_3,VR_2	Compare	QV	A5A8	IC
VCR	M_1,VR_3,VR_2	Compare	VV	A528	IC
VCS	$M_1,GR_3,RS_2(RT_2)$	Compare	QST	A4A8	IC
VCVM		Complement VMR	RRE	A641	NC
VCZVM	GR_1	Count Left Zeros in VMR	RRE	A642	NC c
VDD	$VR_1,VR_3,RS_2(RT_2)$	Divide (L)	VST	A413	IM
VDDQ	VR_1,FR_3,VR_2	Divide (L)	QV	A593	IM
VDDR	VR_1,VR_3,VR_2	Divide (L)	VV	A513	IM
VDDS	$VR_1,FR_3,RS_2(RT_2)$	Divide (L)	QST	A493	IM
VDE	$VR_1,VR_3,RS_2(RT_2)$	Divide (S)	VST	A403	IM
VDEQ	VR_1,FR_3,VR_2	Divide (S)	QV	A583	IM
VDER	VR_1,VR_3,VR_2	Divide (S)	VV	A503	IM
VDES	$VR_1,FR_3,RS_2(RT_2)$	Divide (S)	QST	A483	IM
VL	$VR_1,RS_2(RT_2)$	Load	VST	A409	IC
VLBIX	$VR_1,GR_3,D_2(B_2)$	Load Bit Index	RSE	E428	IG c
VLCDR	VR_1,VR_2	Load Complement (L)	VV	A552	IM
VLCER	VR_1,VR_2	Load Complement (S)	VV	A542	IM
VLCR	VR_1,VR_2	Load Complement	VV	A562	IM
VLCVM	RS_2	Load VMR Complement	VS	A681	NC
VLD	$VR_1,RS_2(RT_2)$	Load (L)	VST	A419	IC
VLDQ	VR_1,FR_2	Load (L)	QV	A599	IC
VLDR	VR_1,VR_2	Load (L)	VV	A519	IC
VLE	$VR_1,RS_2(RT_2)$	Load (S)	VST	A409	IC
VLEL	VR_1,GR_3,GR_2	Load Element	VR	A628	N1
VLELD	VR_1,FR_3,GR_2	Load Element (L)	VR	A618	N1
VLELE	VR_1,FR_3,GR_2	Load Element (S)	VR	A608	N1
VLEQ	VR_1,FR_2	Load (S)	QV	A589	IC
VLER	VR_1,VR_2	Load (S)	VV	A509	IC
VLH	$VR_1,RS_2(RT_2)$	Load Halfword	VST	A429	IC
VLI	$VR_1,VR_3,D_2(B_2)$	Load Indirect	RSE	E400	IC
VLID	$VR_1,VR_3,D_2(B_2)$	Load Indirect (L)	RSE	E410	IC
VLIE	$VR_1,VR_3,D_2(B_2)$	Load Indirect (S)	RSE	E400	IC
VLINT	$VR_1,RS_2(RT_2)$	Load Integer Vector	VST	A42A	IC
VLM	$VR_1,RS_2(RT_2)$	Load Matched	VST	A40A	IC
VLMD	$VR_1,RS_2(RT_2)$	Load Matched (L)	VST	A41A	IC
VLMDQ	VR_1,FF_2	Load Matched (L)	QV	A59A	IC
VLMDR	VR_1,VR_2	Load Matched (L)	VV	A51A	IC
VLME	$VR_1,RS_2(RT_2)$	Load Matched (S)	VST	A40A	IC
VLMEQ	VR_1,FF_2	Load Matched (S)	QV	A58A	IC
VLMER	VR_1,VR_2	Load Matched (S)	VV	A50A	IC
VLMQ	VR_1,GR_2	Load Matched	QV	A5AA	IC
VLMR	VR_1,VR_2	Load Matched	VV	A50A	IC
VLNDR	VR_1,VR_2	Load Negative (L)	VV	A551	IM
VLNER	VR_1,VR_2	Load Negative (S)	VV	A541	IM
VLNR	VR_1,VR_2	Load Negative	VV	A561	IM

MACHINE INSTRUCTIONS (Cont'd)

By Mnemonic (Cont'd)

Mne-monic	Operands	Name	For-mat	Op Code	Class & Notes
VLPDR	VR_1,VR_2	Load Positive (L)	VV	A550	IM
VLPER	VR_1,VR_2	Load Positive (S)	VV	A540	IM
VLPR	VR_1,VR_2	Load Positive	VV	A560	IM
VLQ	VR_1,GR_2	Load	QV	A5A9	IC
VLR	VR_1,VR_2	Load	VV	A509	IC
VLVCA	$D_2(B_2)$	Load VCT from Address	S	A6C4	NO c
VLVCU	GR_1	Load VCT and Update	RRE	A645	NO c
VLVM	RS_2	Load VMR	VS	A680	NC
VLY	$VR_1,RS_2(RT_2)$	Load Expanded	VST	A40B	IC
VLYD	$VR_1,RS_2(RT_2)$	Load Expanded (L)	VST	A41B	IC
VLYE	$VR_1,RS_2(RT_2)$	Load Expanded (S)	VST	A40B	IC
VLZDR	VR_1	Load Zero (L)	VV	A51B	IC
VLZER	VR_1	Load Zero (S)	VV	A50B	IC
VLZR	VR_1	Load Zero	VV	A50B	IC
VM	$VR_1,VR_3,RS_2(RT_2)$	Multiply	VST	A422	IM
VMAD	$VR_1,VR_3,RS_2(RT_2)$	Multiply and Add (L)	VST	A414	IM
VMADQ	VR_1,FR_3,VR_2	Multiply and Add (L)	QV	A594	IM
VMADS	$VR_1,FR_3,RS_2(RT_2)$	Multiply and Add (L)	QST	A494	IM
VMAE	$VR_1,VR_3,RS_2(RT_2)$	Multiply and Add (S/L)	VST	A404	IM
VMAEQ	VR_1,FR_3,VR_2	Multiply and Add (S/L)	QV	A584	IM
VMAES	$VR_1,FR_3,RS_2(RT_2)$	Multiply and Add (S/L)	QST	A484	IM
VMCD	$VR_1,VR_3,RS_2(RT_2)$	Multiply and Accumulate (L)	VST	A416	IM
VMCDR	VR_1,VR_3,VR_2	Multiply and Accumulate (L)	VV	A516	IM
VMCE	$VR_1,VR_3,RS_2(RT_2)$	Multiply and Accumulate (S/L)	VST	A406	IM
VMCER	VR_1,VR_3,VR_2	Multiply and Accumulate (S/L)	VV	A506	IM
VMD	$VR_1,VR_3,RS_2(RT_2)$	Multiply (L)	VST	A412	IM
VMDQ	VR_1,FR_3,VR_2	Multiply (L)	QV	A592	IM
VMDR	VR_1,VR_3,VR_2	Multiply (L)	VV	A512	IM
VMDS	$VR_1,FR_3,RS_2(RT_2)$	Multiply (L)	QST	A492	IM
VME	$VR_1,VR_3,RS_2(RT_2)$	Multiply (S/L)	VST	A402	IM
VMEQ	VR_1,FR_3,VR_2	Multiply (S/L)	QV	A582	IM
VMER	VR_1,VR_3,VR_2	Multiply (S/L)	VV	A502	IM
VMES	$VR_1,FR_3,RS_2(RT_2)$	Multiply (S/L)	QST	A482	IM
VMNSD	VR_1,FR_3,GR_2	Minimum Signed (L)	VR	A611	IM
VMNSE	VR_1,FR_3,GR_2	Minimum Signed (S)	VR	A601	IM
VMQ	VR_1,GR_3,VR_2	Multiply	QV	A5A2	IM
VMR	VR_1,VR_3,VR_2	Multiply	VV	A522	IM
VMRRS	$D_2(B_2)$	Restore VMR	S	A6C3	NZ
VMRSV	$D_2(B_2)$	Save VMR	S	A6C1	NZ
VMS	$VR_1,GR_3,RS_2(RT_2)$	Multiply	QST	A4A2	IM
VMSD	$VR_1,VR_3,RS_2(RT_2)$	Multiply and Subtract (L)	VST	A415	IM
VMSDQ	VR_1,FR_3,VR_2	Multiply and Subtract (L)	QV	A595	IM
VMSDS	$VR_1,FR_3,RS_2(RT_2)$	Multiply and Subtract (L)	QST	A495	IM
VMSE	$VR_1,VR_3,RS_2(RT_2)$	Multiply and Subtract (S/L)	VST	A405	IM
VMSEQ	VR_1,FR_3,VR_2	Multiply and Subtract (S/L)	QV	A585	IM
VMSES	$VR_1,FR_3,RS_2(RT_2)$	Multiply and Subtract (S/L)	QST	A485	IM
VMXAD	VR_1,FR_3,GR_2	Maximum Absolute (L)	VR	A612	IM
VMXAE	VR_1,FR_3,GR_2	Maximum Absolute (S)	VR	A602	IM
VMXSD	VR_1,FR_3,GR_2	Maximum Signed (L)	VR	A610	IM
VMXSE	VR_1,FR_3,GR_2	Maximum Signed (S)	VR	A600	IM
VN	$VR_1,VR_3,RS_2(RT_2)$	AND	VST	A424	IM
VNQ	VR_1,GR_3,VR_2	AND	QV	A5A4	IM
VNR	VR_1,VR_3,VR_2	AND	VV	A524	IM
VNS	$VR_1,GR_3,RS_2(RT_2)$	AND	QST	A4A4	IM
VNVM	RS_2	AND to VMR	VS	A684	NC
VO	$VR_1,VR_3,RS_2(RT_2)$	OR	VST	A425	IM
VOQ	VR_1,GR_3,VR_2	OR	QV	A5A5	IM
VOR	VR_1,VR_3,VR_2	OR	VV	A525	IM
VOS	$VR_1,GR_3,RS_2(RT_2)$	OR	QST	A4A5	IM
VOVM	RS_2	OR to VMR	VS	A685	NC
VRCL	$D_2(B_2)$	Clear VR	S	A6C5	IZ
VRRS	GR_1	Restore VR	RRE	A648	IZ xc
VRSV	GR_1	Save VR	RRE	A64A	IZ c
VRSVC	GR_1	Save Changed VR	RRE	A649	IZ pc
VS	$VR_1,VR_3,RS_2(RT_2)$	Subtract	VST	A421	IM

MACHINE INSTRUCTIONS (Cont'd)

By Mnemonic (Cont'd)

Mnemonic	Operands	Name	Format	Op Code	Class & Notes
VSD	$VR_1,VR_3,RS_2(RT_2)$	Subtract (L)	VST	A411	IM
VSDQ	VR_1,FR_3,VR_2	Subtract (L)	QV	A591	IM
VSDR	VR_1,VR_3,VR_2	Subtract (L)	VV	A511	IM
VSDS	$VR_1,FR_3,RS_2(RT_2)$	Subtract (L)	QST	A491	IM
VSE	$VR_1,VR_3,RS_2(RT_2)$	Subtract (S)	VST	A401	IM
VSEQ	VR_1,FR_3,VR_2	Subtract (S)	QV	A581	IM
VSER	VR_1,VR_3,VR_2	Subtract (S)	VV	A501	IM
VSES	$VR_1,FR_3,RS_2(RT_2)$	Subtract (S)	QST	A481	IM
VSLL	$VR_1,VR_3,D_2(B_2)$	Shift Left Single Logical	RSE	E425	IM
VSPSD	VR_1,FR_2	Sum Partial Sums (L)	VR	A61A	IP
VSQ	VR_1,GR_3,VR_2	Subtract	QV	A5A1	IM
VSR	VR_1,VR_3,VR_2	Subtract	VV	A521	IM
VSRL	$VR_1,VR_3,D_2(B_2)$	Shift Right Single Logical	RSE	E424	IM
VSRRS	$D_2(B_2)$	Restore VSR	S	A6C2	IZ x
VSRSV	$D_2(B_2)$	Save VSR	S	A6C0	NO x
VSS	$VR_1,GR_3,RS_2(RT_2)$	Subtract	QST	A4A1	IM
VST	$VR_1,RS_2(RT_2)$	Store	VST	A40D	IC
VSTD	$VR_1,RS_2(RT_2)$	Store (L)	VST	A41D	IC
VSTE	$VR_1,RS_2(RT_2)$	Store (S)	VST	A40D	IC
VSTH	$VR_1,RS_2(RT_2)$	Store Halfword	VST	A42D	IC
VSTI	$VR_1,VR_3,D_2(B_2)$	Store Indirect	RSE	E401	IC
VSTID	$VR_1,VR_3,D_2(B_2)$	Store Indirect (L)	RSE	E411	IC
VSTIE	$VR_1,VR_3,D_2(B_2)$	Store Indirect (S)	RSE	E401	IC
VSTK	$VR_1,RS_2(RT_2)$	Store Compressed	VST	A40F	IC
VSTKD	$VR_1,RS_2(RT_2)$	Store Compressed (L)	VST	A41F	IC
VSTKE	$VR_1,RS_2(RT_2)$	Store Compressed (S)	VST	A40F	IC
VSTM	$VR_1,RS_2(RT_2)$	Store Matched	VST	A40E	IC
VSTMD	$VR_1,RS_2(RT_2)$	Store Matched (L)	VST	A41E	IC
VSTME	$VR_1,RS_2(RT_2)$	Store Matched (S)	VST	A40E	IC
VSTVM	RS_2	Store VMR	VS	A682	NC
VSTVP	$D_2(B_2)$	Store Vector Parameters	S	A6C8	NO
VSVMM	$D_2(B_2)$	Set Vector Mask Mode	S	A6C6	NO
VTVM		Test VMR	RRE	A640	NC c
VX	$VR_1,VR_3,RS_2(RT_2)$	Exclusive OR	VST	A426	IM
VXEL	VR_1,GR_3,GR_2	Extract Element	VR	A629	N1
VXELD	VR_1,FR_3,GR_2	Extract Element (L)	VR	A619	N1
VXELE	VR_1,FR_3,GR_2	Extract Element (S)	VR	A609	N1
VXQ	VR_1,GR_3,VR_2	Exclusive OR	QV	A5A6	IM
VXR	VR_1,VR_3,VR_2	Exclusive OR	VV	A526	IM
VXS	$VR_1,GR_3, RS_2(RT_2)$	Exclusive OR	QST	A4A6	IM
VXVC	GR_1	Extract VCT	RRE	A644	NO
VXVM	RS_2	Exclusive OR to VMR	VS	A686	NC
VXVMM	GR_1	Extract Vector Mask Mode	RRE	A646	NO
VZPSD	VR_1	Zero Partial Sums (L)	VR	A61B	IP

Floating-point operand lengths:

- (E) Extended source and result.
- (E/L) Extended source, long result.
- (L/E) Long source, extended result.
- (L) Long source and result.
- (L/S) Long source, short result.
- (S/L) Short source, long result.
- (S) Short source and result.

Notes:

- c. Condition code set.
- i. Interruptible instruction.
- n. New condition code loaded.
- p. Privileged instruction.
- q. Semiprivileged instruction.
- x. Execution in problem state and supervisor state differs.
- y. Condition code may be set.

Class (for instructions subject to vector-control bit, CR 0 bit 14)

- IC: Interruptible, (VCT − VIX) elements processed.
- IG: Interruptible, either (bit count in a general register) elements or (section-size − VIX) elements processed, whichever is fewer.
- IM: Interruptible, (VCT − VIX) elements processed, vector-mask mode.
- IP: Interruptible, (partial-sum-number − VIX) elements processed.
- IZ: Interruptible, (section-size) elements processed.
- NC: Not interruptible; (VCT) elements processed.
- NZ: Not interruptible; (section-size) elements processed.
- NO: Not interruptible; no elements processed (VSR/VAC housekeeping).
- N1: Not interruptible; one element processed.

MACHINE INSTRUCTIONS (Cont'd)

By Mnemonic (Cont'd)

Mnemonic	Operands	Name	Format	Op Code	Class & Notes
X	$R_1,D_2(X_2,B_2)$	Exclusive OR	RX	57	c
XC	$D_1(L,B_1),D_2(B_2)$	Exclusive OR	SS	D7	c
XI	$D_1(B_1),I_2$	Exclusive OR	SI	97	c
XR	R_1,R_2	Exclusive OR	RR	17	c
ZAP	$D_1(L_1,B_1),D_2(L_2,B_2)$	Zero and Add	SS	F8	c
--	Model-dependent	Diagnose	--	83	py

Floating-point operand lengths:
(E) Extended source and result.
(E/L) Extended source, long result.
(L/E) Long source, extended result.
(L) Long source and result.
(L/S) Long source, short result.
(S/L) Short source, long result.
(S) Short source and result.

Notes:
c. Condition code set.
i. Interruptible instruction.
n. New condition code loaded.
p. Privileged instruction.
q. Semiprivileged instruction.
x. Execution in problem state and supervisor state differs.
y. Condition code may be set.

Class (for instructions subject to vector-control bit, CR 0 bit 14)
IC: Interruptible; (VCT – VIX) elements processed.
IG: Interruptible; either (bit count in a general register) elements or (section-size – VIX) elements processed, whichever is fewer.
IM: Interruptible; (VCT – VIX) elements processed, vector-mask mode.
IP: Interruptible; (partial-sum-number – VIX) elements processed.
IZ: Interruptible; (section-size) elements processed.
NC: Not interruptible; (VCT) elements processed.
NZ: Not interruptible; (section-size) elements processed.
NO: Not interruptible; no elements processed (VSR/VAC housekeeping).
N1: Not interruptible; one element processed.

MACHINE INSTRUCTIONS (Cont'd)

By Operation Code

Op Code	Mne-monic
0102	UPT
04	SPM
05	BALR
06	BCTR
07	BCR
0A	SVC
0B	BSM
0C	BASSM
0D	BASR
0E	MVCL
0F	CLCL
10	LPR
11	LNR
12	LTR
13	LCR
14	NR
15	CLR
16	OR
17	XR
18	LR
19	CR
1A	AR
1B	SR
1C	MR
1D	DR
1E	ALR
1F	SLR
20	LPDR
21	LNDR
22	LTDR
23	LCDR
24	HDR
25	LRDR
26	MXR
27	MXDR
28	LDR
29	CDR
2A	ADR
2B	SDR
2C	MDR
2D	DDR
2E	AWR
2F	SWR
30	LPER
31	LNER
32	LTER
33	LCER
34	HER
35	LRER
36	AXR
37	SXR
38	LER
39	CER
3A	AER
3B	SER
3C	MER
3D	DER
3E	AUR
3F	SUR
40	STH
41	LA
42	STC
43	IC
44	EX
45	BAL
46	BCT

Op Code	Mne-monic
47	BC
48	LH
49	CH
4A	AH
4B	SH
4C	MH
4D	BAS
4E	CVD
4F	CVB
50	ST
54	N
55	CL
56	O
57	X
58	L
59	C
5A	A
5B	S
5C	M
5D	D
5E	AL
5F	SL
60	STD
67	MXD
68	LD
69	CD
6A	AD
6B	SD
6C	MD
6D	DD
6E	AW
6F	SW
70	STE
78	LE
79	CE
7A	AE
7B	SE
7C	ME
7D	DE
7E	AU
7F	SU
80	SSM
82	LPSW
83	Diagnose
86	BXH
87	BXLE
88	SRL
89	SLL
8A	SRA
8B	SLA
8C	SRDL
8D	SLDL
8E	SRDA
8F	SLDA
90	STM
91	TM
92	MVI
93	TS
94	NI
95	CLI
96	OI
97	XI
98	LM
99	TRACE
A400	VAE
A401	VSE

Op Code	Mne-monic
A402	VME
A403	VDE
A404	VMAE
A405	VMSE
A406	VMCE
A407	VACE
A408	VCE
A409	VL
A409	VLE
A40A	VLM
A40A	VLME
A40B	VLY
A40B	VLYE
A40D	VST
A40D	VSTE
A40E	VSTM
A40E	VSTME
A40F	VSTK
A40F	VSTKE
A410	VAD
A411	VSD
A412	VMD
A413	VDD
A414	VMAD
A415	VMSD
A416	VMCD
A417	VACD
A418	VCD
A419	VLD
A41A	VLMD
A41B	VLYD
A41D	VSTD
A41E	VSTMD
A41F	VSTKD
A420	VA
A421	VS
A422	VM
A424	VN
A425	VO
A426	VX
A428	VC
A429	VLH
A42A	VLINT
A42D	VSTH
A480	VAES
A481	VSES
A482	VMES
A483	VDES
A484	VMAES
A485	VMSES
A488	VCES
A490	VADS
A491	VSDS
A492	VMDS
A493	VDDS
A494	VMADS
A495	VMSDS
A498	VCDS
A4A0	VAS
A4A1	VSS
A4A2	VMS
A4A4	VNS
A4A5	VOS
A4A6	VXS
A4A8	VCS
A500	VAER

MACHINE INSTRUCTIONS (Cont'd)

By Operation Code (Cont'd)

Op Code	Mne-monic
A501	VSER
A502	VMER
A503	VDER
A506	VMCER
A507	VACER
A508	VCER
A509	VLER
A509	VLR
A50A	VLMER
A50A	VLMR
A50B	VLZER
A50B	VLZR
A510	VADR
A511	VSDR
A512	VMDR
A513	VDDR
A516	VMCDR
A517	VACDR
A518	VCDR
A519	VLDR
A51A	VLMDR
A51B	VLZDR
A520	VAR
A521	VSR
A522	VMR
A524	VNR
A525	VOR
A526	VXR
A528	VCR
A540	VLPER
A541	VLNER
A542	VLCER
A550	VLPDR
A551	VLNDR
A552	VLCDR
A560	VLPR
A561	VLNR
A562	VLCR
A580	VAEQ
A581	VSEQ
A582	VMEQ
A583	VDEQ
A584	VMAEQ
A585	VMSEQ
A588	VCEQ
A589	VLEQ
A58A	VLMEQ
A590	VADQ
A591	VSDQ
A592	VMDQ
A593	VDDQ
A594	VMADQ
A595	VMSDQ
A598	VCDQ
A599	VLDQ
A59A	VLMDQ
A5A0	VAQ
A5A1	VSQ
A5A2	VMQ
A5A4	VNQ
A5A5	VOQ
A5A6	VXQ
A5A8	VCQ
A5A9	VLQ
A5AA	VLMQ
A600	VMXSE

Op Code	Mne-monic
A601	VMNSE
A602	VMXAE
A608	VLELE
A609	VXELE
A610	VMXSD
A611	VMNSD
A612	VMXAD
A618	VLELD
A619	VXELD
A61A	VSPSD
A61B	VZPSD
A628	VLEL
A629	VXEL
A640	VTVM
A641	VCVM
A642	VCZVM
A643	VCOVM
A644	VXVC
A645	VLVCU
A646	VXVMM
A648	VRRS
A649	VRSVC
A64A	VRSV
A680	VLVM
A681	VLCVM
A682	VSTVM
A684	VNVM
A685	VOVM
A686	VXVM
A6C0	VSRSV
A6C1	VMRSV
A6C2	VSRRS
A6C3	VMRRS
A6C4	VLVCA
A6C5	VRCL
A6C6	VSVMM
A6C8	VSTVP
A6CA	VACSV
A6CB	VACRS
AC	STNSM
AD	STOSM
AE	SIGP
AF	MC
B1	LRA
B202	STIDP
B204	SCK
B205	STCK
B206	SCKC
B207	STCKC
B208	SPT
B209	STPT
B20A	SPKA
B20B	IPK
B20D	PTLB
B210	SPX
B211	STPX
B212	STAP
B214	SIE
B218	PC
B219	SAC
B21A	CFC
B221	IPTE
B222	IPM
B223	IVSK
B224	IAC
B225	SSAR

Op Code	Mne-monic
B226	EPAR
B227	ESAR
B228	PT
B229	ISKE
B22A	RRBE
B22B	SSKE
B22C	TB
B22D	DXR
B230	CSCH
B231	HSCH
B232	MSCH
B233	SSCH
B234	STSCH
B235	TSCH
B236	TPI
B237	SAL
B238	RSCH
B239	STCRW
B23A	STCPS
B23B	RCHP
B23C	SCHM
B6	STCTL
B7	LCTL
BA	CS
BB	CDS
BD	CLM
BE	STCM
BF	ICM
D1	MVN
D2	MVC
D3	MVZ
D4	NC
D5	CLC
D6	OC
D7	XC
D9	MVCK
DA	MVCP
DB	MVCS
DC	TR
DD	TRT
DE	ED
DF	EDMK
E400	VLI
E400	VLIE
E401	VSTI
E401	VSTIE
E410	VLID
E411	VSTID
E424	VSRL
E425	VSLL
E428	VLBIX
E500	LASP
E501	TPROT
E8	MVCIN
F0	SRP
F1	MVO
F2	PACK
F3	UNPK
F8	ZAP
F9	CP
FA	AP
FB	SP
FC	MP
FD	DP

ASSEMBLER INSTRUCTIONS

Function	Mnemonic	Meaning
Data definition	DC	Define constant
	DS	Define storage
	CCW	Define channel command word
	CCW0	Define format-0 channel command word
	CCW1	Define format-1 channel command word
Program sectioning and linking	START	Start assembly
	LOCTR	Specify multiple location counters
	CSECT	Identify control section
	DSECT	Identify dummy section
	DXD	Define external dummy section
	CXD	Cumulative length of external dummy section
	COM	Identify blank common control section
	AMODE	Specify addressing mode
	RMODE	Specify residence mode
	ENTRY	Identify entry-point symbol
	EXTRN	Identify external symbol
	WXTRN	Identify weak external symbol
Base register assignment	USING	Use base address register
	DROP	Drop base address register
Control of listings	TITLE	Identify assembly output
	EJECT	Start new page
	SPACE	Space listing
	PRINT	Print optional data
Program Control	ICTL	Input format control
	ISEQ	Input sequence checking
	PUNCH	Punch a card
	REPRO	Reproduce following card
	ORG	Set location counter
	EQU	Equate symbol
	OPSYN	Equate operation code
	PUSH	Save current PRINT or USING status
	POP	Restore PRINT or USING status
	LTORG	Begin literal pool
	CNOP	Conditional no operation
	COPY	Copy predefined source coding
	END	End assembly
Macro definition	MACRO	Macro definition header
	MEXIT	Macro definition exit
	MEND	Macro definition trailer
	AREAD	Assign card to SETC symbol
Conditional assembly	ACTR	Conditional assembly loop counter
	AGO	Unconditional branch
	AIF	Conditional branch
	ANOP	Assembly no operation
	GBLA	Define global SETA symbol
	GBLB	Define global SETB symbol
	GBLC	Define global SETC symbol
	LCLA	Define local SETA symbol
	LCLB	Define local SETB symbol
	LCLC	Define local SETC symbol
	MNOTE	Generate error message
	MHELP	Trace macro flow
	SETA	Set arithmetic variable symbol
	SETB	Set binary variable symbol
	SETC	Set character variable symbol

Source: GC26-4037.

EXTENDED MNEMONIC INSTRUCTIONS

Use	Extended Mnemonic* (RX or RR)	Meaning	Machine Instr.* (RX or RR)
General	B or BR	Unconditional Branch	BC or BCR 15,
	NOP or NOPR	No Operation	BC or BCR 0,
After Compare Instructions (A:B)	BH or BHR	Branch on A High	BC or BCR 2,
	BL or BLR	Branch on A Low	BC or BCR 4,
	BE or BER	Branch on A Equal B	BC or BCR 8,
	BNH or BNHR	Branch on A Not High	BC or BCR 13,
	BNL or BNLR	Branch on A Not Low	BC or BCR 11,
	BNE or BNER	Branch on A Not Equal B	BC or BCR 7,
After Arithmetic Instructions	BP or BPR	Branch on Plus	BC or BCR 2,
	BM or BMR	Branch on Minus	BC or BCR 4,
	BZ or BZR	Branch on Zero	BC or BCR 8,
	BO or BOR	Branch on Overflow	BC or BCR 1,
	BNP or BNPR	Branch on Not Plus	BC or BCR 13,
	BNM or BNMR	Branch on Not Minus	BC or BCR 11,
	BNZ or BNZR	Branch on Not Zero	BC or BCR 7,
	BNO or BNOR	Branch on No Overflow	BC or BCR 14,
After Test under Mask Instruction	BO or BOR	Branch if Ones	BC or BCR 1,
	BM or BMR	Branch if Mixed	BC or BCR 4,
	BZ or BZR	Branch if Zeros	BC or BCR 8,
	BNO or BNOR	Branch if Not Ones	BC or BCR 14,
	BNM or BNMR	Branch if Not Mixed	BC or BCR 11,
	BNZ or BNZR	Branch if Not Zeros	BC or BCR 7,

Source: GC26-4037.
*Second operand, not shown, is $D_2(X_2,B_2)$ for RX format and R_2 for RR format.

CNOP ALIGNMENT

<table>
<tr><td colspan="8">DOUBLEWORD</td></tr>
<tr><td colspan="4">WORD</td><td colspan="4">WORD</td></tr>
<tr><td colspan="2">HALFWORD</td><td colspan="2">HALFWORD</td><td colspan="2">HALFWORD</td><td colspan="2">HALFWORD</td></tr>
<tr><td>BYTE</td><td>BYTE</td><td>BYTE</td><td>BYTE</td><td>BYTE</td><td>BYTE</td><td>BYTE</td><td>BYTE</td></tr>
<tr><td>0,4
0,8</td><td></td><td>2,4
2,8</td><td></td><td>0,4
4,8</td><td></td><td>2,4
6,8</td><td></td></tr>
</table>

Source: GC26-4037.

SUMMARY OF CONSTANTS

Type	Implied Length, Bytes	Alignment	Format	Truncation/ Padding
C	–	byte	characters	right
G	(even)	byte	graphic (double-byte) characters	right
X	–	byte	hexadecimal digits	left
B	–	byte	binary digits	left
F	4	word	fixed-point binary	left
H	2	halfword	fixed-point binary	left
E	4	word	short floating-point	right
D	8	doubleword	long floating-point	right
L	16	doubleword	extended floating-point	right
P	–	byte	packed decimal	left
Z	–	byte	zoned decimal	left
A	4	word	value of address	left
Y	2	halfword	value of address	left
S	2	halfword	address in base-displacement form	–
V	4	word	externally defined address value	left
Q	4	word	symbol naming a DXD or DSECT	left

Source: GC26-4037.

PROGRAM-STATUS WORD

0	R	000	T	I	E	PSW key	1	M	W	P	S	0	CC	Program mask	0000 0000
0			5			8	12				16		18	20	24 31

A	Instruction address
32	33 63

1 (R) Program-event-recording mask
5 (T = 1) DAT mode
6 (I) Input/output mask
7 (E) External mask
13 (M) Machine-check mask
14 (W = 1) Wait state
15 (P = 1) Problem state
16 (S = 1) Secondary-space mode
18-19 (CC) Condition code
20 Fixed-point-overflow mask
21 Decimal-overflow mask
22 Exponent-underflow mask
23 Significance mask
32 (A = 1) 31-bit addressing mode

EXTERNAL-INTERRUPTION CODES

At real storage address 134-135 (hex 86-87)

Code (Hex)	Condition
0040	Interrupt key
1003	TOD-clock-sync check
1004	Clock comparator
1005	CPU timer
1200	Malfunction alert
1201	Emergency signal
1202	External call
2401	Service signal

PROGRAM-INTERRUPTION CODES

At real storage address 142-143 (hex 8E-8F)

Code (hex)	Condition
0001	Operation exception
0002	Privileged-operation exception
0003	Execute exception
0004	Protection exception
0005	Addressing exception
0006	Specification exception
0007	Data exception
nn08*	Fixed-point overflow exception
0009	Fixed-point divide exception
000A	Decimal-overflow exception
000B	Decimal-divide exception
nn0C*	Exponent-overflow exception
nn0D*	Exponent-underflow exception
nn0E*	Significance exception
nn0F*	Floating-point divide exception
0010	Segment-translation exception
0011	Page-translation exception
0012	Translation-specification exception
0013	Special-operation exception
0015	Operand exception
0016	Trace-table exception
0017	ASN-translation specification exception
0019	Vector-operation exception
001C	Space-switch event
nn1E*	Unnormalized-operand exception
001F	PC-translation specification exception
0020	AFX-translation exception
0021	ASX-translation exception
0022	LX-translation exception
0023	EX-translation exception
0024	Primary-authority exception
0025	Secondary-authority exception
0040	Monitor event
0080	PER event (code may be combined with another code)

*Use the Exception-Extension code table below for bits 0-7 (nn) of the program-interruption code.

EXCEPTION-EXTENSION CODE

```
| a v w w r r r r |
0               7
```

Bit	Meaning
0(a)	Arithmetic-partial-completion bit 0 Completion or suppression of instruction and bits 1-7 of the exception-extension code are also zero 1 Partial completion of vector instruction
1(v)	Arithmetic-result location 0 Scalar register 1 Vector register
2-3(ww)	Arithmetic-result width 01 4-byte result 10 8-byte result
4-7(rrrr)	Register number of result register designated by the interrupted instruction

FIXED STORAGE LOCATIONS

Area, dec.	Addr type	Hex addr	Function
0- 7	A	0	Initial-program-loading PSW
0- 7	R	0	Restart new PSW
8- 15	A	8	Initial-program-loading CCW1
8- 15	R	8	Restart old PSW
16- 23	A	10	Initial-program-loading CCW2
24- 31	R	18	External old PSW
32- 39	R	20	Supervisor-call old PSW
40- 47	R	28	Program old PSW
48- 55	R	30	Machine-check old PSW
56- 63	R	38	Input/output old PSW
88- 95	R	58	External new PSW
96-103	R	60	Supervisor-call new PSW
104-111	R	68	Program new PSW
112-119	R	70	Machine-check new PSW
120-127	R	78	Input/output new PSW
128-131	R	80	External-interruption parameter for service signal
132-133	R	84	CPU address associated with external interruption, or zeros
134-135	R	86	External-interruption code (see table)
136-139	R	88	SVC interruption (0-12 zeros, 13-14 ILC, 15:0, 16-31 code)
140-143	R	8C	Program interruption (0-12 zeros, 13-14 ILC, 15:0, 16-31 code)
144-147	R	90	Translation-exception ID (see table)
148-149	R	94	Monitor class (0-7 zeros, 8-15 class number)
150-151	R	96	PER code (0-3 code, 4-15 zeros)
152-155	R	98	PER address (0:0, 1-31 address)
156-159	R	9C	Monitor code
184-187	R	B8	Subsystem-identification word (0-14 zeros, 15:1, 16-31 subchannel number)
188-191	R	BC	I/O interruption parameter (from the associated subchannel)
216-223	A	D8	Store-status CPU-timer save area
216-223	R	D8	Machine-check CPU-timer save area
224-231	A	E0	Store-status clock-comparator save area
224-231	R	E0	Machine-check clock-comparator save area
232-239	R	E8	Machine-check-interruption code (see diagram)
244-247	R	F4	External-damage code (see diagram)
248-251	R	F8	Failing-storage address (0:0, 1-31 address)
256-263	A	100	Store-status PSW save area
256-271	R	100	Fixed-logout area*
264-267	A	108	Store-status prefix save area
352-383	A	160	Store-status floating-point-register save area
352-383	R	160	Machine-check floating-point-register save area
384-447	A	180	Store-status general-register save area
384-447	R	180	Machine-check general-register save area
448-511	A	1C0	Store-status control-register save area
448-511	R	1C0	Machine-check control-register save area

A = Absolute address

R = Real address

*Contents may vary among models; see System Library manuals for specific model.

OPERATION-REQUEST BLOCK

Word	Fields
0	Interruption parameter
1	Key | S | 000 | F | P | I | A | U | 000 | LPM | L | 000 0000
2	Channel-program address

Bit positions: 0, 8, 16, 24, 31

Word	Bit
1	0-3 (Key) Subchannel key
1	4 (S) Suspend control
1	8 (F) CCW-format control
1	9 (P) Prefetch control
1	10 (I) Initial-status-interruption control
1	11 (A) Address-limit-checking control
1	12 (U) Suppress-suspended-interruption control
1	16-23 (LPM) Logical-path mask
1	24 (L) Incorrect-length-suppression mode

CHANNEL-COMMAND WORD

Format-0 CCW

Command code	Data address
0	8–31

Flags	0	//////	Byte count
32	39	40	48–63

CD – bit 32 (80) causes use of data-address portion of next CCW.
CC – bit 33 (40) causes use of command code and data address of next CCW.
SLI – bit 34 (20) causes suppression of possible incorrect-length indication.
Skip – bit 35 (10) suppresses transfer of information to main storage.
PCI – bit 36 (08) causes an intermediate-interruption condition to occur.
IDA – bit 37 (04) causes bits 8-31 of CCW to specify location of first IDAW.
Suspend – bit 38 (02) causes suspension before execution of this CCW.

Format-1 CCW

Command code	Flags	0	Byte count
0	8	15	16–31

0	Data address
32	33–63

CD – bit 8 (80) causes use of data-address portion of next CCW.
CC – bit 9 (40) causes use of command code and data address of next CCW.
SLI – bit 10 (20) causes suppression of possible incorrect-length indication.
Skip – bit 11 (10) suppresses transfer of information to main storage.
PCI – bit 12 (08) causes an intermediate-interruption condition to occur.
IDA – bit 13 (04) causes bits 33-63 of CCW to specify location of first IDAW.
Suspend – bit 14 (02) causes suspension before execution of this CCW.

I/O COMMAND CODES

Standard Command-Code Assignments (CCW bits 0-7)

x x x x	0 0 0 0	Invalid Command	mmmm	0 1 0 0	Sense	
mmmm	mm0 1	Write	0 0 0 0	0 1 0 0	– Basic Sense	
mmmm	mm1 0	Read	1 1 1 0	0 1 0 0	– Sense ID	
0 0 0 0	0 0 1 0	–Read IPL	x x x x	1 0 0 0	Transfer in Channel	(a)
mmmm	mm1 1	Control	0 0 0 0	1 0 0 0	Transfer in Channel	(b)
0 0 0 0	0 0 1 1	– Control No Operation	mmmm	1 0 0 0	Invalid Command	(c)
			mmmm	1 1 0 0	Read Backward	

x – Bit Ignored
m – Modifier bit for specific type of I/O device

a Format-0 CCW
b Format-1 CCW
c Format-1 CCW and nonzero m bit

Standard Meanings of Bits of First Sense Byte

Bit	Designation	Bit	Designation
0	Command reject	4	Data check
1	Intervention required	5	Overrun
2	Bus-out check	6	(Device–dependent)
3	Equipment check	7	(Device–dependent)

Console Printer Channel Commands

Write, No Carrier Return	01	Sense	04
Write, Auto Carrier Return	09	Audible Alarm	0B
Read Inquiry	0A	No Operation	03

Card Reader and Card Punch Channel Commands

3504, 3505 Card Readers/3525 Card Punch (GA21-9124)

Channel Command	Binary		Bit Meanings	
Sense	0 0 0 0	0 1 0 0	SS	Stacker
Feed, Select Stacker	S S 1 0	F 0 1 1	00	1
Read Only*	1 1 D 0	F 0 1 0	01/10	2
Diagnostic Read (invalid for 3504)	1 1 0 1	0 0 1 0		
Read, Feed, Select Stacker*	S S D 0	F 0 1 0	F	Format Mode
Write RCE Format*	0 0 0 1	0 0 0 1	0	Unformatted
			1	Formatted
3504, 3505 only				
Write OMR Format†	0 0 1 1	0 0 0 1	D	Data Mode
			0	1–EBCDIC
3525 only			1	2–Card image
Write, Feed, Select Stacker	S S D 0	0 0 0 1		
Print Line*	L L L L	L 1 0 1	L	Line Position
			(5-bit binary value)	

*Special feature on 3525
†Special feature

I/O COMMAND CODES (Cont'd)

Printer Channel Commands

COMMANDS VALID FOR ALL PRINTERS (Except 3800-3, -6 when in Page Mode)	
No Operation	03
Space 1 Line Immediate	0B
Space 2 Lines Immediate	13
Space 3 Lines Immediate	1B
Block Data Check	73
Allow Data Check	7B
Skip to Channel 1 Immediate	8B
Skip to Channel 2 Immediate	93
Skip to Channel 3 Immediate	9B
Skip to Channel 4 Immediate	A3
Skip to Channel 5 Immediate	AB
Skip to Channel 6 Immediate	B3
Skip to Channel 7 Immediate	BB
Skip to Channel 8 Immediate	C3
Skip to Channel 9 Immediate	CB
Skip to Channel 10 Immediate	D3
Skip to Channel 11 Immediate	DB
Skip to Channel 12 Immediate	E3
Write Without Spacing	01
Write and Space 1 Line	09
Write and Space 2 Lines	11
Write and Space 3 Lines	19
Write and Skip to Channel 1	89
Write and Skip to Channel 2	91
Write and Skip to Channel 3	99
Write and Skip to Channel 4	A1
Write and Skip to Channel 5	A9
Write and Skip to Channel 6	B1
Write and Skip to Channel 7	B9
Write and Skip to Channel 8	C1
Write and Skip to Channel 9	C9
Write and Skip to Channel 10	D1
Write and Skip to Channel 11	D9
Write and Skip to Channel 12	E1
Basic Sense	04

3800-3, -6 PAGE MODE COMMANDS (See Note Y)	
No Operation	03
Load Font Index	0F
Load Font Control	1F
Load Font	2F
Execute Order Any State	33
Load Font Equivalence	3F
Delete Font	4F
Begin Page Segment	5F
Delete Page Segment	6F
Include Page Segment	7F
Execute Order Home State	8F
Set Home State	97
Load Copy Control	9F
Begin Page	AF
End Page	BF
Load Page Description	CF
Begin Overlay	DF
Delete Overlay	EF
Write Factored Text Control	0D
Write Text	2D
Write Image Control	3D
Write Image	4D
End	5D
Load Page Position	6D
Basic Sense	04
Sense Intermediate Buffer	14
Sense Error Log	24
Sense ID	E4

3800-1 Reference: GA26-1635
3800-3, -6 Reference: GA32-0050

Note X: For 3800-3, -6 only, Set Home State (97) command will be accepted, but with command retry; the retry will succeed because Page Mode will have been set.

Note Y: Other 3800-3, -6 commands accepted, but with command retry; the retry will succeed because Page Mode will have been reset.

IMPACT PRINTERS – ADDITIONAL COMMANDS

Printer	Column	Reference
1403-N1	A	GA24-3312
3203-5	B	GA33-1529
3211	B	GA24-3543
4248-1 <3211 mode>	B	GA24-3927
4248-2 <3211 mode>	B	GA24-3991
3262-5 <3262-1 mode>	C	GA24-3936
4245-1	C	GA33-1541
4245-12, -20	C	GA33-1579
3262-5 <4248 mode>	D	GA24-3936
4248-1 <native mode>	D	GA24-3927
4248-2 <native mode>	D	GA24-3991
6262-014	D	GA24-4134

Use column A, B, C, or D.		A	B	C	D
Unfold	23	.	X	X	X
Execute Order	33	.	.	.	X
Fold	43	.	X	X	X
Load Forms Control Buffer	63	.	X	X	X
Raise Cover	6B	.	1	2	
Signal Attention	6B	.			3
Skip to Channel 0 Immediate	83	.	4	.	2
Clear Printer	87	.	.	X	X
UCS Gate Load	EB	X	.	.	.
Load UCS Buffer and Fold	F3	X	.	.	
Verify Band ID	F3		.	.	X
Load UCS Buffer (No Fold)	FB	X	X	X	
Verify Band ID	FB				X
Release CU and Device	14	5	.	.	
Sense Intermediate Buffer	14		.	.	X
Release CU, Reserve Device	34	5	.	.	.
Reserve CU, Release Device	54	5	.	.	.
Reserve CU and Device	74	5	.	.	.
Release Device	94	5	.	.	.
Reserve Device	B4	5	.	.	.
Release CU	D4	5	.	.	.
Sense ID	E4	.	.	X	X
Reserve CU	F4	5	.	.	.
Read Band ID	0A	.			X
Diagnostic Read PLB	02	X	X	6	2
Diagnostic Write	05	7	8	6	2
Diagnostic Check Read	06	X	X	X	2
Diagnostic Gate	07	.	X	X	2
Diagnostic Read UCS Buffer	0A	.	X	X	
Diagnostic Read FCB	12	.	X	X	X

X = Valid
. = Invalid
Blank = Not applicable.

1 = No action occurs (except 3211).
2 = No action occurs.
3 = No action occurs on 3262-5.
4 = 3211 only (no action occurs on 4248 <3211 mode>.
5 = Two-channel switch feature only.
6 = No action occurs (except 4245).
7 = 1403-N1 also uses command codes 0D, 15, 1D, 8D, 95, 9D, A5, AD, B5, BD, C5, CD, D5, DD, and E5.
8 = 3211 and 4248 <3211 mode> only.

3800 - ADDITIONAL COMMANDS (Except 3800-3, -6 when in Page Mode; see Note X)	
End of Transmission	07
Mark Form	17
Load Copy Number	23
Execute Order Any State	33
Initialize Printer	37
Load Forms Overlay Seq Control	43
Select Translate Table 0	47
Load Writable Char Gen Module	53
Select Translate Table 1	57
Load Forms Control Buffer	63
Select Translate Table 2	67
Select Translate Table 3	77
Load Translate Table	83
Clear Printer	87
Load Graphic Char Modification	25
Load Copy Modification	35
Sense Intermediate Buffer	14
Sense Error Log	24
Sense ID	E4

I/O COMMAND CODES (Cont'd)

Magnetic-Tape Channel Commands

Channel Command	Hex Code	3420-3 3420-5 3420-7	3420-4 3420-6 3420-8	3422 3430	3480
No Operation	03	X	X	X	X
Rewind	07	X	X	X	X
Rewind Unload	0F	X	X	X	X
Modeset-1 (200/Odd/DC)	13	(a)	(b)		(b)
Erase Gap	17	X	X	X	X
Request Track-In-Error	1B	X	X	(c)	
Write Tape Mark	1F	X	X	X	X
Modeset-1 (200/Even/Normal)	23	(a)	(b)		(b)
Backspace Block	27	X	X	X	X
Modeset-1 (200/Even/TR)	2B	(a)	(b)		(b)
Backspace File	2F	X	X	X	X
Modeset-1 (200/Odd/Normal)	33	(a)	(b)		(b)
Forward Space Block	37	X	X	X	X
Modeset-1 (200/Odd/TR)	3B	(a)	(b)		(b)
Forward Space File	3F	X	X	X	X
Synchronize	43				X
Locate Block	4F				X
Modeset-1 (556/Odd/DC)	53	(d)	(b)		(b)
Suspend Multipath Reconnection	5B				(b)
Modeset-1 (556/Even/Normal)	63	(d)	(b)		(b)
Modeset-1 (556/Even/TR)	6B	(d)	(b)		(b)
Modeset-1 (556/Odd/Normal)	73	(d)	(b)		(b)
Modeset-1 (556/Odd/TR)	7B	(d)	(b)		(b)
Modeset-1 (800/Odd/DC)	93	(d)	(b)		(b)
Data Security Erase	97	X	X	X	X
Load Display	9F				X
Modeset-1 (800/Even/Normal)	A3	(d)	(b)		(b)
Modeset-1 (800/Even/TR)	AB	(d)	(b)		(b)
Set Path Group ID	AF				X
Modeset-1 (800/Odd/Normal)	B3	(d)	(b)		(b)
Assign	B7				X
Modeset-1 (800/Odd/TR)	BB	(d)	(b)		(b)
Modeset-2 (1600 bpi PE)	C3	(e)	(f)	X	–
Set Tape-Write-Immediate	C3	–	–	–	X
Unassign	C7				X
Modeset-2 (800 bpi NRZI)	CB	(e)	(b)		(b)
Modeset-2 (6250 bpi GCR)	D3		(f)	X	(b)
Mode Set	DB				X
Control Access	E3				X
Write	01	X	X	X	X
Read	02	X	X	X	X
Read Buffer	12				X
Read Block ID	22				X
Read Backward	0C	X	X	X	X
Basic Sense	04	X	X	X	X
Read Buffered Log	24				X
Sense Path Group ID	34				X
Release	D4	(g)	(g)	(g)	
Sense ID	E4			X	X
Reserve	F4	(g)	(g)	(g)	
Diagnostic Mode Set	0B	X	X		
Set Diagnose	4B	X	X	(c)	
Loop Write-To-Read	8B	X	X	X	

Notes:
a No action occurs unless 7-track feature is installed; if present, density set is 200 bpi by 3803-2 Tape Control, 556 bpi by 3803-1.
b Valid command, but no action occurs.
c Invalid command for 3422.
d No action occurs unless 7-track feature is installed.
e No action occurs unless 800 bpi density feature is installed.
f No action occurs unless 1600 bpi density feature is installed.
g Requires two-channel switch feature; invalid for 3430.

For hex code C3, the meaning depends on the machine type; hyphens signify that the alternative meaning is used.

Modeset-1 command (for 7-track drives): density (200, 556, 800 bpi)/parity (even, odd)/mode (Normal, DC = data converter, TR = translator). Modeset-2 command (for 9-track drives): density (800, 1600, 6250 bpi).

Sources:
3420-3, -5, -7 (GA32-0020)
3420-4, -6, -8 (GA32-0021)
3422 (GA32-0089)
3430 (GA32-0076)
3480 (GA32-0042)

I/O COMMAND CODES (Cont'd)

Direct Access Storage Devices

Use this chart to find the proper column in the DASD Channel Commands table and to find order numbers for DASD reference manuals. See DASD manuals for the restrictions and details of operations.

	Count/Key/Data Devices							FBA Device	
Controller	**2305**	**3330 3333**	**3340 3344**	**3350**	**3375**	**3380 -0-A**	**3380 -D-E -J-K**	**3370**	**Controller Manual**
ISC		col2	col2	col2					GA26-1620
ISC-SA		col2		col2					GA32-0036
2835-2	col1								GA26-1589
3380-CJ2							*col5		GC26-4497
3830-2		col2	col2	col2					GA26-1617
3830-3		col2		col2					GA32-0036
3880-1		col2	col2	col2	col4			col6	GA26-1661
3880-2		col2	col2	col2	col4	col4		col6	GA26-1661
3880-3						col4	col4		GA26-1661
3880-4					col4			col6	GA26-1661
3880-11(ND)		col2		col2					GA32-0061
3880-11(PD)				col2					GA32-0061
3880-11(PP)				col3					GA32-0061
3880-13						col5			GA32-0067
3880-21(PD)				col2					GA32-0031
3880-21(PP)				col3					GA32-0031
3880-23						*col5	col5		GA32-0083
3990-1, -2, -3						*col5	col5		GA32-0099
Device Manual	GA26 1589	GA26 1615	GA26 1619	GA26 1638	GA26 1666	GC26 4491	GC26 4491	GA26 1657	

ISC = Integrated Storage Controller
ISC-SA = Integrated Storage Controller with Staging Adapter
ND = Nonpaging director
PD = Paging director, direct mode
PP = Paging director, paging mode
3380-0-A = 3380 Direct Access Storage Models AA4, A04, and B04
3380-D-E = 3380 Direct Access Storage Models AD4, AE4, BD4, and BE4
3380-J,-K = 3380 Direct Access Storage Models AJ4, AK4, BJ4, and BK4
* = 3380-A04 does not attach to 3380-23 or 3990; only 3380-BJ4 and -BK4 attach to 3380-CJ2

I/O COMMAND CODES (Cont'd)

DASD Channel Commands

Channel Command	Hex Code	2305	3330 3340 3350	3350	3375 3380	3380	3370	Typical Transfer Count
		1	2	3	4	5	6	
Control								
No Operation	03	X	X	X	X	X	X	None
Seek	07	X	X	X	X	X		6
Seek Cylinder	0B	X	X	X	X	X		6
Space Count	0F	X	X		X	X		3
Recalibrate (No Op on 2305-2)	13	X	X		X	X		None
Restore (executed as No-Op)	17	X	X		X	X		None
Seek Head	1B	X	X	X	X	X		6
Set File Mask	1F	X	X		X	X		1
Set Sector (3340 RPS is optional)	23	X	X	X	X	X		1
Vary Sensing	27	X						1
Perform Subsystem Function	27					(u)		Variable
Orient (No-Op on 2305-2)	2B	X						None
Set High Performance Storage Limits	3B					(a)		10
Locate	43						X	8
Locate Record	47				(b)	(c)		16
Suspend Multipath Reconnection	5B				(d)	X		None
Define Extent	63				(b)	X	X	16
Set Subsystem Mode	87		(e)			(r)		2
Set Paging Parameters	8B			X				10
Discard Block	8F			X				2 + (5 × n)
Set Path Group ID	AF				(d)	X		12
Search								
Search Key Equal (*A9)	29	X	X		X	X		KL
Search ID Equal (*B1)	31	X	X	X	X	X		5
Search Home Address Equal (*B9)	39	X	X		X	X		4
Search Key High (*C9)	49	X	X		X	X		KL
Search ID High (*D1)	51	X	X		X	X		5
Search Key Equal or High (*E9)	69	X	X		X	X		KL
Search ID Equal or High (*F1)	71	X	X		X	X		5
Read								
Read Initial Program Load	02	X	X		X	X	X	DL or 512
Read Data (*86)	06	X	X	X	X	X		DL
Read Key & Data (*BE)	0E	X	X		X	X		KL + DL
Read Count (*92)	12	X	X		X	X		8
Read Record Zero (*96)	16	X	X		X	X		8 + KL + DL
Read Home Address (*9A)	1A	X	X		X	X		5
Read Count Key & Data (*9E)	1E	X	X		X	X		8 + KL + DL
Read Sector (3340 RPS is optional)	22	X	X		X	X		1
Read Subsystem Data	3E					(u)		Variable
Read	42						X	512 × n
Read Message ID	4E					(v)		11
Read Multiple Count Key & Data	5E		(f)		X	X		n × (8 + KL + DL)
Read Track	DE					(t)		Variable
Read Configuration Data	FA					(u)		256
Write								
Write Special Count Key & Data	01	X	X					8 + KL + DL
Write Data	05	X	X	X	X	X		DL
Write Key & Data	0D	X	X		X	X		KL + DL
Erase	11	X	X		X	X		8 + KL + DL
Write Record Zero	15	X	X		X	X		8 + KL + DL
Write Home Address	19	X	X		X	X		5, 7, or 11
Write Count Key & Data	1D	X	X		X	X		8 + KL + DL
Write	41						X	512 × n
Write Update Data	85				(b)	(c)		DL
Write Update Key & Data	8D				(b)	(c)		KL + DL
Write Count Key & Data Next Track	9D				(b)	(c)		8 + KL + DL
		1	2	3	4	5	6	

I/O COMMAND CODES (Cont'd)

DASD Channel Commands (Cont'd)

Channel Command		Hex Code	2305	3330 3340 3350	3350	3375 3380	3380	3370	Typical Transfer Count
			1	2	3	4	5	6	
Sense									
Basic Sense		04	X	X	X	X	X	X	24 or 32
Unconditional Reserve	(g)	14		(h,j)		(d,h, j)	X	(h,j)	24 or 32
Read Buffered Log		24	X						128
Sense Path Group ID		34				(d)	X		12
Reset Allegiance		44					(t)		32
Sense Subsystem Status		54		(k)			X		40
Read Device Characteristics		64					(c)	X	32
Sense Subsystem Counts		74		(k)			(s)		80
Device Release		94	(j)	(h,j)		(d,h, j)	X	(h,j)	24
Read and Reset Buffered Log		A4		X		X	X	X	24 or 32
Device Reserve		B4	(j)	(h,j)		(d,h, j)	X	(h,j)	24 or 32
Sense ID	(f)	E4		X	X	X	X	X	7
Diagnostic									
Diagnostic Write Home Address		09				X	X		27 or 28
Diagnostic Read Home Address		0A				X	X		27 or 28
Diagnostic Sense #		44	X	(m)					16 or 512
Diagnostic Load		53	X	(m)					1
Diagnostic Write		73	X	(m)					8 or 512
Diagnostic Sense/Read		C4		(p)		X	X	X	Variable
Diagnostic Control		F3		(q)		(q)	X	X	4 + n
			1	2	3	4	5	6	

a Valid only for 3880-13
b Speed matching buffer feature
c Not valid for 3880-13
d Dynamic path selection (only valid on 3380-AA4, -AD4, -AE4, -AJ4, -AK4 strings)
e Valid only for 3880-21
f Not valid for 3330/3333 on ISC-SA; 3830-2, -3, and ISC require 3344/3350 microcode
g Not valid on ISC-SA; not valid on 3330/3333, 3340/3344
h String-switching feature
j Channel-switching feature
k Valid only for 3880-11 paging director and 3880-21
m Not valid on 3880-21
p Valid only for 3880-1, -2, -11, -21
q Valid only for 3330/3350 on 3880-1, -2, and for 3380 on 3880-2, -3 without 3380-speed matching-buffer feature
r Valid only for 3880-13, -23, and 3990-3
s Valid only for 3880-13, -23
t Not valid for 3880-13, -23
u Valid only for 3990
v Valid only for 3990-3
* Multi track command codes (standard)
# Also called "Read Diagnostic Status 1"

CODE ASSIGNMENTS

Code Tables

Dec.	Hex	Graphics and Controls BCDIC	EBCDIC	ASCII	7-Track Tape BCDIC	Card Code EBCDIC	Binary
0	00		NUL	NUL		12-0-1-8-9	0000 0000
1	01		SOH	SOH		12-1-9	0000 0001
2	02		STX	STX		12-2-9	0000 0010
3	03		ETX	ETX		12-3-9	0000 0011
4	04		SEL	EOT		12-4-9	0000 0100
5	05		HT	ENQ		12-5-9	0000 0101
6	06		RNL	ACK		12-6-9	0000 0110
7	07		DEL	BEL		12-7-9	0000 0111
8	08		GE	BS		12-8-9	0000 1000
9	09		SPS	HT		12-1-8-9	0000 1001
10	0A		RPT	LF		12-2-8-9	0000 1010
11	0B		VT	VT		12-3-8-9	0000 1011
12	0C		FF	FF		12-4-8-9	0000 1100
13	0D		CR	CR		12-5-8-9	0000 1101
14	0E		SO	SO		12-6-8-9	0000 1110
15	0F		SI	SI		12-7-8-9	0000 1111
16	10		DLE	DLE		12-11-1-8-9	0001 0000
17	11		DC1	DC1		11-1-9	0001 0001
18	12		DC2	DC2		11-2-9	0001 0010
19	13		DC3	DC3		11-3-9	0001 0011
20	14		RES/ENP	DC4		11-4-9	0001 0100
21	15		NL	NAK		11-5-9	0001 0101
22	16		BS	SYN		11-6-9	0001 0110
23	17		POC	ETB		11-7-9	0001 0111
24	18		CAN	CAN		11-8-9	0001 1000
25	19		EM	EM		11-1-8-9	0001 1001
26	1A		UBS	SUB		11-2-8-9	0001 1010
27	1B		CU1	ESC		11-3-8-9	0001 1011
28	1C		IFS	FS		11-4-8-9	0001 1100
29	1D		IGS	GS		11-5-8-9	0001 1101
30	1E		IRS	RS		11-6-8-9	0001 1110
31	1F		ITB/IUS	US		11-7-8-9	0001 1111
32	20		DS	SP		11-0-1-8-9	0010 0000
33	21		SOS	!		0-1-9	0010 0001
34	22		FS	"		0-2-9	0010 0010
35	23		WUS	#		0-3-9	0010 0011
36	24		BYP/INP	$		0-4-9	0010 0100
37	25		LF	%		0-5-9	0010 0101
38	26		ETB	&		0-6-9	0010 0110
39	27		ESC	'		0-7-9	0010 0111
40	28		SA	(		0-8-9	0010 1000
41	29		SFE	)		0-1-8-9	0010 1001
42	2A		SM/SW	*		0-2-8-9	0010 1010
43	2B		CSP	+		0-3-8-9	0010 1011
44	2C		MFA	,		0-4-8-9	0010 1100
45	2D		ENQ	–		0-5-8-9	0010 1101
46	2E		ACK	.		0-6-8-9	0010 1110
47	2F		BEL	/		0-7-8-9	0010 1111
48	30			0		12-11-0-1-8-9	0011 0000
49	31			1		1-9	0011 0001
50	32		SYN	2		2-9	0011 0010
51	33		IR	3		3-9	0011 0011
52	34		PP	4		4-9	0011 0100
53	35		TRN	5		5-9	0011 0101
54	36		NBS	6		6-9	0011 0110
55	37		EOT	7		7-9	0011 0111
56	38		SBS	8		8-9	0011 1000
57	39		IT	9		1-8-9	0011 1001
58	3A		RFF	:		2-8-9	0011 1010
59	3B		CU3	;		3-8-9	0011 1011
60	3C		DC4	<		4-8-9	0011 1100
61	3D		NAK	=		5-8-9	0011 1101
62	3E			>		6-8-9	0011 1110
63	3F		SUB	?		7-8-9	0011 1111

CODE ASSIGNMENTS (Cont'd)

Code Tables (Cont'd)

Dec.	Hex	Graphics and Controls BCDIC	EBCDIC(1)		ASCII	7-Track Tape BCDIC(2)	Card Code EBCDIC	Binary
64	40	SP	SP	SP	@	(3)	no punches	0100 0000
65	41		RSP		A		12-0-1-9	0100 0001
66	42				B		12-0-2-9	0100 0010
67	43				C		12-0-3-9	0100 0011
68	44				D		12-0-4-9	0100 0100
69	45				E		12-0-5-9	0100 0101
70	46				F		12-0-6-9	0100 0110
71	47				G		12-0-7-9	0100 0111
72	48				H		12-0-8-9	0100 1000
73	49				I		12-1-8	0100 1001
74	4A		¢	¢	J		12-2-8	0100 1010
75	4B	.	.	.	K	B A 8 2 1	12-3-8	0100 1011
76	4C	¤)	<	<	L	B A 8 4	12-4-8	0100 1100
77	4D	[	(	(	M	B A 8 4 1	12-5-8	0100 1101
78	4E	<	+	+	N	B A 8 4 2	12-6-8	0100 1110
79	4F	‡	|	|	O	B A 8 4 2 1	12-7-8	0100 1111
80	50	& +	&	&	P	B A	12	0101 0000
81	51				Q		12-11-1-9	0101 0001
82	52				R		12-11-2-9	0101 0010
83	53				S		12-11-3-9	0101 0011
84	54				T		12-11-4-9	0101 0100
85	55				U		12-11-5-9	0101 0101
86	56				V		12-11-6-9	0101 0110
87	57				W		12-11-7-9	0101 0111
88	58				X		12-11-8-9	0101 1000
89	59				Y		11-1-8	0101 1001
90	5A		!	!	Z		11-2-8	0101 1010
91	5B	$	$	$	[	B 8 2 1	11-3-8	0101 1011
92	5C	*	*	*	\	B 8 4	11-4-8	0101 1100
93	5D	]	)	)	]	B 8 4 1	11-5-8	0101 1101
94	5E	;	;	;	^	B 8 4 2	11-6-8	0101 1110
95	5F	Δ	¬	¬	_	B 8 4 2 1	11-7-8	0101 1111
96	60	-	-	-	`	B	11	0110 0000
97	61	/	/	/	a	A 1	0-1	0110 0001
98	62				b		11-0-2-9	0110 0010
99	63				c		11-0-3-9	0110 0011
100	64				d		11-0-4-9	0110 0100
101	65				e		11-0-5-9	0110 0101
102	66				f		11-0-6-9	0110 0110
103	67				g		11-0-7-9	0110 0111
104	68				h		11-0-8-9	0110 1000
105	69				i		0-1-8	0110 1001
106	6A		¦		j		12-11	0110 1010
107	6B	,	,	,	k	A 8 2 1	0-3-8	0110 1011
108	6C	%(	%	%	l	A 8 4	0-4-8	0110 1100
109	6D	γ	_	_	m	A 8 4 1	0-5-8	0110 1101
110	6E	\	>	>	n	A 8 4 2	0-6-8	0110 1110
111	6F	⧻	?	?	o	A 8 4 2 1	0-7-8	0110 1111
112	70				p		12-11-0	0111 0000
113	71				q		12-11-0-1-9	0111 0001
114	72				r		12-11-0-2-9	0111 0010
115	73				s		12-11-0-3-9	0111 0011
116	74				t		12-11-0-4-9	0111 0100
117	75				u		12-11-0-5-9	0111 0101
118	76				v		12-11-0-6-9	0111 0110
119	77				w		12-11-0-7-9	0111 0111
120	78				x		12-11-0-8-9	0111 1000
121	79		`		y		1-8	0111 1001
122	7A	ƀ	:	:	z	A	2-8	0111 1010
123	7B	# =	#	#	{	8 2 1	3-8	0111 1011
124	7C	@ '	@	@	|	8 4	4-8	0111 1100
125	7D	:	'	'	}	8 4 1	5-8	0111 1101
126	7E	>	=	=	~	8 4 2	6-8	0111 1110
127	7F	√	"	"	DEL	8 4 2 1	7-8	0111 1111

CODE ASSIGNMENTS (Cont'd)

Code Tables (Cont'd)

Dec.	Hex	Graphics and Controls BCDIC EBCDIC(1) ASCII	7-Track Tape BCDIC	Card Code EBCDIC	Binary
128	80			12-0-1-8	1000 0000
129	81	a a		12-0-1	1000 0001
130	82	b b		12-0-2	1000 0010
131	83	c c		12-0-3	1000 0011
132	84	d d		12-0-4	1000 0100
133	85	e e		12-0-5	1000 0101
134	86	f f		12-0-6	1000 0110
135	87	g g		12-0-7	1000 0111
136	88	h h		12-0-8	1000 1000
137	89	i i		12-0-9	1000 1001
138	8A			12-0-2-8	1000 1010
139	8B	{		12-0-3-8	1000 1011
140	8C	≤		12-0-4-8	1000 1100
141	8D	$^{(}$ See Note		12-0-5-8	1000 1101
142	8E	$^{+}$ See Note		12-0-6-8	1000 1110
143	8F	+		12-0-7-8	1000 1111
144	90			12-11-1-8	1001 0000
145	91	j j		12-11-1	1001 0001
146	92	k k		12-11-2	1001 0010
147	93	l l		12-11-3	1001 0011
148	94	m m		12-11-4	1001 0100
149	95	n n		12-11-5	1001 0101
150	96	o o		12-11-6	1001 0110
151	97	p p		12-11-7	1001 0111
152	98	q q		12-11-8	1001 1000
153	99	r r		12-11-9	1001 1001
154	9A			12-11-2-8	1001 1010
155	9B	}		12-11-3-8	1001 1011
156	9C	¤		12-11-4-8	1001 1100
157	9D	$^{)}$ See Note		12-11-5-8	1001 1101
158	9E	±		12-11-6-8	1001 1110
159	9F	■		12-11-7-8	1001 1111
160	A0	$^{-}$ See Note		11-0-1-8	1010 0000
161	A1	~ °		11-0-1	1010 0001
162	A2	s s		11-0-2	1010 0010
163	A3	t t		11-0-3	1010 0011
164	A4	u u		11-0-4	1010 0100
165	A5	v v		11-0-5	1010 0101
166	A6	w w		11-0-6	1010 0110
167	A7	x x		11-0-7	1010 0111
168	A8	y y		11-0-8	1010 1000
169	A9	z z		11-0-9	1010 1001
170	AA			11-0-2-8	1010 1010
171	AB	└		11-0-3-8	1010 1011
172	AC	┌		11-0-4-8	1010 1100
173	AD	[		11-0-5-8	1010 1101
174	AE	≥		11-0-6-8	1010 1110
175	AF	•		11-0-7-8	1010 1111
176	B0	^{0} See Note		12-11-0-1-8	1011 0000
177	B1	^{1} See Note		12-11-0-1	1011 0001
178	B2	^{2} See Note		12-11-0-2	1011 0010
179	B3	^{3} See Note		12-11-0-3	1011 0011
180	B4	^{4} See Note		12-11-0-4	1011 0100
181	B5	^{5} See Note		12-11-0-5	1011 0101
182	B6	^{6} See Note		12-11-0-6	1011 0110
183	B7	^{7} See Note		12-11-0-7	1011 0111
184	B8	^{8} See Note		12-11-0-8	1011 1000
185	B9	^{9} See Note		12-11-0-9	1011 1001
186	BA			12-11-0-2-8	1011 1010
187	BB	┘		12-11-0-3-8	1011 1011
188	BC	┐		12-11-0-4-8	1011 1100
189	BD	]		12-11-0-5-8	1011 1101
190	BE	≠		12-11-0-6-8	1011 1110
191	BF	—		12-11-0-7-8	1011 1111

Note: This character is an EBCDIC superscript character.

CODE ASSIGNMENTS (Cont'd)

Code Tables (Cont'd)

Dec.	Hex	Graphics and Controls BCDIC	EBCDIC(1)	ASCII	7-Track Tape BCDIC(2)	Card Code EBCDIC	Binary
192	C0	?	{		B A 8 2	12-0	1100 0000
193	C1	A	A	A	B A 1	12-1	1100 0001
194	C2	B	B	B	B A 2	12-2	1100 0010
195	C3	C	C	C	B A 2 1	12-3	1100 0011
196	C4	D	D	D	B A 4	12-4	1100 0100
197	C5	E	E	E	B A 4 1	12-5	1100 0101
198	C6	F	F	F	B A 4 2	12-6	1100 0110
199	C7	G	G	G	B A 4 2 1	12-7	1100 0111
200	C8	H	H	H	B A 8	12-8	1100 1000
201	C9	I	I	I	B A 8 1	12-9	1100 1001
202	CA		SHY			12-0-2-8-9	1100 1010
203	CB					12-0-3-8-9	1100 1011
204	CC					12-0-4-8-9	1100 1100
205	CD					12-0-5-8-9	1100 1101
206	CE					12-0-6-8-9	1100 1110
207	CF					12-0-7-8-9	1100 1111
208	D0	!	}		B 8 2	11-0	1101 0000
209	D1	J	J	J	B 1	11-1	1101 0001
210	D2	K	K	K	B 2	11-2	1101 0010
211	D3	L	L	L	B 2 1	11-3	1101 0011
212	D4	M	M	M	B 4	11-4	1101 0100
213	D5	N	N	N	B 4 1	11-5	1101 0101
214	D6	O	O	O	B 4 2	11-6	1101 0110
215	D7	P	P	P	B 4 2 1	11-7	1101 0111
216	D8	Q	Q	Q	B 8	11-8	1101 1000
217	D9	R	R	R	B 8 1	11-9	1101 1001
218	DA					12-11-2-8-9	1101 1010
219	DB					12-11-3-8-9	1101 1011
220	DC					12-11-4-8-9	1101 1100
221	DD					12-11-5-8-9	1101 1101
222	DE					12-11-6-8-9	1101 1110
223	DF					12-11-7-8-9	1101 1111
224	E0	‡	\		A 8 2	0-2-8	1110 0000
225	E1		NSP			11-0-1-9	1110 0001
226	E2	S	S	S	A 2	0-2	1110 0010
227	E3	T	T	T	A 2 1	0-3	1110 0011
228	E4	U	U	U	A 4	0-4	1110 0100
229	E5	V	V	V	A 4 1	0-5	1110 0101
230	E6	W	W	W	A 4 2	0-6	1110 0110
231	E7	X	X	X	A 4 2 1	0-7	1110 0111
232	E8	Y	Y	Y	A 8	0-8	1110 1000
233	E9	Z	Z	Z	A 8 1	0-9	1110 1001
234	EA					11-0-2-8-9	1110 1010
235	EB					11-0-3-8-9	1110 1011
236	EC					11-0-4-8-9	1110 1100
237	ED					11-0-5-8-9	1110 1101
238	EE					11-0-6-8-9	1110 1110
239	EF					11-0-7-8-9	1110 1111
240	F0	0	0	0	8 2	0	1111 0000
241	F1	1	1	1	1	1	1111 0001
242	F2	2	2	2	2	2	1111 0010
243	F3	3	3	3	2 1	3	1111 0011
244	F4	4	4	4	4	4	1111 0100
245	F5	5	5	5	4 1	5	1111 0101
246	F6	6	6	6	4 2	6	1111 0110
247	F7	7	7	7	4 2 1	7	1111 0111
248	F8	8	8	8	8	8	1111 1000
249	F9	9	9	9	8 1	9	1111 1001
250	FA					12-11-0-2-8-9	1111 1010
251	FB					12-11-0-3-8-9	1111 1011
252	FC					12-11-0-4-8-9	1111 1100
253	FD					12-11-0-5-8-9	1111 1101
254	FE					12-11-0-6-8-9	1111 1110
255	FF		EO			12-11-0-7-8-9	1111 1111

1. Two columns of EBCDIC graphics are shown. The first gives IBM standard U.S. bit pattern assignments. The second shows the T-11 and TN text printing chains (120 graphics).
2. Add C (check bit) for odd or even parity as needed, except as noted.
3. For even parity, use CA.

HEXADECIMAL AND DECIMAL CONVERSION

From hex: locate each hex digit in its corresponding column position and note the decimal equivalents. Add these to obtain the decimal value.

From decimal: (1) locate the largest decimal value in the table that will fit into the decimal number to be converted, and (2) note its hex equivalent and hex column position. (3) Find the decimal remainder. Repeat the process on this and subsequent remainders

Note: Decimal, hexadecimal, and binary equivalents of all numbers from 0 to 255 are listed in the code tables.

WORD															
HALFWORD								HALFWORD							
BYTE				BYTE				BYTE				BYTE			
BITS: 0123		4567		0123		4567		0123		4567		0123		4567	
Hex	Decimal	Hex	Decimal	Hex	Decimal	Hex	Decimal	Hex	Decimal	Hex	Decimal	Hex	Decimal	Hex	Decimal
0	0	0	0	0	0	0	0	0	0	0	0	0	0	0	0
1	268,435,456	1	16,777,216	1	1,048,576	1	65,536	1	4,096	1	256	1	16	1	1
2	536,870,912	2	33,554,432	2	2,097,152	2	131,072	2	8,192	2	512	2	32	2	2
3	805,306,368	3	50,331,648	3	3,145,728	3	196,608	3	12,288	3	768	3	48	3	3
4	1,073,741,824	4	67,108,864	4	4,194,304	4	262,144	4	16,384	4	1,024	4	64	4	4
5	1,342,177,280	5	83,886,080	5	5,242,880	5	327,680	5	20,480	5	1,280	5	80	5	5
6	1,610,612,736	6	100,663,296	6	6,291,456	6	393,216	6	24,576	6	1,536	6	96	6	6
7	1,879,048,192	7	117,440,512	7	7,340,032	7	458,752	7	28,672	7	1,792	7	112	7	7
8	2,147,483,648	8	134,217,728	8	8,388,608	8	524,288	8	32,768	8	2,048	8	128	8	8
9	2,415,919,104	9	150,994,944	9	9,437,184	9	589,824	9	36,864	9	2,304	9	144	9	9
A	2,684,354,560	A	167,772,160	A	10,485,760	A	655,360	A	40,960	A	2,560	A	160	A	10
B	2,952,790,016	B	184,549,376	B	11,534,336	B	720,896	B	45,056	B	2,816	B	176	B	11
C	3,221,225,472	C	201,326,592	C	12,582,912	C	786,432	C	49,152	C	3,072	C	192	C	12
D	3,489,660,928	D	218,103,808	D	13,631,488	D	851,968	D	53,248	D	3,328	D	208	D	13
E	3,758,096,384	E	234,881,024	E	14,680,064	E	917,504	E	57,344	E	3,584	E	224	E	14
F	4,026,531,840	F	251,658,240	F	15,728,640	F	983,040	F	61,440	F	3,840	F	240	F	15
8		7		6		5		4		3		2		1	

HEXADECIMAL AND DECIMAL CONVERSION (Cont'd)

Powers of 2 and 16

m	n	2^m and 16^n
0	0	1
1		2
2		4
3		8
4	1	16
5		32
6		64
7		128
8	2	256
9		512
10		1 024
11		2 048
12	3	4 096
13		8 192
14		16 384
15		32 768
16	4	65 536
17		131 072
18		262 144
19		524 288
20	5	1 048 576
21		2 097 152
22		4 194 304
23		8 388 608
24	6	16 777 216
25		33 554 432
26		67 108 864
27		134 217 728
28	7	268 435 456
29		536 870 912
30		1 073 741 824
31		2 147 483 648

m	n	2^m and 16^n
32	8	4 294 967 296
33		8 589 934 592
34		17 179 869 184
35		34 359 738 368
36	9	68 719 476 736
37		137 438 953 472
38		274 877 906 944
39		549 755 813 888
40	10	1 099 511 627 776
41		2 199 023 255 552
42		4 398 046 511 104
43		8 796 093 022 208
44	11	17 592 186 044 416
45		35 184 372 088 832
46		70 368 744 177 664
47		140 737 488 355 328
48	12	281 474 976 710 656
49		562 949 953 421 312
50		1 125 899 906 842 624
51		2 251 799 813 685 248
52	13	4 503 599 627 370 496
53		9 007 199 254 740 992
54		18 014 398 509 481 984
55		36 028 797 018 963 968
56	14	72 057 594 037 927 936
57		144 115 188 075 855 872
58		288 230 376 151 711 744
59		576 460 752 303 423 488
60	15	1 152 921 504 606 846 976
61		2 305 843 009 213 693 952
62		4 611 686 018 427 387 904
63		9 223 372 036 854 775 808

Symbol	Value
K (kilo)	$1,024 = 2^{10}$
M (mega)	$1,048,576 = 2^{20}$
G (giga)	$1,073,741,824 = 2^{30}$

Appendix B

Examples of the Use and Description of Machine Instructions

This appendix consists of pages reproduced from IBM Form SA22-7085, System/370 Extended Architecture: Principles of Operations. It is intended as an introductory guide to the use of that publication.

Page B-2 consists of the detailed explanation of the Load (L and LR), Load Address (LA), and Load and Test (LTR) instructions. These descriptions are reproduced from Chapter 7 (General Instructions) of SA22-7085.

Page B-3 consists of examples of use of the Load (L) and Load Address (LA) instructions. These descriptions are reproduced from Appendix A (Number Representations and Instruction-Use Examples) of SA22-7085.

Page B-4 consists of the detailed explanation of the Add Decimal (AP) and Compare Decimal (CP) instructions. These descriptions are reproduced from Chapter 10 (Decimal Instructions) of SA22-7085.

Pages B-5 and B-6 consists of examples of use of the Unpack (UNPK), Add Decimal (AP), Compare Decimal (CP), and Divide Decimal (DP) instructions. These descriptions are also reproduced from Appendix A of SA22-7085.

INSERT CHARACTER

IC $R_1,D_2(X_2,B_2)$ [RX]

'43'	R_1	X_2	B_2	D_2
0	8	12	16	20 31

The byte at the second-operand location is inserted into bit positions 24-31 of general register R_1. The remaining bits in the register remain unchanged.

Condition Code: The code remains unchanged.

Program Exceptions:

Access (fetch, operand 2)

INSERT CHARACTERS UNDER MASK

ICM $R_1,M_3,D_2(B_2)$ [RS]

'BF'	R_1	M_3	B_2	D_2
0	8	12	16	20 31

Bytes from contiguous locations beginning at the second-operand address are inserted into general register R_1 under control of a mask.

The contents of the M_3 field are used as a mask. These four bits, left to right, correspond one for one with the four bytes, left to right, of general register R_1. The byte positions corresponding to ones in the mask are filled, left to right, with bytes from successive storage locations beginning at the second-operand address. When the mask is not zero, the length of the second operand is equal to the number of ones in the mask. The bytes in the general register corresponding to zeros in the mask remain unchanged.

The resulting condition code is based on the mask and on the value of the bits inserted. When the mask is zero or when all inserted bits are zeros, the condition code is set to 0. When the inserted bits are not all zeros, the code is set according to the leftmost bit of the storage operand: if this bit is one, the code is set to 1; if this bit is zero, the code is set to 2.

When the mask is not zero, exceptions associated with storage-operand access are recognized only for the number of bytes specified by the mask. When the mask is zero, access exceptions are recognized for one byte at the second-operand address.

Resulting Condition Code:

0 All inserted bits zeros, or mask bits all zeros
1 Leftmost inserted bit one
2 Leftmost inserted bit zero, and not all inserted bits zeros
3 --

Program Exceptions:

Access (fetch, operand 2)

Programming Notes

1. Examples of the use of the INSERT CHARACTERS UNDER MASK instruction are given in Appendix A.

2. The condition code for INSERT CHARACTERS UNDER MASK is defined such that, when the mask is 1111, the instruction causes the same condition code to be set as for LOAD AND TEST. Thus, the instruction may be used as a storage-to-register load-and-test operation.

3. INSERT CHARACTERS UNDER MASK with a mask of 1111 or 0001 performs a function similar to that of a LOAD (L) or INSERT CHARACTER (IC) instruction, respectively, with the exception of the condition-code setting. However, the performance of INSERT CHARACTERS UNDER MASK may be slower.

INSERT PROGRAM MASK

IPM R_1 [RRE]

'B222'	////////	R_1	////
0	16	24	28 31

The condition code and program mask from the current PSW are inserted into bit positions 2-3 and 4-7, respectively, of general register R_1. Bits 0 and 1 of the register are set to zeros; bits 8-31 are left unchanged.

Bits 16-23 and 28-31 of the instruction are ignored.

Condition Code: The code remains unchanged.

Program Exceptions: None.

LOAD

LR R_1,R_2 [RR]

'18'	R_1	R_2
0	8	12 15

L $R_1,D_2(X_2,B_2)$ [RX]

'58'	R_1	X_2	B_2	D_2
0	8	12	16	20 31

The second operand is placed unchanged at the first-operand location.

Condition Code: The code remains unchanged.

Program Exceptions:

Access (fetch, operand 2 of L only)

Programming Note

An example of the use of the LOAD instruction is given in Appendix A.

LOAD ADDRESS

LA $R_1,D_2(X_2,B_2)$ [RX]

'41'	R_1	X_2	B_2	D_2
0	8	12	16	20 31

The address specified by the X_2, B_2, and D_2 fields is placed in general register R_1. The address computation follows the rules for address arithmetic.

In the 24-bit addressing mode, the address is placed in bit positions 8-31, and bits 0-7 are set to zeros. In the 31-bit addressing mode, the address is placed in bit positions 1-31, and bit 0 is set to zero.

No storage references for operands take place, and the address is not inspected for access exceptions.

Condition Code: The code remains unchanged.

Program Exceptions: None.

Programming Notes

1. An example of the use of the LOAD ADDRESS instruction is given in Appendix A.

2. LOAD ADDRESS may be used to increment the rightmost bits of a general register, other than register 0, by the contents of the D_2 field of the instruction. The register to be incremented should be designated by R_1 and by either X_2 (with B_2 set to zero) or B_2 (with X_2 set to zero). The instruction updates 24 bits in the 24-bit addressing mode and updates 31 bits in the 31-bit addressing mode.

LOAD AND TEST

LTR R_1,R_2 [RR]

'12'	R_1	R_2
0	8	12 15

The second operand is placed unchanged at the first-operand location, and the sign and magnitude of the second operand, treated as a 32-bit signed binary integer, are indicated in the condition code.

Resulting Condition Code:

0 Result zero
1 Result less than zero
2 Result greater than zero
3 --

Program Exceptions: None.

Programming Note

When the R_1 and R_2 fields designate the same register, the operation is equivalent to a test without data movement.

LOAD COMPLEMENT

LCR R_1,R_2 [RR]

'13'	R_1	R_2
0	8	12 15

The two's complement of the second operand is placed at the first-operand location. The second operand and result are treated as 32-bit signed binary integers.

ADD DECIMAL

AP $D_1(L_1,B_1),D_2(L_2,B_2)$ [SS]

'FA'	L_1	L_2	B_1	D_1	B_2	D_2
0	8	12	16	20	32	36 47

The second operand is added to the first operand, and the resulting sum is placed at the first-operand location. The operands and result are in the packed format.

Addition is algebraic, taking into account the signs and all digits of both operands. All sign and digit codes are checked for validity.

If the first operand is too short to contain all leftmost nonzero digits of the sum, decimal overflow occurs. The operation is completed. The result is obtained by ignoring the overflow digits, and condition code 3 is set. If the decimal-overflow mask is one, a program interruption for decimal overflow occurs.

The sign of the sum is determined by the rules of algebra. In the absence of overflow, the sign of a zero result is made positive. If overflow occurs, a zero result is given either a positive or negative sign, as determined by what the sign of the correct sum would have been.

<u>Resulting Condition Code</u>:

0 Result zero; no overflow
1 Result less than zero; no overflow
2 Result greater than zero; no overflow
3 Overflow

<u>Program Exceptions</u>:

Access (fetch, operand 2; fetch and store, operand 1)
Data
Decimal overflow

<u>Programming Note</u>

An example of the use of the ADD DECIMAL instruction is given in Appendix A.

COMPARE DECIMAL

CP $D_1(L_1,B_1),D_2(L_2,B_2)$ [SS]

'F9'	L_1	L_2	B_1	D_1	B_2	D_2
0	8	12	16	20	32	36 47

The first operand is compared with the second operand, and the result is indicated in the condition code. The operands are in the packed format.

Comparison is algebraic and follows the procedure for decimal subtraction, except that both operands remain unchanged. When the difference is zero, the operands are equal. When a nonzero difference is positive or negative, the first operand is high or low, respectively.

Overflow cannot occur because the difference is discarded.

All sign and digit codes are checked for validity.

<u>Resulting Condition Code</u>:

0 Operands equal
1 First operand low
2 First operand high
3 --

<u>Program Exceptions</u>:

Access (fetch, operands 1 and 2)
Data

<u>Programming Notes</u>

1. An example of the use of the COMPARE DECIMAL instruction is given in Appendix A.

2. The preferred and alternate sign codes for a particular sign are treated as equivalent for comparison purposes.

3. A negative zero and a positive zero compare equal.

DIVIDE DECIMAL

DP $D_1(L_1,B_1),D_2(L_2,B_2)$ [SS]

'FD'	L_1	L_2	B_1	D_1	B_2	D_2
0	8	12	16	20	32	36 47

The first operand (the dividend) is divided by the second operand (the divisor). The resulting quotient and remainder are placed at the first-operand location. The operands and results are in the packed format.

The quotient is placed leftmost in the first-operand location. The number of bytes in the quotient field is equal to the difference between the dividend and divisor lengths ($L_1 - L_2$). The remainder is placed rightmost in the first-operand location and has a length equal to the divisor length. Together, the quotient and remainder fields occupy the entire first operand; therefore, the address of the quotient is the address of the first operand.

The divisor length cannot exceed 15 digits and sign (L_2 not greater than seven) and must be less than the dividend length (L_2 less than L_1); otherwise, a specification exception is recognized.

The dividend, divisor, quotient, and remainder are each signed decimal integers in the packed format and are right-aligned in their fields. All sign and digit codes of the dividend and divisor are checked for validity.

The sign of the quotient is determined by the rules of algebra from the dividend and divisor signs. The sign of the remainder has the same value as the dividend sign. These rules hold even when the quotient or remainder is zero.

Overflow cannot occur. If the divisor is zero or the quotient is too large to be represented by the number of digits specified, a decimal-divide exception is recognized. This includes the case of division of zero by zero. The decimal-divide exception is indicated only if the sign codes of both the dividend and divisor are valid, and only if the digit or digits used in establishing the exception are valid.

Condition Code: The code remains unchanged.

Program Exceptions:

Access (fetch, operand 2; fetch and store, operand 1)
Data
Decimal divide
Specification

Programming Notes

1. An example of the use of the DIVIDE DECIMAL instruction is given in Appendix A.

2. The dividend cannot exceed 31 digits and sign. Since the remainder cannot be shorter than one digit and sign, the quotient cannot exceed 29 digits and sign.

3. The condition for a decimal-divide exception can be determined by a trial comparison. The leftmost digit of the divisor is aligned one digit to the right of the leftmost dividend digit. When the divisor, so aligned, is less than or equal to the dividend, ignoring signs, a divide exception is indicated.

4. If a data exception does not exist, a decimal-divide exception occurs when the leftmost dividend digit is not zero.

EDIT

ED $D_1(L,B_1),D_2(B_2)$ [SS]

'DE'	L	B_1	D_1	B_2	D_2
0	8	16	20	32	36 47

The second operand (the source), which normally contains one or more decimal numbers in the packed format, is changed to the zoned format and modified under the control of the first operand (the pattern). The edited result replaces the first operand.

The length field specifies the length of the first operand, which may contain bytes of any value.

The length of the source is determined by the operation according to the contents of the pattern. The source normally consists of one or more decimal numbers, each in the packed format. The leftmost four bits of each source byte must specify a decimal-digit code (0000-1001); a sign code (1010-1111) is recognized as a data exception. The rightmost four bits may specify either a sign code or a decimal-digit code. Access and data exceptions are recognized only for those bytes in the second operand which are actually required.

The result is obtained as if both operands were processed left to right one byte at a time. Overlapping pattern and source fields give unpredictable results.

During the editing process, each byte of the pattern is affected in one of three ways:

1. It is left unchanged.

2. It is replaced by a source digit expanded to the zoned format.

3. It is replaced by the first byte in the pattern, called the fill byte.

Further assume that at storage address 5000, the following EXECUTE instruction is located:

Machine Format

Op Code	R_1	X_2	B_2	D_2
44	1	0	A	000

Assembler Format

Op Code	$R_1,D_2(X_2,B_2)$
EX	1,0(0,10)

where register 10 contains 00 00 38 20 and register 1 contains 00 0F F0 03.

When the instruction at 5000 is executed, the rightmost byte of register 1 is ORed with the second byte of the target instruction:

```
Instruction byte:     0000 0000{2} = 00
Register byte:        0000 0011{2} = 03
---------------------------------------
Result:               0000 0011{2} = 03
```

causing the instruction at 3820 to be executed as if it originally were:

Machine Format

Op Code	L	B_1	D_1	B_2	D_2
D2	03	C	003	D	000

Assembler Format

Op Code	$D_1(L,B_1),D_2(B_2)$
MVC	3(4,12),0(13)

However, after execution:

Register 1 is unchanged.
The instruction at 3820 is unchanged.
The contents of the four bytes starting at location 90A0 have been moved to the four bytes starting at location 8916.
The CPU next executes the instruction at address 5004 (PSW bits 40-63 contain 00 50 04).

INSERT CHARACTERS UNDER MASK (ICM)

The INSERT CHARACTERS UNDER MASK (ICM) instruction may be used to replace all or selected bytes in a general register with bytes from storage and to set the condition code to indicate the value of the inserted field.

For example, if it is desired to insert a three-byte address from FIELDA into register 5 and leave the leftmost byte of the register unchanged, assume:

Machine Format

Op Code	R_1	M_3	S_2
BF	5	7	* * * *

Assembler Format

Op Code	R_1,M_3,S_2
ICM	5,B'0111',FIELDA

FIELDA:	FE DC BA
Register 5 (before):	12 34 56 78
Register 5 (after):	12 FE DC BA
Condition code (after):	1 (leftmost bit of inserted field is one)

As another example:

Machine Format

Op Code	R_1	M_3	S_2
BF	6	9	* * * *

Assembler Format

Op Code	R_1,M_3,S_2
ICM	6,B'1001',FIELDB

FIELDB:	12 34
Register 6 (before):	00 00 00 00
Register 6 (after):	12 00 00 34
Condition code (after):	2 (inserted field is nonzero with left-most zero bit)

When the mask field contains 1111, the ICM instruction produces the same result as LOAD (L) (provided that the indexing capability of the RX format is not needed), except that ICM also sets the condition code. The condition-code setting is useful when an all-zero field (condition code 0) or a leftmost one bit (condition code 1) is used as a flag.

LOAD (L, LR)

The LOAD instruction takes four bytes from storage or from a general register and place them unchanged into a general register. For example, assume that the four bytes starting with location 21003 are to be loaded into register 10. Initially:

- Register 5 contains 00 02 00 00.
- Register 6 contains 00 00 10 03.
- The contents of register 10 are not significant.
- Storage locations 21003-21006 contain 00 00 AB CD.

To load register 10, the RX form of the instruction can be used:

Machine Format

Op Code	R_1	X_2	B_2	D_2
58	A	5	6	000

Assembler Format

```
Op Code  R1,D2(X2,B2)
   L      10,0(5,6)
```

After the instruction is executed, register 10 contains 00 00 AB CD.

LOAD ADDRESS (LA)

The LOAD ADDRESS instruction provides a convenient way to place a nonnegative binary integer up to 4095{10} in a register without first defining a constant and then using it as an operand. For example, the following instruction places the number 2048{10} in register 1:

Machine Format

Op Code	R_1	X_2	B_2	D_2
41	1	0	0	800

Assembler Format

```
Op Code  R1,D2(X2,B2)
   LA     1,2048(0,0)
```

The LOAD ADDRESS instruction can also be used to increment a register by an amount up to 4095{10} specified in the D_2 field. Depending on the addressing mode, only the rightmost 24 or 31 bits of the sum are retained, however. The leftmost bits of the 32-bit result are set to zeros. For example, assume that register 5 contains 00 12 34 56.

The instruction:

Machine Format

Op Code	R_1	X_2	B_2	D_2
41	5	0	5	00A

Assembler Format

```
Op Code  R1,D2(X2,B2)
   LA     5,10(0,5)
```

adds 10 (decimal) to the contents of register 5 as follows:

```
Register 5 (old): 00 12 34 56
D2 field:         00 00 00 0A
-----------------------------
Register 5 (new): 00 12 34 60
```

The register may be specified as either B_2 or X_2. Thus, the instruction LA 5,10(5,0) produces the same result.

As the most general example, the instruction LA 6,10(5,4) forms the sum of three values: the contents of register 4, the contents of register 5, and a displacement of 10 and places the 24-bit or 31-bit sum with zeros appended on the left in register 6.

LOAD HALFWORD (LH)

The LOAD HALFWORD instruction places unchanged a halfword from storage into the right half of a register. The left half of the register is loaded with zeros or ones according to the sign (leftmost bit) of the halfword.

For example, assume that the two bytes in storage locations 1803-1804 are to be loaded into register 6. Also assume:

- The contents of register 6 are not significant.
- Register 14 contains 00 00 18 03.
- Locations 1803-1804 contain 00 20.

The instruction required to load the register is:

	0	1	2	3	4	5	6	7	8	9	A	B	C	D	E	F
200_	40	40	40	40	40	40	40	40	40	40	40	40	40	40	40	40
201_	40	40	40	40	40	40	40	40	40	40	40	40	40	40	40	40
202_	40	40	40	40	40	40	40	40	40	40	40	40	40	40	40	40
203_	40	40	40	40	40	40	40	40	40	40	40	40	40	40	40	40
204_	04	40	40	40	40	40	40	40	40	40	40	08	40	0C	10	40
205_	14	40	40	40	40	40	40	40	40	40	40	18	1C	20	40	40
206_	24	28	40	40	40	40	40	40	40	40	40	2C	40	40	40	40
207_	40	40	40	40	40	40	40	40	40	40	40	30	34	38	3C	40
208_	40	40	40	40	40	40	40	40	40	40	40	40	40	40	40	40
209_	40	40	40	40	40	40	40	40	40	40	40	40	40	40	40	40
20A_	40	40	40	40	40	40	40	40	40	40	40	40	40	40	40	40
20B_	40	40	40	40	40	40	40	40	40	40	40	40	40	40	40	40
20C_	40	00	00	00	00	00	00	00	00	00	40	40	40	40	40	40
20D_	40	00	00	00	00	00	00	00	00	00	40	40	40	40	40	40
20E_	40	40	00	00	00	00	00	00	00	00	40	40	40	40	40	40
20F_	00	00	00	00	00	00	00	00	00	00	40	40	40	40	40	40

Note: If the character codes in the statement being translated occupy a range smaller than 00 through FF{16}, a table of fewer than 256 bytes can be used.

Translate and Test Table

The table entries for the alphameric characters in EBCDIC are 00; thus, the letter A (code C1) corresponds to byte location 20C1, which contains 00.

The 15 special symbols have nonzero entries from 04{16} to 3C{16} in increments of 4. Thus, the blank (code 40) has the entry 04{16}, the period (code 4B) has the entry 08{16}, and so on.

All other table positions have the entry 40{16} to indicate an invalid character.

The table entries are chosen so that they may be used to select one of a list of 16 words containing addresses of different routines to be entered for each special symbol or invalid character encountered during the scan.

Assume that this list of 16 branch addresses is stored at locations 3004-3043.

Starting at storage location CA80, there is the following sequence of 21{10} EBCDIC characters, where "b" stands for a blank.

Locations CA80-CA94:

UNPKbPROUT(9),WORD(5)

Also assume:

Register 1 contains 00 00 CA 7F.
Register 2 contains 00 00 30 00.
Register 15 contains 00 00 20 00.

As the instruction:

Machine Format

Op Code	L	B_1	D_1	B_2	D_2
DD	14	1	001	F	000

Assembler Format

Op Code	$D_1(L,B_1),D_2(B_2)$
TRT	1(21,1),0(15)

is executed, the value of the first source byte, the EBCDIC code for the letter U, is added to the starting address of the table to produce the address of the table entry to be examined:

Table starting address	2000
First source byte (U)	E4
Address of table entry	20E4

Because zeros were placed in storage location 20E4, no special action occurs. The operation continues with the second and subsequent source bytes until it reaches the blank in location CA84. When this symbol is reached, its value is added to the starting address of the table, as usual:

Table starting address	2000
Source byte (blank)	40
Address of table entry	2040

Because location 2040 contains a nonzero value, the following actions occur:

1. The address of the source byte, 00CA84, is placed in the rightmost 24 bits of register 1.
2. The table entry, 04, is placed in the rightmost eight bits of register 2, which now contains 00 00 30 04.
3. Condition code 1 is set (scan not completed).

The TRANSLATE AND TEST instruction may be followed by instructions to branch to the routine at the address found at location 3004, which corresponds to the blank character encountered in the scan. When this routine is completed, program control may return to the TRANSLATE AND TEST instruction to continue the scan, except that the length must first be adjusted for the characters already scanned.

For this purpose, the TRANSLATE AND TEST may be executed by the use of an EXECUTE instruction, which supplies the length specification from a general register. In this way, a complete statement scan can be performed with a single TRANSLATE AND TEST instruction used repeatedly by means of EXECUTE, and without modifying any instructions in storage. In the example, after the first execution of TRANSLATE AND TEST, register 1 contains the address of the last source byte translated. It is then a simple matter to subtract this address from the address of the last source byte (CA94) to produce a length specification. This length minus one is placed in the register that is referenced as the R1 field of the EXECUTE instruction. (Note that the length code in the machine format is one less than the total number of bytes in the field.) The second-operand address of the EXECUTE instruction points to the TRANSLATE AND TEST instruction, which is the same as illustrated above, except for the length (L) which is set to zero.

UNPACK (UNPK)

Assume that storage locations 2501-2502 contain a signed, packed-decimal number that is to be unpacked and placed in storage locations 1000-1004. Also assume:

Register 12 contains 00 00 10 00.
Register 13 contains 00 00 25 00.
Storage locations 2501-2502 contain 12 3D.
The initial contents of storage locations 1000-1004 are not significant.

After the instruction:

Machine Format

Op Code	L_1	L_2	B_1	D_1	B_2	D_2
F3	4	1	C	000	D	001

Assembler Format

Op Code	$D_1(L_1,B_1),D_2(L_2,B_2)$
UNPK	0(5,12),1(2,13)

is executed, the storage locations 1000-1004 contain F0 F0 F1 F2 D3.

DECIMAL INSTRUCTIONS

(See Chapter 8 for a complete description of the decimal instructions.)

ADD DECIMAL (AP)

Assume that the signed, packed-decimal number at storage locations 500-503 is to be added to the signed, packed-decimal number at locations 2000-2002. Also assume:

Register 12 contains 00 00 20 00.
Register 13 contains 00 00 05 00.
Storage locations 2000-2002 contain 38 46 0D (a negative number).
Storage locations 500-503 contain 01 12 34 5C (a positive number).

After the instruction:

Machine Format

Op Code	L_1	L_2	B_1	D_1	B_2	D_2
FA	2	3	C	000	D	000

Assembler Format

Op Code $D_1(L_1,B_1),D_2(L_2,B_2)$

```
AP     0(3,12),0(4,13)
```

is executed, the storage locations 2000-2002 contain 73 88 5C; condition code 2 is set to indicate that the result is greater than zero. Note that:

1. Because the two numbers had different signs, they were in effect subtracted.
2. Although the second operand is longer than the first operand, no overflow interruption occurs because the result can be entirely contained within the first operand.

COMPARE DECIMAL (CP)

Assume that the signed, packed-decimal contents of storage locations 700-703 are to be algebraically compared with the signed, packed-decimal contents of locations 500-502. Also assume:

Register 12 contains 00 00 06 00.
Register 13 contains 00 00 03 00.
Storage locations 700-703 contain 17 25 35 6D.
Storage locations 500-502 contain 72 14 2D.

After the instruction:

Machine Format

Op Code	L_1	L_2	B_1	D_1	B_2	D_2
F9	3	2	C	100	D	200

Assembler Format

Op Code $D_1(L_1,B_1),D_2(L_2,B_2)$

```
CP   X'100'(4,12),X'200'(3,13)
```

is executed, condition code 1 is set, indicating that the first operand (the contents of locations 700-703) is less than the second.

DIVIDE DECIMAL (DP)

Assume that the signed, packed-decimal number at storage locations 2000-2004 (the dividend) is to be divided by the signed, packed-decimal number at locations 3000-3001 (the divisor). Also assume:

Register 12 contains 00 00 20 00.
Register 13 contains 00 00 30 00.
Storage locations 2000-2004 contain 01 23 45 67 8C.
Storage locations 3000-3001 contain 32 1D.

After the instruction:

Machine Format

Op Code	L_1	L_2	B_1	D_1	B_2	D_2
FD	4	1	C	000	D	000

Assembler Format

Op Code $D_1(L_1,B_1),D_2(L_2,B_2)$

```
DP     0(5,12),0(2,13)
```

is executed, the dividend is entirely replaced by the signed quotient and remainder, as follows:

	2000				2004
Locations 2000-2004	38	46	0D	01	8C
	quotient			remainder	

Notes:

1. Because the dividend and divisor have different signs, the quotient receives a negative sign.
2. The remainder receives the sign of the dividend and the length of the divisor.
3. If an attempt were made to divide the dividend by the one-byte field at location 3001, the quotient would be too long to fit within the four bytes allotted to it. A decimal-divide exception would exist, causing a program interruption.

EDIT (ED)

Before decimal data in the packed format can be used in a printed report, digits and signs must be converted to printable characters. Moreover, punctuation marks, such as commas and decimal points, may have to be inserted in appropriate places. The highly flexible EDIT instruction performs these functions in a single instruction execution.

This example shows step-by-step one way that the EDIT instruction can be used. The field to be edited (the source) is four bytes long; it is edited against a pattern 13 bytes long. The following symbols are used:

Symbol	Meaning
b (Hexadecimal 40)	Blank character
((Hexadecimal 21)	Significance starter
d (Hexadecimal 20)	Digit selector

Assume that register 12 contains:

00 00 10 00

and that the source and pattern fields are:

Source

1200 1203

02	57	42	6C

↑ +

Pattern

1000 100C

40	20	20	6B	20	21	20	4B	20	20	40	C3	D9
b	d	d	,	d	(	d	.	d	d	b	C	R

Execution of the instruction:

Machine Format

Op Code	L	B_1	D_1	B_2	D_2
DE	0C	C	000	C	200

Assembler Format

Op Code $D_1(L,B_1),D_2(B_2)$

```
ED     0(13,12),X'200'(12)
```

alters the pattern field as follows:

Appendix C

Frequency of Machine Instruction Usage

The following tabulation was created by counting the use of machine instructions from a random sampling of programs that were written by a single programmer. It is presented as an indication of a subset of instructions that might be considered a sufficient repertoire for general programming. Such usage will vary widely among programmers, applications, experience, etc.

COUNT	%	CODE	INSTRUCTION
94	0.313	BALR	BRANCH AND LINK
362	1.209	BCTR	BRANCH ON COUNT
108	0.360	BCR	BRANCH ON CONDITION
6	0.020	SVC	SUPERVISOR CALL
12	0.040	MVCL	MOVE LONG
2	0.006	CLR	COMPARE LOGICAL LONG
5	0.016	LPR	LOAD POSITIVE
3	0.010	LNR	LOAD NEGATIVE
177	0.591	LTR	LOAD AND TEST
2	0.006	LCR	LOAD COMPLIMENT
2	0.006	NR	AND
1	0.003	OR	OR
224	0.748	XR	EXCLUSIVE OR
602	2.010	LR	LOAD
102	0.340	CR	COMPARE
152	0.507	AR	ADD
254	0.848	SR	SUBTRACT
2	0.006	MR	MULTIPLY
18	0.060	DR	DIVIDE
2	0.006	SLR	SUBTRACT LOGICAL
156	0.521	STH	STORE HALFWORD
2362	7.888	LA	LOAD ADDRESS
107	0.357	STC	STORE CHARACTER
116	0.387	IC	INSERT CHARACTER
396	1.322	EX	EXECUTE
1674	5.590	BAL	BRANCH AND LINK
101	0.337	BCT	BRANCH ON COUNT
6042	20.179	BC	BRANCH ON CONDITION
298	0.995	LH	LOAD HALFWORD
166	0.554	CH	COMPARE HALFWORD
138	0.460	AH	ADD HALFWORD
114	0.380	SH	SUBTRACT HALFWORD
63	0.210	MH	MULTIPLY HALFWORD
237	0.791	CVD	CONVERT TO DECIMAL
153	0.511	CVB	CONVERT TO BINARY
591	1.973	ST	STORE
28	0.093	N	AND
986	3.293	CLC	COMPARE LOGICAL
2	0.006	O	OR
1117	3.730	L	LOAD
73	0.243	C	COMPARE
70	0.233	A	ADD
29	0.096	S	SUBTRACT
58	0.193	M	MULTIPLY

COUNT	%	CODE	INSTRUCTION
74	0.247	D	DIVIDE
1	0.003	SL	SUBTRACT LOGICAL
3	0.010	BXH	BRANCH ON INDEX HIGH
148	0.494	BXLE	BRANCH ON INDEX LOW OR EQUAL
82	0.273	SRL	SHIFT RIGHT SINGLE LOGICAL
66	0.220	SLL	SHIFT LEFT SINGLE LOGICAL
43	0.143	SRA	SHIFT RIGHT SINGLE
2	0.006	SLDL	SHIFT LEFT DOUBLE LOGICAL
1	0.003	SRDA	SHIFT RIGHT DOUBLE
62	0.207	STM	STORE MULTIPLE
518	1.730	TM	TEST UNDER MASK
1756	5.864	MVI	MOVE (IMMEDIATE)
1	0.003	TS	TEST AND SET
158	0.527	NI	AND (IMMEDIATE)
1402	4.682	CLI	COMPARE LOGICAL (IMMEDIATE)
506	1.689	OI	OR (IMMEDIATE)
25	0.083	XI	EXCLUSIVE OR (IMMEDIATE)
174	0.581	LM	LOAD MULTIPLE
1	0.003	CS	COMPARE AND SWAP
10	0.033	CLM	COMPARE LOGICAL CHARACTER UNDER MASK
43	0.143	STCM	STORE CHARACTER UNDER MASK
101	0.337	ICM	INSERT CHARACTER UNDER MASK
2	0.006	MVN	MOVE NUMERICS
3613	12.067	MVC	MOVE (CHARACTER)
261	0.871	NC	AND (CHARACTER)
123	0.410	OC	OR (CHARACTER)
235	0.784	XC	EXCLUSIVE OR (CHARACTER)
379	1.265	TR	TRANSLATE
139	0.464	TRT	TRANSLATE AND TEST
349	1.165	ED	EDIT
72	0.240	EDMK	EDIT AND MARK
4	0.013	SRP	SHIFT AND ROUND DECIMAL
1	0.003	MVO	MOVE WITH OFFSET
299	0.998	PACK	PACK
563	1.880	UNPK	UNPACK
425	1.419	ZAP	ZERO AND ADD
224	0.748	CP	COMPARE DECIMAL
595	1.987	AP	ADD DECIMAL
223	0.744	SP	SUBTRACT DECIMAL
21	0.070	MP	MULTIPLY DECIMAL
28	0.093	DP	DIVIDE DECIMAL
1	0.003	STCK	STORE CLOCK
434	1.449	BR	*UNCONDITIONAL BRANCH
19	0.063	BHR	*BRANCH ON A HIGH

COUNT	%	CODE	INSTRUCTION
13	0.043	BLR	*BRANCH ON A LOW
45	0.150	BER	*BRANCH ON A EQUAL B
2	0.006	BNHR	*BRANCH ON A NOT HIGH
15	0.050	BNER	*BRANCH ON A NOT EQUAL B)
18	0.060	BOR	*BRANCH ON OVERFLOW (IF ONES)
3	0.010	BNOR	*BRANCH ON NO OVERFLOW (IF NOT ONES)
34	0.113	BMR	*BRANCH ON MINUS (IF MIXED)
2	0.006	BNPR	*BRANCH ON NOT PLUS
2	0.006	BNMR	*BRANCH ON NOT MINUS (IF NOT MIXED)
8	0.026	BNZR	*BRANCH ON NOT ZERO (IF NOT ZEROS)
24	0.080	BZR	*BRANCH ON ZERO (IF ZEROS)
1748	5.838	B	*UNCONDITIONAL BRANCH
147	0.490	BH	*BRANCH ON A HIGH
181	0.604	BL	*BRANCH ON A LOW
1427	4.766	BE	*BRANCH ON A EQUAL B
166	0.554	BNH	*BRANCH ON A NOT HIGH
852	2.845	BNE	*BRANCH ON A NOT EQUAL B)
148	0.494	BO	*BRANCH ON OVERFLOW (IF ONES)
10	0.033	BNO	*BRANCH ON NO OVERFLOW (IF NOT ONES)
32	0.106	BP	*BRANCH ON PLUS)
45	0.150	BM	*BRANCH ON MINUS (IF MIXED)
70	0.233	BNP	*BRANCH ON NOT PLUS
9	0.030	BNM	*BRANCH ON NOT MINUS (IF NOT MIXED)
154	0.514	BNZ	*BRANCH ON NOT ZERO (IF NOT ZEROS)
430	1.436	BZ	*BRANCH ON ZERO (IF ZEROS)
29941		TOTAL, SUBSET SIZE= 86	

* These instructions are assembler instructions which generate machine instructions. They do not participate in the above totals. Their respective usage counts have been added to the proper machine instruction usage counts.

Appendix D
Sample Programs

```
SAMPLE ASSEMBLER PROGRAM--EXAMPLE 1

                                                                                        ASM H V 02 08.08 07/28/88
  LOC  OBJECT CODE    ADDR1 ADDR2  STMT   SOURCE STATEMENT
                                      2 ***********************************************************************
                                      3 * THIS IS A SAMPLE ASSEMBLER PROGRAM TO DEMONSTRATE THE FORMAT OF     *
                                      4 * ASSEMBLER OUTPUT.                                                   *
                                      5 ***********************************************************************

000000                                7          START X'0'          ADJUST LOCATION COUNTER FOR MVS/XA
                                      8 * THE FOLLOWING STATEMENT ASSEMBLES THE ASSEMBLY DATE AND TIME INTO
                                      9 * THE OUTPUT.

                                     11          DC    C'SAMPLE1--ASSEMBLED &SYSDATE-&SYSTIME'
000000 E2C1D4D7D3C5F160                +         DC    C'SAMPLE1--ASSEMBLED 07/28/88-08.08'

                                     13 * THE LABEL "BEGIN" IS IDENTIFIED AS THE STARTING LOCATION BY THE
                                     14 * 'END' STATEMENT AT THE END OF THE PROGRAM.

                                     16 * THE FOLLOWING STATEMENT IS A MACRO THAT GENERATES THE INSTRUCTION
                                     17 * TO SAVE THE REGISTERS UPON ENTRY TO THE PROGRAM.  NOTE THAT THIS IS
                                     18 * USED IN ALL MVS PROGRAM MODULES BUT IN DOS IT IS USED ONLY WITHIN
                                     19 * SUBROUTINES.

                                     21 BEGIN    SAVE  (14,12)               SAVE REGISTERS
000022                               22+BEGIN    DS    0H                                                 01-SAVE
000022 90EC D00C             0000C   23+         STM   14,12,12(13)                   SAVE REGISTERS      01-SAVE
000026 05C0                          24          BALR  12,0                 LOAD BASE REGISTER
                             00028   25          USING *,12                 ESTABLISH ADDRESSABILITY
000028 50D0 C02C             00054   26          ST    13,SAVEAREA+4        SAVE ENTRY REGISTER
00002C 41D0 C028             00050   27          LA    13,SAVEAREA          POINT TO SAVE AREA

000030 5810 C070             00098   29          L     1,A                  LOAD THE CONTENTS AT "A" INTO REG 1  R 1
000034 5A10 C074             0009C   30          A     1,B                  ADD THE CONTENTS OF "B"
000038 5010 C078             000A0   31          ST    1,C                  SAVE RESULT AT "C"
00003C FA41 C07C C081 000A4  000A9   32          AP    X,Y                  ADD THE CONTENTS OF "Y" TO "X"
000042 1B22                          33          SR    2,2                  SET REGISTER 2 TO ZERO

000044 58D0 C02C             00054   35 RETURN   L     13,SAVEAREA+4        RESTORE ENTRY REGISTER
                                     36          RETURN (14,12)             RESTORE REGISTERS/RETURN
000048 98EC D00C             0000C   37+         LM    14,12,12(13)                   RESTORE THE REGISTERS  01-RETUR
00004C 07FE                          38+         BR    14                             RETURN                 01-RETUR
00004E 0000
000050 0000000000000000              39 SAVEAREA DC    18F'0'
000098 00000064                      40 A        DC    F'100'
00009C 000000C8                      41 B        DC    F'200'
0000A0                               42 C        DS    F
0000A4 000000100C                    43 X        DC    PL5'100'
0000A9 200C                          44 Y        DC    P'200'
000022                               45          END   BEGIN


                                      CROSS REFERENCE

                                                                                        ASM H V 02 08.08 07/28/88
SYMBOL     LEN    VALUE  DEFN  REFERENCES

A         00004  000098 0040  0029
B         00004  00009C 0041  0030
BEGIN     00002  000022 0022  0045
C         00004  0000A0 0042  0031
RETURN    00004  000044 0035
SAVEAREA  00004  000050 0039  0026 0027 0035
X         00005  0000A4 0043  0032
Y         00002  0000A9 0044  0032
```

```
     SAMPLE ASSEMBLER PROGRAM--SAMPLE2

  LOC  OBJECT CODE    ADDR1 ADDR2  STMT   SOURCE STATEMENT                                          ASM H V 02 08.59 08/03/88

                                      2 ***********************************************************************
                                      3 * THIS PROGRAM READS A SET OF CARD IMAGES FROM A SEQUENTIAL DATASET,  *
                                      4 * EXTRACTS TWO DECIMAL FIELDS, AND PRINTS THE SUM OF THE TWO VALUES.  *
                                      5 *---------------------------------------------------------------------*
                                      6 * THE TWO INPUT VALUES ARE LEFT JUSTIFIED IN POSITIONS 1-10 AND 11-20.*
                                      7 ***********************************************************************
000000                                9          START X'0'             ADJUST LOCATION COUNTER FOR MVS/XA
                                     10          PRINT NOGEN

                                     12          DC    C'SAMPLE2--ASSEMBLED &SYSDATE-&SYSTIME'

                                     14 BEGIN    SAVE  (14,12)                SAVE REGISTERS
000026 05C0                          17          BALR  12,0                   LOAD BASE REGISTER
                            00028    18          USING *,12                   ESTABLISH ADDRESSABILITY
000028 50D0 C0B4            000DC    19          ST    13,SAVEAREA+4          SAVE ENTRY REGISTER
00002C 41D0 C0B0            000D8    20          LA    13,SAVEAREA            POINT TO SAVE AREA

                                     22          OPEN  (CARDS,,PRINTER,OUTPUT) OPEN FILES                          R 1
                                     30          PUT   PRINTER,HEADING        PRINT PAGE HEADING

                                     36 READLOOP GET   CARDS,CARD             READ CARD
00005A F249 C0F8 C107 00120 0012F    41          PACK  A,INPUTA               PACK FIRST FIELD
000060 F249 C0FD C111 00125 00139    42          PACK  B,INPUTB                " SECOND FIELD
000066 F844 C102 C0F8 0012A 00120    43          ZAP   APLUSB,A               INITIALIZE SUM
00006C FA44 C102 C0FD 0012A 00125    44          AP    APLUSB,B               ADD SECOND VALUE
000072 D209 C158 C107 00180 0012F    45          MVC   OUTPUTA,INPUTA         MOVE FIRST OPERAND TO OUTPUT
000078 D209 C162 C111 0018A 00139    46          MVC   OUTPUTB,INPUTB          " 2ND FIELD
                                     47          FORMAT APLUSB,OUTPUTC        FORMAT A+B
                                     58          PUT   PRINTER,LINE           PRINT LINE
0000BC 47F0 C024            0004C    63          B     READLOOP               GO GET NEXT RECORD

                                     65 CARDEOF  CLOSE (CARDS,,PRINTER)       CLOSE FILES

0000CE 58D0 C0B4            000DC    74 RETURN   L     13,SAVEAREA+4          RESTORE ENTRY REGISTER
                                     75          RETURN (14,12)               RESTORE REGISTERS/RETURN
0000D8 0000000000000000              78 SAVEAREA DC    18F'0'
000120                               79 A        DS    PL5
000125                               80 B        DS    PL5
00012A                               81 APLUSB   DS    PL5
00012F                               82 CARD     DS    CL80
00017F                      0012F    83          ORG   CARD
00012F                               84 INPUTA   DS    CL10
000139                               85 INPUTB   DS    CL10
000143                      0017F    86          ORG
00017F F040404040404040              87 LINE     DC    CL133'0'
000204                      00180    88          ORG   LINE+1
000180                               89 OUTPUTA  DS    CL10
00018A                               90 OUTPUTB  DS    CL10
000194                               91 OUTPUTC  DS    CL10
00019E                      00204    92          ORG
000204 F140404040404040              93 HEADING  DC    CL133'1'
000289                      0020A    94          ORG   HEADING+6
00020A C140404040404040              95          DC    CL10'A'
000214 C240404040404040              96          DC    CL10'B'
00021E C14EC24040404040              97          DC    CL10'A+B'
000228                      00289    98          ORG

                                    100 CARDS    DCB   DDNAME=SYSIN,          DATA DEFINITION NAME                 -
                                                       DSORG=PS,              DATA SET ORGNAZIATION=PHYS. SEQ.     -
                                                       MACRF=GM,              MACRO INSTR. FORM=GET,MOVE           -
                                                       EODAD=CARDEOF          END OF DATA ADDRESS

                                    155 PRINTER  DCB   DDNAME=PRINTER,DSORG=PS,                                    -
                                                       MACRF=PM,              MACRO INSTRUCTION FORM=PUT,MOVE      -
                                                       LRECL=133,             LOGICAL RECORD LENGTH                -
                                                       BLKSIZE=133,           BLOCK SIZE                           -
                                                       RECFM=FBA              RECORD FORMAT=FIXED-BLOCKED,FORMAT-A
000022                              209          END   BEGIN
000350 4020                         210                =X'4020'
```

```
                                   CROSS REFERENCE

SYMBOL     LEN     VALUE  DEFN  REFERENCES                                                        ASM H V 02 08.59 08/03/88

A          00005   000120 0079  0041 0043
APLUSB     00005   00012A 0081  0043 0044 0053 0053 0057 0057
B          00005   000125 0080  0042 0044
BEGIN      00002   000022 0015  0209
CARD       00080   00012F 0082  0038 0083
CARDEOF    00004   0000C0 0067  0122
CARDS      00004   00028C 0104  0026 0037 0069
HEADING    00133   000204 0093  0032 0094
INPUTA     00010   00012F 0084  0041 0045
INPUTB     00010   000139 0085  0042 0046
LINE       00133   00017F 0087  0060 0088
OUTPUTA    00010   000180 0089  0045
OUTPUTB    00010   00018A 0090  0046
OUTPUTC    00010   000194 0091  0048 0049 0049 0049 0050 0050 0051 0053 0054 0055 0057 0057 0057

PRINTER    00004   0002EC 0159  0028 0031 0059 0071
READLOOP   00004   00004C 0037  0063
RETURN     00004   0000CE 0074
SAVEAREA   00004   0000D8 0078  0019 0020 0074
=X'4020'   00002   000350 0210  0048
```

```
A          B          A+B
    5          6         11
 1000        299       1299
89999          1      90000
```

```
SAMPLE ASSEMBLER PROGRAM--SAMPLE3

  LOC  OBJECT CODE    ADDR1 ADDR2  STMT   SOURCE STATEMENT                                          ASM H V 02 07.52 08/12/88

                                      2 ************************************************************************
                                      3 * THIS PROGRAM READS A SET OF CARD IMAGES FROM A SEQUENTIAL DATASET,   *
                                      4 * EXTRACTS TWO DECIMAL FIELDS AND EXAMINES AN OPERATION FIELD.  THE   *
                                      5 * THE SUM, DIFFERENCE, PRODUCT, OR QUOTIENT IS COMPUTED.  THIS RESULT *
                                      6 * DEPENDS ON THE OPERATION FIELD ('+', '-', '*', OR '/', RESPECTIVELY).*
                                      7 * IN THE CASE OF DIVISION THE FIRST FIELD IS THE DIVIDEND AND THE     *
                                      8 * SECOND FIELD IS THE DIVISOR.                                        *
                                      9 *---------------------------------------------------------------------*
                                     10 * THE OPERATOR IS IN THE FIRST BYTE OF THE INPUT RECORD.  THE TWO     *
                                     11 * DECIMAL VALUES ARE RIGHT JUSTIFIED IN POSITIONS 2-10 AND 12-20.     *
                                     12 ************************************************************************
000000                               14          START X'0'           ADJUST LOCATION COUNTER FOR MVS/XA
                                     15          PRINT NOGEN
                                     17          DC    C'SAMPLE3--ASSEMBLED &SYSDATE-&SYSTIME'
                                     19 BEGIN    SAVE  (14,12)                   SAVE REGISTERS
000026 05C0                          22          BALR  12,0                      LOAD BASE REGISTER
                            00028    23          USING *,12                      ESTABLISH ADDRESSABILITY
000028 50D0 C0EC            00114    24          ST    13,SAVEAREA+4             SAVE ENTRY REGISTER
00002C 41D0 C0E8            00110    25          LA    13,SAVEAREA               POINT TO SAVE AREA
                                     27          OPEN  (CARDS,,PRINTER,OUTPUT) OPEN FILES                  R 1
                                     36 READLOOP GET   CARDS,CARD                READ CARD
00004C F248 C130 C143 00158 0016B    41          PACK  A,INPUTA                  PACK FIRST FIELD
000052 F248 C135 C14D 0015D 00175    42          PACK  B,INPUTB                   " SECOND FIELD
000058 F874 C13A C130 00162 00158    43          ZAP   RESULT,A                  INITIALIZE RESULT TO FIRST OPERAND
00005E 954E C142      0016A          45          CLI   OPCODE,C'+'               SUM VALUES?
000062 4780 C0B2            000DA    46          BE    SUM                        YES
000066 9560 C142      0016A          47          CLI   OPCODE,C'-'               COMPUTE DIFFERENCE?
00006A 4780 C0BC            000E4    48          BE    SUBTRACT                   YES
00006E 955C C142      0016A          49          CLI   OPCODE,C'*'               COMPUTE PRODUCT?
000072 4780 C0C6            000EE    50          BE    PRODUCT                    YES
000076 FD74 C13A C135 00162 0015D    52          DP    RESULT,B                  COMPUTE QUOTIENT
00007C F872 C13A C13A 00162 00162    53          ZAP   RESULT,RESULT(L'RESULT-L'B) OVERLAY REMAINDER
000082 D200 C19D C142 001C5 0016A    55 OUTPUT   MVC   OUTPUTOP,OPCODE           MOVE OPERATION CODE
000088 D209 C193 C143 001BB 0016B    56          MVC   OUTPUTA,INPUTA            MOVE FIRST OPERAND TO OUTPUT
00008E D209 C19E C14D 001C6 00175    57          MVC   OUTPUTB,INPUTB             " 2ND FIELD
                                     58          FORMAT RESULT,OUTPUTC           FORMAT RESULT OF OPERATION
                                     69          PUT   PRINTER,LINE              PRINT LINE
0000D2 92F0 C192      001BA          74          MVI   LINE,C'0'                 SET TO DOUBLE SPACE AFTER FIRST TIME
0000D6 47F0 C016            0003E    75          B     READLOOP                  GO GET NEXT RECORD
0000DA FA74 C13A C135 00162 0015D    77 SUM      AP    RESULT,B                  ADD SECOND VALUE
0000E0 47F0 C05A            00082    78          B     OUTPUT                    GO SETUP PRINT LINE/PRINT
0000E4 FB74 C13A C135 00162 0015D    80 SUBTRACT SP    RESULT,B                  SUBTRACT SECOND VALUE
0000EA 47F0 C05A            00082    81          B     OUTPUT                    GO SETUP PRINT LINE/PRINT
0000EE|FC74 C13A C135 00162 0015D    83 PRODUCT  MP    RESULT,B       |          MULTIPLY BY ADD SECOND VALUE
0000F4|47F0 C05A            00082    84          B     OUTPUT         |          GO SETUP PRINT LINE/PRINT
```

```
        SAMPLE ASSEMBLER PROGRAM--SAMPLE3

                                                                                    ASM H V 02 07.52 08/12/88
 LOC  OBJECT CODE    ADDR1 ADDR2  STMT   SOURCE STATEMENT

                                    86 CARDEOF  CLOSE (CARDS,,PRINTER)     CLOSE FILES

000106 58D0 C0EC           00114    95 RETURN   L     13,SAVEAREA+4        RESTORE ENTRY REGISTER
                                    96          RETURN (14,12)             RESTORE REGISTERS/RETURN
000110 0000000000000000             99 SAVEAREA DC    18F'0'
000158                             100 A        DS    PL5
00015D                             101 B        DS    PL5
000162                             102 RESULT   DS    PL8
00016A                             103 CARD     DS    CL80
0001BA                     0016A   104          ORG   CARD
00016A                             105 OPCODE   DS    C
00016B                             106 INPUTA   DS    CL9,C
000175                             107 INPUTB   DS    CL9
00017E                     001BA   108          ORG
0001BA F140404040404040            109 LINE     DC    CL133'1'
00023F                     001BB   110          ORG   LINE+1
0001BB                             111 OUTPUTA  DS    CL10
0001C5                             112 OUTPUTOP DS    C
0001C6                             113 OUTPUTB  DS    CL10
0001D0 7E                          114          DC    C'='
0001D1                             115 OUTPUTC  DS    CL10
0001DB                     0023F   116          ORG

                                   118 CARDS    DCB   DDNAME=SYSIN,        DATA DEFINITION NAME                 -
                                                      DSORG=PS,            DATA SET ORGNAZIATION=PHYS. SEQ.     -
                                                      MACRF=GM,            MACRO INSTR. FORM=GET,MOVE           -
                                                      EODAD=CARDEOF        END OF DATA ADDRESS

                                   173 PRINTER  DCB   DDNAME=PRINTER,DSORG=PS,                                  -
                                                      MACRF=PM,            MACRO INSTRUCTION FORM=PUT,MOVE      -
                                                      LRECL=133,           LOGICAL RECORD LENGTH                -
                                                      BLKSIZE=133,         BLOCK SIZE                           -
                                                      RECFM=FBA            RECORD FORMAT=FIXED-BLOCKED,FORMAT-A
000022                             227          END   BEGIN
000300 4020                        228                =X'4020'
```

```
                                         CROSS REFERENCE

SYMBOL    LEN    VALUE  DEFN  REFERENCES                                          ASM H V 02 07.52 08/12/88

A         00005  000158 0100  0041 0043
B         00005  00015D 0101  0042 0052 0053 0077 0080 0083
BEGIN     00002  000022 0020  0227
CARD      00080  00016A 0103  0038 0104
CARDEOF   00004  0000F8 0088  0140
CARDS     00004  000240 0122  0031 0037 0090
INPUTA    00009  00016B 0106  0041 0056
INPUTB    00009  000175 0107  0042 0057
LINE      00133  0001BA 0109  0071 0074 0110
OPCODE    00001  00016A 0105  0045 0047 0049 0055
OUTPUT    00006  000082 0055  0078 0081 0084

OUTPUTA   00010  0001BB 0111  0056
OUTPUTB   00010  0001C6 0113  0057
OUTPUTC   00010  0001D1 0115  0059 0060 0060 0060 0061 0061 0062 0064 0065 0066 0068 0068 0068

OUTPUTOP  00001  0001C5 0112  0055
PRINTER   00004  0002A0 0177  0033 0070 0092
PRODUCT   00006  0000EE 0083  0050
READLOOP  00004  00003E 0037  0075
RESULT    00008  000162 0102  0043 0052 0053 0053 0053 0064 0064 0068 0068 0077 0080 0083
RETURN    00004  000106 0095
SAVEAREA  00004  000110 0099  0024 0025 0095
SUBTRACT  00006  0000E4 0080  0048
SUM       00006  0000DA 0077  0046

=X'4020'  00002  000300 0228  0059
```

```
SAMPLE ASSEMBLER PROGRAM--SAMPLE4

  LOC  OBJECT CODE    ADDR1 ADDR2  STMT   SOURCE STATEMENT                                   ASM H V 02 11.08 09/03/88

                                      2 ***********************************************************************
                                      3 * THIS PROGRAM OBTAINS THE DATE AND TIME BY USING THE MVS 'TIME'      *
                                      4 * MACRO.  THE DATE IS CONVERTED FROM 00YYDDDF TO MM/DD/YY.  THE TIME  *
                                      5 * IS CONVERTED FROM HHMMSSTH TO HH:MM:SS.T XXXX AND THE CLOCK IS CON- *
                                      6 * VERTED FROM THE 24-HOUR TO THE 12-HOUR CONVENTION.  XXXX IS EITHER  *
                                      7 * 'A.M.', 'P.M.', 'NOON', OR 'M.N.'.                                  *
                                      8 ***********************************************************************

000000                               10          START X'0'              ADJUST LOCATION COUNTER FOR MVS/XA
                                     11          PRINT NOGEN

                                     13          DC    C'SAMPLE4--ASSEMBLED &SYSDATE-&SYSTIME'

                                     15 BEGIN    SAVE  (14,12)                SAVE REGISTERS
000026 05C0                          18          BALR  12,0                   LOAD BASE REGISTER
                             00028   19          USING *,12                   ESTABLISH ADDRESSABILITY
000028 50D0 C124             0014C   20          ST    13,SAVEAREA+4          SAVE ENTRY REGISTER
00002C 41D0 C120             00148   21          LA    13,SAVEAREA            POINT TO SAVE AREA

                                     23          OPEN  (PRINTER,OUTPUT)       OPEN PRINT DCB                      R 1

                                     30          TIME                         GET DATE AND TIME
000040 9001 C168             00190   35          STM   0,1,HHMMSSTH           SAVE TIME AND DATE
000044 DE0B C199 C168 001C1 00190    36          ED    CLOCK24,HHMMSSTH       FORMAT 24 HOUR CLOCK
00004A 960F C16B       00193         37          OI    HHMMSSTH+L'HHMMSSTH-1,X'F'  OVERLAY HUNDREDTHS WITH SIGN
00004E 9512 C168       00190         38          CLI   HHMMSSTH,X'12'         AFTER MORNING?
000052 47B0 C04E             00076   39          BNL   AFTERAM                 YES
000056 9500 C168       00190         40          CLI   HHMMSSTH,0             1:00 AM OR LATER?
00005A 4770 C074             0009C   41          BNE   TIMEDONE                YES
00005E 9212 C168       00190         42          MVI   HHMMSSTH,X'12'         CONVERT 00 HOURS TO 12
000062 F920 C169 C11C 00191 00144    43          CP    HHMMSSTH+1(L'HHMMSSTH-1),=P'0' MIDNIGHT?
000068 4780 C074             0009C   44          BE    TIMEDONE                NO
00006C D203 C1D6 C100 001FE 00128    45          MVC   SUFFIX,=C'M.N.'        SET MIDNIGHT INDICATOR
000072 47F0 C074             0009C   46          B     TIMEDONE               GO FORMAT TIME

000076 92D7 C1D6       001FE         48 AFTERAM  MVI   SUFFIX,C'P'            SET TO P.M.
00007A 9512 C168       00190         49          CLI   HHMMSSTH,X'12'         BEFORE 1:00 PM?
00007E 4780 C064             0008C   50          BE    BEFORE1P                YES
000082 FB33 C168 C104 00190 0012C    51          SP    HHMMSSTH,=P'1200000'  CONVERT TO 12-HOUR CLOCK
000088 47F0 C074             0009C   52          B     TIMEDONE               GO FORMAT TIME

00008C F920 C169 C11C 00191 00144    54 BEFORE1P CP    HHMMSSTH+1(L'HHMMSSTH-1),=P'0' EXACTLY NOON?
000092 4770 C074             0009C   55          BNE   TIMEDONE                NO
000096 D203 C1D6 C108 001FE 00130    56          MVC   SUFFIX,=C'NOON'        SET NOON INDICATOR

00009C DE0A C1CA C168 001F2 00190    58 TIMEDONE ED    CLOCK12,HHMMSSTH       FORMAT 12 HOUR CLOCK

0000A2 DE06 C1B3 C16D 001DB 00195    60          ED    JULIAN,ZZYYDDDC+1      FORMAT JULIAN DATE
0000A8 F811 C172 C118 0019A 00140    61          ZAP   FEBRUARY,=P'28'        ASSUME NOT LEAP YEAR (NOT NECESSARY)
0000AE F810 C188 C11C 001B0 00144    62          ZAP   MONTHS,=P'0'           INITIALIZE MONTH
0000B4 9835 C10C             00134   63          LM    3,5,=A(JANUARY,L'JANUARY,DECEMBER)
0000B8 9101 C16D       00195         64          TM    ZZYYDDDC+1,1           LEAP YEAR?
0000BC 4710 C0A6             000CE   65          BO    MNTHLOOP                NO
0000C0 9112 C16D       00195         66          TM    ZZYYDDDC+1,X'12'
0000C4 4740 C0A6             000CE   67          BM    MNTHLOOP                NO
```

```
SAMPLE ASSEMBLER PROGRAM--SAMPLE4

  LOC  OBJECT CODE      ADDR1 ADDR2  STMT   SOURCE STATEMENT                                    ASM H V 02 11.08 09/03/88
0000C8 F811 C172 C11A 0019A 00142    68            ZAP   FEBRUARY,=P'29'      SET DAYS FOR LEAP YEAR

0000CE FA10 C188 C11D 001B0 00145    70 MNTHLOOP AP    MONTHS,=P'1'         INCREMENT MONTH
0000D4 F911 C16E 3000 00196 00000    71          CP    ZZYYDDDC+2(2),0(L'JANUARY,3) DAYS EXCEED DAYS OF MONTH?
0000DA 47D0 C0C0            000E8    72          BNH   MOFOUND              NO
0000DE FB11 C16E 3000 00196 00000    73          SP    ZZYYDDDC+2(2),0(L'JANUARY,3) SUBTRACT DAYS IN CURRENT MO TH
0000E4 8734 C0A6            000CE    74          BXLE  3,4,MNTHLOOP         CONTINUE

0000E8 F311 C1EB C188 00213 001B0    76 MOFOUND  UNPK  GREG(2),MONTHS       UNPACK 0MMC   TO FMCM
0000EE F311 C1EE C16E 00216 00196    77          UNPK  GREG+3(2),ZZYYDDDC+2(2) " 0DDC   TO       FDCD
0000F4 F321 C1F1 C16D 00219 00195    78          UNPK  GREG+6(3),ZZYYDDDC+1(2) " YYOD   TO            FYFYDO
0000FA 96F0 C1EC      00214          79          OI    GREG+1,C'0'          FORCE UNITS DIGIT OF MM NUMERIC
0000FE 96F0 C1EF      00217          80          OI    GREG+4,C'0'          FORCE UNITS DIGIT OF DD NUMERIC
000102 924B C1F3      0021B          81          MVI   GREG+8,C'.'          OVERLAY OD WITH TERMINATING PERIOD
                                     82          PUT   PRINTER,LINE         PRINT LINE

                                     88          CLOSE (PRINTER)            CLOSE PRINT FILE

00011E 58D0 C124            0014C    95 RETURN   L     13,SAVEAREA+4        RESTORE ENTRY REGISTER
                                     96          RETURN (14,12)             RESTORE REGISTERS/RETURN
000128                               99          LTORG
000128 D44BD54B                     100                =C'M.N.'
00012C 1200000C                     101                =P'1200000'
000130 D5D6D6D5                     102                =C'NOON'
000134 0000019800000002             103                =A(JANUARY,L'JANUARY,DECEMBER)
000140 028C                         104                =P'28'
000142 029C                         105                =P'29'
000144 0C                           106                =P'0'
000145 1C                           107                =P'1'
000146 0000
000148 0000000000000000             108 SAVEAREA DC    18F'0'
000190                              109 HHMMSSTH DS    F
000194                              110 ZZYYDDDC DS    F
000198 031C028C031C030C             111 JANUARY  DC    P'31,28,31,30,31,30,31,31,30,31,30'
                            0019A   112 FEBRUARY EQU   JANUARY+L'JANUARY
0001AE 031C                         113 DECEMBER DC    P'31'
0001B0                              114 MONTHS   DS    PL2
0001B2 F140404040404040             115 LINE     DC    CL133'1'
000237                      001B3   116          ORG   LINE+1
0001B3 F2F460C8D6E4D940             117          DC    C'24-HOUR CLOCK='
0001C1                              118 CLOCK24  DS    0CL12
0001C1 4021207A20207A20             119          DC    X'402120',C':',2X'20',C':',2X'20',C'.',2X'20'
0001CD 6B40D1E4D3C9C1D5             120          DC    C', JULIAN DATE='
0001DB                              121 JULIAN   DS    0CL7
0001DB 40212061202020               122          DC    X'402120',C'/',3X'20'
0001E2 6B40F1F260C8D6E4             123          DC    C', 12-HOUR CLOCK='
0001F2                              124 CLOCK12  DS    0CL11
0001F2 4021207A20207A20             125          DC    X'402120',C':',2X'20',C':',2X'20',C'.',X'2040'
0001FE C14BD44B                     126 SUFFIX   DC    C'A.M.'
000202 6B40C7D9C5C7D6D9             127          DC    C', GREGORIAN DATE='
000213 D4D461C4C461E8E8             128 GREG     DC    CL8'MM/DD/YY',C'.'
00021C                      00237   129          ORG

                                    131 PRINTER  DCB   DDNAME=PRINTER,DSORG=PS,                                    -
                                                       MACRF=PM,            MACRO INSTRUCTION FORM=PUT,MOVE        -
                                                       LRECL=133,           LOGICAL RECORD LENGTH                  -
                                                       BLKSIZE=133,         BLOCK SIZE                             -
                                                       RECFM=FBA            RECORD FORMAT=FIXED-BLOCKED,FORMAT-A
000022                              185          END   BEGIN
```

```
                                   CROSS REFERENCE

SYMBOL    LEN    VALUE  DEFN REFERENCES                                              ASM H V 02 11.08 09/03/88

AFTERAM  00004   000076 0048 0039
BEFORE1P 00006   00008C 0054 0050
BEGIN    00002   000022 0016 0185
CLOCK12  00011   0001F2 0124 0058
CLOCK24  00012   0001C1 0118 0036
DECEMBER 00002   0001AE 0113 0103
FEBRUARY 00002 0000019A 0112 0061 0068
GREG     00008   000213 0128 0076 0077 0078 0079 0080 0081
HHMMSSTH 00004   000190 0109 0035 0036 0037 0037 0038 0040 0042 0043 0043 0049 0051 0054 0054 0058
JANUARY  00002   000198 0111 0071 0073 0103 0103 0112 0112
JULIAN   00007   0001DB 0121 0060
LINE     00133   0001B2 0115 0084 0116
MNTHLOOP 00006   0000CE 0070 0065 0067 0074
MOFOUND  00006   0000E8 0076 0072
MONTHS   00002   0001B0 0114 0062 0070 0076
PRINTER  00004   000238 0135 0027 0083 0092
RETURN   00004   00011E 0095
SAVEAREA 00004   000148 0108 0020 0021 0095
SUFFIX   00004   0001FE 0126 0045 0048 0056
TIMEDONE 00006   00009C 0058 0041 0044 0046 0052 0055
ZZYYDDDC 00004   000194 0110 0060 0064 0066 0071 0073 0077 0078
=A(JANUARY,L'JANUARY,DECEMBER)
          00004  000134 0103 0063
=C'M.N.' 00004   000128 0100 0045
=C'NOON' 00004   000130 0102 0056
=P'0'    00001   000144 0106 0043 0054 0062
=P'1'    00001   000145 0107 0070
=P'1200000'
          00004  00012C 0101 0051
=P'28'   00002   000140 0104 0061
=P'29'   00002   000142 0105 0068

  24-HOUR CLOCK= 11:13:12.74, JULIAN DATE= 88/247, 12-HOUR CLOCK= 11:13:12.7 A.M., GREGORIAN DATE=09/03/88.
```

```
SAMPLE ASSEMBLER PROGRAM--SAMPLE5

 LOC  OBJECT CODE    ADDR1 ADDR2  STMT   SOURCE STATEMENT                                  ASM H V 02 11.08 09/03/88

                                     2 ************************************************************************
                                     3 * THIS PROGRAM READS A SET OF CARD IMAGES FROM A SEQUENTIAL DATASET,   *
                                     4 * EXTRACTS A DECIMAL FIELD OF 10 DIGITS, COMPUTES THE MODULUS 10 SELF *
                                     5 * CHECKING DIGIT OF THIS FIELD, AND COMPARES IT TO THE ENTERED VALUE. *
                                     6 *----------------------------------------------------------------------*
                                     7 * THE INPUT NUMBER IS IN BYTES 1-10 OF THE INPUT RECORD.  BYTE 11      *
                                     8 * CONTAINS THE INPUT SCD.                                              *
                                     9 ************************************************************************
000000                              11          START X'0'            ADJUST LOCATION COUNTER FOR MVS/XA
                                    12          PRINT NOGEN

                                    14          DC    C'SAMPLE5--ASSEMBLED &SYSDATE-&SYSTIME'

                                    16 BEGIN    SAVE  (14,12)              SAVE REGISTERS
000026 05C0                         19          BALR  12,0                 LOAD BASE REGISTER
                             00028  20          USING *,12                 ESTABLISH ADDRESSABILITY
000028 50D0 C0A8             000D0  21          ST    13,SAVEAREA+4        SAVE ENTRY REGISTER
00002C 41D0 C0A4             000CC  22          LA    13,SAVEAREA          POINT TO SAVE AREA

                                    24          OPEN  (CARDS,,PRINTER,OUTPUT) OPEN FILES                    R 1

                                    33 READLOOP GET   CARDS,CARD           READ CARD
00004C F800 C101 C2BE 00129 002E6   38          ZAP   SCD,=P'0'            INITIALIZE                        00292
000052 98F1 C2B0             002D8  39          LM    15,1,=A(IDNUMBER,2,IDNUMBER+9)                         00294

000056 D201 C102 F000 0012A 00000   41 SCDLOOP  MVC   X(2),0(15)           MOVE EVEN/ODD PAIR OF DIGHTS      00301
00005C D401 C102 C2BC 0012A 002E4   42          NC    X(2),=2X'F'          REMOVE ZONE BITS
000062 DC00 C102 C1D9 0012A 00201   43          TR    X,EVENS              TRANSLATE TO 10-DIGIT             00302
000068 FA00 C101 C102 00129 0012A   44          AP    SCD,X                ACCUMULATE EVEN FACTOR            00303
00006E DC00 C103 C1E3 0012B 0020B   45          TR    Y,ODDS               TRANSLATE TO 10-2*DIGIT OR 10-SUM(D) 00305
000074 FA00 C101 C103 00129 0012D   46          AP    SCD,Y                ACCUMULATE                        00306
00007A 87F0 C02E             00056  47          BXLE  15,0,SCDLOOP         CONTINUE UNTIL ALL PAIRS PROCESSED 00307

00007E F300 C101 C101 00129 00129   49          UNPK  SCD,SCD              UNPACK S-C-D                      00309
000084 96F0 C101       00129        50          OI    SCD,C'0'             FORCE TO NUMERIC                  00310
000088 D247 C155 C104 0017D 0012C   51          MVC   OUTCARD,CARD         MOVE CARD IMAGE
00008E D500 C101 C10E 00129 00136   52          CLC   SCD,CARDSCD          INPUT S-C-D CORRECT?
000094 4780 C076             0009E  53          BE    PRINT                 YES
000098 D215 C163 C0EC 0018B 00114   54          MVC   OUTERROR,ERROR       MOVE ERROR MESSAGE
                                    55 PRINT    PUT   PRINTER,LINE         PRINT LINE
0000AC 92F0 C154       0017C        60          MVI   LINE,C'0'            SET TO DOUBLE SPACE AFTER FIRST TIME
0000B0 47F0 C016             0003E  61          B     READLOOP             GO GET NEXT RECORD

                                    63 CARDEOF  CLOSE (CARDS,,PRINTER)     CLOSE FILES

0000C2 58D0 C0A8             000D0  72 RETURN   L     13,SAVEAREA+4        RESTORE ENTRY REGISTER
                                    73          RETURN (14,12)             RESTORE REGISTERS/RETURN
0000CC 0000000000000000             76 SAVEAREA DC    18F'0'
000114 5C5C40C5D9D9D6D9             77 ERROR    DC    C'** ERROR ** S-C-D IS '
000129                              78 SCD      DS    C
00012A                              79 X        DS    C
00012B                              80 Y        DS    C
00012C                              81 CARD     DS    CL80
00017C                       0012C  82          ORG   CARD
```

```
SAMPLE ASSEMBLER PROGRAM--SAMPLE5

                                                                                      ASM H V 02 11.08 09/03/88
  LOC  OBJECT CODE    ADDR1 ADDR2  STMT   SOURCE STATEMENT
00012C                              83 IDNUMBER DS    CL10
000136                              84 CARDSCD  DS    C
000137                        0017C 85          ORG
00017C F140404040404040             86 LINE     DC    CL133'1'
000201                        0017D 87          ORG   LINE+1
00017D                              88 OUTCARD  DS    CL72
0001C5                        0018B 89          ORG   LINE+15
00018B                              90 OUTERROR DS    CL(L'ERROR+1)
0001A1                        00201 91          ORG
000201 0C9C8C7C6C5C4C3C             92 EVENS    DC    PL1'0,9,8,7,6,5,4,3,2,1'                           00318
00020B 0C8C6C4C2C9C7C5C             93 ODDS     DC    PL1'0,8,6,4,2,9,7,5,3,1'                           00319

                                    95 CARDS    DCB   DDNAME=SYSIN,       DATA DEFINITION NAME          -
                                                      DSORG=PS,           DATA SET ORGNAZIATION=PHYS. SEQ.  -
                                                      MACRF=GM,           MACRO INSTR. FORM=GET,MOVE    -
                                                      EODAD=CARDEOF       END OF DATA ADDRESS

                                   150 PRINTER  DCB   DDNAME=PRINTER,DSORG=PS,                          -
                                                      MACRF=PM,           MACRO INSTRUCTION FORM=PUT,MOVE  -
                                                      LRECL=133,          LOGICAL RECORD LENGTH         -
                                                      BLKSIZE=133,        BLOCK SIZE                    -
                                                      RECFM=FBA           RECORD FORMAT=FIXED-BLOCKED,FORMAT-A
000022                             204          END   BEGIN
0002D8 0000012C00000002            205                =A(IDNUMBER,2,IDNUMBER+9)
0002E4 0F0F                        206                =2X'F'
0002E6 0C                          207                =P'0'
```

```
                                   CROSS REFERENCE                                            ASM H V 02 11.08 09/03/88

SYMBOL     LEN     VALUE  DEFN  REFERENCES

BEGIN      00002   000022 0017  0204
CARD       00080   00012C 0081  0035 0051 0082
CARDEOF    00004   0000B4 0065  0117
CARDS      00004   000218 0099  0028 0034 0067
CARDSCD    00001   000136 0084  0052
ERROR      00021   000114 0077  0054 0090
EVENS      00001   000201 0092  0043
IDNUMBER   00010   00012C 0083  0205 0205
LINE       00133   00017C 0086  0057 0060 0087 0089
ODDS       00001   00020B 0093  0045
OUTCARD    00072   00017D 0088  0051
OUTERROR   00022   00018B 0090  0054
PRINT      00004   00009E 0056  0053
PRINTER    00004   000278 0154  0030 0056 0069
READLOOP   00004   00003E 0034  0061
RETURN     00004   0000C2 0072
SAVEAREA   00004   0000CC 0076  0021 0022 0072
SCD        00001   000129 0078  0038 0044 0046 0049 0049 0050 0052
SCDLOOP    00006   000056 0041  0047
X          00001   00012A 0079  0041 0042 0043 0044
Y          00001   00012B 0080  0045 0046
=A(IDNUMBER,2,IDNUMBER+9)
           00004   0002D8 0205  0039
=P'0'      00001   0002E6 0207  0038
=2X'F'     00001   0002E4 0206  0042
```

```
12345678903
12345678908    ** ERROR ** S-C-D IS 3
09876543217
09876543218    ** ERROR ** S-C-D IS 7
11111111115
11111111118    ** ERROR ** S-C-D IS 5
99999999990
99999999998    ** ERROR ** S-C-D IS 0
```

```
SAMPLE ASSEMBLER PROGRAM--SAMPLE6, SORT ROUTINE

  LOC  OBJECT CODE    ADDR1 ADDR2  STMT   SOURCE STATEMENT                                          ASM H V 02 11.06 09/03/88

                                      2 ***********************************************************************
                                      3 * THIS SUBROUTINE SORTS AN ARRAY IN ASCENDING ORDER.  THE ARRAY, THE  *
                                      4 * NUMBER OF ENTRIES, AND THE SIZE OF THE ENTRIES ARE SPECIFIED BY      *
                                      5 * PARAMETERS.                                                         *
                                      6 *---------------------------------------------------------------------*
                                      7 * USAGE:                                                              *
                                      8 *                                                                     *
                                      9 * 1)  ASSEMBLER                                                       *
                                     10 *                                                                     *
                                     11 *     CALL KHNSORT,(ARRAY,N,LEN)                                      *
                                     12 *                                                                     *
                                     13 * 2)  COBOL                                                           *
                                     14 *                                                                     *
                                     15 *     CALL 'KHNSORT' USING ARRAY, N, LEN.                             *
                                     16 *                                                                     *
                                     17 * WHERE:                                                              *
                                     18 *                                                                     *
                                     19 *     ARRAY = ARRAY NAME                                              *
                                     20 *                                                                     *
                                     21 *     N = NUMBER OF ENTRIES (FULL WORD BINARY)                        *
                                     22 *                                                                     *
                                     23 *     LEN = LENGTH OF EACH ENTRY (HALF WORD BINARY AND LEN NOT > 256) *
                                     24 ***********************************************************************

                                     26          ENTRY KHNSORT         DEFINE ENTRY POINT
                                     27          PRINT NOGEN

                                     29 KHNSORT  SAVE  (14,12)                  SAVE REGISTERS
000004 05C0                          32          BALR  12,0                     LOAD BASE REGISTER
                              00006  33          USING *,12                     ESTABLISH ADDRESSABILITY
000006 50D0 C062              00068  34          ST    13,SAVEAREA+4            SAVE ENTRY REGISTER
00000A 41D0 C05E              00064  35          LA    13,SAVEAREA              POINT TO SAVE AREA

00000E 9824 1000              00000  37          LM    2,4,0(1)                 LOAD ADDRESSES OF PARAMETERS
000012 5873 0000              00000  38          L     7,0(3)                   LOAD NUMBER OF ENTRIES
000016 4814 0000              00000  39          LH    1,0(4)                   LOAD SIZE OF ENTRY
00001A 0670                          40          BCTR  7,0                      DECREMENT NUMBER OF ENTRIES
00001C 1277                          41          LTR   7,7                      AT LEAST TWO ENTRIES?
00001E 47D0 C054              0005A  42          BNP   RETURN                    NO
000022 1C61                          43          MR    6,1                      LEN*(N-1)
000024 4172 7000              00000  44          LA    7,0(2,7)                 ADDRESS OF LAST ENTRY
000028 1852                          45          LR    5,2                      ADDRESS OF FIRST ENTRY (FOR MAINLINE
00002A 18A1                          46          LR    10,1                     LOAD LENGTH OF ENTRY(FOR LEVEL2 BXLE
00002C 1861                          47          LR    6,1                       " (FOR MAINLINE BXLE)
00002E 18B7                          48          LR    11,7                     LOAD ADDRESS OF LAST ELEMENT (LEVEL2
000030 1B71                          49          SR    7,1                      GET ADDRESS OF PREVIOUS ENTRY
000032 1211                          50          LTR   1,1                      LENGTH POSITIVE?
000034 47D0 C054              0005A  51          BNP   RETURN                    NO
000038 0610                          52          BCTR  1,0                      COMPUTE LENGTH - 1

00003A 419A 5000              00000  54 MAINLINE LA    9,0(10,5)                ENTRY AFTER CURRENT (TOP) ENTRY

00003E 4410 C0A6              000AC  56 LEVEL2   EX    1,COMPARE                TOP ENTRY OKAY?
000042 47D0 C04C              00052  57          BNH   TOPOKAY                   YES
000046 4410 C0AC              000B2  58          EX    1,XCAB                   XC A,B (EXCHANGE TOP ENTRY
00004A 4410 C0B2              000B8  59          EX    1,XCBA                   XC B,A     WITH
00004E 4410 C0AC              000B2  60          EX    1,XCAB                   XC A,B        CURRENT ENTRY)

000052 879A C038              0003E  62 TOPOKAY  BXLE  9,10,LEVEL2              CONTINUE UNTIL ALL BUBBLES FLOATED

000056 8756 C034              0003A  64          BXLE  5,6,MAINLINE             CONTINUE UNTIL PERCOLATETED

00005A 58D0 C062              00068  66 RETURN   L     13,SAVEAREA+4            RESTORE ENTRY REGISTER
                                     67          RETURN (14,12)                 RESTORE REGISTERS/RETURN
000064 0000000000000000              70 SAVEAREA DC    18F'0'

0000AC D500 5000 9000 00000 00000    72 COMPARE  CLC   0(*-*,5),0(9)
0000B2 D700 5000 9000 00000 00000    73 XCAB     XC    0(*-*,5),0(9)
0000B8 D700 9000 5000 00000 00000    74 XCBA     XC    0(*-*,9),0(5)
                                     75          END
```

```
                                   CROSS REFERENCE                                           ASM H V 02 11.06 09/03/88

SYMBOL     LEN      VALUE  DEFN  REFERENCES

COMPARE   00006    0000AC 0072  0056
KHNSORT   00002    000000 0030  0026
LEVEL2    00004    00003E 0056  0062
MAINLINE  00004    00003A 0054  0064
RETURN    00004    00005A 0066  0042 0051
SAVEAREA  00004    000064 0070  0034 0035 0066
TOPOKAY   00004    000052 0062  0057
XCAB      00006    0000B2 0073  0058 0060
XCBA      00006    0000B8 0074  0059


LISTING OF INPUT--UNSORTED

12345678903
12345678908
09876543217
09876543218
11111111115
11111111118
99999999990
99999999998
WASHINGTON, GEORGE
DOE, JANE
SMITH, WILLIAM
SMITH, MARY
SMITH, JOHN


LISTING OF INPUT--SORTED

DOE, JANE
SMITH, JOHN
SMITH, MARY
SMITH, WILLIAM
WASHINGTON, GEORGE
09876543217
09876543218
11111111115
11111111118
12345678903
12345678908
99999999990
99999999998
```

```
SAMPLE ASSEMBLER PROGRAM--SAMPLE6

  LOC  OBJECT CODE    ADDR1 ADDR2  STMT   SOURCE STATEMENT                                        ASM H V 02 11.35 09/03/88
                                      2 ********************************************************************
                                      3 * THIS PROGRAM READS A SET OF CARD IMAGES FROM A SEQUENTIAL DATASET,  *
                                      4 * EXTRACTS AND PRINTS THE DATA CONTAINED IN THE FIRST 20 BYTES OF THE *
                                      5 * RECORD, SORTS IT USING KHNSORT, AND PRINTS THE SORTED DATA.         *
                                      6 *--------------------------------------------------------------------*
                                      7 * THE INPUT FIELD IS IN BYTES 1-20 OF THE INPUT RECORD.              *
                                      8 ********************************************************************
000000                               10          START X'0'            ADJUST LOCATION COUNTER FOR MVS/XA
                                     11          PRINT NOGEN
                                     13          DC    C'SAMPLE6--ASSEMBLED &SYSDATE-&SYSTIME'
                                     15 BEGIN    SAVE  (14,12)               SAVE REGISTERS
000026 05C0                          18          BALR  12,0                  LOAD BASE REGISTER
                              00028  19          USING *,12                  ESTABLISH ADDRESSABILITY
000028 50D0 C0A8              000D0  20          ST    13,SAVEAREA+4         SAVE ENTRY REGISTER
00002C 41D0 C0A4              000CC  21          LA    13,SAVEAREA           POINT TO SAVE AREA
                                     23          OPEN  (CARDS,,PRINTER,OUTPUT) OPEN FILES                   R 1
00003E 45B0 C112              0013A  31          BAL   11,HEADPAGE           PRINT FIRST PAGE HEADING
000042 9835 C140              00168  33          LM    3,5,=A(FIRST,L'FIRST,LAST)
000046 1722                          34          XR    2,2                   CLEAR CARD COUNTER
                                     36 READLOOP GET   CARDS,CARD            READ CARD
000056 D213 3000 C15A 00000 00182    41          MVC   0(L'FIRST,3),CARD     MOVE TO ARRAY
00005C D247 C1AB C15A 001D3 00182    42          MVC   OUTCARD,CARD          MOVE TO PRINT LINE
000062 45B0 C0F8              00120  43          BAL   11,PRINT              PRINT INPUT IMAGE
000066 4122 0001              00001  44          LA    2,1(2)                COUNT CARD IMAGE
00006A 1863                          45          LR    6,3                   SAVE ADDRESS OF CURRENT ENTRY
00006C 8734 C020              00048  46          BXLE  3,4,READLOOP          CONTINUE UNTIL ARRAY FULL
000070 5020 C154              0017C  48 CARDEOF  ST    2,COUNT               STORE NUMBER OF CARDS
                                     49          PRINT GEN                   SHOW EXPANSION OF CALL MACRO
                                     50          CALL  KHNSORT,(FIRST,COUNT,SIZE) GO SORT ARRAY
000074                               51+         CNOP  0,4                                                      01-CALL
000074 47F0 C054              0007C  52+         B     *+8                              BRANCH AROUND VCON      01-CALL
000078 00000000                      53+IHB0005B DC    V(KHNSORT)                       ENTRY POINT ADDRESS     01-CALL
00007C                               54+         CNOP  0,4                                                      02-IHBOP
00007C 4110 C05C              00084  55+         LA    1,IHB0006                        LIST ADDRESS  @ZMC3742  02-IHBOP
000080 47F0 C068              00090  56+         B     IHB0006A                         BYPASS LIST   @ZMC3742  02-IHBOP
                              00084  57+IHB0006  EQU   *                                                        02-IHBOP
000084 0000039C                      58+         DC    A(FIRST)              PROB.PROG.PARAMETER                02-IHBOP
000088 0000017C                      59+         DC    A(COUNT)              PROB.PROG.PARAMETER                02-IHBOP
00008C 00000180                      60+         DC    A(SIZE)                                        @G860P40  02-IHBOP
                              00090  61+IHB0006A EQU   *                                                        02-IHBOP
000090 58F0 C050              00078  62+         L     15,IHB0005B                      LOAD 15 WITH ENTRY ADR  01-CALL
000094 05EF                          63+         BALR  14,15                            BRANCH TO ENTRY POINT   01-CALL
                                     64          PRINT NOGEN                 RESUME SUPPRESSION OF EXPANSIONS   T
000096 4130 C374              0039C  66          LA    3,FIRST               LOAD ADDRESS OF FIRST SORTED ENTRY
00009A 1856                          67          LR    5,6                   LOAD ADDRESS OF LAST ENTRY
00009C D207 C242 C244 0026A 0026C    68          MVC   UNSORTED,UNSORTED+2   CHANGE 'UNSORTED' TO 'SORTED  '
0000A2 45B0 C112              0013A  69          BAL   11,HEADPAGE           PRINT NEW PAGE HEADING
```

```
SAMPLE ASSEMBLER PROGRAM--SAMPLE6

  LOC  OBJECT CODE    ADDR1 ADDR2  STMT   SOURCE STATEMENT                                ASM H V 02 11.35 09/03/88

0000A6 D213 C1AB 3000 001D3 00000    71 PRTLOOP  MVC   OUTCARD(L'FIRST),0(3) MOVE SORTED DATA TO PRINT LINE
0000AC 45B0 C0F8            00120    72          BAL   11,PRINT              PRINT SORTED IMAGE
0000B0 8734 C07E            000A6    73          BXLE  3,4,PRTLOOP           CONTINUE UNTIL ALL IMAGES SORTED

                                     75          CLOSE (CARDS,,PRINTER)      CLOSE FILES

0000C2 58D0 C0A8            000D0    84 RETURN   L     13,SAVEAREA+4         RESTORE ENTRY REGISTER
                                     85          RETURN (14,12)              RESTORE REGISTERS/RETURN
0000CC 0000000000000000              88 SAVEAREA DC    18F'0'
000118                               89 DOUBLE   DS    D

                                     91 PRINT    PUT   PRINTER,LINE          PRINT REPORT LINE
00012E 9240 C1AA      001D2          96          MVI   LINE,C' '             SET SEED
000132 D283 C1AB C1AA 001D3 001D2    97          MVC   LINE+1(L'LINE-1),LINE CLEAR TO BLANKS
000138 06AB                          98          BCTR  10,11                 RETURN IF PAGE NOT FULL

00013A FA10 C151 C150 00179 00178   100 HEADPAGE AP    PAGES,=P'1'           INCREMENT PAGE COUNT
000140 D203 C2B0 C14C 002D8 00174   101          MVC   PAGENO,=X'40202120'   SET EDIT PATTTERN

000146 DE03 C2B0 C151 002D8 00179   102          ED    PAGENO,PAGES          FORMAT PAGE NUMBER
                                    103          PUT   PRINTER,HEADING       PRINT PAGE HEADING
00015A 41A0 0038            00038   108          LA    10,56                 SET LINES/PAGE
00015E 92F0 C1AA      001D2         109          MVI   LINE,C'0'             SET TO DOUBLE SPACE
000162 07FB                         110          BR    11                    RETURN

000168                              112          LTORG
000168 0000039C00000014             113                =A(FIRST,L'FIRST,LAST)
000174 40202120                     114                =X'40202120'
000178 1C                           115                =P'1'
000179 000C                         116 PAGES    DC    PL2'0'
00017C                              117 COUNT    DS    F
000180 0014                         118 SIZE     DC    AL2(L'FIRST)
000182                              119 CARD     DS    CL80
0001D2 F140404040404040             120 LINE     DC    CL133'1'
000257                      001D3   121          ORG   LINE+1
0001D3                              122 OUTCARD  DS    CL72
00021B                      00257   123          ORG
000257 F140404040404040             124 HEADING  DC    CL133'1'                                    00318
0002DC                      00258   125          ORG   HEADING+1                                   00319
000258 D3C9E2E3C9D5C740             126          DC    C'LISTING OF INPUT--'
00026A E4D5E2D6D9E3C5C4             127 UNSORTED DC    C'UNSORTED'
000272                      00295   128          ORG   HEADING+L'HEADING/2-4
000295                              129 TODAY    DS    CL8
00029D                      002D4   130          ORG   HEADING+L'HEADING-8
0002D4 D7C1C7C5                     131          DC    C'PAGE'
0002D8                              132 PAGENO   DS    CL4
0002DC                      002DC   133          ORG

                                    135 CARDS    DCB   DDNAME=SYSIN,         DATA DEFINITION NAME              -
                                                       DSORG=PS,             DATA SET ORGNAZIATION=PHYS. SEQ.  -
                                                       MACRF=GM,             MACRO INSTR. FORM=GET,MOVE        -
                                                       EODAD=CARDEOF         END OF DATA ADDRESS

                                    190 PRINTER  DCB   DDNAME=PRINTEP,DSORG=PS,                                -
                                                       MACRF=PM,             MACRO INSTRUCTION FORM=PUT,MOVE   -

                                                       LRECL=133,            LOGICAL RECORD LENGTH             -
                                                       BLKSIZE=133,          BLOCK SIZE                        -
                                                       RECFM=FBA             RECORD FORMAT=FIXED-BLOCKED,FORMAT-A

00039C                              245 FIRST    DS    100CL20
000B6C                              246 LAST     DS    CL(L'FIRST)
000022                              247          END   BEGIN
```

```
                                        CROSS REFERENCE

SYMBOL     LEN     VALUE  DEFN  REFERENCES                                          ASM H V 02 11.35 09/03/88

BEGIN     00002   000022 0016  0247
CARD      00080   000182 0119  0038 0041 0042
CARDEOF   00004   000070 0048  0157
CARDS     00004   0002DC 0139  0027 0037 0079
COUNT     00004   00017C 0117  0048 0059
DOUBLE    00008   000118 0089
FIRST     00020   00039C 0245  0041 0058 0066 0071 0113 0113 0118 0246
HEADING   00133   000257 0124  0105 0125 0128 0128 0130 0130
HEADPAGE  00006   00013A 0100  0031 0069
IHB0005B  00004   000078 0053  0062
IHB0006   00001 00000084 0057  0055
IHB0006A  00001 00000090 0061  0056
LAST      00020   000B6C 0246  0113
LINE      00133   0001D2 0120  0093 0096 0097 0097 0097 0109 0121
OUTCARD   00072   0001D3 0122  0042 0071
PAGENO    00004   0002D8 0132  0101 0102
PAGES     00002   000179 0116  0100 0102
PRINT     00004   000120 0092  0043 0072
PRINTER   00004   00033C 0194  0029 0081 0092 0104
PRTLOOP   00006   0000A6 0071  0073
READLOOP  00004   000048 0037  0046
RETURN    00004   0000C2 0084
SAVEAREA  00004   0000CC 0088  0020 0021 0084
SIZE      00002   000180 0118  0060
TODAY     00008   000295 0129
UNSORTED  00008   00026A 0127  0068 0068
=A(FIRST,L'FIRST,LAST)
          00004   000168 0113  0033
=P'1'     00001   000178 0115  0100
=X'40202120'
          00004   000174 0114  0101
```

```
LOC  OBJECT CODE    ADDR1 ADDR2  STMT   SOURCE STATEMENT                          ASM H V 02 10.13 10/15/88

                                               MACRO
                                       &NAME    MOVE   &A,&B,&DBL=DOUBLE,&R=0
                                       .* THIS MACRO MOVES THE CONTENTS OF THE FIRST OPERAND TO THE SECOND
                                       .* OPERAND.  THE KEYWORD '&DBL' IS USED TO SPECIFY A DOUBLE WORD WORK
                                       .* AREA AND '&R' IS USED TO SPECIFY A WORK REGISTER.  THE DATA TYPES
                                       .* OF THE FIRST TWO OPERANDS ARE EXAMINED TO GENERATE THE PROPER
                                       .* INSTRUCTIONS BASED ON THE DECISION TABLE GIVEN BELOW.  DATA TYPES
                                       .* ARE RESTRICTED TO FULL WORDS, HALF WORDS, ZONED DECIMAL, AND PACKED
                                       .* DECIMAL.
                                       .*
                                       .* T'&A | T'&B='F'      | T'&B='H'       | T'&B='Z'       | T'&B='P'       |
                                       .*-----+---------------+----------------+----------------+----------------|
                                       .* 'F' | MVC  &B,&A    | MVC  &B,&A+2   | L    &R,&A     | L    $R,&A     |
                                       .*     |               |                | CVD  &R,&DBL   | CVD  &R,&DBL   |
                                       .*     |               |                | UNPK &B,&DBL   | ZAP  &B,&DBL   |
                                       .*-----+---------------+----------------+----------------+----------------|
                                       .* 'H' | LH   &R,&A    | MVC  &B,&A     | LH   &R,&A     | LH   &R,&A     |
                                       .*     | ST   &R,&B    |                | CVD  &R,&DBL   | CVD  &R,&DBL   |
                                       .*     |               |                | UNPK &B,&DBL   | ZAP  &B,&DBL   |
                                       .*-----+---------------+----------------+----------------+----------------|
                                       .* 'Z' | PACK &DBL,&A  | PACK &DBL,&A   | PACK &DBL,&A   | PACK &B,&A     |
                                       .*     | CVB  &R,&DBL  | PACK &R,&DBL   | UNPK &B,&DBL   |                |
                                       .*     | ST   &R,&B    | STH  &R,&B     |                |                |
                                       .*-----+---------------+----------------+----------------+----------------|
                                       .* 'P' | ZAP  &DBL,&A  | ZAP  &DBL,&A   | UNPK &B,&A     | ZAP  &B,&A     |
                                       .*     | CVB  &R,&DBL  | PACK &R,&DBL   |                |                |
                                       .*     | ST   &R,&B    | STH  &R,&B     |                |                |
                                       .*-----+---------------+----------------+----------------+----------------|
                                       .*
                                                LCLC   &OP1,&OP2
                                                AIF    (T'&A NE 'F').ANOTF
                                                AIF    (T'&B EQ 'F').FF
                                                AIF    (T'&B EQ 'H').FH
                                       &OP1     SETC   'L'
                                       &OP2     SETC   'UNPK'
                                                AIF    (T'&B EQ 'Z').FZP
                                       &OP2     SETC   'ZAP'
                                                AIF    (T'&B EQ 'P').FZP
                                       .ERROR   MNOTE  2,'INVALID DATA TYPE'
                                                MEXIT
                                       .FF      ANOP
                                       &NAME    MVC    &B,&A
                                                MEXIT
                                       .FH      ANOP
                                       &NAME    MVC    &B,&A+2
                                                MEXIT
                                       .FZP     ANOP
                                       &NAME    &OP1   &R,&A
                                                CVD    &R,&DBL
                                                &OP2   &B,&DBL
                                                MEXIT
                                       .ANOTF   AIF    (T'&A NE 'H').ANOTH
                                                AIF    (T'&B EQ 'F').HF
                                                AIF    (T'&B EQ 'H').FF
                                       &OP1     SETC   'LH'
                                       &OP2     SETC   'UNPK'
                                                AIF    (T'&B EQ 'Z').FZP
                                       &OP2     SETC   'ZAP'
                                                AIF    (T'&B EQ 'P').FZP
                                                AGO    .ERROR
                                       .HF      ANOP
                                       &NAME    LH     &R,&A
                                                ST     &R,&B
                                                MEXIT
                                       .ANOTH   AIF    (T'&A NE 'Z').ANOTZ
                                       &OP1     SETC   'PACK'
                                       &OP2     SETC   'ST'
                                                AIF    (T'&B EQ 'F').ZFH
                                       &OP2     SETC   'STH'
                                                AIF    (T'&B EQ 'H').ZFH
```

```
LOC  OBJECT CODE    ADDR1 ADDR2  STMT   SOURCE STATEMENT                                   ASM H V 02 10.13 10/15/88
                                   71            AIF    (T'&B EQ 'Z').ZZ
                                   72            AIF    (T'&B EQ 'P').ZP
                                   73            AGO    .ERROR
                                   74  .ZFH      ANOP
                                   75  &NAME     &OP1   &DBL,&A
                                   76            CVB    &R,&DBL
                                   77            &OP2   &R,&B
                                   78            MEXIT
                                   79  .ZZ       ANOP
                                   80  &NAME     PACK   &DBL,&A
                                   81            UNPK   &B,&DBL
                                   82            MEXIT
                                   83  .ZP       ANOP
                                   84  &NAME     PACK   &B,&A
                                   85            MEXIT
                                   86  .ANOTZ    AIF    (T'&A NE 'P').ERROR
                                   87  &OP1      SETC   'PACK'
                                   88  &OP2      SETC   'ST'
                                   89            AIF    (T'&B EQ 'F').ZFH
                                   90  &OP2      SETC   'STH'
                                   91            AIF    (T'&B EQ 'H').ZFH
                                   92            AIF    (T'&B EQ 'Z').PZ
                                   93            AIF    (T'&B NE 'P').ERROR
                                   94  &NAME     ZAP    &B,&A
                                   95            MEXIT
                                   96  .PZ       UNPK   &B,&A
                                   97            MEND
                                   98            MACRO
                                   99  &NAME     NFACT  &N,&NFACT
                                  100            GBLB   &FIRST
                                  101            LCLA   &X
                                  102            AIF    (&FIRST).NOT1ST
                                  103  &FIRST    SETB   1
                                  104  &NAME     ZAP    &NFACT,=P'1'
                                  105  .NOT1ST   AIF    (&N LE 1).END
                                  106            MP     &NFACT,=P'&N'
                                  107  &X        SETA   &N-1
                                  108            NFACT  &X,&NFACT
                                  109            MEXIT
                                  110  .END      ANOP
                                  111  &FIRST    SETB   0
                                  112            MEND
                                  113            MACRO
                                  114  &NAME     SUM    &A,&B,&RESULT=SUM
                                  115  &NAME     ZAP    &RESULT,&A
                                  116            AP     &RESULT,&B
                                  117            MEND
                                  118            MACRO
                                  119  &NAME     MSUM   &A,&B,&C
                                  120            LCLA   &I
                                  121            AIF    (T'&NAME EQ 'O').LOOP
                                  122  &NAME     DS     OH
                                  123  .LOOP     AIF    (&I GE N'&B).END
                                  124  &I        SETA   &I+1
                                  125            ZAP    &SYSLIST(3,&I),&A
                                  126            AP     &SYSLIST(3,&I),&SYSLIST(2,&I)
                                  127            AGO    .LOOP
                                  128  .END      MEND
                                  129            MACRO
                                  130  &NAME     EXPDATE &CENTURY=19
                                  131            LCLA   &I
                                  132            LCLC   &M(12),&X,&Y,&Z
                                  133  &M(10)    SETC   'OCTOBER'
                                  134  &X        SETC   '&SYSDATE'(1,2)
                                  135  &I        SETA   &X
                                  136  &Y        SETC   '&SYSDATE'(4,2)
                                  137  &Z        SETC   '&SYSDATE'(7,2)
                                  138            AIF    ('&Y'(1,1) NE 'O').AFTER9
                                  139  &Y        SETC   '&Y'(2,1)
                                  140  .AFTER9   ANOP
```

```
  LOC  OBJECT CODE    ADDR1 ADDR2  STMT   SOURCE STATEMENT                                    ASM H V 02 10.13 10/15/88
                                    141 &NAME      DC     C'&M(&X) &Y, &CENTURY&Z'
                                    142            MEND
                              00000 143            USING  *,15
                                    144            SUM    ALPHA,BETA,RESULT=GAMMA
000000 F844 F12C F122 0012C 00122   145+           ZAP    GAMMA,ALPHA                                          01-00115
000006 FA44 F12C F127 0012C 00127   146+           AP     GAMMA,BETA                                           01-00116
                                    147            SUM    Z,=P'10'
00000C F844 F131 F136 00131 00136   148+           ZAP    SUM,Z                                                01-00115
000012 FA41 F131 F178 00131 00178   149+           AP     SUM,=P'10'                                           01-00116
                                    150 TEST       MSUM   ALPHA,BETA,GAMMA
000018                              151+TEST       DS     0H                                                   01-00122
000018 F844 F12C F122 0012C 00122   152+           ZAP    GAMMA,ALPHA                                          01-00125
00001E FA44 F12C F127 0012C 00127   153+           AP     GAMMA,BETA                                           01-00126
                                    154            MSUM   ALPHA,(B1,B2,B3),(C1,C2,C3)
000024 F844 F14A F122 0014A 00122   155+           ZAP    C1,ALPHA                                             01-00125
00002A FA44 F14A F13B 0014A 0013B   156+           AP     C1,B1                                                01-00126
000030 F844 F14F F122 0014F 00122   157+           ZAP    C2,ALPHA                                             01-00125
000036 FA44 F14F F140 0014F 00140   158+           AP     C2,B2                                                01-00126
00003C F844 F154 F122 00154 00122   159+           ZAP    C3,ALPHA                                             01-00125
000042 FA44 F154 F145 00154 00145   160+           AP     C3,B3                                                01-00126
                                    161            EXPDATE CENTURY=20
000048 D6C3E3D6C2C5D940             162+           DC     C'OCTOBER 15, 2088'                                  01-00141
                                    163 DATE       EXPDATE
000058 D6C3E3D6C2C5D940             164+DATE       DC     C'OCTOBER 15, 1988'                                  01-00141
                                    165 MOVEFF     MOVE   FULL,FULL
000068 D203 F15C F15C 0015C 0015C   166+MOVEFF     MVC    FULL,FULL                                            01-00042
                                    167 MOVEFH     MOVE   FULL,HALF
00006E D201 F160 F15E 00160 0015E   168+MOVEFH     MVC    HALF,FULL+2                                          01-00045
                                    169 MOVEFZ     MOVE   FULL,ZONED
000074 5800 F15C            0015C   170+MOVEFZ     L      0,FULL                                               01-00048
000078 4E00 F170            00170   171+           CVD    0,DOUBLE                                             01-00049
00007C F377 F167 F170 00167 00170   172+           UNPK   ZONED,DOUBLE                                         01-00050
                                    173 MOVEFP     MOVE   FULL,PACKED
000082 5800 F15C            0015C   174+MOVEFP     L      0,FULL                                               01-00048
000086 4E00 F170            00170   175+           CVD    0,DOUBLE                                             01-00049
00008A F847 F162 F170 00162 00170   176+           ZAP    PACKED,DOUBLE                                        01-00050
                                    177 MOVEHF     MOVE   HALF,FULL
000090 4800 F160            00160   178+MOVEHF     LH     0,HALF                                               01-00062
000094 5000 F15C            0015C   179+           ST     0,FULL                                               01-00063
                                    180 MOVEHH     MOVE   HALF,HALF
000098 D201 F160 F160 00160 00160   181+MOVEHH     MVC    HALF,HALF                                            01-00042
                                    182 MOVEHZ     MOVE   HALF,ZONED
00009E 4800 F160            00160   183+MOVEHZ     LH     0,HALF                                               01-00048
0000A2 4E00 F170            00170   184+           CVD    0,DOUBLE                                             01-00049
0000A6 F377 F167 F170 00167 00170   185+           UNPK   ZONED,DOUBLE                                         01-00050
                                    186 MOVEHP     MOVE   HALF,PACKED
0000AC 4800 F160            00160   187+MOVEHP     LH     0,HALF                                               01-00048
0000B0 4E00 F170            00170   188+           CVD    0,DOUBLE                                             01-00049
0000B4 F847 F162 F170 00162 00170   189+           ZAP    PACKED,DOUBLE                                        01-00050
                                    190            MHELP  B'1'                MACRO CALL TRACE
                                    191 MOVEZF     MOVE   ZONED,FULL

                                       ++//MHELP CALL TO MACRO MOVE        DEPTH=001   SYSNDX=0000015   STMT=00191

0000BA F277 F170 F167 00170 00167   192+MOVEZF     PACK   DOUBLE,ZONED                                         01-00075
0000C0 4F00 F170            00170   193+           CVB    0,DOUBLE                                             01-00076
0000C4 5000 F15C            0015C   194+           ST     0,FULL                                               01-00077
                                    195            MHELP  B'10'               MACRO BRANCH TRACE
                                    196 MOVEZH     MOVE   ZONED,HALF

                                       ++//MHELP  BRANCH FROM STMT 00031 TO STMT 00052 IN MACRO MOVE

                                       ++//MHELP  BRANCH FROM STMT 00052 TO STMT 00065 IN MACRO MOVE

                                       ++//MHELP  BRANCH FROM STMT 00070 TO STMT 00075 IN MACRO MOVE

0000C8 F277 F170 F167 00170 00167   197+MOVEZH     PACK   DOUBLE,ZONED                                         01-00075
0000CE 4F00 F170            00170   198+           CVB    0,DOUBLE                                             01-00076
```

```
  LOC  OBJECT CODE    ADDR1 ADDR2  STMT   SOURCE STATEMENT                               ASM H V 02 10.13 10/15/88

0000D2 4000 F160            00160  199+           STH   0,HALF                                             01-00077
                                   200            MHELP B'100'               MACRO AIF TRACE
                                   201 MOVEZZ     MOVE  ZONED,ZONED

                                        //MHELP AIF IN    MOVE      MODEL STMT=00031 DEPTH=001 SYSNDX=0000017 KWCNT=002
                                        ////SET SYMBOLS (SKIPPED NUMBERS MAY BE SEQUENCE SYMBOLS).//
                                        //0000 LCLC       OP1                                        LNTH= 0
                                        //0001 LCLC       OP2                                        LNTH= 0
                                        //MHELP AIF IN    MOVE      MODEL STMT=00052 DEPTH=001 SYSNDX=0000017 KWCNT=002
                                        ////SET SYMBOLS (SKIPPED NUMBERS MAY BE SEQUENCE SYMBOLS).//
                                        //0000 LCLC       OP1                                        LNTH= 0
                                        //0001 LCLC       OP2                                        LNTH= 0

                                        //MHELP AIF IN    MOVE      MODEL STMT=00065 DEPTH=001 SYSNDX=0000017 KWCNT=002
                                        ////SET SYMBOLS (SKIPPED NUMBERS MAY BE SEQUENCE SYMBOLS).//
                                        //0000 LCLC       OP1                                        LNTH= 0
                                        //0001 LCLC       OP2                                        LNTH= 0

                                        //MHELP AIF IN    MOVE      MODEL STMT=00068 DEPTH=001 SYSNDX=0000017 KWCNT=002
                                        ////SET SYMBOLS (SKIPPED NUMBERS MAY BE SEQUENCE SYMBOLS).//
                                        //0000 LCLC       OP1                                        LNTH= 004
                                        //     VAL=PACK
                                        //0001 LCLC       OP2                                        LNTH= 002
                                        //     VAL=ST

                                        //MHELP AIF IN    MOVE      MODEL STMT=00070 DEPTH=001 SYSNDX=0000017 KWCNT=002
                                        ////SET SYMBOLS (SKIPPED NUMBERS MAY BE SEQUENCE SYMBOLS).//
                                        //0000 LCLC       OP1                                        LNTH= 004
                                        //     VAL=PACK
                                        //0001 LCLC       OP2                                        LNTH= 003
                                        //     VAL=STH

                                        //MHELP AIF IN    MOVE      MODEL STMT=00071 DEPTH=001 SYSNDX=0000017 KWCNT=002
                                        ////SET SYMBOLS (SKIPPED NUMBERS MAY BE SEQUENCE SYMBOLS).//
                                        //0000 LCLC       OP1                                        LNTH= 004
                                        //     VAL=PACK
                                        //0001 LCLC       OP2                                        LNTH= 003
                                        //     VAL=STH
0000D6 F277 F170 F167 00170 00167  202+MOVEZZ     PACK  DOUBLE,ZONED                                       01-00080
0000DC F377 F167 F170 00167 00170  203+           UNPK  ZONED,DOUBLE                                       01-00081
                                   204            MHELP B'1000'              MACRO EXIT TRACE
                                   205 MOVEZP     MOVE  ZONED,PACKED
0000E2 F247 F162 F167 00162 00167  206+MOVEZP     PACK  PACKED,ZONED                                       01-00084

                                        //MHELP EXIT FROM MOVE      MODEL STMT=00085 DEPTH=001 SYSNDX=0000018 KWCNT=002
                                        ////SET SYMBOLS (SKIPPED NUMBERS MAY BE SEQUENCE SYMBOLS).//
                                        //0000 LCLC       OP1                                        LNTH= 004
                                        //     VAL=PACK
                                        //0001 LCLC       OP2                                        LNTH= 003
                                        //     VAL=STH

                                   207            MHELP B'10000'             MACRO ENTRY TRACE
                                   208 MOVEPF     MOVE  PACKED,FULL

                                        //MHELP ENTRY TO  MOVE      MODEL STMT=00000 DEPTH=001 SYSNDX=0000019 KWCNT=002
                                        ////PARAMETERS (SYSNDX,SYSECT,SYSLOC,SYSTIME,SYSDATE,SYSPARM,NAME,KWS,PPS) ///
                                        //NUM  LNTH  VALUE (64 CHARS/LINE)
                                        //0000  004  0019
                                        //0001  NUL
                                        //0002  NUL
                                        //0003  005   10.13
                                        //0004  008   10/15/88
                                        //0005  NUL
                                        //0006  006   MOVEPF
                                        //0007  006   DOUBLE
```

```
LOC    OBJECT CODE     ADDR1 ADDR2  STMT    SOURCE STATEMENT                                ASM H V 02 10.13 10/15/88
                                           //0008  001  0
                                           //0009  006  PACKED
                                           //0010  004  FULL
0000E8 F274 F170 F162 00170 00162   209+MOVEPF    PACK  DOUBLE,PACKED                                    01-00075
0000EE 4F00 F170            00170   210+          CVB   0,DOUBLE                                         01-00076
0000F2 5000 F15C            0015C   211+          ST    0,FULL                                           01-00077
                                    212           MHELP B'1000100'          MACRO HEX DUMP W/ AIF TRACE
                                    213 MOVEPH    MOVE  PACKED,HALF

                                           //MHELP AIF IN    MOVE      MODEL STMT=00031 DEPTH=001 SYSNDX=0000020 KWCNT=002
                                           ////SET SYMBOLS (SKIPPED NUMBERS MAY BE SEQUENCE SYMBOLS).//
                                           //0000 LCLC        OP1                                     LNTH= 0
                                           //0001 LCLC        OP2                                     LNTH= 0

                                           //MHELP AIF IN    MOVE      MODEL STMT=00052 DEPTH=001 SYSNDX=0000020 KWCNT=002
                                           ////SET SYMBOLS (SKIPPED NUMBERS MAY BE SEQUENCE SYMBOLS).//
                                           //0000 LCLC        OP1                                     LNTH= 0
                                           //0001 LCLC        OP2                                     LNTH= 0

                                           //MHELP AIF IN    MOVE      MODEL STMT=00065 DEPTH=001 SYSNDX=0000020 KWCNT=002
                                           ////SET SYMBOLS (SKIPPED NUMBERS MAY BE SEQUENCE SYMBOLS).//
                                           //0000 LCLC        OP1                                     LNTH= 0
                                           //0001 LCLC        OP2                                     LNTH= 0

                                           //MHELP AIF IN    MOVE      MODEL STMT=00086 DEPTH=001 SYSNDX=0000020 KWCNT=002
                                           ////SET SYMBOLS (SKIPPED NUMBERS MAY BE SEQUENCE SYMBOLS).//
                                           //0000 LCLC        OP1                                     LNTH= 0
                                           //0001 LCLC        OP2                                     LNTH= 0

                                           //MHELP AIF IN    MOVE      MODEL STMT=00089 DEPTH=001 SYSNDX=0000020 KWCNT=002
                                           ////SET SYMBOLS (SKIPPED NUMBERS MAY BE SEQUENCE SYMBOLS).//
                                           //0000 LCLC        OP1                                     LNTH= 004
                                           //     VAL=PACK
                                           //0001 LCLC        OP2                                     LNTH= 002
                                           //     VAL=ST

                                           //MHELP AIF IN    MOVE      MODEL STMT=00091 DEPTH=001 SYSNDX=0000020 KWCNT=002
                                           ////SET SYMBOLS (SKIPPED NUMBERS MAY BE SEQUENCE SYMBOLS).//
                                           //0000 LCLC        OP1                                     LNTH= 004
                                           //     VAL=PACK
                                           //0001 LCLC        OP2                                     LNTH= 003
                                           //     VAL=STH
0000F6 F274 F170 F162 00170 00162   214+MOVEPH    PACK  DOUBLE,PACKED                                    01-00075
0000FC 4F00 F170            00170   215+          CVB   0,DOUBLE                                         01-00076
000100 4000 F160            00160   216+          STH   0,HALF                                           01-00077
                                    217           MHELP B'1001000'          MACRO HEX DUMP W/ EXIT TRACE
                                    218 MOVEPZ    MOVE  PACKED,ZONED
000104 F374 F167 F162 00167 00162   219+          UNPK  ZONED,PACKED                                     01-00096

                                           //MHELP EXIT FROM MOVE      MODEL STMT=00097 DEPTH=001 SYSNDX=0000021 KWCNT=002
                                           ////SET SYMBOLS (SKIPPED NUMBERS MAY BE SEQUENCE SYMBOLS).//
                                           //0000 LCLC        OP1                                     LNTH= 004
                                           //     VAL=PACK
                                           //0001 LCLC        OP2                                     LNTH= 003
                                           //     VAL=STH

                                    220           MHELP B'1010000'          MACRO HEX DUMP W/ ENTRY TRACE
                                    221 MOVEPP    MOVE  PACKED,PACKED

                                           //MHELP ENTRY TO  MOVE      MODEL STMT=00000 DEPTH=001 SYSNDX=0000022 KWCNT=002
                                           ////PARAMETERS (SYSNDX,SYSECT,SYSLOC,SYSTIME,SYSDATE,SYSPARM,NAME,KWS,PPS) ///
                                           //NUM  LNTH  VALUE (64 CHARS/LINE)
                                           //0000  004  0022
                                           //0001  NUL
```

```
LOC   OBJECT CODE    ADDR1 ADDR2  STMT   SOURCE STATEMENT                                   ASM H V 02 10.13 10/15/88
                                         //0002  NUL
                                         //0003  005   10.13
                                         //0004  008   10/15/88
                                         //0005  NUL
                                         //0006  006   MOVEPP
                                         //0007  006   DOUBLE
                                         //0008  001   0
                                         //0009  006   PACKED
                                         //0010  006   PACKED
00010A F844 F162 F162 00162 00162   222+MOVEPP   ZAP    PACKED,PACKED                                         01-00094
                                    223          MHELP  B'1011111'          ALL MACRO TRACE & DUMP OPTIONS
                                    224 NFACT    NFACT  3,DOUBLE
                                         ++//MHELP CALL TO MACRO NFACT       DEPTH=001   SYSNDX=0000023   STMT=00224

                                         //MHELP ENTRY TO  NFACT    MODEL STMT=00000 DEPTH=001 SYSNDX=0000023 KWCNT=000
                                         ////PARAMETERS (SYSNDX,SYSECT,SYSLOC,SYSTIME,SYSDATE,SYSPARM,NAME,KWS,PPS) ///
                                         //NUM   LNTH  VALUE (64 CHARS/LINE)
                                         //0000  004   0023
                                         //0001  NUL
                                         //0002  NUL
                                         //0003  005   10.13
                                         //0004  008   10/15/88
                                         //0005  NUL
                                         //0006  005   NFACT
                                         //0007  001   3
                                         //0008  006   DOUBLE

                                         //MHELP AIF IN    NFACT    MODEL STMT=00102 DEPTH=001 SYSNDX=0000023 KWCNT=000
                                         ////SET SYMBOLS (SKIPPED NUMBERS MAY BE SEQUENCE SYMBOLS).//
                                         //0000 GBLB       FIRST                                              VAL=0
                                         //0001 LCLA       X                                                  VAL=   0000000000
000110 F870 F170 F17A 00170 0017A   225+NFACT    ZAP    DOUBLE,=P'1'                                          01-00104
                                         //MHELP AIF IN    NFACT    MODEL STMT=00105 DEPTH=001 SYSNDX=0000023 KWCNT=000
                                         ////SET SYMBOLS (SKIPPED NUMBERS MAY BE SEQUENCE SYMBOLS).//
                                         //0000 GBLB       FIRST                                              VAL=1
                                         //0001 LCLA       X                                                  VAL=   0000000000
000116 FC70 F170 F17B 00170 0017B   226+         MP     DOUBLE,=P'3'                                          01-00106
                                         ++//MHELP CALL TO MACRO NFACT       DEPTH=002   SYSNDX=0000024   STMT=00108

                                         //MHELP ENTRY TO  NFACT    MODEL STMT=00000 DEPTH=002 SYSNDX=0000024 KWCNT=000
                                         ////PARAMETERS (SYSNDX,SYSECT,SYSLOC,SYSTIME,SYSDATE,SYSPARM,NAME,KWS,PPS) ///
                                         //NUM   LNTH  VALUE (64 CHARS/LINE)
                                         //0000  004   0024
                                         //0001  NUL
                                         //0002  NUL
                                         //0003  005   10.13
                                         //0004  008   10/15/88
                                         //0005  NUL
                                         //0006  NUL
                                         //0007  001   2
                                         //0008  006   DOUBLE

                                         //MHELP AIF IN    NFACT    MODEL STMT=00102 DEPTH=002 SYSNDX=0000024 KWCNT=000
                                         ////SET SYMBOLS (SKIPPED NUMBERS MAY BE SEQUENCE SYMBOLS).//
                                         //0000 GBLB       FIRST                                              VAL=1
                                         //0001 LCLA       X                                                  VAL=   0000000000

                                         ++//MHELP  BRANCH FROM STMT 00102 TO STMT 00105 IN MACRO NFACT
```

```
LOC    OBJECT CODE      ADDR1 ADDR2  STMT   SOURCE STATEMENT                                          ASM H V 02 10.13 10/15/88
                                            //MHELP AIF IN     NFACT    MODEL STMT=00105 DEPTH=002 SYSNDX=0000024 KWCNT=000
                                            ////SET SYMBOLS (SKIPPED NUMBERS MAY BE SEQUENCE SYMBOLS).//
                                            //0000 GBLB        FIRST                                    VAL=1
                                            //0001 LCLA        X                                        VAL=  0000000000
00011C FC70 F170 F17C 00170 0017C    227+          MP    DOUBLE,=P'2'                                            02-00106
                                            ++//MHELP CALL TO MACRO NFACT       DEPTH=003   SYSNDX=0000025   STMT=00108

                                            //MHELP ENTRY TO  NFACT    MODEL STMT=00000 DEPTH=003 SYSNDX=0000025 KWCNT=000
                                            ////PARAMETERS (SYSNDX,SYSECT,SYSLOC,SYSTIME,SYSDATE,SYSPARM,NAME,KWS,PPS) ///
                                            //NUM  LNTH  VALUE (64 CHARS/LINE)
                                            //0000  004  0025
                                            //0001  NUL
                                            //0002  NUL
                                            //0003  005  10.13
                                            //0004  008  10/15/88
                                            //0005  NUL
                                            //0006  NUL
                                            //0007  001  1
                                            //0008  006  DOUBLE

                                            //MHELP AIF IN     NFACT    MODEL STMT=00102 DEPTH=003 SYSNDX=0000025 KWCNT=000
                                            ////SET SYMBOLS (SKIPPED NUMBERS MAY BE SEQUENCE SYMBOLS).//
                                            //0000 GBLB        FIRST                                    VAL=1
                                            //0001 LCLA        X                                        VAL=  0000000000

                                            ++//MHELP  BRANCH FROM STMT 00102 TO STMT 00105 IN MACRO NFACT

                                            //MHELP AIF IN     NFACT    MODEL STMT=00105 DEPTH=003 SYSNDX=0000025 KWCNT=000
                                            ////SET SYMBOLS (SKIPPED NUMBERS MAY BE SEQUENCE SYMBOLS).//
                                            //0000 GBLB        FIRST                                    VAL=1
                                            //0001 LCLA        X                                        VAL=  0000000000

                                            ++//MHELP  BRANCH FROM STMT 00105 TO STMT 00111 IN MACRO NFACT

                                            //MHELP EXIT FROM NFACT    MODEL STMT=00112 DEPTH=003 SYSNDX=0000025 KWCNT=000
                                            ////SET SYMBOLS (SKIPPED NUMBERS MAY BE SEQUENCE SYMBOLS).//
                                            //0000 GBLB        FIRST                                    VAL=0
                                            //0001 LCLA        X                                        VAL=  0000000000

                                            //MHELP EXIT FROM NFACT    MODEL STMT=00109 DEPTH=002 SYSNDX=0000024 KWCNT=000
                                            ////SET SYMBOLS (SKIPPED NUMBERS MAY BE SEQUENCE SYMBOLS).//
                                            //0000 GBLB        FIRST                                    VAL=0
                                            //0001 LCLA        X                                        VAL=  0000000001

                                            //MHELP EXIT FROM NFACT    MODEL STMT=00109 DEPTH=001 SYSNDX=0000023 KWCNT=000
                                            ////SET SYMBOLS (SKIPPED NUMBERS MAY BE SEQUENCE SYMBOLS).//
                                            //0000 GBLB        FIRST                                    VAL=0
                                            //0001 LCLA        X                                        VAL=  0000000002

000122                               229 ALPHA    DS    PL5
000127                               230 BETA     DS    PL5
00012C                               231 GAMMA    DS    PL5
000131                               232 SUM      DS    PL5
000136                               233 Z        DS    PL5
00013B                               234 B1       DS    PL5
000140                               235 B2       DS    PL5
000145                               236 B3       DS    PL5
00014A                               237 C1       DS    PL5
00014F                               238 C2       DS    PL5
000154                               239 C3       DS    PL5
```

```
  LOC  OBJECT CODE    ADDR1 ADDR2  STMT   SOURCE STATEMENT                                     ASM H V 02 10.13 10/15/88

00015C                              240 FULL      DS    F
000160                              241 HALF      DS    H
000162                              242 PACKED    DS    PL5
000167                              243 ZONED     DS    ZL8
                                    244           AIF   (D'DOUBLE EQ 1).END

000170                              245 DOUBLE    DS    D
                                    246 .END      END
000178 010C                         247                 =P'10'
00017A 1C                           248                 =P'1'
00017B 3C                           249                 =P'3'
00017C 2C                           250                 =P'2'
```

```
                                    CROSS REFERENCE

SYMBOL    LEN     VALUE  DEFN  REFERENCES                                                     ASM H V 02 10.13 10/15/88

ALPHA     00005   000122 0229  0145 0152 0155 0157 0159
BETA      00005   000127 0230  0146 0153
B1        00005   00013B 0234  0156
B2        00005   000140 0235  0158
B3        00005   000145 0236  0160
C1        00005   00014A 0237  0155 0156
C2        00005   00014F 0238  0157 0158
C3        00005   000154 0239  0159 0160
DATE      00016   000058 0164
DOUBLE    00008   000170 0245  0171 0172 0175 0176 0184 0185 0188 0189 0192 0193 0197 0198 0202 0203 0209 0210 0214 0215
                               0225 0226 0227
FULL      00004   00015C 0240  0166 0166 0168 0170 0174 0179 0194 0211
GAMMA     00005   00012C 0231  0145 0146 0152 0153
HALF      00002   000160 0241  0168 0178 0181 0181 0183 0187 0199 0216
MOVEFF    00006   000068 0166
MOVEFH    00006   00006E 0168
MOVEFP    00004   000082 0174
MOVEFZ    00004   000074 0170
MOVEHF    00004   000090 0178
MOVEHH    00006   000098 0181
MOVEHP    00004   0000AC 0187
MOVEHZ    00004   00009E 0183
MOVEPF    00006   0000E8 0209
MOVEPH    00006   0000F6 0214
MOVEPP    00006   00010A 0222
MOVEZF    00006   0000BA 0192
MOVEZH    00006   0000C8 0197
MOVEZP    00006   0000E2 0206
MOVEZZ    00006   0000D6 0202
NFACT     00006   000110 0225
PACKED    00005   000162 0242  0176 0189 0206 0209 0214 0219 0222 0222
SUM       00005   000131 0232  0148 0149
TEST      00002   000018 0151
Z         00005   000136 0233  0148
ZONED     00008   000167 0243  0172 0185 0192 0197 0202 0203 0206 0219
=P'1'     00001   00017A 0248  0225
=P'10'    00002   000178 0247  0149
=P'2'     00001   00017C 0250  0227
=P'3'     00001   00017B 0249  0226
```

```
SAMPLE ASSEMBLER PROGRAM--SAMPLE7

  LOC  OBJECT CODE    ADDR1 ADDR2  STMT   SOURCE STATEMENT                                          ASM H V 02 07.59 01/04/89

                                      2 *********************************************************************
                                      3 * THIS PROGRAM DEMONSTRATES THE 'XDAP' MACRO FOR BUILDING AND EXE-    *
                                      4 * CUTION OF DIRECT ACCESS CHANNEL PROGRAMS.                          *
                                      5 *                                                                    *
                                      6 * ADDITIONALLY FACILITIES DEMONSTRATED ARE:                          *
                                      7 *                                                                    *
                                      8 * 1) THE 'DEVTYPE' MACRO TO OBTAIN DASD CHARACTERISTICS.             *
                                      9 *                                                                    *
                                     10 * 2) THE 'CVTPCNVT' ROUTINE TO CONVERT FROM RELATIVE TO ABSOLUTE     *
                                     11 *    DASD ADDRESSES.                                                 *
                                     12 *                                                                    *
                                     13 * 3) THE 'CVT' DSECT MACRO TO SYMBOLICALLY ACCESS FIELDS WITHIN THE  *
                                     14 *    CVT (COMMUNICATIONS VECTOR TABLE).                              *
                                     15 *                                                                    *
                                     16 * 4) THE 'DCBD' DSECT MACRO TO SYMBOLICALLY ACCESS FIELDS WITHIN THE *
                                     17 *    DCB.                                                            *
                                     18 *                                                                    *
                                     19 * 5) THE 'IEZIOB' DSECT MACRO TO SYMBOLICALLY ACCESS FIELDS WITHIN   *
                                     20 *    IOB (INPUT/OUTPUT BLOCK).                                       *
                                     21 *********************************************************************
000000                               23          START X'0'          ADJUST LOCATION COUNTER FOR MVS/XA
                                     24          PRINT NOGEN

                                     26 BEGIN    SAVE  (14,12)            SAVE REGISTERS
000004 05C0                          29          BALR  12,0               LOAD BASE REGISTER
                              00006  30          USING *,12               ESTABLISH ADDRESSABILITY
000006 50D0 C28E              00294  31          ST    13,SAVEAREA+4      SAVE ENTRY REGISTER
00000A 41D0 C28A              00290  32          LA    13,SAVEAREA        POINT TO SAVE AREA

                                     34          OPEN  (DISKIN,,PRINTER,OUTPUT)                               R 1
00001E 45B0 C32E              00334  42          BAL   11,HEADPAGE        GO PRINT PAGE HEADING
                                     43          DEVTYPE DDNAME,DASDINFO,DEVTAB GET DASD CHARACTERISTICS
00002E 4140 0005              00005  48          LA    4,5                SET WORD COUNT
000032 4130 C562              00568  49          LA    3,DASDINFO         POINT TO FIRST WORD
000036 D20B C5DB C442 005E1  00448  50          MVC   LINE+21(12),=C'DEVTYPE INFO'

00003C 45B0 C2FA              00300  52 INFOLOOP BAL   11,FORMAT          FORMAT DASD WORD
000040 4640 C036              0003C  53          BCT   4,INFOLOOP         CONTINUE FOR ALL WORDS

000044 9200 C59E        005A4        55          MVI   RC,0               INITIALIZE RETURN CODE
000048 5810 0010              00010  56          L     1,16               ADDR OF COMMUNICATIONS VECTOR TABLE
                              00000  57          USING CVT,1              ESTABLISH ADDRESSABILITY TO CVT
00004C 58F0 101C              0001C  58          L     15,CVTPCNVT        LOAD ADDRESS OF IECPCNVT)
                                     59          DROP  1                  DE-ESTABLISH ADDRESSABILITY TO CVT
000050 1700                          60          XR    0,0                INITIAL RELATIVE DASD ADDRESS (TTRN)  0)
000052 5810 C766              0076C  61          L     1,DISKIN+DCBDEBAD-DCBRELAD GET ADDR OF DEB FROM DCB
000056 4120 C3C2              003C8  62          LA    2,MBBCCHHR         POINT TO ABSOLUTE ADDRESS
00005A 908D C35A              00360  63          STM   8,13,SAVE8#13      SAVE WORK REGISTERS
00005E 188C                          64          LR    8,12               SAVE BASE REGISTER
000060 05EF                          65          BALR  14,15              CONVERT REL TTRN TO ABS MBBCCHHR      TE ADDR
000062 18C8                          66          LR    12,8               RESTORE BASE REGISTER
000064 988D C35A              00360  67          LM    8,13,SAVE8#13      RESTORE REGISTERS
000068 12FF                          68          LTR   15,15              VALID ADDRESS?
00006A 4770 C2D2              002D8  69          BNZ   EXTERROR            NO
```

```
SAMPLE ASSEMBLER PROGRAM--SAMPLE7

  LOC  OBJECT CODE    ADDR1 ADDR2  STMT   SOURCE STATEMENT                                    ASM H V 02 07.59 01/04/89

00006E 9620 C40E      00414          70          OI    INECB+64,X'20'      TURN ON SLI INDICATIOR (SUP INC LEN)
000072 1711                          71 READLOOP XR    1,1                 CLEAR REGISTER
000074 4310 C3C9            003CF    72          IC    1,RECORD            INSERT RECORD NUMBER
000078 4111 0001            00001    73          LA    1,1(1)              INCREMENT RECORD NUMBER
00007C 4210 C3C9            003CF    74          STC   1,RECORD            SAVE RECORD NUMBER
                                     75          PRINT GEN
                                     76          XDAP  INECB,,,,,,MBBCCHHR,MF=E READ DASD
000080 4110 C3D2            003D8    77+         LA    1,INECB+4                      LOAD IOB ADDRESS        01-XDAP
000084 D207 1020 C3C2 00020 003C8    78+         MVC   32(8,1),MBBCCHHR                 MOVE BLKREF TO IOB    01-XDAP
00008A 9601 1000      00000          79+         OI    0(1),X'01'                       SVC ISSUE EXCP Y02072 01-XDAP
00008E 0A00                          80+         SVC   0                                EXCP SVC              01-XDAP
                                     81          WAIT  ECB=INECB           WAIT FOR READ TO COMPLETE
000090 4110 C3CE            003D4    82+         LA    1,INECB                        LOAD PARAMETER REG 1    02-IHBIN
000094 4100 0001            00001    83+         LA    0,1(0,0)                   COUNT OMITTED 1 USED        01-WAIT
000098 0A01                          84+         SVC   1                              LINK TO WAIT ROUTINE    01-WAIT
                                     85          PRINT NOGEN
00009A 957F C3CE      003D4          86          CLI   INECB,X'7F'         ANY EXCEPTIONS
00009E 4780 C120            00126    87          BE    READOKAY             NO
0000A2 9542 C3CE      003D4          88          CLI   INECB,X'42'
0000A6 4780 C116            0011C    89          BE    EOE                  YES, END OF EXTENT

                                     90 *        B     ERROR                YES, OTHER

0000AA 4110 C3D2            003D8    92 ERROR    LA    1,INECB+4           POINT TO IOB
                            00010    93          USING IOBSTDRD,1          ESTABLISH ADDRESSABILITY
0000AE 910E 100C      0001C          94          TM    IOBUSTAT,X'E'       CHAN. END, DEVICE END, UNIT CHECK?
0000B2 47E0 C108            0010E    95          BNO   NOTINDEX             NO
                                     96          DROP  1                   DE-ESTABILISH ADDRESSABILITY
0000B6 D213 C5C6 C44E 005CC 00454    97          MVC   LINE(20),=C'*** END OF TRACK ***' SET INDICATOR
0000BC 45B0 C32C            00332    98          BAL   11,DOUBLESP         ALLOW FOR DOUBLE SPACE
0000C0 45B0 C314            0031A    99          BAL   11,PRINT            PRINT INDICATOR LINE
0000C4 1733                         100          XR    3,3                 CLEAR REGISTER
0000C6 BF33 C3C7            003CD   101          ICM   3,3,HEAD            INSERT CURRENT TRACK
0000CA 4133 0001            00001   102          LA    3,1(3)              INCREMENT TRACK
0000CE 4930 C56C            00572   103          CH    3,TRACKS            MAXIMUM TRACKS?
0000D2 4740 C0EC            000F2   104          BL    TRACKOK              NO
0000D6 D216 C5C6 C484 005CC 0048A   105          MVC   LINE(23),=C'*** END OF CYLINDER ***' SET INDICATOR
0000DC 45B0 C32C            00332   106          BAL   11,DOUBLESP         ALLOW FOR DOUBLE SPACE
0000E0 45B0 C314            0031A   107          BAL   11,PRINT            PRINT INDICATOR LINE
0000E4 BF33 C3C5            003CB   108          ICM   3,3,CYLINDER        INSERT CYLINDER NUMBER
0000E8 4133 0001            00001   109          LA    3,1(3)              INCREMENT CYLINDER
0000EC BE33 C3C5            003CB   110          STCM  3,3,CYLINDER        SAVE INCREMENTED VALUE
0000F0 1733                         111          XR    3,3                 INITIALIZE TRACK

0000F2 BE33 C3C7            003CD   113 TRACKOK  STCM  3,3,HEAD            SAVE UPDATED TRACK
0000F6 9200 C3C9      003CF         114          MVI   RECORD,0            INITIALIZE RECORD NUMBER
0000FA FA20 C59B C49B 005A1 004A1   115          AP    ERRORS,=P'1'        COUNT END OF TRACKS
000100 F921 C59B C46E 005A1 00474   116          CP    ERRORS,=P'20'       COUNT EXCEEDED
000106 4740 C06C            00072   117          BL    READLOOP            NO
00010A 47F0 C268            0026E   118          B     EOF                  YES

00010E D20C C5F8 C49C 005FE 004A2   120 NOTINDEX MVC   LINE+50(13),=C'ERROR OCCURED'
000114 9608 C59E      005A4         121          OI    RC,8                FLAG ERROR CONDITION
000118 47F0 C120            00126   122          B     READOKAY            GO DISPLAY DATA

00011C D20C C5F8 C4A9 005FE 004AF   124 EOE      MVC   LINE+50(13),=C'END OF EXTENT'
```

```
SAMPLE ASSEMBLER PROGRAM--SAMPLE7

  LOC  OBJECT CODE    ADDR1 ADDR2  STMT   SOURCE STATEMENT                                      ASM H V 02 07.59 01/04/89
000122 9604 C59E       005A4        125           OI    RC,4                 FLAG ERROR CONDITION

000126 FA20 C598 C49B 0059E 004A1   127 READOKAY AP    BLOCKS,=P'1'         INCREMENT BLOCK COUNT
00012C F384 C5B6 C3C2 005BC 003C8   128          UNPK  ABSADDR(9),MBBCCHHR(5) UNPACK FIRST 8 NYBLS (MBBC)
000132 F384 C5BE C3C6 005C4 003CC   129          UNPK  ABSADDR+8(9),MBBCCHHR+4(5) " SECOND 8 (CHHR)
000138 9240 C5C6       005CC        130          MVI   ABSADDR+16,C' '      CLEAR FOLLOWING BYTE
00013C D40F C5B6 C576 005BC 0057C   131          NC    ABSADDR,MASK         MASK OUT ZONE BITS
000142 DC0F C5B6 C586 005BC 0058C   132          TR    ABSADDR,HEX          CONVERT TO HEX DISPLAY
000148 D226 C5C7 C59F 005CD 005A5   133          MVC   LINE+1(LDETAIL1),DETAIL1 MOVE IMAGE TO PRINT LINE
00014E DE05 C5CC C598 005D2 0059E   134          ED    BLOCK-DETAIL1+LINE+1,BLOCKS FORMAT BLOCK COUNT
000154 45B0 C314             0031A  135          BAL   11,PRINT             PRINT DETAIL 1 LINE
000158 45B0 C32C             00332  136          BAL   11,DOUBLESP          ALLOW FOR DOUBLE SPACE
00015C D203 C5C6 C462 005CC 00468   137          MVC   LINE(4),=C'0ECB'     SET CC FOR DOUBLE SPACE, ECB ID
000162 4130 C3CE             003D4  138          LA    3,INECB              POINT TO ECB
000166 45B0 C2FA             00300  139          BAL   11,FORMAT            PRINT DETAIL 1 LINE
00016A 45B0 C32C             00332  140          BAL   11,DOUBLESP          ALLOW FOR DOUBLE SPACE
00016E D203 C5C6 C466 005CC 0046C   141          MVC   LINE(4),=C'0IOB'     SET CC FOR DOUBLE SPACE, ECB ID
000174 D222 C5D7 C4B6 005DD 004BC   142          MVC   LINE+17(35),=C'IOBFLAG1,IOBFLAG2,IOBSENS0,IOBSENS1'
00017A 45B0 C2FA             00300  143          BAL   11,FORMAT            GO FORMAT HEX NYBLS

00017E D201 C5CB C470 005D1 00476   145          MVC   LINE+5(2),=C'+4'     SET ID FOR SECOND WORD IOB
000184 D210 C5D7 C4D9 005DD 004DF   146          MVC   LINE+17(17),=C'IOBECBCC,IOBECBPT'
00018A 45B0 C2FA             00300  147          BAL   11,FORMAT            GO FORMAT HEX NYBLS

00018E D201 C5CB C472 005D1 00478   149          MVC   LINE+5(2),=C'+8'     SET ID FOR THIRD WORD OF IOB
000194 D212 C5D7 C4EA 005DD 004F0   150          MVC   LINE+17(19),=C'IOBFLAG3,IOBCSW 0-2'
00019A 45B0 C2FA             00300  151          BAL   11,FORMAT            GO FORMAT HEX NYBLS

00019E D202 C5CA C4FD 005D0 00503   153          MVC   LINE+4(3),=C'+12'    SET ID FOR FOURTH WORD OF IOB
0001A4 D209 C5D7 C474 005DD 0047A   154          MVC   LINE+17(10),=C'IOBCSW 3-6'
0001AA 45B0 C2FA             00300  155          BAL   11,FORMAT            GO FORMAT HEX NYBLS

0001AE D202 C5CA C500 005D0 00506   157          MVC   LINE+4(3),=C'+16'    SET ID FOR FIFTH WORD OF IOB
0001B4 D210 C5D7 C503 005DD 00509   158          MVC   LINE+17(17),=C'IOBSIOCC,IOBSTART'
0001BA 45B0 C2FA             00300  159          BAL   11,FORMAT            GO FORMAT HEX NYBLS

0001BE D202 C5CA C514 005D0 0051A   161          MVC   LINE+4(3),=C'+20'    SET ID FOR SIXTH WORD OF IOB
0001C4 D210 C5D7 C517 005DD 0051D   162          MVC   LINE+17(17),=C'RESERVED,IOBDCBPT'
0001CA 45B0 C2FA             00300  163          BAL   11,FORMAT            GO FORMAT HEX NYBLS

0001CE D202 C5CA C528 005D0 0052E   165          MVC   LINE+4(3),=C'+24'    SET ID FOR SEVENTH WORD OF IOB
0001D4 D207 C5D7 C412 005DD 00418   166          MVC   LINE+17(08),=C'IOBRESTR'
0001DA 45B0 C2FA             00300  167          BAL   11,FORMAT            GO FORMAT HEX NYBLS

0001DE D202 C5CA C52B 005D0 00531   169          MVC   LINE+4(3),=C'+28'    SET ID FOR EIGHTH WORD OF IOB
0001E4 D210 C5D7 C52E 005DD 00534   170          MVC   LINE+17(17),=C'IOBINCAM,IOBERRCT'
0001EA 45B0 C2FA             00300  171          BAL   11,FORMAT            GO FORMAT HEX NYBLS

0001EE D202 C5CA C53F 005D0 00545   173          MVC   LINE+4(3),=C'+32'    SET ID FOR NINETH WORD OF IOB
0001F4 D20A C5D7 C542 005DD 00548   174          MVC   LINE+17(11),=C'IOBSEEK 0-3'
0001FA 45B0 C2FA             00300  175          BAL   11,FORMAT            GO FORMAT HEX NYBLS

0001FE D202 C5CA C54D 005D0 00553   177          MVC   LINE+4(3),=C'+36'    SET ID FOR TENTH WORD OF IOB
000204 D20A C5D7 C550 005DD 00556   178          MVC   LINE+17(11),=C'IOBSEEK 4-7'
00020A 45B0 C2FA             00300  179          BAL   11,FORMAT            GO FORMAT HEX NYBLS
```

```
SAMPLE ASSEMBLER PROGRAM--SAMPLE7

  LOC  OBJECT CODE    ADDR1 ADDR2  STMT   SOURCE STATEMENT                                       ASM H V 02 07.59 01/04/89
00020E 45B0 C32C            00332   180          BAL   11,DOUBLESP             ALLOW FOR DOUBLE SPACE

000212 D205 C5C6 C47E 005CC 00484   182          MVC   LINE(6),=C'OCCW-1'     SET ID FOR CCWS
000218 45B0 C2E4            002EA   183          BAL   11,FORMAT2              FORMAT CCW-1
00021C 4133 0004            00004   184          LA    3,4(3)                  SKIP SECOND WORD OF CCW
000220 92F2 C5CB      005D1         185          MVI   LINE+5,C'2'             SET ID FOR CCW-2
000224 45B0 C2E4            002EA   186          BAL   11,FORMAT2              FORMAT CCW-2
000228 4133 0004            00004   187          LA    3,4(3)                  SKIP SECOND WORD OF CCW
00022C 92F3 C5CB      005D1         188          MVI   LINE+5,C'3'             SET ID FOR CCW-3
000230 45B0 C2E4            002EA   189          BAL   11,FORMAT2              FORMAT CCW-3
000234 45B0 C32C            00332   190          BAL   11,DOUBLESP             ALLOW FOR DOUBLE SPACE
000238 D204 C5C6 C55B 005CC 00561   191          MVC   LINE(5),=C'ODATA'
00023E 9836 C41A            00420   192          LM    3,6,=A(INAREA,4,INAREA+40,LINE+6)
000242 F384 6000 3000 00000 00000   193 DATALOOP UNPK  0(9,6),0(5,3)           UNPACK NYBLS OF DATA WORD
000248 D407 6000 C576 00000 0057C   194          NC    0(8,6),MASK             MASK OUT ZONE NYBLS
00024E DC07 6000 C586 00000 0058C   195          TR    0(8,6),HEX              CONVERT TO DISPLAY HEX
000254 9240 6008      00008         196          MVI   8(6),C' '               SET SEPARATOR
000258 4166 0009            00009   197          LA    6,9(6)                  POINT TO NEXT LINE POSITION
00025C 8734 C23C            00242   198          BXLE  3,4,DATALOOP            CONTINUE UNTIL LINE FORMATTED
000260 45B0 C314            0031A   199          BAL   11,PRINT                PRINT DATA LINE
000264 F921 C598 C46E 0059E 00474   200          CP    BLOCKS,=P'20'           LIMIT REACHED?
00026A 4740 C06C            00072   201          BL    READLOOP                 NO

00026E 17FF                         203 EOF      XR    15,15                   INITIALIZE RETURN CODE REGISTER
000270 43F0 C59E            005A4   204          IC    15,RC                   LOAD RETURN CODE
                                    205 WRAPUP   CLOSE (DISKIN,,PRINTER)
000282 58D0 C28E            00294   213 RETURN   L     13,SAVEAREA+4           RESTORE ENTRY REGISTER
                                    214          RETURN (14,12),RC=(15)        RESTORE REGISTERS/RETURN
000290 0000000000000000             218 SAVEAREA DC    18F'0'

0002D8 D217 C5C7 C42A 005CD 00430   220 EXTERROR MVC   LINE+1(24),=C'INVALID RELATIVE ADDRESS'
0002DE 45B0 C314            0031A   221          BAL   11,PRINT                PRINT ERROR MESSAGE
0002E2 41F0 000C            0000C   222          LA    15,12                   SET ERROR RETURN
0002E6 47F0 C26E            00274   223          B     WRAPUP                  GO EXIT


0002EA F384 C5D7 3004 005DD 00004   225 FORMAT2  UNPK  LINE+17(9),4(5,3)       UNPACK HEX NYBLS OF SECOND WORD
0002F0 D407 C5D7 C576 005DD 0057C   226          NC    LINE+17(8),MASK         CLEAR ZONE NYBLS
0002F6 DC07 C5D7 C586 005DD 0058C   227          TR    LINE+17(8),HEX          CONVERT TO DISPLAY HEX
0002FC 9240 C5DF      005E5         228          MVI   LINE+25,C' '            CLEAR TRAILING POSITION

000300 F384 C5CE 3000 005D4 00000   230 FORMAT   UNPK  LINE+8(9),0(5,3)        UNPACK HEX NYBLS
000306 D407 C5CE C576 005D4 0057C   231          NC    LINE+8(8),MASK          CLEAR ZONE NYBLS
00030C DC07 C5CE C586 005D4 0058C   232          TR    LINE+8(8),HEX           SET TO DISPLAY HEX
000312 9240 C5D6      005DC         233          MVI   LINE+16,C' '            CLEAR TRAILING POSITION
000316 4133 0004            00004   234          LA    3,4(3)                  POINT TO NEXT WORD

                                    236 PRINT    PUT   PRINTER,LINE            PRINT REPORT LINE
000328 9240 C5C6      005CC         241          MVI   LINE,C' '               SET SEED
00032C D283 C5C7 C5C6 005CD 005CC   242          MVC   LINE+1(L'LINE-1),LINE CLEAR TO BLANKS
000332 06AB                         243 DOUBLESP BCTR  10,11                   RETURN IF PAGE NOT FULL

000334 FA10 C596 C49B 0059C 004A1   245 HEADPAGE AP    PAGES,=P'1'             INCREMENT PAGE COUNT
00033A D203 C6CC C46A 006D2 00470   246          MVC   PAGENO,=X'40202120'     SET EDIT PATTTERN
000340 DE03 C6CC C596 006D2 0059C   247          ED    PAGENO,PAGES            FORMAT PAGE NUMBER
```

```
SAMPLE ASSEMBLER PROGRAM--SAMPLE7

  LOC  OBJECT CODE    ADDR1 ADDR2  STMT   SOURCE STATEMENT                                      ASM H V 02 07.59 01/04/89
                                    248              PUT   PRINTER,HEADING     PRINT PAGE HEADING
000354 41A0 0038            00038   253              LA    10,56               SET LINES/PAGE
000358 92F0 C5C6      005CC         254              MVI   LINE,C'0'           SET TO DOUBLE SPACE
00035C 07FB                         255              BR    11                  RETURN

000360                              257 SAVE8#13 DS    6F
000378                              258 INAREA   DS    CL80
0003C8                              259 MBBCCHHR DS    0D
0003C8 00                           260 EXTENT   DC    X'0'
0003C9 0000                         261          DC    2X'0'
0003CB 0064                         262 CYLINDER DC    AL2(100)
0003CD 0005                         263 HEAD     DC    AL2(5)
0003CF 03                           264 RECORD   DC    AL1(3)

                                    266          PRINT GEN
                                    267          XDAP  INECB,RI,DISKIN,INAREA,L'INAREA,,MBBCCHHR,,MF=L
0003D0 07000700                     268+         CNOP  4,8                                                01-XDAP
0003D4 00000000                     269+INECB    DC    1F'0'                    EVENT CONTROL BLOCK      01-XDAP
0003D8 42                           270+         DC    X'42'                     IOB START FLAG          01-XDAP
0003D9 00000000                     271+         DC    X'00000000'                                       01-XDAP
0003DD 0003D4                       272+         DC    AL3(INECB)                ECB ADDRESS             01-XDAP
0003E0 0000000000000000             273+         DC    2F'0'                     3RD WORD                01-XDAP
0003E8 00                           274+         DC    X'00'                     4TH WORD START          01-XDAP
0003E9 000400                       275+         DC    AL3(INECB+44)            CCW1 ADDRESS             01-XDAP
0003EC 00                           276+         DC    X'00'                                             01-XDAP
0003ED 000740                       277+         DC    AL3(DISKIN)               DCB ADDRESS             01-XDAP
0003F0 0000000000000000             278+         DC    2F'0'                     FIFTH DOUBLE WORD       01-XDAP
0003F8 0000000000000000             279+IHB0014  DC    2F'0'                     BLKREF FIELD            01-XDAP
000400 31                           280+IHB0014A DC    X'31'                     SET OPCODE IN CCW-1     01-XDAP
000401 0003FB                       281+         DC    AL3(IHB0014+3)            SET UP IOBSEEK+3        01-XDAP
000404 40                           282+         DC    X'40'                     FLAG BYTE               01-XDAP
000405 00                           283+         DC    X'00'                                             01-XDAP
000406 0005                         284+         DC    H'05'                     SET UP COUNT FIELD      01-XDAP
000408 08                           285+         DC    X'08'                     CCW2                    01-XDAP
000409 000400                       286+         DC    AL3(IHB0014A)                                     01-XDAP
00040C 00000000                     287+         DC    X'00000000'               2ND WD IN CCW2          01-XDAP
000410 0E                           288+         DC    AL1(14)                  CCW3 OPCODE              01-XDAP
000411 000378                       289+         DC    AL3(INAREA)               SET AREA ADDR IN CCW3   01-XDAP
000414 00                           290+         DC    X'00'                     FLAG BYTE IN CCW3       01-XDAP
000415 00                           291+         DC    X'00'                                             01-XDAP
000416 0050                         292+         DC    AL2(L'INAREA)            LENGTH IN CCW3           01-XDAP
                                    293          PRINT NOGEN
000418                              294          LTORG
000418 C9D6C2D9C5E2E3D9             295                =C'IOBRESTR'
000420 0000037800000004             296                =A(INAREA,4,INAREA+40,LINE+6)
000430 C9D5E5C1D3C9C440             297                =C'INVALID RELATIVE ADDRESS'
000448 C4C5E5E3E8D7C540             298                =C'DEVTYPE INFO'
000454 5C5C5C40C5D5C440             299                =C'*** END OF TRACK ***'
000468 F0C5C3C2                     300                =C'0ECB'
00046C F0C9D6C2                     301                =C'0IOB'
000470 40202120                     302                =X'40202120'
000474 020C                         303                =P'20'
000476 4EF4                         304                =C'+4'
000478 4EF8                         305                =C'+8'
00047A C9D6C2C3E2E640F3             306                =C'IOBCSW 3-6'
```

```
SAMPLE ASSEMBLER PROGRAM--SAMPLE7

  LOC  OBJECT CODE    ADDR1 ADDR2  STMT   SOURCE STATEMENT                                         ASM H V 02 07.59 01/04/89

000484 F0C3C3E660F1                 307                  =C'OCCW-1'
00048A 5C5C5C40C5D5C440             308                  =C'*** END OF CYLINDER ***'
0004A1 1C                           309                  =P'1'
0004A2 C5D9D9D6D940D6C3             310                  =C'ERROR OCCURED'
0004AF C5D5C440D6C640C5             311                  =C'END OF EXTENT'
0004BC C9D6C2C6D3C1C7F1             312                  =C'IOBFLAG1,IOBFLAG2,IOBSENS0,IOBSENS1'
0004DF C9D6C2C5C3C2C3C3             313                  =C'IOBECBCC,IOBECBPT'
0004F0 C9D6C2C6D3C1C7F3             314                  =C'IOBFLAG3,IOBCSW 0-2'
000503 4EF1F2                       315                  =C'+12'
000506 4EF1F6                       316                  =C'+16'
000509 C9D6C2E2C9D6C3C3             317                  =C'IOBSIOCC,IOBSTART'
00051A 4EF2F0                       318                  =C'+20'
00051D D9C5E2C5D9E5C5C4             319                  =C'RESERVED,IOBDCBPT'
00052E 4EF2F4                       320                  =C'+24'
000531 4EF2F8                       321                  =C'+28'
000534 C9D6C2C9D5C3C1D4             322                  =C'IOBINCAM,IOBERRCT'
000545 4EF3F2                       323                  =C'+32'
000548 C9D6C2E2C5C5D240             324                  =C'IOBSEEK 0-3'
000553 4EF3F6                       325                  =C'+36'
000556 C9D6C2E2C5C5D240             326                  =C'IOBSEEK 4-7'
000561 F0C4C1E3C1                   327                  =C'ODATA'
000568                              328 DASDINFO DS      2F
000570                              329 CYLS     DS      H
000572                              330 TRACKS   DS      H
000574                              331          DS      2F
00057C 0F0F0F0F0F0F0F0F             332 MASK     DC      16X'F'
00058C F0F1F2F3F4F5F6F7             333 HEX      DC      C'0123456789ABCDEF'
00059C 000C                         334 PAGES    DC      PL2'0'
00059E 00000C                       335 BLOCKS   DC      PL3'0'
0005A1 00000C                       336 ERRORS   DC      PL3'0'
0005A4                              337 RC       DS      X
0005A5 C2D3D6C3D2                   338 DETAIL1  DC      C'BLOCK'
0005AA 4020202021204B40             339 BLOCK    DC      X'402020202120',C'.  MBBCCHHR='
0005BC                              340 ABSADDR  DS      CL16
                            00027   341 LDETAIL1 EQU     *-DETAIL1
0005CC F140404040404040             342 LINE     DC      CL133'1'
000651 F140404040404040             343 HEADING  DC      CL133'1'                                         00318
0006D6                      00652   344          ORG     HEADING+1                                        00319
000652 E7C4C1D740C961D6             345          DC      C'XDAP I/O TEST'
00065F                      006CE   346          ORG     HEADING+L'HEADING-8
0006CE D7C1C7C5                     347          DC      C'PAGE'
0006D2                              348 PAGENO   DS      CL4
0006D6                      006D6   349          ORG

                                    351 PRINTER  DCB     DDNAME=PRINTER,DSORG=PS,MACRF=PM,LRECL=133,BLKSIZE=133, -
                                                         RECFM=FBA

000738 C4C9E2D2C9D54040             406 DDNAME   DC      CL8'DISKIN'
                                    407 DISKIN   DCB     DDNAME=DISKIN,MACRF=(E),DSORG=PS,DEVD=DA,EODAD=EOF
                                    439          PRINT   GEN
```

```
SAMPLE ASSEMBLER PROGRAM--SAMPLE7

LOC    OBJECT CODE    ADDR1 ADDR2  STMT   SOURCE STATEMENT                                     ASM H V 02 07.59 01/04/89
                                   441          DCBD   DEVD=DA              DATA CONTROL BLOCK DSECT
                                   442+*,***   IHB068  NO VALID DSORG SPECIFIED-EXCP ASSUMED                      02-IHBER

                                   444+*                               DCB SYMBOLIC DEFINITION FOR
                                   445+*                               EXCP WITH EXTENSION

000000                             447+IHADCB    DSECT , -                  DCBPTR                          @ZA05613 01-DCBD

                                   449+*
                                   450+*******************************************************************************
                                   451+*DATA CONTROL BLOCK DEFINITION
                                   452+*
                                   453+*$MAC(DCBD):
                                   454+*
                                   455+*   STATUS - MVS/XA DFP RELEASE 2.0
                                   456+*
                                   457+*******************************************************************************

                        00080      459+DCBBIT0   EQU   128                                                  @ZA05613 01-DCBD
                        00040      460+DCBBIT1   EQU   64                                                   @ZA05613 01-DCBD
                        00020      461+DCBBIT2   EQU   32                                                   @ZA05613 01-DCBD
                        00010      462+DCBBIT3   EQU   16                                                   @ZA05613 01-DCBD
                        00008      463+DCBBIT4   EQU   8                                                    @ZA05613 01-DCBD
                        00004      464+DCBBIT5   EQU   4                                                    @ZA05613 01-DCBD
                        00002      465+DCBBIT6   EQU   2                                                    @ZA05613 01-DCBD
                        00001      466+DCBBIT7   EQU   1                                                    @ZA05613 01-DCBD
                                   468+*******************************************************************************

                                   470+*******************************************************************************
                                   471+*                             DEVICE INTERFACES
                                   472+*******************************************************************************

                                   474+*******************************************************************************
                                   475+*                             DIRECT ACCESS DEVICES
                                   476+*******************************************************************************
000000                             478+DCBRELAD DS    CL4 -          PARTITIONED ORGANIZATION DATA SET -        01-DCBD
                                   479+*                             ADDRESS (IN THE FORM TTRN) OF MEMBER
                                   480+*                             CURRENTLY USED.  ---
                                   481+*                             SYS1.LOGREC DATA SET - IF CCH OPTION HAS
                                   482+*                             BEEN SPECIFIED IN SYSGEN PROCESS, ADDRESS
                                   483+*                             OF A 12-BYTE PARAMETER IN THE EXPANSION
                                   484+*                             OF MACRO INSTRUCTION IGFCATAP
000004                             485+DCBKEYCN DS    FL1 -          KEYED BLOCK OVERHEAD CONSTANT              01-DCBD
000005                             486+DCBFDAD  DS    CL8 -          FULL DISK ADDRESS IN THE FORM OF MBBCCHHR  01-DCBD
                                   487+*                             OF RECORD THAT WAS JUST READ OR WRITTEN

00000D                  0000C      489+          ORG   DCBFDAD+7                                            01-DCBD
00000C                             490+DCBDVTBL DS    0A -           SAME AS DCBDVTBA BELOW                     01-DCBD
00000C                             491+          DS    X -           LAST BYTE OF DCBFDAD                       01-DCBD
```

Pages 9-13 contain only unreferenced DCB expansions and are deleted.

```
SAMPLE ASSEMBLER PROGRAM--SAMPLE7

  LOC  OBJECT CODE    ADDR1 ADDR2  STMT   SOURCE STATEMENT                                         ASM H V 02 07.59 01/04/89
                            00001   767+DCBMRDMD EQU   DCBBIT7 -        DATA MODE (QSAM)                               01-DCBD
                            00001   768+DCBMRSTI EQU   DCBBIT7 -        SETL BY ID (QISAM) ---                         01-DCBD
                                    769+*                               ALWAYS ZERO (BISAM) ---
                                    770+*                               RESERVED (BPAM, QTAM, BTAM)
                                    771+*        AIF   (NOT &DSORGXE).C8A8                                     @L1A
                            00034   772+DCBLNGXE EQU   *-IHADCB         LENGTH OF DCB FOR EXCP WITH            @L1A 01-DCBD
                                    773+*                               EXTENSION INTERFACE                    @L1A

                                    775+*******************************************************************
                                    776+*                        FOUNDATION AFTER OPEN
                                    777+*******************************************************************
000034                      00028   779+         ORG   IHADCB+40                                                     01-DCBD
000028                              780+DCBTIOT  DS    AL2              OFFSET FROM TIOT ORIGIN TO TIOELNGH FIELD    01-DCBD
                                    781+*                               IN TIOT ENTRY FOR DD STATEMENT ASSOCIATED
                                    782+*                               WITH THIS DCB
00002A                              783+DCBMACRF DS    OBL2 -           SAME AS DCBMACR BEFORE OPEN                  01-DCBD
00002A                              784+DCBMACF1 DS    BL1 -            FIRST BYTE OF DCBMACRF                       01-DCBD
00002B                              785+DCBMACF2 DS    BL1 -            SECOND BYTE OF DCBMACRF                      01-DCBD
00002C                              786+DCBDEBAD DS    OA -             ADDRESS OF ASSOCIATED DEB                    01-DCBD
00002C                              787+DCBIFLGS DS    BL1 -            SAME AS DCBIFLG BEFORE OPEN                  01-DCBD
                            000C0   788+DCBIFEC  EQU   DCBBIT0+DCBBIT1 - ERROR CORRECTION INDICATOR                  01-DCBD
                            00030   789+DCBIFPCT EQU   DCBBIT2+DCBBIT3 - PRINTER CARRIAGE TAPE PUNCH INDICATOR       01-DCBD
                            0000C   790+DCBIFIOE EQU   DCBBIT4+DCBBIT5 - IOS ERROR ROUTINE USE INDICATOR             01-DCBD
                            00002   791+DCBIFLDT EQU   DCBBIT6 -        POSSIBLE LOST DATA CONDITION       @42480LP  01-DCBD
                                    792+*                               SUCH AS FOR A PRINTER              @42480LP
00002D                              793+DCBDEBA  DS    AL3 -            ADDRESS OF ASSOCIATED DEB                    01-DCBD


000030                      00034   797+         ORG   IHADCB+52                                                     01-DCBD
000034                              798+DCBOPTCD DS    OBL1 -                     OPTION CODE                        01-DCBD
                                    801          CVT   DSECT=YES,LIST=YES  COMMUNICATIONS VECTOR TABLE DSECT
                                    802+*%CVTL1 : ;
                                    803+*/*                                                                  */
                                    804+*/*       COMMUNICATION VECTOR TABLE                                 */
                                    805+*/*                                                                  */
                                    806+*/*   COPYRIGHT=                                                @P7C*/
                                    807+*/*       5740-XC6                                                   */
                                    808+*/*       CONTAINS RESTRICTED MATERIALS OF IBM                       */
                                    809+*/*       (C) COPYRIGHT IBM CORP. 1977, 1986                         */
                                    810+*/*       LICENSED MATERIALS - PROPERTY OF IBM                       */
                                    811+*/*       REFER TO COPYRIGHT INSTRUCTIONS                            */
                                    812+*/*       FORM NUMBER G120-2083.                                     */
                                    813+*/*                                                                  */
                                    814+*/*   STATUS= OS/VS2 JBB2220                                    @P7C*/
                                    815+*/*                                                                  */
                                    816+*/*   METHOD OF ACCESS                                               */
                                    817+*/*       PL/S - DCL CVTPTR PTR                                      */
                                    818+*/*       BAL  - DSECT=YES SHOULD BE SPECIFIED ON MACRO CALL EXCEPT  */
                                    819+*/*              WHEN CALLED BY IEAVCVT TO CREATE CSECT.  CVT FOR    */
                                    820+*/*              OS/VS2 IS MAPPED UNLESS SYS=AOS1 IS SPECIFIED.  THE */
                                    821+*/*              PREFIX IS NOT MAPPED UNLESS PREFIX=YES IS SPECIFIED.*/
                                    822+*/*              A USING ON CVTMAP OR DSECT NAME WILL ESTABLISH      */
                                    823+*/*              ADDRESSABILITY FOR ALL SYMBOLS EXCEPT IN THE 2      */
                                    824+*/*              EXTENSIONS.  TO ESTABLISH ADDRESSABILITY FOR THE    */
                                    825+*/*              OS - OS/VS COMMON EXTENSION, YOU SHOULD CODE        */
                                    826+*/*                                                                  */
                                    827+*/*              L      REG,CVTEXT1                                  */
                                    828+*/*              USING CVTXTNT1,REG                                  */
                                    829+*/*                                                                  */
                                    830+*/*              TO ESTABLISH ADDRESSABILITY FOR THE OS/VS2          */
                                    831+*/*              COMMON EXTENSION, YOU SHOULD CODE                   */
                                    832+*/*                                                                  *
```

```
SAMPLE ASSEMBLER PROGRAM--SAMPLE7

  LOC  OBJECT CODE    ADDR1 ADDR2  STMT   SOURCE STATEMENT                                              ASM H V 02 07.59 01/04/89

                                   833+*/*              L      REG,CVTEXT2                                     */
                                   834+*/*              USING CVTXTNT2,REG                                     */
                                   835+*/*                                                                     */
                                   836+*/*              WHERE REG IN EITHER CASE IS ANY REGISTER OTHER         */
                                   837+*/*              THAN ZERO.                                             */
                                   838+*/*                                                                     */
                                   839+*/*              WHEN LISTING IS SUPPRESSED, YOU CAN DETERMINE WHICH    */
                                   840+*/*              DSECT A SYMBOL IS IN BY USING THE STATEMENT NUMBER     */
                                   841+*/*              IN THE DEFN COLUMN IN THE CROSS REFERENCE LISTING.     */
                                   842+*/*              FOR EXAMPLE, ANY SYMBOL DEFINED BETWEEN THE            */
                                   843+*/*              STATEMENT NUMBERS FOR CVTXTNT1 AND CVTXTNT2 IS IN      */
                                   844+*/*              THE OS - OS/VS COMMON EXTENSION.                       */
                                   845+*/*                                                                     */
                                   846+*/*  F.E.'S                                                             */
                                   847+*/*      MICROFICHE LISTING - CVT                                       */
                                   848+*/*                                                                     */
                                   849+*/*  DEVELOPERS                                                         */
                                   850+*/*      BAL LISTING  - SPECIFY LIST=YES ON MACRO CALL                  */
                                   851+*/*      PL/S LISTING - SPECIFY %IHALIST='YES' BEFORE INCLUDE           */
                                   852+*/*                                                                     */
                                   853+*/*      FOR INTEGRATION, A LISTING MUST NOT BE REQUESTED UNLESS        */
                                   854+*/*      YOUR MODULE CREATES THE CSECT.                                 */
                                   855+*
                                   856+*%GOTO CVTL2;   /*
                                   857+         PUSH  PRINT                                                       01-CVT
                      00010        858+CVTPTR   EQU   16 -          ABSOLUTE ADDRESS OF POINTER TO CVT            01-CVT
                                   859+*
                                   860+*              BEGINNING OF CVT PROPER
                                   861+*
000000                             862+CVT      DSECT                                                             01-CVT
                      00000        863+CVTMAP   EQU   * -           CVTPTR CONTENT POINTS HERE                    01-CVT
                                   864+*
000000 00000000                    865+CVTTCBP  DC    V(IEATCBP) -  ADDRESS OF A DOUBLE WORD, THE FIRST           01-CVT
                                   866+*                            CONTAINING THE NEXT-TO-BE-DISPATCHED TCB
                                   867+*                            ADDRESS, THE SECOND CONTAINING THE LAST
                                   868+*                            (CURRENT) TCB ADDRESS.  BOTH WORDS ARE
                                   869+*                            IDENTICAL UNLESS THE TASK GOES INTO A
                                   870+*                            WAIT STATE.  WHEN IN A WAIT STATE, THE
                                   871+*                            FIRST WORD IS SET TO ZERO UNTIL THE
                                   872+*                            WAITING IS OVER AND THEN BOTH WORDS ARE
                                   873+*                            ONCE AGAIN IDENTICAL.
                                   874+*                            ADDRESS OF 4-WORD LIST OF ADDRESSES -
                                   875+*                            THE NEXT TCB, THE CURRENT TCB, THE NEXT
                                   876+*                            ASCB AND THE CURRENT ASCB, IN THAT
                                   877+*                            ORDER                               MDC026
000004 00000000                    878+CVTOEF00 DC    V(IEAOEF00) - ADDRESS OF ROUTINE TO SCHEDULE                01-CVT
                                   879+*                            ASYNCHRONOUS EXITS
000008 00000000                    880+CVTLINK  DC    V(IEFLINK) -  ADDRESS OF DCB FOR SYS1.LINKLIB DATA SET      01-CVT
00000C 00000000                    881+CVTAUSCB DC    V(IEFAUSDM) - ADDRESS OF ASSIGN/UNASSIGN SERVICE     @H1A   01-CVT
                                   882+*                            DATA MODULE.                         @H1A
000010 00000000                    883+CVTBUF   DC    A(0) -        ADDRESS OF THE BUFFER OF THE RESIDENT         01-CVT
                                   884+*                            CONSOLE INTERRUPT ROUTINE
000014 00000000                    885+CVTXAPG  DC    V(IECXAPG) -  ADDRESS OF I/O SUPERVISOR APPENDAGE VECTOR    01-CVT
                                   886+*                            TABLE
000018 00000000                    887+CVTOVL00 DC    V(IEAOVL00) - ADDRESS OF ENTRY POINT OF THE TASK            01-CVT
                                   888+*                            SUPERVISOR'S ADDRESS VALIDITY CHECKING
```

```
SAMPLE ASSEMBLER PROGRAM--SAMPLE7

  LOC  OBJECT CODE    ADDR1 ADDR2  STMT   SOURCE STATEMENT                                     ASM H V 02 07.59 01/04/89
                                   889+*                                  ROUTINE
00001C 00000000                    890+CVTPCNVT DC    V(IECPCNVT) - ADDRESS OF ENTRY POINT OF THE ROUTINE       01-CVT
                                   891+*                                  WHICH CONVERTS A RELATIVE TRACK ADDRESS
                                   892+*                                  (TTR) TO AN ABSOLUTE TRACK ADDRESS
                                   893+*                                  (MBBCCHHR)
000020 00000000                    894+CVTPRLTV DC    V(IECPRLTV) - ADDRESS OF ENTRY POINT OF THE ROUTINE       01-CVT
                                   895+*                                  WHICH CONVERTS AN ABSOLUTE TRACK ADDRESS
                                   896+*                                  (MBBCCHHR) TO A RELATIVE TRACK ADDRESS
                                   897+*                                  (TTR)
000024 00000000                    898+CVTLLCB  DC    V(CSVLLCB) -  ADDRESS OF THE LLCB.                   @P1M 01-CVT
000028 00000000                    899+CVTLLTRM DC    V(CSVLLTRM) - ADDRESS OF LLA'S MEMORY TERNIMATION    @P1M 01-CVT
                                   900+*                                  RESOURCE MANAGER.                      @P1M
00002C 00000000                    901+CVTXTLER DC    V(IECXTLER) - ADDRESS OF ERROR RECOVERY PROCEDURE (ERP)   01-CVT
                                   902+*                                  LOADER (IECVERPL) ENTRY POINT IECXTLER
                                   903+*                                  (MDC349)                          @Z40AQ9A
000030 00000000                    904+CVTSYSAD DC    A(0) -        UCB ADDRESS FOR THE SYSTEM RESIDENCE      01-CVT
                                   905+*                                  VOLUME               (MDCXXX) @G860PVB
000034 00000000                    906+CVTBTERM DC    V(IEAVTRG1) - ADDRESS OF ENTRY POINT OF THE ABTERM        01-CVT
                                   907+*                                  ROUTINE                 @(DCR854) @G860P46
000038 00000000                    908+CVTDATE  DC    F'0' -        CURRENT DATE IN PACKED DECIMAL             01-CVT
00003C 00000000                    909+CVTMSLT  DC    V(IEEMSER) -  ADDRESS OF THE MASTER COMMON AREA IN        01-CVT
                                   910+*                                  MASTER SCHEDULER RESIDENT DATA AREA.
```

Pages 17-33 contain only unreferenced CVT expansions and are deleted.

```
                                  1822          IEZIOB DSECT=YES          INPUT/OUTPUT BLOCK TABLE DSECT
                                  1823+*%IOBL1 : ;
                                  1824+*
                                  1825+*/*              INPUT/OUTPUT BLOCK                                  */
                                  1826+*/*                                                                  */
                                  1827+*/*   OS/VS2 SU30, 01/18/77, LEVEL=1                                 */
                                  1828+*/*                                                                  */
                                  1829+*/*   METHOD OF ACCESS                                               */
                                  1830+*/*       BAL  - DSECT IS PRODUCED UNLESS DSECT=NO IS SPECIFIED.     */
                                  1831+*/*              USING ON IOB GIVES ADDRESSABILITY FOR ALL SYMBOLS.  */
                                  1832+*/*       PL/S - DCL (IOBPRPTR,IOBSTPTR) PTR                         */
                                  1833+*/*                                                                  */
                                  1834+*%GOTO IOBL2;  /*
000000                            1836+IOB      DSECT , -       IOBSTDRD-16                                 01-IEZIO
                                  1838+*********************************************************************
                                  1839+*                                                                   *
                                  1840+*                          PREFIX SECTIONS OF THE IOB               *
                                  1841+*                                                                   *
                                  1842+*********************************************************************
000000                            1844+IOBPREFX DS    0D                                                    01-IEZIO
                                  1846+*                            ***************************************
                                  1847+*                            *                                     *
                                  1848+*                            *        QSAM,BSAM,BPAM PREFIX        *
                                  1849+*                            *   CHAINED SCHEDULING *** 16 BYTES   *
                                  1850+*                            *                                     *
                                  1851+*                            ***************************************
000000                            1853+IOBQSAMC DS    0D                                                    01-IEZIO
000000                            1854+IOBBSAMC DS    0D                                                    01-IEZIO
000000                            1855+IOBBPAMC DS    0D                                                    01-IEZIO
000000                            1856+IOBCFLG1 DS    B -       I/O INDICATORS                              01-IEZIO
                      00080       1857+IOBV6CHN EQU   X'80' -   I/O CHAINED BIT SET BY IGG019V6   @ZA56251  01-IEZIO
```

```
SAMPLE ASSEMBLER PROGRAM--SAMPLE7

  LOC  OBJECT CODE    ADDR1 ADDR2  STMT   SOURCE STATEMENT                                              ASM H V 02 07.59 01/04/89

                            00040 1858+IOBRSV02 EQU   X'40',,C'X'  RESERVED                                        01-IEZIO
                            00020 1859+IOBRSV03 EQU   X'20',,C'X'  RESERVED                                        01-IEZIO
                            00010 1860+IOBRSV04 EQU   X'10',,C'X'  RESERVED                                        01-IEZIO
                            00008 1861+IOBPTST  EQU   X'08' -   NOTE OR POINT OPERATION IS IN PROCESS             01-IEZIO
                            00004 1862+IOBABAPP EQU   X'04' -   ERROR HAS BEEN PROCESSED ONCE BY ABNORMAL-END     01-IEZIO
                                  1863+*                        APPENDAGE ROUTINE
                            00002 1864+IOBRSTCH EQU   X'02' -   RESTART CHANNEL                                   01-IEZIO
                            00001 1865+IOBPCI   EQU   X'01' -   SET WHEN A PROGRAM-CONTROLLED INTERRUPTION        01-IEZIO
                                  1866+*                        (PCI) OCCURS
000001                            1867+IOBRSV05 DS    XL1 -     RESERVED                                          01-IEZIO
000002                            1868+IOBCINOP DS    CL1 -     OFFSET OF THE LAST I/O COMMAND FOR INPUT          01-IEZIO
                                  1869+*                        OPERATION (NOP CCW) FROM THE ORIGIN OF THE ICB
000003                            1870+IOBCONOP DS    CL1 -     OFFSET OF THE LAST I/O COMMAND FOR AN OUTPUT      01-IEZIO
                                  1871+*                        OPERATION (NOP CCW) FROM THE ORIGIN OF THE ICB
000004                            1872+IOBCECB  DS    F -       EVENT CONTROL BLOCK USED BY BSAM OR QSAM.         01-IEZIO
                                  1873+*                        SHOWS THE STATUS OF THE I/O OPERATION.
000008                            1874+IOBCICB  DS    A -       ADDRESS OF THE FIRST INTERRUPT CONTROL BLOCK      01-IEZIO
                                  1875+*                        (ICB) ON THE ICB QUEUE
00000C                            1876+IOBCNOPA DS    A -       ADDRESS OF THE NOP COMMAND AT THE END OF THE      01-IEZIO
                                  1877+*                        QUEUE

000010                      00008 1879+         ORG   IOBPREFX+8                                                    01-IEZIO
                                  1881+*                           ****************************************
                                  1882+*                           *                                      *
                                  1883+*                           *        QSAM,BSAM,BPAM PREFIX         *
                                  1884+*                           *   NORMAL SCHEDULING *** 8 BYTES      *
                                  1885+*                           *                                      *
                                  1886+*                           ****************************************
000008                            1888+IOBQSAMN DS    0D                                                        01-IEZIO
000008                            1889+IOBBSAMN DS    0D                                                        01-IEZIO
000008                            1890+IOBBPAMN DS    0D                                                        01-IEZIO
000008                            1891+IOBNIOBA DS    0A -      ADDRESS OF THE NEXT IOB ASSOCIATED WITH ONE       01-IEZIO
                                  1892+*                        PARTICULAR DCB.  THE IOB'S ARE CHAINED IN
                                  1893+*                        SEQUENTIAL ORDER.
000008                            1894+IOBNFLG1 DS    B -       FLAG BYTE                                         01-IEZIO
                            00080 1895+IOBPRTOV EQU   X'80' -   PRTOV HAS OCCURRED (PRINTER DEVICES)              01-IEZIO
                                  1896+*                        (MDC331)                           @Z40FP9A
                            00080 1897+IOBSEGMT EQU   X'80' -   SEGMENTING OF A SPANNED RECORD IS IN PROCESS      01-IEZIO
                                  1898+*                        (QSAM LOCATE MODE, LOGICAL RECORD INTERFACE,
                                  1899+*                        UPDATE PROCESSING) (DIRECT ACCESS) (OS/VS2)
                                  1900+*                        (MDC332)                           @Z40FP9A
                            00040 1901+IOBWRITE EQU   X'40' -   A WRITE OPERATION IS IN PROCESS                   01-IEZIO
                            00020 1902+IOBREAD  EQU   X'20' -   A READ OPERATION IS IN PROCESS                    01-IEZIO
                            00010 1903+IOBUPDAT EQU   X'10' -   UPDATE FLAG.  SET ON TOGETHER WITH BIT 1 OF       01-IEZIO
                                  1904+*                        THIS BYTE TO SHOW THAT THE BLOCK IS TO BE
                                  1905+*                        UPDATED.  CAN ONLY OCCUR IF THE OPEN
                                  1906+*                        PARAMETER IS UPDAT.
                            00008 1907+IOBBKSPC EQU   X'08' -   IOB BEING USED FOR BACKSPACE, CONTROL OR          01-IEZIO
                                  1908+*                        NOTE/POINT OPERATION
                            00004 1909+IOBSPAN  EQU   X'04' -   THE RECORD CURRENTLY BEING PROCESSED HAS MORE     01-IEZIO
                                  1910+*                        THAN ONE SEGMENT (QSAM LOCATE MODE, LOGICAL
                                  1911+*                        RECORD INTERFACE, UPDATE PROCESSING OF
                                  1912+*                        SPANNED RECORDS)
                            00002 1913+IOBUPERR EQU   X'02' -   UPDATE CHANNEL PROGRAM HAS BEEN SPLIT INTO        01-IEZIO
                                  1914+*                        TWO PARTS                             MDC036
                            00001 1915+IOBFIRST EQU   X'01' -   THIS IS THE FIRST IOB ON CHAIN                    01-IEZIO
000009                            1916+IOBNIOBB DS    AL3 -     ADDRESS OF THE NEXT IOB ASSOCIATED WITH ONE       01-IEZIO
                                  1917+*                        PARTICULAR DCB.  THE IOB'S ARE CHAINED IN
                                  1918+*                        SEQUENTIAL ORDER.
00000C                            1919+IOBNECB  DS    F -       EVENT CONTROL BLOCK USED BY QSAM TO INDICATE      01-IEZIO
                                  1920+*                        THE STATUS OF THE I/O EVENT
```

```
SAMPLE ASSEMBLER PROGRAM--SAMPLE7

  LOC  OBJECT CODE    ADDR1 ADDR2  STMT   SOURCE STATEMENT                                       ASM H V 02 07.59 01/04/89

000010                      00008  1922+          ORG   IOBPREFX+8                                             01-IEZIO
                                   1924+*                               ***************************************
                                   1925+*                               *                                     *
                                   1926+*                               *      BDAM PREFIX *** 8 BYTES        *
                                   1927+*                               *                                     *
                                   1928+*                               ***************************************
000008                             1930+IOBBDAM   DS    0D                                                      01-IEZIO
000008                             1931+IOBDQADA  DS    0A -      ADDRESS OF THE OTHER IOB REFERRED TO IN      01-IEZIO
                                   1932+*                         DESCRIPTION OF IOBDEQ BELOW
000008                             1933+IOBDEQIN  DS    B -       DEQUEUE LOOP INDICATOR                        01-IEZIO
                            00080  1934+IOBDEQ    EQU   X'80' -   THIS IOB IS USING A TRACK THAT WAS DEQUEUED BY 01-IEZIO
                                   1935+*                         ANOTHER IOB WHICH IS NOW WAITING TO DEQUEUE
                                   1936+*                         ANOTHER TRACK.  THE OTHER IOB ENQUEUED ON TWO
                                   1937+*                         OR MORE TRACKS TO FIND SPACE IN WHICH TO
                                   1938+*                         WRITE/ADD A SPANNED RECORD.  THE OTHER IOB
                                   1939+*                         REMAINED ENQUEUED UNTIL IT EITHER WROTE THE
                                   1940+*                         RECORD OR DETERMINED THAT THERE WAS ENOUGH
                                   1941+*                         CONTIGUOUS FREE SPACE ON THE TRACKS TO CONTAIN
                                   1942+*                         THE RECORD.  AFTER THE OTHER IOB DEQUEUED THE
                                   1943+*                         CURRENT TRACK, THE DEQUEUEING WAS INTERRUPTED
                                   1944+*                         BY THE NEED OF THIS IOB FOR THE CURRENT TRACK.
                            00040  1945+IOBRSV07  EQU   X'40',,C'X' RESERVED                                    01-IEZIO
                            00020  1946+IOBRSV08  EQU   X'20',,C'X' RESERVED                                    01-IEZIO
                            00010  1947+IOBRSV09  EQU   X'10',,C'X' RESERVED                                    01-IEZIO
                            00008  1948+IOBRSV10  EQU   X'08',,C'X' RESERVED                                    01-IEZIO
                            00004  1949+IOBRSV11  EQU   X'04',,C'X' RESERVED                                    01-IEZIO
                            00002  1950+IOBRSV12  EQU   X'02',,C'X' RESERVED                                    01-IEZIO
                            00001  1951+IOBRSV13  EQU   X'01',,C'X' RESERVED                                    01-IEZIO
000009                             1952+IOBDQADB  DS    AL3 -     ADDRESS OF THE OTHER IOB REFERRED TO IN      01-IEZIO
                                   1953+*                         DESCRIPTION OF IOBDEQ ABOVE
00000C                             1954+IOBSWAP   DS    A -       ADDRESS OF THE SEGMENT WORK AREA USED BY THIS 01-IEZIO
                                   1955+*                         IOB TO READ OR WRITE A RECORD OF A FORMAT VS
                                   1956+*                         DATA SET

000010                      0000C  1958+          ORG   IOBPREFX+12                                            01-IEZIO
                                   1960+*                               ***************************************
                                   1961+*                               *                                     *
                                   1962+*                               *      GAM,QISAM PREFIX *** 4 BYTES   *
                                   1963+*                               *                                     *
                                   1964+*                               ***************************************
                            0000C  1966+IOBGAM    EQU   *                                                       01-IEZIO
                            0000C  1967+IOBQISAM  EQU   *                                                       01-IEZIO
00000C                             1968+IOBGQECB  DS    F -       EVENT CONTROL BLOCK THAT IS WITHIN FIRST IOB  01-IEZIO
                                   1969+*                         ONLY  (GAM)
                                   1970+*                         EVENT CONTROL BLOCK USED TO INDICATE STATUS
                                   1971+*                         OF AN I/O EVENT  (QISAM)

                                   1973+***********************************************************************
                                   1974+*                                                                     *
                                   1975+*                         STANDARD SECTION OF THE IOB                 *
                                   1976+*                                                                     *
                                   1977+***********************************************************************
000010                             1979+IOBSTDRD  DS    0D                                                      01-IEZIO
000010                             1981+IOBFLAG1  DS    B -       FLAG BYTE 1                                   01-IEZIO
```

```
SAMPLE ASSEMBLER PROGRAM--SAMPLE7

LOC    OBJECT CODE  ADDR1 ADDR2  STMT   SOURCE STATEMENT                                                                ASM H V 02 07.59 01/04/89

                          00080  1982+IOBDATCH EQU  X'80'  -  DATA CHAINING USED IN CHANNEL PROGRAM              01-IEZIO
                          00040  1983+IOBCMDCH EQU  X'40'  -  COMMAND CHAINING USED IN CHANNEL PROGRAM           01-IEZIO
                          00020  1984+IOBERRTN EQU  X'20'  -  ERROR ROUTINE IS IN CONTROL                        01-IEZIO
                          00010  1985+IOBRPSTN EQU  X'10'  -  DEVICE IS TO BE REPOSITIONED                       01-IEZIO
                          00008  1986+IOBCYCCK EQU  X'08'  -  CYCLIC REDUNDANCY CHECK (CRC) NEEDED (TAPE)        01-IEZIO
                          00008  1987+IOBFCREX EQU  X'08'  -  FETCH COMMAND RETRY EXIT (DIRECT ACCESS)           01-IEZIO
                          00004  1988+IOBIOERR EQU  X'04'  -  EXCEPTIONAL CONDITION.  AFTER THE ERROR            01-IEZIO
                                 1989+*                       ROUTINE RETURNS AND THIS BIT IS ON, THE ERROR
                                 1990+*                       IS CONSIDERED PERMANENT.
                          00002  1991+IOBUNREL EQU  X'02'  -  IOB UNRELATED FLAG (I.E., NONSEQUENTIAL)           01-IEZIO
                          00001  1992+IOBRSTRT EQU  X'01'  -  IF 1, RESTART ADDRESS IN IOB TO BE USED.           01-IEZIO
                                 1993+*                       IF 0, START.  (OS/VS1)                    MDC034
                          00001  1994+IOBSPSVC EQU  X'01'  -  FOR SAM/PAM, SET BY SVC IF I/O APPENDAGE           01-IEZIO
                                 1995+*                       SHOULD NOT PROCESS INTERRUPT (OS/VS2)     MDC035
000011                           1996+IOBFLAG2 DS   B      -  FLAG BYTE 2                                        01-IEZIO
                          00080  1997+IOBHALT  EQU  X'80'  -  HALT I/O HAS BEEN ISSUED BY SVC PURGE ROUTINE      01-IEZIO
                          00040  1998+IOBSENSE EQU  X'40'  -  SENSE WILL NOT BE PERFORMED UNTIL THE DEVICE       01-IEZIO
                                 1999+*                       IS FREE
                          00020  2000+IOBPURGE EQU  X'20'  -  IOB HAS BEEN PURGED TO ALLOW I/O ACTIVITY TO       01-IEZIO
                                 2001+*                       QUIESCE.  (OS/VS1)                        MDC046
                          00020  2002+IOBRRT3  EQU  X'20'  -  TYPE 3 RELATED REQUEST (OS/VS2)           MDC048   01-IEZIO
                          00010  2003+IOBRDHAO EQU  X'10'  -  HOME ADDRESS (RO) RECORD IS TO BE READ.  SEEK      01-IEZIO
                                 2004+*                       COMMAND NOT NEEDED.  (OS/VS1)             MDC047
                          00010  2005+IOBRRT2  EQU  X'10'  -  TYPE 2 RELATED REQUEST (OS/VS2)           MDC049   01-IEZIO
                          00008  2006+IOBALTTR EQU  X'08'  -  NO TEST FOR OUT-OF-EXTENT.  AN ALTERNATE TRACK     01-IEZIO
                                 2007+*                       IS IN USE.
                          00004  2008+IOBSKUPD EQU  X'04'  -  SEEK ADDRESS IS BEING UPDATED.  CYLINDER END       01-IEZIO
                                 2009+*                       OR FILE MASK VIOLATION HAS OCCURRED.
                          00002  2010+IOBSTATO EQU  X'02'  -  DEVICE END STATUS HAS BEEN OR'ED WITH CHANNEL      01-IEZIO
                                 2011+*                       END STATUS  (GRAPHICS DEVICE)
                          00001  2012+IOBPNCH  EQU  X'01'  -  ERROR RECOVERY IN CONTROL FOR A 2540 CARD          01-IEZIO
                                 2013+*                       PUNCH WITH THREE BUFFERS  (QSAM)
                                 2014+*                       RESETPL MACRO INSTRUCTION WAS USED  (BTAM)
000012                           2015+IOBSENS0 DS   B      -  FIRST SENSE BYTE                                   01-IEZIO
                          00080  2016+IOBS0B0  EQU  X'80'  -  BIT 0 (DEVICE DEPENDENT)                           01-IEZIO
                          00040  2017+IOBS0B1  EQU  X'40'  -  BIT 1 (DEVICE DEPENDENT)                           01-IEZIO
                          00020  2018+IOBS0B2  EQU  X'20'  -  BIT 2 (DEVICE DEPENDENT)                           01-IEZIO
                          00010  2019+IOBS0B3  EQU  X'10'  -  BIT 3 (DEVICE DEPENDENT)                           01-IEZIO
                          00008  2020+IOBS0B4  EQU  X'08'  -  BIT 4 (DEVICE DEPENDENT)                           01-IEZIO
                          00004  2021+IOBS0B5  EQU  X'04'  -  BIT 5 (DEVICE DEPENDENT)                           01-IEZIO
                          00002  2022+IOBS0B6  EQU  X'02'  -  BIT 6 (DEVICE DEPENDENT)                           01-IEZIO
                          00001  2023+IOBS0B7  EQU  X'01'  -  BIT 7 (DEVICE DEPENDENT)                           01-IEZIO
                          00001  2024+IOBSNSC9 EQU  X'01'  -  CHANNEL 9 SENSED IN CARRIAGE TAPE                  01-IEZIO
000013                           2025+IOBSENS1 DS   B      -  SECOND SENSE BYTE                                  01-IEZIO
                          00080  2026+IOBS1B0  EQU  X'80'  -  BIT 0 (DEVICE DEPENDENT)                           01-IEZIO
                          00040  2027+IOBS1B1  EQU  X'40'  -  BIT 1 (DEVICE DEPENDENT)                           01-IEZIO
                          00020  2028+IOBS1B2  EQU  X'20'  -  BIT 2 (DEVICE DEPENDENT)                           01-IEZIO
                          00010  2029+IOBS1B3  EQU  X'10'  -  BIT 3 (DEVICE DEPENDENT)                           01-IEZIO
                          00008  2030+IOBS1B4  EQU  X'08'  -  BIT 4 (DEVICE DEPENDENT)                           01-IEZIO
                          00004  2031+IOBS1B5  EQU  X'04'  -  BIT 5 (DEVICE DEPENDENT)                           01-IEZIO
                          00002  2032+IOBS1B6  EQU  X'02'  -  BIT 6 (DEVICE DEPENDENT)                           01-IEZIO
                          00001  2033+IOBS1B7  EQU  X'01'  -  BIT 7 (DEVICE DEPENDENT)                           01-IEZIO
000014                           2034+IOBECBPT DS   0A     -  ADDRESS OF ECB TO BE POSTED ON I/O COMPLETION      01-IEZIO
000014                           2035+IOBECBCC DS   CL1    -  COMPLETION CODE FOR AN I/O REQUEST.  THIS CODE     01-IEZIO
                                 2036+*                       WILL APPEAR IN THE FIRST BYTE OF AN ECB.
```

```
SAMPLE ASSEMBLER PROGRAM--SAMPLE7

  LOC  OBJECT CODE    ADDR1 ADDR2  STMT   SOURCE STATEMENT                                            ASM H V 02 07.59 01/04/89
000015                             2037+IOBECBPB DS    AL3 -       ADDRESS OF THE ECB TO BE POSTED UPON THE          01-IEZIO
                                   2038+*                          COMPLETION OF AN I/O EVENT.  FOR BSAM/BPAM,
                                   2039+*                          ECB IS IN THE DECB.  FOR QSAM, ECB IS IN THE
                                   2040+*                          QSAM PREFIX OF THE IOB.
000018                             2041+IOBFLAG3 DS    OB -        I/O SUPERVISOR ERROR ROUTINE FLAG BYTE            01-IEZIO
                                   2042+*                          (DEVICE DEPENDENT)
000018                             2043+IOBFL3   DS    B -         FLAG 3 - STATUS ERROR COUNTS FOR MAGNETIC         01-IEZIO
                                   2044+*                          DOCUMENT READER (3890) OR FLAGS FOR 3800
                                   2045+*                          (OS/VS1)  (MDC307)                       @X50AD9A
                          00080    2046+IOBCCC   EQU   X'80' -     CHANNEL CONTROL CHECK ERROR COUNT (3890)          01-IEZIO
                                   2047+*                                                                   MDC038
                          00040    2048+IOBICC   EQU   X'40' -     INTERFACE CONTROL CHECK ERROR COUNT (3890)        01-IEZIO
                                   2049+*                                                                   MDC039
                          00020    2050+IOBCDC   EQU   X'20' -     CHANNEL DATA CHECK ERROR (3890)          MDC040 01-IEZIO
                          00010    2051+IOBACU   EQU   X'10' -     ATTENTION/CONTROL UNIT ERROR (3890)      MDC041 01-IEZIO
                          00008    2052+IOBCNC   EQU   X'08' -     CHAIN CHECK ERROR (3890)                 MDC042 01-IEZIO
                          00008    2053+IOBSDR   EQU   X'08' -     STATISTICS ONLY FLAG (3800) (MDC306)   @X50AD9A 01-IEZIO
                          00004    2054+IOBMSG   EQU   X'04' -     MESSAGE FLAG (3890 OR 3800) (MDC308)   @X50AD9A 01-IEZIO
                          00002    2055+IOBICL   EQU   X'02' -     INCORRECT LENGTH ERROR (3890)            MDC020 01-IEZIO
                          00002    2056+IOBJAM   EQU   X'02' -     SET ON WHEN JES SUBSYSTEM HAS DETECTED A          01-IEZIO
                                   2057+*                          PAPER JAM SO 3800 ERP WILL SUPPRESS ITS
                                   2058+*                          INTERVENTION REQUIRED MESSAGE (3800)
                                   2059+*                          (MDC330)                               @X50AD9A
                          00001    2060+IOBLOG   EQU   X'01' -     LOG OUT FLAG (3890 OR 3800) (MDC309)   @X50AD9A 01-IEZIO
000019                             2061+IOBCSW   DS    OCL7 -      LOW-ORDER SEVEN BYTES OF THE LAST CSW THAT        01-IEZIO
                                   2062+*                          REFLECTS THE STATUS FOR THIS REQUEST
000019                             2063+IOBIOCSW DS    OCL5 -      LOW-ORDER BYTES OF CSW FOR MAGNETIC DOCUMENT      01-IEZIO
                                   2064+*                          READER (3890) (OS/VS1)                   MDC022
000019                             2065+IOBCMDA  DS    AL3 -       COMMAND ADDRESS (3890)                   MDC023 01-IEZIO
00001C                             2066+IOBSTBYT DS    OBL2 -      STATUS BITS 32-47 (3890)                 MDC024 01-IEZIO
00001C                             2067+IOBUSTAT DS    B -         CSW UNIT STATUS FLAGS (3800) (MDC311)  @Z40MP9A 01-IEZIO
                          00080    2068+IOBUSB0  EQU   X'80' -     ATTENTION  (MDC312)                    @Z40MP9A 01-IEZIO
                          00040    2069+IOBUSB1  EQU   X'40' -     STATUS MODIFIER  (MDC313)              @Z40MP9A 01-IEZIO
                          00020    2070+IOBUSB2  EQU   X'20' -     CONTROL UNIT END  (MDC314)             @Z40MP9A 01-IEZIO
                          00010    2071+IOBUSB3  EQU   X'10' -     BUSY  (MDC315)                         @Z40MP9A 01-IEZIO
                          00008    2072+IOBUSB4  EQU   X'08' -     CHANNEL END  (MDC316)                  @Z40MP9A 01-IEZIO
                          00004    2073+IOBUSB5  EQU   X'04' -     DEVICE END  (MDC317)                   @Z40MP9A 01-IEZIO
                          00002    2074+IOBUSB6  EQU   X'02' -     UNIT CHECK  (MDC318)                   @Z40MP9A 01-IEZIO
                          00001    2075+IOBUSB7  EQU   X'01' -     UNIT EXCEPTION  (MDC319)               @Z40MP9A 01-IEZIO
00001D                             2076+IOBCSTAT DS    B -         CSW CHANNEL STATUS FLAGS (3800)                   01-IEZIO
                                   2077+*                          (MDC320)                               @Z40MP9A
                          00080    2078+IOBCSB0  EQU   X'80' -     PROGRAM CONTROL INTERRUPT  (MDC321)    @Z40MP9A 01-IEZIO
                          00040    2079+IOBCSB1  EQU   X'40' -     INCORRECT LENGTH  (MDC322)             @Z40MP9A 01-IEZIO
                          00020    2080+IOBCSB2  EQU   X'20' -     PROGRAM CHECK  (MDC323)                @Z40MP9A 01-IEZIO
                          00010    2081+IOBCSB3  EQU   X'10' -     PROTECTION CHECK  (MDC324)             @Z40MP9A 01-IEZIO
                          00008    2082+IOBCSB4  EQU   X'08' -     CHANNEL DATA CHECK  (MDC325)           @Z40MP9A 01-IEZIO
                          00004    2083+IOBCSB5  EQU   X'04' -     CHANNEL CONTROL CHECK  (MDC326)        @Z40MP9A 01-IEZIO
                          00002    2084+IOBCSB6  EQU   X'02' -     INTERFACE CONTROL CHECK  (MDC327)      @Z40MP9A 01-IEZIO
                          00001    2085+IOBCSB7  EQU   X'01' -     CHAINING CHECK  (MDC328)               @Z40MP9A 01-IEZIO
00001E                             2086+         DS    XL2 -       LAST TWO BYTES OF IOBCSW                          01-IEZIO
000020                             2087+IOBSTART DS    OA -        ADDRESS OF CHANNEL PROGRAM TO BE EXECUTED         01-IEZIO
000020                             2088+IOBSIOCC DS    B -         SIO CODE.  BITS 2 AND 3 CONTAIN CONDITION CODE    01-IEZIO
                                   2089+*                          RETURNED AFTER EXECUTION OF SIO INSTRUCTION
                                   2090+*                          FOR THIS I/O EVENT.
000021                             2091+IOBSTRTB DS    AL3 -       ADDRESS OF CHANNEL PROGRAM TO BE EXECUTED         01-IEZIO
```

```
SAMPLE ASSEMBLER PROGRAM--SAMPLE7

  LOC  OBJECT CODE    ADDR1 ADDR2  STMT   SOURCE STATEMENT                                               ASM H V 02 07.59 01/04/89
000024                              2092+IOBDCBPT DS    0A -       ADDRESS OF DCB ASSOCIATED WITH THIS IOB              01-IEZIO
000024                              2093+IOBFLAG4 DS    B -        FLAG BYTE                                    MDC011  01-IEZIO
                              00080 2094+IOBGDPOL EQU   X'80' -    RE-ENTER SIO APPENDAGE FOR OLTEP GUARANTEED          01-IEZIO
                                    2095+*                         DEVICE PATH                                  MDC012
                              00040 2096+IOBCC3WE EQU   X'40' -    USER REQUESTS THAT IOS POST A X'6D' FOR A            01-IEZIO
                                    2097+*                         CONDITION CODE 3 ON ATTEMPTED I/O OPERATIONS
                                    2098+*                         (OS/VS2)  (MDC310)                        @Z309P9A
                              00020 2099+IOBPMERR EQU   X'20' -    VTAM SETS THIS BIT ON TO INDICATE TO IOS THAT        01-IEZIO
                                    2100+*                         VTAM SHOULD BE POSTED WITH A PERMANENT I/O
                                    2101+*                         ERROR BECAUSE ALL ALTERNATE PATHS TO THE 3705
                                    2102+*                         HAVE BEEN TRIED (OS/VS1)  (MDC329)        @X04BH9A
                              00010 2103+IOBRSV40 EQU   X'10',,C'X' - RESERVED                                          01-IEZIO
                              00008 2104+IOBRSV41 EQU   X'08',,C'X' - RESERVED                                          01-IEZIO
                              00004 2105+IOBRSV42 EQU   X'04',,C'X' - RESERVED                                          01-IEZIO
                              00002 2106+IOBJES3I EQU   X'02' -    JES3 INTERVENTION REQUIRED NOTIFICATION.             01-IEZIO
                                    2107+*                         SETTING THIS BIT WILL RESULT IN TURNING ON BIT
                                    2108+*                         IOSPGDPX IN THE IOSB.  (OS/VS2)
                                    2109+*                         (MDC305)                                  @Y02BP9A
                              00001 2110+IOBRSV44 EQU   X'01',,C'X' - RESERVED                                          01-IEZIO
000025                              2111+IOBDCBPB DS    AL3 -      ADDRESS OF DCB ASSOCIATED WITH THIS IOB              01-IEZIO
000028                              2112+IOBRESTR DS    0A -       AFTER SVC 16 (PURGE) - QUIESCE - ADDRESS OF          01-IEZIO
                                    2113+*                         THE NEXT IOB IN THE PURGE CHAIN.  (LAST IOB IN
                                    2114+*                         THE CHAIN, BYTE 4 IS FF.)
                                    2115+*                         DURING I/O SUPERVISOR WRITE-TO-OPERATOR
                                    2116+*                         ROUTINE CONTROL - CCHH PART OF THE ADDRESS OF
                                    2117+*                         A DEFECTIVE TRACK.
                                    2118+*                         DURING I/O ERROR CORRECTION (MEANINGFUL ONLY
                                    2119+*                         IF BIT 3 IN THE IOBFLAG1 FIELD IS ON) -
                                    2120+*                         ADDRESS OF THE CHANNEL PROGRAM USED TO CORRECT
                                    2121+*                         AN ERROR CONDITION.
                                    2122+*                         AFTER I/O ERROR CORRECTION - IF A CHANNEL
                                    2123+*                         PROGRAM IS RESTARTED THROUGH A CCW OTHER THAN
                                    2124+*                         THE ONE POINTED TO BY THE IOBSTART FIELD, ITS
                                    2125+*                         ADDRESS IS HERE.
000028                              2126+IOBREPOS DS    CL1 -      DURING I/O ERROR CORRECTION (MEANINGFUL ONLY         01-IEZIO
                                    2127+*                         IF BIT 3 IN THE IOBFLAG1 FIELD IS ON) FOR
                                    2128+*                         MAGNETIC TAPE ONLY - THE CONTROL COMMAND
                                    2129+*                         (BSR, FSR, ERG) REQUIRED TO REPOSITION OVER A
                                    2130+*                         BLOCK.
000029                              2131+IOBRSTRB DS    AL3 -      SAME AS IOBRESTR ABOVE                               01-IEZIO
00002C                              2132+IOBINCAM DS    0H -       QSAM, BSAM, EXCP ACCESS METHOD -- NORMAL             01-IEZIO
                                    2133+*                         SCHEDULING - VALUE USED TO INCREMENT BLOCK
                                    2134+*                         COUNT FIELD IN DCB FOR MAGNETIC TAPE.
                                    2135+*                         CHAINED SCHEDULING - ZEROS.
                                    2136+*                         QSAM, BSAM -- OPERATION CODE OF WRITE CCW WHEN
                                    2137+*                         A USASI CONTROL CHARACTER AND NO DATA IS TO BE
                                    2138+*                         WRITTEN (PRINTER AND CARD PUNCH ONLY)
00002C                              2139+IOBBTAMF DS    B -        FLAG BYTE FOR BTAM                                   01-IEZIO
                              00080 2140+IOBPRMER EQU   X'80' -    SAD OR ENABLE ISSUED BY OPEN RESULTED IN A           01-IEZIO
                                    2141+*                         PERMANENT I/O ERROR
                              00040 2142+IOBINUSE EQU   X'40' -    THIS IOB IS CURRENTLY IN USE BY AN I/O               01-IEZIO
                                    2143+*                         OPERATION
                              00020 2144+IOBRSV14 EQU   X'20',,C'X' RESERVED                                            01-IEZIO
                              00010 2145+IOBRSV15 EQU   X'10',,C'X' RESERVED                                            01-IEZIO
                              00008 2146+IOBRSV16 EQU   X'08',,C'X' RESERVED                                            01-IEZIO
```

```
SAMPLE ASSEMBLER PROGRAM--SAMPLE7

  LOC  OBJECT CODE    ADDR1 ADDR2  STMT   SOURCE STATEMENT                                       ASM H V 02 07.59 01/04/89
                            00004  2147+IOBRSV17 EQU   X'04',,C'X' RESERVED                                        01-IEZIO
                            00002  2148+IOBRFTMG EQU   X'02' -     A REQUEST-FOR-TEST MESSAGE RECEIVED FROM A      01-IEZIO
                                   2149+*                          REMOTE 3270 DISPLAY STATION              ICB478
                            00001  2150+IOBOLTST EQU   X'01' -     LINE IS UNDER ON-LINE TEST OPERATION            01-IEZIO
00002D                             2151+IOBRSV19 DS    XL1 -       RESERVED                                        01-IEZIO

00002E                      0002C  2153+         ORG   IOBINCAM                                                    01-IEZIO
00002C                             2154+IOBFL4   DS    B -         FLAG 4 - SENSE ERROR COUNTS FOR MAGNETIC        01-IEZIO
                                   2155+*                          DOCUMENT READER (3890) (OS/VS1) OR ERROR CODE
                                   2156+*                          PASSBACK BYTE FOR 3895 (FOR ERROR CODE VALUES
                                   2157+*                          SEE IBM 3895 DOCUMENT READER/INSCRIBER MACHINE
                                   2158+*                          AND PROGRAMMING DESCRIPTION, GA24-3620)
                                   2159+*                          (MDC333)                              @G30HP9A
                            00080  2160+IOBOVR   EQU   X'80' -     OVERRUN ERROR (3890)  (MDC026)        @G30HP9A 01-IEZIO
                            00040  2161+IOBREJ   EQU   X'40' -     COMMAND REJECT ERROR (3890) (MDC027)  @G30HP9A 01-IEZIO
                            00020  2162+IOBDCK   EQU   X'20' -     DATA CHECK ERROR (3890)  (MDC028)     @G30HP9A 01-IEZIO
                            00010  2163+IOBBUS   EQU   X'10' -     BUS-OUT ERROR (3890)  (MDC029)        @G30HP9A 01-IEZIO
                            00008  2164+IOBEQP   EQU   X'08' -     EQUIPMENT CHECK ERROR (3890) (MDC030) @G30HP9A 01-IEZIO
                            00004  2165+IOBENT   EQU   X'04' -     FIRST TIME ENTRY SWITCH (3890)                 01-IEZIO
                                   2166+*                          (MDC045)                              @G30HP9A
                            00002  2167+IOBRSV47 EQU   X'02',,C'X' - RESERVED FOR 3890                    MDC044 01-IEZIO
                            00001  2168+IOBRSV46 EQU   X'01',,C'X' - RESERVED FOR 3890                    MDC033 01-IEZIO

00002D                      0002C  2170+         ORG   IOBINCAM                                                    01-IEZIO
00002C                             2171+IOBCRDCC DS    CL1 -       DATA CHECK ERROR COUNT  (OPTICAL READER)        01-IEZIO
00002D                             2172+IOBCRILC DS    CL1 -       INCORRECT LENGTH ERROR COUNT  (OPTICAL READER) 01-IEZIO

00002E                             2174+IOBERRCT DS    H -         USED BY I/O SUPERVISOR ERROR ROUTINES TO COUNT 01-IEZIO
                                   2175+*                          TEMPORARY ERRORS DURING RETRY

                                   2177+***********************************************************************
                                   2178+*                                                                     *
                                   2179+*                     EXTENSION SECTIONS OF THE IOB                   *
                                   2180+*                                                                     *
                                   2181+***********************************************************************

000030                             2183+IOBEXTEN DS    0D                                                          01-IEZIO

                                   2185+*                               ***************************************
                                   2186+*                               *                                     *
                                   2187+*                               *  DIRECT ACCESS EXTENSION *** 8 BYTES *
                                   2188+*                               *                                     *
                                   2189+*                               ***************************************

000030                             2191+IOBSEEK  DS    0CL8 -      A SEEK ADDRESS (IN THE FORMAT MBBCCHHR) USED    01-IEZIO
                                   2192+*                          WITH A CHANNEL PROGRAM
000030                             2193+IOBM     DS    CL1 -       THE NUMBER OF THE DEB EXTENT TO BE USED FOR     01-IEZIO
                                   2194+*                          THIS REQUEST.  THE FIRST EXTENT IS NUMBER 0.
000031                             2195+IOBBB    DS    0CL2 -      BIN NUMBER(DATA CELL)                           01-IEZIO
000031                             2196+IOBBB1   DS    CL1                                                         01-IEZIO
```

```
         SAMPLE ASSEMBLER PROGRAM--SAMPLE7

  LOC  OBJECT CODE    ADDR1 ADDR2  STMT   SOURCE STATEMENT                                    ASM H V 02 07.59 01/04/89
000032                             2197+IOBBB2   DS    CL1                                                  01-IEZIO
000033                             2198+IOBCC    DS    OCL2 -    CYLINDER NUMBER                            01-IEZIO
000033                             2199+IOBCC1   DS    CL1                                                  01-IEZIO
000034                             2200+IOBCC2   DS    CL1                                                  01-IEZIO
000035                             2201+IOBHH    DS    OCL2 -    TRACK NUMBER                               01-IEZIO
000035                             2202+IOBHH1   DS    CL1                                                  01-IEZIO
000036                             2203+IOBHH2   DS    CL1                                                  01-IEZIO
000037                             2204+IOBR     DS    CL1 -     RECORD NUMBER                              01-IEZIO

000038                       00030 2206+         ORG   IOBEXTEN                                             01-IEZIO
                                   2208+*                  ****************************************
                                   2209+*                  *                                      *
                                   2210+*                  *        BTAM EXTENSION ***            *
                                   2211+*                  *     40 BYTES + CHANNEL PROGRAM       *
                                   2212+*                  *                                      *
                                   2213+*                  ****************************************
000030                             2215+IOBUCBX  DS    CL1 -     UCB INDEX.  THE LINE NUMBER IS USED AS AN   01-IEZIO
                                   2216+*                  INDEX TO LOCATE THE PROPER UCB ADDRESS IN THE
                                   2217+*                  DEB.
000031                             2218+IOBWORK  DS    CL5 -     WORK AREA USED BY ERROR ROUTINES AND ON-LINE 01-IEZIO
                                   2219+*                  TERMINAL TEST ROUTINES
000036                             2220+IOBRCVPT DS    CL1 -     RECEIVED ACK (ACK-0 OR ACK-1)               01-IEZIO
000037                             2221+IOBSNDPT DS    CL1 -     SENT ACK (ACK-0 OR ACK-1)                   01-IEZIO
000038                             2222+IOBERCCW DS    CL8 -     CCW AREA USED BY THE BTAM ERROR RECOVERY    01-IEZIO
                                   2223+*                  ROUTINES
000040                             2224+IOBERINF DS    CL16 -    ERROR INFORMATION FIELD USED BY THE BTAM ERROR 01-IEZIO
                                   2225+*                  RECOVERY ROUTINES
000050                             2226+IOBCPA   DS    0D -      CHANNEL PROGRAMS AREA.  THE LENGTH DEPENDS ON 01-IEZIO
                                   2227+*                  THE TERMINAL AND THE OPTIONS.

000050                       00038 2229+         ORG   IOBSEEK+8                                            01-IEZIO
                                   2231+*                  ****************************************
                                   2232+*                  *                                      *
                                   2233+*                  *     BISAM EXTENSION *** 16 BYTES     *
                                   2234+*                  *                                      *
                                   2235+*                  ****************************************
000038                             2237+IOBCCWAD DS    A -       FOR FIXED LENGTH RECORDS, ADDRESS OF FIRST  01-IEZIO
                                   2238+*                  CCW OF CHANNEL PROGRAM.
                                   2239+*                  FOR VARIABLE LENGTH RECORDS, ADDRESS OF
                                   2240+*                  BUFFER, IF DYNAMIC BUFFERING SPECIFIED, AFTER
                                   2241+*                  COMPLETION OF A READ FOR UPDATE (READ KU)
00003C                             2242+IOBINDCT DS    B -       INDICATORS                                  01-IEZIO
                             00080 2243+IOBDEQCP EQU   X'80' -   DEQUEUE CHANNEL PROGRAM FROM QUEUE          01-IEZIO
                             00040 2244+IOBUNSCH EQU   X'40' -   UNSCHEDULED QUEUE                           01-IEZIO
                             00020 2245+IOBOVPTR EQU   X'20' -   IF 0, DECBAREA + 6 POINTS TO OVERFLOW RECORD 01-IEZIO
                                   2246+*                  DATA.
                                   2247+*                  IF 1, DCBMSWA POINTS TO OVERFLOW RECORD KEY
                                   2248+*                  FOLLOWED BY DATA.
                             00010 2249+IOBKEYAD EQU   X'10' -   IF 0, DECBKEY POINTS TO OVERFLOW RECORD KEY. 01-IEZIO
```

Pages 42-44 contain only unreferenced IOB expansions and are deleted.

```
SAMPLE ASSEMBLER PROGRAM--SAMPLE7

  LOC  OBJECT CODE    ADDR1 ADDR2  STMT   SOURCE STATEMENT                                             ASM H V 02 07.59 01/04/89
                                   2410+*                                ****************************************
                                   2411+*                                *                                      *
                                   2412+*                                *      VTAM EXTENSION (OS/VS1 ONLY)    *
                                   2413+*                                *            *** 24 BYTES              *
                                   2414+*                                *                                      *
                                   2415+*                                ****************************************
000030                             2417+IOBERCT  DS    OA -      POINTER TO COUNTERS FOR SIO AND TEMPORARY            01-IEZIO
                                   2418+*                        ERRORS                                       MDC001
000030                             2419+IOBUCBXV DS    OFL1 -    UCB INDEX                                    MDC050 01-IEZIO
000030                             2420+IOBRTYPE DS    C -       RECORD TYPE FOR OBR                          MDC002 01-IEZIO
000031                             2421+IOBERCTA DS    AL3 -     POINTER TO COUNTERS FOR SIO AND TEMPORARY            01-IEZIO
                                   2422+*                        ERRORS                                       MDC003
000034                             2423+IOBNAME  DS    OA -      POINTER TO TERMINAL NAME                     MDC004 01-IEZIO
000034                             2424+IOBNAMSZ DS    FL1 -     SIZE OF TERMINAL NAME                        MDC005 01-IEZIO
000035                             2425+IOBNAMEA DS    AL3 -     POINTER TO TERMINAL NAME                     MDC006 01-IEZIO
000038                             2426+IOBMDREC DS    A -       POINTER TO RECORD BEING PASSED TO                    01-IEZIO
                                   2427+*                        MISCELLANEOUS DATA RECORDER                  MDC007
00003C                             2428+IOBRCD   DS    A -       POINTER TO QUEUE OF OBR RECORDS PASSED FROM          01-IEZIO
                                   2429+*                        3705                                         MDC008
000040                             2430+IOBSENSV DS    X -       SENSE BYTE SAVE AREA                         MDC009 01-IEZIO
000041                             2431+IOBCSWSV DS    XL7 -     SAVE AREA FOR LAST 7 BYTES OF CSW            MDC010 01-IEZIO

000048                      00030  2433+         ORG   IOBEXTEN -                                           @Z30OP9A 01-IEZIO
                                   2435+*                                ****************************************
                                   2436+*                                *                                      *
                                   2437+*                                *  3540 EXTENSION *** 4 BYTES  @Z30OP9A*
                                   2438+*                                *                                      *
                                   2439+*                                ****************************************
000030                             2441+IOBSKADR DS    OCL4 -    3540 SEEK ADDRESS  (MDC300)                 @Z30OP9A 01-IEZIO
000030                             2442+IOBSKRV  DS    XL1 -     RESERVED  (MDC301)                          @Z30OP9A 01-IEZIO
000031                             2443+IOBSKTT  DS    XL1 -     TRACK NUMBER  (MDC302)                      @Z30OP9A 01-IEZIO
000032                             2444+IOBSKO   DS    XL1 -     MUST BE ZERO  (MDC303)                      @Z30OP9A 01-IEZIO
000033                             2445+IOBSKSS  DS    XL1 -     SECTOR NUMBER  (MDC304)                     @Z30OP9A 01-IEZIO
                                   2446+*                   RESET LOCATION COUNTER TO END OF IOB             @ZA93383
000034                      00060  2447+         ORG                                                                 01-IEZIO
000000                             2448          END   BEGIN
```

```
                                  CROSS REFERENCE

SYMBOL    LEN    VALUE   DEFN  REFERENCES                                                              ASM H V 02 07.59 01/04/89

ABSADDR   00016   0005BC 0340  0128 0129 0130 0131 0132
BEGIN     00002   000000 0027  2448
BLOCK     00006   0005AA 0339  0134
BLOCKS    00003   00059E 0335  0127 0134 0200
CVT       00001 00000000 0862  0057
CVTBRET   00002   000052 0921  1366 1444
CVTPCNVT  00004   00001C 0890  0058
CVTVSTGX  00001 00000000 1717  1674
CVTXTNT1  00001 00000000 1756  1092
CVTXTNT2  00001 00000000 1764  1158
CVT4MS1   00001 00000010 0946  0952
CVT6DAT   00001 00000002 0948  0952
CYLINDER  00002   0003CB 0262  0108 0110
DASDINFO  00004   000568 0328  0045 0049
DATALOOP  00006   000242 0193  0198
DCBBIT0   00001 00000080 0459  0545 0553 0566 0590 0623 0625 0626 0628 0651 0654 0674 0678 0693 0730 0788
DCBBIT1   00001 00000040 0460  0546 0554 0568 0591 0592 0601 0607 0623 0625 0627 0628 0656 0674 0676 0678 0696 0697 0698
                               0733 0734 0788
DCBBIT2   00001 00000020 0461  0547 0555 0569 0570 0571 0591 0592 0596 0602 0607 0623 0624 0629 0658 0679 0680 0701 0702
                               0703 0737 0738 0789
DCBBIT3   00001 00000010 0462  0548 0569 0571 0572 0591 0604 0630 0661 0679 0682 0705 0706 0707 0741 0742 0789
DCBBIT4   00001 00000008 0463  0556 0605 0606 0607 0631 0662 0684 0689 0690 0710 0711 0745 0746 0748 0749 0790
DCBBIT5   00001 00000004 0464  0557 0612 0634 0635 0664 0684 0686 0687 0690 0714 0716 0717 0718 0752 0753 0754 0755 0790
DCBBIT6   00001 00000002 0465  0549 0613 0614 0617 0634 0636 0665 0721 0722 0723 0724 0758 0759 0760 0761 0791
DCBBIT7   00001 00000001 0466  0550 0613 0615 0617 0638 0669 0726 0727 0764 0765 0767 0768
DCBDEBAD  00004   00002C 0786  0061
DCBFDAD   00008   000005 0486  0489
DCBRELAD  00004   000000 0478  0061
DDNAME    00008   000738 0406  0044
DETAIL1   00005   0005A5 0338  0133 0134 0341
DISKIN    00004   000740 0411  0038 0061 0209 0277
DOUBLESP  00002   000332 0243  0098 0106 0136 0140 0180 0190
EOE       00006   00011C 0124  0089
EOF       00002   00026E 0203  0118 0429
ERRORS    00003   0005A1 0336  0115 0116
EXTERROR  00006   0002D8 0220  0069
FORMAT    00006   000300 0230  0052 0139 0143 0147 0151 0155 0159 0163 0167 0171 0175 0179
FORMAT2   00006   0002EA 0225  0183 0186 0189
HEAD      00002   0003CD 0263  0101 0113
HEADING   00133   000651 0343  0250 0344 0346 0346
HEADPAGE  00006   000334 0245  0042
HEX       00016   00058C 0333  0132 0195 0227 0232
IHADCB    00001 00000000 0447  0527 0576 0647 0772 0779 0797
IHB0014   00004   0003F8 0279  0281
IHB0014A  00001   000400 0280  0286
INAREA    00080   000378 0258  0289 0292 0296 0296
INECB     00004   0003D4 0269  0070 0077 0082 0086 0088 0092 0138 0272 0275
INFOLOOP  00004   00003C 0052  0053
IOBEXTEN  00008   000030 2183  2206 2275 2408 2433
IOBINCAM  00002   00002C 2132  2153 2170
IOBPREFX  00008   000000 1844  1879 1922 1958
IOBSEEK   00008   000030 2191  2229 2301 2313 2387
IOBSTDRD  00008   000010 1979  0093
IOBUSTAT  00001   00001C 2067  0094
LDETAIL1  00001 00000027 0341  0133
```

```
                                    CROSS REFERENCE

SYMBOL    LEN     VALUE  DEFN  REFERENCES                                                         ASM H V 02 07.59 01/04/89

LINE      00133   0005CC 0342  0050 0097 0105 0120 0124 0133 0134 0137 0141 0142 0145 0146 0149 0150 0153 0154 0157 0158
                               0161 0162 0165 0166 0169 0170 0173 0174 0177 0178 0182 0185 0188 0191 0220 0225 0226 0227
                               0228 0230 0231 0232 0233 0238 0241 0242 0242 0242 0254 0296
MASK      00001   00057C 0332  0131 0194 0226 0231
MBBCCHHR  00008   0003C8 0259  0062 0078 0128 0129
NOTINDEX  00006   00010E 0120  0095
PAGENO    00004   0006D2 0348  0246 0247
PAGES     00002   00059C 0334  0245 0247
PRINT     00004   00031A 0237  0099 0107 0135 0199 0221
PRINTER   00004   0006D8 0355  0040 0211 0237 0249
RC        00001   0005A4 0337  0055 0121 0125 0204
READLOOP  00002   000072 0071  0117 0201
READOKAY  00006   000126 0127  0087 0122
RECORD    00001   0003CF 0264  0072 0074 0114
SAVEAREA  00004   000290 0218  0031 0032 0213
SAVE8#13  00004   000360 0257  0063 0067
TRACKOK   00004   0000F2 0113  0104
TRACKS    00002   000572 0330  0103
WRAPUP    00004   000274 0207  0223
=A(INAREA,4,INAREA+40,LINE+6)
          00004   000420 0296  0192
=C'+12'   00003   000503 0315  0153
=C'+16'   00003   000506 0316  0157
=C'+20'   00003   00051A 0318  0161
=C'+24'   00003   00052E 0320  0165
=C'+28'   00003   000531 0321  0169
=C'+32'   00003   000545 0323  0173
=C'+36'   00003   000553 0325  0177
=C'+4'    00002   000476 0304  0145
=C'+8'    00002   000478 0305  0149
=C'*** END OF CYLINDER ***'
          00023   00048A 0308  0105
=C'*** END OF TRACK ***'
          00020   000454 0299  0097
=C'DEVTYPE INFO'
          00012   000448 0298  0050
=C'END OF EXTENT'
          00013   0004AF 0311  0124
=C'ERROR OCCURED'
          00013   0004A2 0310  0120
=C'INVALID RELATIVE ADDRESS'
          00024   000430 0297  0220
=C'IOBCSW 3-6'
          00010   00047A 0306  0154
=C'IOBECBCC,IOBECBPT'
          00017   0004DF 0313  0146
=C'IOBFLAG1,IOBFLAG2,IOBSENS0,IOBSENS1'
          00035   0004BC 0312  0142
=C'IOBFLAG3,IOBCSW 0-2'
          00019   0004F0 0314  0150
=C'IOBINCAM,IOBERRCT'
          00017   000534 0322  0170
=C'IOBRESTR'
          00008   000418 0295  0166
=C'IOBSEEK 0-3'
          00011   000548 0324  0174
=C'IOBSEEK 4-7'
          00011   000556 0326  0178
=C'IOBSIOCC,IOBSTART'
          00017   000509 0317  0158
=C'RESERVED,IOBDCBPT'
          00017   00051D 0319  0162
=C'OCCW-1'
          00006   000484 0307  0182
=C'ODATA'
          00005   000561 0327  0191
```

```
                                          CROSS REFERENCE

SYMBOL    LEN    VALUE  DEFN  REFERENCES                                               ASM H V 02 07.59 01/04/89

=C'OECB' 00004  000468 0300  0137
=C'OIOB' 00004  00046C 0301  0141
=P'1'    00001  0004A1 0309  0115 0127 0245
=P'20'   00002  000474 0303  0116 0200
=X'40202120'
         00004  000470 0302  0246
XDAP I/O TEST

         3010200E     DEVTYPE INFO
         00007FF8
         06EB000F
         BB600100
         2010010B
BLOCK       1.  MBBCCHHR=00000000A7000001

ECB      7F000000

IOB      43000000 IOBFLAG1,IOBFLAG2,IOBSENSO,IOBSENS1
      +4 7F006C5C IOBECBCC,IOBECBPT
      +8 00006CA0 IOBFLAG3,IOBCSW 0-2
     +12 0C000000 IOBCSW 3-6
     +16 00006C88 IOBSIOCC,IOBSTART
     +20 00006FC8 RESERVED,IOBDCBPT
     +24 00000000 IOBRESTR
     +28 00000000 IOBINCAM,IOBERRCT
     +32 00000000 IOBSEEK 0-3
     +36 A7000001 IOBSEEK 4-7

CCW-1    31006C83 40000005
    2    08006C88 00000000
    3    0E006C00 20000050

DATA 7FAB0000 00200000 10000008 C9C4D9C5 C3D6D9C4 C1C4C3D6 C1D7C3E3 1506372F 0188094F 00350000 46000008
** END OF TRACK ***
BLOCK       2.  MBBCCHHR=00000000A7000101

ECB      7F000000

IOB      43000000 IOBFLAG1,IOBFLAG2,IOBSENSO,IOBSENS1
      +4 7F006C5C IOBECBCC,IOBECBPT
      +8 00006CA0 IOBFLAG3,IOBCSW 0-2
     +12 0C000000 IOBCSW 3-6
     +16 00006C88 IOBSIOCC,IOBSTART
     +20 00006FC8 RESERVED,IOBDCBPT
     +24 00000000 IOBRESTR
     +28 00000000 IOBINCAM,IOBERRCT
     +32 00000000 IOBSEEK 0-3
     +36 A7000101 IOBSEEK 4-7

CCW-1    31006C83 40000005
    2    08006C88 00000000
    3    0E006C00 20000050

DATA 7CC30000 0FF40000 07030008 0069DC20 00007C20 00005D20 EA000500 0001231C 01000300 006BC760 40404040
** END OF TRACK ***
BLOCK       3.  MBBCCHHR=00000000A7000201

ECB      7F000000

IOB      43000000 IOBFLAG1,IOBFLAG2,IOBSENSO,IOBSENS1
      +4 7F006C5C IOBECBCC,IOBECBPT
      +8 00006CA0 IOBFLAG3,IOBCSW 0-2
```

```
Pages 2-5 contain information simliar to the above and are omitted.

XDAP I/O TEST

   +28 00000000 IOBINCAM,IOBERRCT
   +32 00000000 IOBSEEK 0-3
   +36 A7000C01 IOBSEEK 4-7

CCW-1  31006C83 40000005
    2  08006C88 00000000
    3  0E006C00 20000050

DATA 7B180000 0FF40000 07030008 0069DC20 000075C0 000031E0 E100F400 0031098C 00000000 0000060C 40404040
** END OF TRACK ***
BLOCK     14.  MBBCCHHR=00000000A7000D01

ECB     7F000000

IOB      43000000 IOBFLAG1,IOBFLAG2,IOBSENS0,IOBSENS1
      +4 7F006C5C IOBECBCC,IOBECBPT
      +8 00006CA0 IOBFLAG3,IOBCSW 0-2
     +12 0C000000 IOBCSW 3-6
     +16 00006C88 IOBSIOCC,IOBSTART
     +20 00006FC8 RESERVED,IOBDCBPT
     +24 00000000 IOBRESTR
     +28 00000000 IOBINCAM,IOBERRCT
     +32 00000000 IOBSEEK 0-3
     +36 A7000D01 IOBSEEK 4-7

CCW-1  31006C83 40000005
    2  08006C88 00000000
    3  0E006C00 20000050

DATA 7BBC0000 0FF40000 04030008 0022B000 00004A90 00001260 00000000 00000000 00000000 00000000 00000000
** END OF TRACK ***
BLOCK     15.  MBBCCHHR=00000000A7000E01

ECB     7F000000

IOB      43000000 IOBFLAG1,IOBFLAG2,IOBSENS0,IOBSENS1
      +4 7F006C5C IOBECBCC,IOBECBPT
      +8 00006CA0 IOBFLAG3,IOBCSW 0-2
     +12 0C000000 IOBCSW 3-6
     +16 00006C88 IOBSIOCC,IOBSTART
     +20 00006FC8 RESERVED,IOBDCBPT
     +24 00000000 IOBRESTR
     +28 00000000 IOBINCAM,IOBERRCT
     +32 00000000 IOBSEEK 0-3
     +36 A7000E01 IOBSEEK 4-7

CCW-1  31006C83 40000005
    2  08006C88 00000000
    3  0E006C00 20000050

DATA 7DA90000 0FF40000 20030008 00253808 000090F0 00004260 40C1D540 C9D5E5D9 C5D840C5 D9D9D6D9 40C8C1E2
** END OF TRACK ***
** END OF CYLINDER ***
```

```
SAMPLE8--REVERSE POLISH NOTATION

  LOC  OBJECT CODE    ADDR1 ADDR2  STMT   SOURCE STATEMENT                                         ASM H V 02 10.22 01/13/89

                                      2 ***********************************************************************
                                      3 * THIS PROGRAM DEMONSTRATES TECHNIQUE FOR PARSING SIMPLE ALGEBRATIC     *
                                      4 * EQUATIONS AND CONVERTING FROM INFIX TO REVERSE POLISH NOTATION.       *
                                      5 ***********************************************************************

                                      7          PRINT NOGEN                  SUPPRESS MACRO EXPANSION LISTING     PRPE0080
000000                                8          START 0                                                            00016**2
                                      9 BEGIN    SAVE  (14,12)                SAVE REGISTERS
000004 05C0                          12          BALR  12,0                   LOAD BASE REGISTER
                             00006   13          USING *,12                   ESTABLISH ADDRESSABILITY
000006 50D0 C1DE             001E4   14          ST    13,SAVEAREA+4          SAVE ENTRY REGISTER
00000A 41D0 C1DA             001E0   15          LA    13,SAVEAREA            POINT TO SAVE AREA
                                     16          TIME
000014 5010 C3C2             003C8   21          ST    1,TODAY                SAVE DATE (00YYDDDC)
000018 4510 C308             0030E   22          BAL   1,JULGREG              CONVERT TO MM/DD/YY
                                     23          OPEN  (PRINTER,OUTPUT,CARDS) OPEN CURRENT FILES                   PRPE0120
00002A 45B0 C1B0             001B6   31          BAL   11,HEADPAGE


                                     33 READCARD GET   CARDS,CARDAREA          READ CARD                            PRPE0180
00003C F810 C306 C43C 0030C 00442    38          ZAP   NESTS,=P'0'            INITIALIZE PARENTHICAL EXPRESSIONS
000042 4160 C494             0049A   39          LA    6,CARDAREA             POINT TO BEGINNING OF INPUT
000046 4180 0048             00048   40          LA    8,72                   SET INPUT LENGTH
00004A D205 C58E C41E 00594 00424    41          MVC   LINE+1(6),=C'INPUT:'   INDENTIFY INPUT
000050 D24F C597 C494 0059D 0049A    42          MVC   LINE+10(80),CARDAREA MOVE CARD IMAGE
000056 45B0 C196             0019C   43          BAL   11,PRINT               GO PRINT INPUT
00005A D206 C58E C43D 00594 00443    44          MVC   LINE+1(7),=C'OUTPUT:'  IDENTIFY OUTOUT (TARGET STRING)
000060 4190 C597             0059D   45          LA    9,LINE+10              POINT TO BEGINNING OF OUTPUT
000064 4150 C617             0061D   46          LA    5,STACK-L'STACK        POINT TO OPERATOR STACK

000068 4140 C10A             00110   48          LA    4,CARDEND              SET NULL RETURN
00006C 45E0 C222             00228   49 OUTLOOP  BAL   14,SCAN                SCAN FOR OPERAND OR OPERATOR
000070 9540 C4E4       004EA         50          CLI   OPERAND,C' '           OPERAND?
000074 4770 C0D0             000D6   51          BNE   ISOPRAND                YES

000078 954D C4ED       004F3         53          CLI   OPERATOR+1,C'('        OPEN PARENTHESIS?
00007C 4780 C0BA             000C0   54          BE    PUSH                    YES

000080 5950 C3E2             003E8   56 NEXTOP   C     5,=A(STACK)            IS STACK EMPTY?
000084 4740 C0BA             000C0   57          BL    PUSH                    YES
000088 D500 C4EC 5000 004F2 00000    58          CLC   OPERATOR(1),0(5)       DID HIERARCHY INCREASE?
00008E 4720 C0AA             000B0   59          BH    PUSHMAYB                YES
000092 D201 9000 5001 00000 00001    60          MVC   0(2,9),1(5)            POP OPERATOR FROM STACK
000098 4B50 C424             0042A   61          SH    5,=AL2(L'STACK)        POINT TO PREVIOUS STACK ENTRY
00009C 4199 0002             00002   62          LA    9,2(9)                 POINT PAST OPERATOR
0000A0 955C 5005       00005         63          CLI   L'STACK+2(5),C'*'      EXPONENTATION?
0000A4 4770 C07A             00080   64          BNE   NEXTOP                  NO
0000A8 4199 0001             00001   65          LA    9,1(9)                 SKIP PAST DOUBLE CHARACTER
0000AC 47F0 C07A             00080   66          B     NEXTOP                 GO CHECK AGAINST NEXT STACK ENTRY


0000B0 955D C4ED       004F3         68 PUSHMAYB CLI   OPERATOR+1,C')'        CLOSING PARENTHESIS?
0000B4 4770 C0BA             000C0   69          BNE   PUSH                    NO
0000B8 4B50 C424             0042A   70          SH    5,=AL2(L'STACK)        POP OPENING PARENTHESIS
0000BC 47F0 C066             0006C   71          B     OUTLOOP                GO GET NEXT UNIT
```

```
SAMPLE8--REVERSE POLISH NOTATION

  LOC  OBJECT CODE    ADDR1 ADDR2  STMT   SOURCE STATEMENT                                    ASM H V 02 10.22 01/13/89

0000C0 4155 0003            00003    73 PUSH     LA    5,L'STACK(5)         INCREMENT TOP OF STACK
0000C4 5950 C3E6            003EC    74          C     5,=A(STACKEND)       STACK OVERFLOW?
0000C8 4720 C0DC            000E2    75          BH    STACKOVF              YES
0000CC D202 5000 C4EC 00000 004F2    76          MVC   0(L'STACK,5),OPERATOR PUSH CURRENT OPERATOR
0000D2 47F0 C066            0006C    77          B     OUTLOOP              GO GET NEXT UNIT

0000D6 4470 C48C            00492    79 ISOPRAND EX    7,MOVERAND           MOVE OPERAND TO OUTPUT (TARGET)
0000DA 4197 9001            00001    80          LA    9,1(7,9)             POINT TO NEXT OUTPUT POSITION
0000DE 47F0 C066            0006C    81          B     OUTLOOP              GO CONTINUE

0000E2 D212 C4EF C444 004F5 0044A    83 STACKOVF MVC   ERROR(19),=C'STACK SIZE EXCEEDED'
0000E8 47F0 C10A            00110    84          B     CARDEND              GO PRINT PROCESSED OUTPUT/ERROR

0000EC D213 C4EF C3EA 004F5 003F0    86 UNPAIRED MVC   ERROR(20),=C'UNPAIRED PARENTHESES'
0000F2 F810 C306 C43C 0030C 00442    87          ZAP   NESTS,=P'0'          RESET TO PREVENT UNENDING LOOP
0000F8 47F0 C10A            00110    88          B     CARDEND              GO PRINT PROCESSED OUTPUT/ERROR

0000FC D216 C4EF C457 004F5 0045D    90 BADOPER  MVC   ERROR(23),=C'TERMINAL OPERATION CODE'
000102 47F0 C10A            00110    91          B     CARDEND              GO PRINT PROCESSED OUTPUT/ERROR

000106 D215 C4EF C426 004F5 0042C    93 TOOLONG  MVC   ERROR(22),=C'SYMBOL EXCEEDS 8 BYTES'
00010C 47F0 C10A            00110    94          B     CARDEND              GO PRINT PROCESSED OUTPUT/ERROR

000110 5950 C3E2            003E8    96 CARDEND  C     5,=A(STACK)          IS STACK EMPTY?
000114 4740 C13E            00144    97          BL    CARDDONE              YES
                                     98          PUT   PRINTER,LINE
000126 D201 9000 5001 00000 00001   103          MVC   0(2,9),1(5)          POP OPERATOR FROM STACK
00012C 4B50 C424            0042A   104          SH    5,=AL2(L'STACK)      POINT TO PREVIOUS STACK ENTRY
000130 4199 0002            00002   105          LA    9,2(9)               POINT PAST OPERATOR
000134 955C 5005      00005         106          CLI   L'STACK+2(5),C'*'    EXPONENTATION?
000138 4770 C10A            00110   107          BNE   CARDEND               NO
00013C 4199 0001            00001   108          LA    9,1(9)               SKIP PAST DOUBLE CHARACTER
000140 47F0 C10A            00110   109          B     CARDEND              GO CHECK AGAINST NEXT STACK ENTRY
000144 45B0 C196            0019C   111 CARDDONE BAL   11,PRINT             PRINT OUTPUT
000148 F910 C306 C43C 0030C 00442   112          CP    NESTS,=P'0'          UNPAIRED PARENTHESES?
00014E 4770 C0E6            000EC   113          BNE   UNPAIRED              YES
000152 D518 C4EF C58D 004F5 00593   114          CLC   ERROR,LINE           ANY ERRORS?
000158 4780 C16E            00174   115          BE    NOERRORS              NO
00015C D21C C58E C46E 00594 00474   116          MVC   LINE+1(29),=C'PROCESSING TERMINATED BECAUSE'
000162 D218 C5AC C4EF 005B2 004F5   117          MVC   LINE+31(L'ERROR),ERROR MOVE ERROR MESSAGE
000168 45B0 C196            0019C   118          BAL   11,PRINT             GO PRINT ERROR MESSAGE
```

```
      SAMPLE8--REVERSE POLISH NOTATION

  LOC  OBJECT CODE      ADDR1 ADDR2  STMT   SOURCE STATEMENT                                        ASM H V 02 10.22 01/13/89
00016C D218 C4EF C58D 004F5 00593    119            MVC    ERROR,LINE            CLEAR ERROR MESSAGE
000172 0000                          120            DC     H'0'

000174 92F0 C58D            00593    122 NOERRORS MVI    LINE,C'0'             SET TO DOUBLE SPACE
000178 45B0 C1AE                  001B4  123            BAL    11,DOUBLESP           COUNT LINE
00017C 47F0 C028                  0002E  124            B      READCARD              GO GET NEXT CARD


                                     126 CARDEOF  CLOSE  (PRINTER,,CARDS)      CLOSE FILES                       PRPE2090
00018E 58D0 C1DE                  001E4  134            L      13,SAVEAREA+4         RESTORE REGISTERS                 00063
                                     135            RETURN (14,12),RC=0


00019C 5810 C3FE                  00404  140 PRINT    L      1,=A(PRINTER)         LOAD ADDRESS OF PRINTER DCB
                                     141            PUT    (1),LINE              PRINT LINE
0001AA 9240 C58D            00593    145            MVI    LINE,C' '             SET TO SINGLE SPACE
0001AE D283 C58E C58D 00594 00593    146            MVC    LINE+1(L'LINE-1),LINE CLEAR TO BLANKS
0001B4 06AB                          147 DOUBLESP BCTR   10,11                 RETURN IF PAGE IS NOT FULL

0001B6 FA10 C492 C48B 00498 00491    149 HEADPAGE AP     PAGES,=P'1'           INCREMENT PAGE HEADING
0001BC D203 C588 C402 0058E 00408    150            MVC    PAGENO,=X'40202120'   SET EDIT PATTERN
0001C2 DE03 C588 C492 0058E 00498    151            ED     PAGENO,PAGES          FORMAT PAGE NUMBER
0001C8 5810 C3FE                  00404  152            L      1,=A(PRINTER)         LOAD ADDRESS OF PRINTER DCB
                                     153            PUT    (1),HEADING           PRINT PAGE HEADING
0001D6 92F0 C58D            00593    157            MVI    LINE,C'0'             SET TO DOUBLE SPACE
0001DA 41A0 0038                  00038  158            LA     10,56                 LINES/PAGE
0001DE 07FB                          159            BR     11                    RETURN


0001E0 0000000000000000              161 SAVEAREA DC     9D'0'                                                   PRPE2330

                                     163 ************************************************************************ KHN00040
                                     164 *  THIS IS AN INTERNAL SUBROUTINE TO SCAN FOR SYMBOLS (OPERANDS) AND  * KHN00050
                                     165 *  OPERATORS). OPERATORS ARE +, -, *, /, **, (, AND ).  SYMBOLS MAY BE* KHN00060
                                     166 *  UP TO 8 BYTES IN LENGTH AND ARE STORED IN 'SYMBOL'.  IMBEDDED       * KHN00070
                                     167 *  BLANKS ARE REMOVED FROM SYMBOLS.  OPERATORS ARE STORED IN THE      * KHN00080
                                     168 *  SECOND BYTE OF 'OPERATOR'.  THE FIRST BYTE IS THE HIERARCHAL VALUE * KHN00080
                                     169 *  OF THE OPERATOR (2,2,3,3,4,0,AND 1; RESPECTIVELY).                 * KHN00080
                                     170 *---------------------------------------------------------------------* KHN00090
                                     171 *  TO REDUCE INSTRUCTION PATH LENGTH THIS SUBROUTINE NEITHER SAVES    * KHN00110
                                     172 *  REGISTERS NOR USES CONVENTIONAL CALLING SEQUENCE.                  * KHN00120
                                     173 *---------------------------------------------------------------------* KHN00130
                                     174 *  USAGE:                                                             * KHN00140
                                     175 *                                                                     * KHN00150
                                     176 *     1)  TO SCAN FOR THE ABOVE TOKENS:                               * KHN00210
                                     177 *                                                                     * KHN00220
                                     178 *         LA    4,NULL                 LOAD ADDRESS OF EOB RETURN     * KHN00230
                                     179 *         BAL   14,SCAN                SCAN FOR NEXT INPUT FIELD      * KHN00240
                                     180 *                                                                     * KHN00250
                                     181 *---------------------------------------------------------------------* KHN00300
                                     182 *  REGISTER USAGE:                                                    * KHN00310
                                     183 *                                                                     * KHN00320
```

```
SAMPLE8--REVERSE POLISH NOTATION

  LOC  OBJECT CODE    ADDR1 ADDR2  STMT   SOURCE STATEMENT                                              ASM H V 02 10.22 01/13/89
                                   184 *     1)  FOR SUBROUTINE 'SCAN' CONTENTS OF REGISTER 1 IS USED AS       * KHN00330
                                   185 *         A WORK REGISTER AND IS NOT RESTORED.                          * KHN00340
                                   186 *     2)  ON ENTRY TO 'SCAN' THE FOLLOWING ASSUMPTIONS ARE MADE:        * KHN00350
                                   187 *         REGISTER 6 POINTS TO THE NEXT SCAN POSITION, REGISTER 8       * KHN00360
                                   188 *         CONTAINS THE REMAINING LENGTH OF INPUT TO BE SCANNED,         * KHN00370
                                   189 *         REGISTER 4 CONTAINS THE ADDRESS TO EXIT ON NULL INPUT, AND    * KHN00380
                                   190 *         REGISTER 14, CONTAINS THE NORMAL RETURN ADDRESS.              * KHN00380
                                   191 *     3)  ON RETURN: REGISTER 7 CONTAINS ONE LESS THAN THE LENGTH       * KHN00390
                                   192 *         OF THE SCANNED UNIT, REGISTER 8 HAS BEEN REDUCED BY THAT      * KHN00400
                                   193 *         LENGTH, AND 'OPERAND' OR 'OPERATOR' HAS BEEN SET AS ABOVE.    * KHN00400
                                   194 *                                                                       * KHN00430
                                   195 *************************************************************************** KHN00440
000228 1288                        197 SCAN     LTR   8,8                 ANY MORE INPUT?                 KHN00550
00022A 0784                        198          BZR   4                    NO                               .
00022C D207 C4E4 C54E 004EA 00554  199          MVC   OPERAND,BLANKS      CLEAR OPERAND                   KHN00550
000232 D202 C4EC C54E 004F2 00554  200          MVC   OPERATOR,BLANKS     " OPERATOR                      KHN00550
000238 41F0 C4E4            004EA  201          LA    15,OPERAND          POINT TO FIRST BYTE             KHN00560
00023C 1722                        202          XR    2,2                 CLEAR REGISTER
00023E 1777                        203          XR    7,7                 CLEAR REGISTER

000240 9540 6000      00000        205 SCANLOOP CLI   0(6),C' '           BLANK CHARACTER?                KHN00580
000244 4780 C2F0            002F6  206          BE    IGNORE               YES

000248 954D 6000      00000        208          CLI   0(6),C'('           OPEN PARENTHESIS?
00024C 4770 C25C            00262  209          BNE   NOTLEFT              NO
000250 9540 C4E4      004EA        210          CLI   OPERAND,C' '        TRAILING '('? (SHOULD NOT HAPPEN)
000254 4770 C2BC            002C2  211          BNE   LEVEL0               YES
000258 FA10 C306 C48B 0030C 00491  212          AP    NESTS,=P'1'         INCREMENT NESTED EXPRESSION COUNT
00025E 47F0 C2BC            002C2  213          B     LEVEL0              GO PROCESS OPERATOR

000262 955D 6000      00000        215 NOTLEFT  CLI   0(6),C')'           CLOSED PARENTHESIS?
000266 4770 C27A            00280  216          BNE   NOTRIGHT             NO
00026A 9540 C4E4      004EA        217          CLI   OPERAND,C' '        TRAILING ')'?
00026E 4770 C2B8            002BE  218          BNE   LEVEL1               YES
000272 FB10 C306 C48B 0030C 00491  219          SP    NESTS,=P'1'         DECREMENT NESTED EXPRESSION COUNT
000278 4740 C0E6            000EC  220          BM    UNPAIRED            UNPAIRED PARENTHESES
00027C 47F0 C2B8            002BE  221          B     LEVEL1              GO PROCESS OPERATOR

000280 954E 6000      00000        223 NOTRIGHT CLI   0(6),C'+'           PLUS SIGN?
000284 4780 C2B4            002BA  224          BE    LEVEL2               YES

000288 9560 6000      00000        226          CLI   0(6),C'-'           MINUS SIGN?
00028C 4780 C2B4            002BA  227          BE    LEVEL2               YES

000290 9561 6000      00000        229          CLI   0(6),C'/'           DIVISION SIGN?
000294 4780 C2B0            002B6  230          BE    LEVEL3               YES

000298 955C 6000      00000        232          CLI   0(6),C'*'           MULTIPLICATION OR EXPONENTIATION?
00029C 4770 C2DE            002E4  233          BNE   NOTSTAR              NO

0002A0 955C 6001      00001        235          CLI   1(6),C'*'           EXPONENTIATION?
0002A4 4770 C2B0            002B6  236          BNE   LEVEL3               NO

0002A8 925C C4EE      004F4        238          MVI   OPERATOR+2,C'*'     SET SECOND BYTE OF OPERATOR
```

```
SAMPLE8--REVERSE POLISH NOTATION

  LOC  OBJECT CODE    ADDR1 ADDR2  STMT   SOURCE  STATEMENT                                       ASM H V 02 10.22 01/13/89

0002AC 0680                         239           BCTR  8,0                     DECREMENT LENGTH FOR SECOND '*'
0002AE 4170 0001            00001   240           LA    7,1                     SET LENGTH=2
0002B2 4122 0001            00001   241           LA    2,1(2)                  INCREMENT HIERARCHY LEVEL

0002B6 4122 0001            00001   243 LEVEL3    LA    2,1(2)                  INCREMENT HIERARCHY LEVEL

0002BA 4122 0001            00001   245 LEVEL2    LA    2,1(2)                  INCREMENT HIERARCHY LEVEL

0002BE 4122 0001            00001   247 LEVEL1    LA    2,1(2)                  INCREMENT HIERARCHY LEVEL

0002C2 9540 C4E4      004EA         249 LEVEL0    CLI   OPERAND,C' '            OPERAND PRESENT?
0002C6 4770 C2FE            00304   250           BNE   ENDORAND                 YES
0002CA D200 C4ED 6000 004F3 00000   251           MVC   OPERATOR+1(1),0(6)      MOVE OPERAND
0002D0 4220 C4EC            004F2   252           STC   2,OPERATOR              STORE HIERARCHIAL LEVEL
0002D4 4166 7001            00001   253           LA    6,1(6,7)                POINT TO NEXT INPUT POSITION
0002D8 068E                         254           BCTR  8,14                    RETURN
0002DA 955D C4ED      004F3         255           CLI   OPERATOR+1,C')'         CLOSING PARENTHESIS?
0002DE 4770 C0F6            000FC   256           BNE   BADOPER                  NO
0002E2 07FE                         257           BR    14                       YES


0002E4 D200 F000 6000 00000 00000   259 NOTSTAR   MVC   0(1,15),0(6)            MOVE CHARACTER TO OPERAND
0002EA 41FF 0001            00001   260           LA    15,1(15)                POINT TO NEXT OUTPUT POSITION
0002EE 59F0 C406            0040C   261           C     15,=A(OPERAND+L'OPERAND) TOO LONG?
0002F2 4720 C100            00106   262           BH    TOOLONG                  YES

0002F6 4166 0001            00001   264 IGNORE    LA    6,1(6)                  POINT TO NEXT INPUT POSITION
0002FA 4680 C23A            00240   265           BCT   8,SCANLOOP              CONTINUE UNTIL UNIT COMPLETE
0002FE 9540 C4E4      004EA         266           CLI   OPERAND,C' '            OPERAND PRESENT?
000302 0784                         267           BER   4                        NO

000304 187F                         269 ENDORAND  LR    7,15                    SET CURRENT OPERAND POSITION
000306 5B70 C40A            00410   270           S     7,=A(OPERAND)           GET LENGTH - 1
00030A 07FE                         271           BR    14                      RETURN


00030C 000C                         273 NESTS     DC    PL2'0'


00030E 5010 C3A2            003A8   275 JULGREG   ST    1,SAVEJRET              SAVE RETURN REGISTER
000312 5810 C3C2            003C8   276           L     1,TODAY                 LOAD YYDDDC
000316 8A10 0010            00010   277           SRA   1,16                    EXTRACT CURRENT YEAR
00031A 8910 0004            00004   278           SLL   1,4                     ALLOW ROOM FOR SIGN
00031E 5010 C3B6            003BC   279           ST    1,YEARS+4               STORE YY0
000322 960C C3B9      003BF         280           OI    YEARS+7,X'C'            SET SIGN
000326 4F10 C3B2            003B8   281           CVB   1,YEARS                 CONVERT TO BINARY
00032A 4210 C3A6            003AC   282           STC   1,LEAPFLAG              SAVE FOR LEAP YEAR TEST
00032E 0610                         283           BCTR  1,0                     LAST YEAR
000330 5C00 C40E            00414   284           M     0,=F'365.25'            100*YEARS*DAYS/YEAR
000334 5D00 0064            00064   285           D     0,100                   DAYS FROM 1/0/00 TO 12/31/(YR-1)
000338 4E10 C3BA            003C0   286           CVD   1,SAVEDAYS              CONVERT TO DECIMAL

00033C F811 C3A7 C3C4 003AD 003CA   287           ZAP   DAYS,TODAY+2(2)         SAVE DAYS FROM BEGINNING OF YEAR
000342 FA71 C3BA C3A7 003C0 003AD   288           AP    SAVEDAYS,DAYS           DAYS FROM 1/0/00 TO TODAY
000348 F810 C3A9 C48B 003AF 00491   289           ZAP   MONTHS,=P'1'            INITIALIZE MONTH
00034E 98F1 C412            00418   290           LM    15,1,=A(JANUARY,L'JANUARY,DECEMBER) DAYS/MONTH TABLE
```

```
SAMPLE8--REVERSE POLISH NOTATION

  LOC  OBJECT CODE    ADDR1 ADDR2  STMT   SOURCE STATEMENT                                  ASM H V 02 10.22 01/13/89

000352 9103 C3A6       003AC        291            TM    LEAPFLAG,3            LEAP YEAR?
000356 4770 C35A             00360  292            BNZ   DDDLOOP                NO
00035A FA10 C3CA C48B 003D0 00491   293            AP    FEBRUARY,=P'1'        ADJUST
000360 F911 C3A7 F000 003AD 00000   294 DDDLOOP    CP    DAYS,0(L'JANUARY,15)  CURRENT MONTH?
000366 47D0 C374             0037A  295            BNH   DDDFOUND               YES
00036A FA10 C3A9 C48B 003AF 00491   296            AP    MONTHS,=P'1'          INCREMENT MONTH
000370 FB11 C3A7 F000 003AD 00000   297            SP    DAYS,0(L'JANUARY,15)  DECREMENT DAYS PER CURRENT MONTH
000376 87F0 C35A             00360  298            BXLE  15,0,DDDLOOP          CONTINUE
00037A F311 C546 C3A9 0054C 003AF   299 DDDFOUND   UNPK  DATE(2),MONTHS        UNPACK MONTH
000380 F311 C549 C3A7 0054F 003AD   300            UNPK  DATE+3(2),DAYS        UNPACK DAY
000386 F317 C54C C3B2 00552 003B8   301            UNPK  DATE+6(2),YEARS       UNPACK YEAR
00038C 9261 C548       0054E        302            MVI   DATE+2,C'/'           SEPARATE MONTH AND DAY
000390 9261 C54B       00551        303            MVI   DATE+5,C'/'           SEPARATE DAY AND YEAR
000394 96F0 C547       0054D        304            OI    DATE+1,C'0'           FORCE MONTH NUMERIC
000398 96F0 C54A       00550        305            OI    DATE+4,C'0'           FORCE DAY NUMERIC
00039C 96F0 C54D       00553        306            OI    DATE+7,C'0'           FORCE YEAR NUMERIC
0003A0 5810 C3A2             003A8  307            L     1,SAVEJRET            RESTORE REGISTER
0003A4 07F1                         308            BR    1                     RETURN

0003A8                              310 SAVEJRET   DS    F


0003AC 00                           312 LEAPFLAG   DC    X'0'
0003AD                              313 DAYS       DS    PL2
0003AF                              314 MONTHS     DS    PL2
0003B1                              315 MMDDYY     DS    CL6
0003B7 00
0003B8 0000000000000000             316 YEARS      DC    D'0'
0003C0                              317 SAVEDAYS   DS    D
0003C8                              318 TODAY      DS    F
0003CC 000C                         319            DC    PL2'0'                MUST IMMEDIATELY PRECEED 'JANUARY'
0003CE 031C                         320 JANUARY    DC    P'31'
                                    321 *                   M   A   M   J   J   A   S   O   N
0003D0 028C031C030C031C             322 FEBRUARY   DC    P'28,31,30,31,30,31,31,30,31,30'
0003E4 031C                         323 DECEMBER   DC    P'31'
0003E8                              324            LTORG
0003E8 00000620                     325                  =A(STACK)
0003EC 0000074C                     326                  =A(STACKEND)
0003F0 E4D5D7C1C9D9C5C4             327                  =C'UNPAIRED PARENTHESES'
000404 000007B0                     328                  =A(PRINTER)
000408 40202120                     329                  =X'40202120'
00040C 000004F2                     330                  =A(OPERAND+L'OPERAND)
000410 000004EA                     331                  =A(OPERAND)
000414 0000016D                     332                  =F'365.25'
000418 000003CE00000002             333                  =A(JANUARY,L'JANUARY,DECEMBER)
000424 C9D5D7E4E37A                 334                  =C'INPUT:'
00042A 0003                         335                  =AL2(L'STACK)
00042C E2E8D4C2D6D340C5             336                  =C'SYMBOL EXCEEDS 8 BYTES'
000442 0C                           337                  =P'0'
000443 D6E4E3D7E4E37A               338                  =C'OUTPUT:'
00044A E2E3C1C3D240E2C9             339                  =C'STACK SIZE EXCEEDED'
00045D E3C5D9D4C9D5C1D3             340                  =C'TERMINAL OPERATION CODE'
000474 D7D9D6C3C5E2E2C9             341                  =C'PROCESSING TERMINATED BECAUSE'
000491 1C                           342                  =P'1'
000492 D200 9000 C4E4 00000 004EA   343 MOVERAND   MVC   0(*-*,9),OPERAND
```

```
SAMPLE8--REVERSE POLISH NOTATION

  LOC  OBJECT CODE      ADDR1 ADDR2  STMT    SOURCE STATEMENT                                                          ASM H V 02 10.22 01/13/89

000498 000C                           344 PAGES     DC     PL2'0'
00049A                                345 CARDAREA  DS     CL80
0004EA 4040404040404040               346 OPERAND   DC     CL8' '
0004F2 404040                         347 OPERATOR  DC     CL3' '
0004F5 4040404040404040               348 ERROR     DC     CL25' '
00050E F140404040404040               349 HEADING   DC     CL133'1'
000593                        0050F   350           ORG    HEADING+1
00050F C6D6D9D4E4D3C140               351           DC     C'FORMULA ANALYSIS'
00051F                        0054C   352           ORG    HEADING+62
00054C D4D461C4C461E8E8               353 DATE      DC     C'MM/DD/YY'
000554 4040404040404040               354 BLANKS    DC     8C' '
00055C                        0058A   355           ORG    HEADING+124
00058A D7C1C7C5                       356           DC     C'PAGE'
00058E                                357 PAGENO    DS     CL4
000592                        00593   358           ORG
000593 F040404040404040               359 LINE      DC     CL133'0'
000618                                360 DOUBLE    DS     D
000620                                361 STACK     DS     100CL3
00074C                                362 STACKEND  DS     CL3


                                      364 CARDS     DCB    DDNAME=SYSIN,DSORG=PS,MACRF=GM,SYNAD=BOMB,    ECL=080,    -
                                                           EODAD=CARDEOF RECFM=F,BLKSIZE=XXXX
                                      418 PRINTER   DCB    DDNAME=PRINTER,DEVD=DA,DSORG=PS,LRECL=133,                -
                                                           BLKSIZE=133,MACRF=PM,RECFM=FBA
000810 00                             472 BOMB      DC     X'0'
                                      473           END                                                          PRPE3480
```

```
                                                  CROSS REFERENCE

SYMBOL    LEN     VALUE  DEFN  REFERENCES                                                          ASM H V 02 10.22 01/13/89

BADOPER   00006   0000FC 0090  0256
BEGIN     00002   000000 0010
BLANKS    00001   000554 0354  0199 0200
BOMB      00001   000810 0472  0401
CARDAREA  00080   00049A 0345  0035 0039 0042
CARDDONE  00004   000144 0111  0097
CARDEND   00004   000110 0096  0048 0084 0088 0091 0094 0107 0109
CARDEOF   00004   000180 0128  0386
CARDS     00004   000750 0368  0029 0034 0132
DATE      00008   00054C 0353  0299 0300 0301 0302 0303 0304 0305 0306
DAYS      00002   0003AD 0313  0287 0288 0294 0297 0300
DDDFOUND  00006   00037A 0299  0295
DDDLOOP   00006   000360 0294  0292 0298
DECEMBER  00002   0003E4 0323  0333
DOUBLE    00008   000618 0360
DOUBLESP  00002   0001B4 0147  0123
ENDORAND  00002   000304 0269  0250
ERROR     00025   0004F5 0348  0083 0086 0090 0093 0114 0117 0117 0119
FEBRUARY  00002   0003D0 0322  0293
HEADING   00133   00050E 0349  0154 0350 0352 0355
HEADPAGE  00006   0001B6 0149  0031
IGNORE    00004   0002F6 0264  0206
ISOPRAND  00004   0000D6 0079  0051
JANUARY   00002   0003CE 0320  0294 0297 0333 0333

JULGREG   00004   00030E 0275  0022
LEAPFLAG  00001   0003AC 0312  0282 0291
LEVEL0    00004   0002C2 0249  0211 0213
LEVEL1    00004   0002BE 0247  0218 0221
LEVEL2    00004   0002BA 0245  0224 0227
LEVEL3    00004   0002B6 0243  0230 0236
LINE      00133   000593 0359  0041 0042 0044 0045 0100 0114 0116 0117 0119 0122 0142 0145 0146 0146 0146 0157

MMDDYY    00006   0003B1 0315
MONTHS    00002   0003AF 0314  0289 0296 0299
MOVERAND  00006   000492 0343  0079
NESTS     00002   00030C 0273  0038 0087 0112 0212 0219
NEXTOP    00004   000080 0056  0064 0066
NOERRORS  00004   000174 0122  0115
NOTLEFT   00004   000262 0215  0209
NOTRIGHT  00004   000280 0223  0216
NOTSTAR   00006   0002E4 0259  0233
OPERAND   00008   0004EA 0346  0050 0199 0201 0210 0217 0249 0266 0330 0330 0331 0343
OPERATOR  00003   0004F2 0347  0053 0058 0068 0076 0200 0238 0251 0252 0255
OUTLOOP   00004   00006C 0049  0071 0077 0081
PAGENO    00004   00058E 0357  0150 0151
PAGES     00002   000498 0344  0149 0151
PRINT     00004   00019C 0140  0043 0111 0118
PRINTER   00004   0007B0 0422  0027 0099 0130 0328
PUSH      00004   0000C0 0073  0054 0057 0069
PUSHMAYB  00004   0000B0 0068  0059
READCARD  00004   00002E 0034  0124
SAVEAREA  00008   0001E0 0161  0014 0015 0134
SAVEDAYS  00008   0003C0 0317  0286 0288
SAVEJRET  00004   0003A8 0310  0275 0307
SCAN      00002   000228 0197  0049
SCANLOOP  00004   000240 0205  0265
```

```
                              CROSS REFERENCE                                       ASM H V 02 10.22 01/13/89

SYMBOL    LEN    VALUE  DEFN  REFERENCES

STACK     00003  000620 0361  0046 0046 0063 0073 0076 0106 0325 0335
STACKEND  00003  00074C 0362  0326
STACKOVF  00006  0000E2 0083  0075
TODAY     00004  0003C8 0318  0021 0276 0287
TOOLONG   00006  000106 0093  0262
UNPAIRED  00006  0000EC 0086  0113 0220
YEARS     00008  0003B8 0316  0279 0280 0281 0301
=A(JANUARY,L'JANUARY,DECEMBER)
          00004  000418 0333  0290
=A(OPERAND+L'OPERAND)
          00004  00040C 0330  0261
=A(OPERAND)
          00004  000410 0331  0270
=A(PRINTER)
          00004  000404 0328  0140 0152
=A(STACK)
          00004  0003E8 0325  0056 0096
=A(STACKEND)
          00004  0003EC 0326  0074
=AL2(L'STACK)
          00002  00042A 0335  0061 0070 0104
=C'INPUT:'
          00006  000424 0334  0041
=C'OUTPUT:'
          00007  000443 0338  0044
=C'PROCESSING TERMINATED BECAUSE'
          00029  000474 0341  0116
=C'STACK SIZE EXCEEDED'
          00019  00044A 0339  0083
=C'SYMBOL EXCEEDS 8 BYTES'
          00022  00042C 0336  0093
=C'TERMINAL OPERATION CODE'
          00023  00045D 0340  0090
=C'UNPAIRED PARENTHESES'
          00020  0003F0 0327  0086
=F'365.25'
          00004  000414 0332  0284
=P'0'     00001  000442 0337  0038 0087 0112
=P'1'     00001  000491 0342  0149 0212 0219 0289 0293 0296
=X'40202120'
          00004  000408 0329  0150
```

```
FORMULA ANALYSIS

INPUT:   ALPHA   +  B E T A
OUTPUT:  ALPHA BETA +

INPUT:   A-B+C
OUTPUT:  A B - C +

INPUT:   A-B*C
OUTPUT:  A B C * -

INPUT:   A+B*C-(D-E)/F
OUTPUT:  A B C * + D E - F / -

INPUT:   A+B*(C-D/(E+F*G))**H
OUTPUT:  A B C D E F G * + / - H ** * +
```

```
SAMPLE ASSEMBLER PROGRAM--SAMPLE9

  LOC  OBJECT CODE    ADDR1 ADDR2  STMT   SOURCE STATEMENT                                     ASM H V 02 17.00 03/28/89

                                      2 ***********************************************************************
                                      3 * THIS PROGRAM READS A SET OF CARD IMAGES FROM A SEQUENTIAL DATASET,   *
                                      4 * EXTRACTS A DECIMAL FIELD WHICH MAY CONTAIN A PRECEEDING MINUS SIGN   *
                                      5 * AND AN IMBEDDED DECIMAL POINT.  THE VALUE IS CONVERTED TO LONG FORM *
                                      6 * FLOATING POINT AND PRINTED OUT IN HEXADECIMAL.  IF NOT NEGATIVE,    *
                                      7 * THE SQUARE ROOT IS COMPUTED, ITS NORMALIZED HEXADECIMAL VALUE(10**7)*
                                      8 * IS PRINTED OUT ALONG WITH ITS UNNORMALIZED VALUE USED IN CONVERSION *
                                      9 * TO FIXED POINT, THE DECIMAL VALUE OF THE SQUARE ROOT, AND THE SQUARE*
                                     10 * OF THE SQUARE ROOT (FOR VERIFICATION).                              *
                                     11 ***********************************************************************

000000                               13          START X'0'            ADJUST LOCATION COUNTER FOR MVS/XA
                                     14          PRINT NOGEN

                                     16          DC    C'SAMPLE9--ASSEMBLED &SYSDATE-&SYSTIME'

                                     18 BEGIN    SAVE  (14,12)               SAVE REGISTERS
000026 05C0                          21          BALR  12,0                  LOAD BASE REGISTER
                              00028  22          USING *,12                  ESTABLISH ADDRESSABILITY
000028 50D0 C244              0026C  23          ST    13,SAVEAREA+4         SAVE ENTRY REGISTER
00002C 41D0 C240              00268  24          LA    13,SAVEAREA           POINT TO SAVE AREA

                                     26          OPEN  (CARDS,,PRINTER,OUTPUT) OPEN FILES                          R 1
                                     34          PUT   PRINTER,HEADING       PRINT PAGE HEADING

                                     40 READLOOP GET   CARDS,CARD            READ CARD
00005A 9240 C360        00388        45          MVI   LINE,C' '             SET SEED
00005E D283 C361 C360   00389 00388  46          MVC   LINE+1(132),LINE      CLEAR LINE
000064 9200 C30E        00336        47          MVI   FLAGS,0               CLEAR FLAGS
000068 9836 C530              00558  48          LM    3,6,=A(CARD,1,CARD+72,0) INITIALIZE REGISTERS
00006C 6800 C290              002B8  49          LD    0,FLOATONE            INITIALIZE DECIMAL PLACES
000070 9540 3000        00000        50 INLOOP   CLI   0(3),C' '             BLANK?
000074 4780 C0BA              000E2  51          BE    BLANK                  YES
000078 954B 3000        00000        52          CLI   0(3),C'.'             DECIMAL POINT?
00007C 4780 C09E              000C6  53          BE    DECIMAL                YES
000080 954E 3000        00000        54          CLI   0(3),C'+'             PLUS?
000084 4780 C0AA              000D2  55          BE    PLUS                   YES
000088 9560 3000        00000        56          CLI   0(3),C'-'             MINUS?
00008C 4780 C0A6              000CE  57          BE    MINUS                  YES
000090 95F0 3000        00000        58          CLI   0(3),C'0'             DECIMAL DIGIT?
000094 4740 C230              00258  59          BL    ERROR                  NO
000098 95F9 3000        00000        60          CLI   0(3),C'9'
00009C 4720 C230              00258  61          BH    ERROR                  NO
0000A0 D200 C30D 3000   00335 00000  62          MVC   HALF+1(1),0(3)        MOVE TO HALFWORD
0000A6 940F C30D        00335        63          NI    HALF+1,X'F'           RETAIN ONLY DECIMAL VALUE
0000AA 4C60 C568              00590  64          MH    6,=H'10'              MULTIPLY PREVIOUS VALUE BY 10
0000AE 4A60 C30C              00334  65          AH    6,HALF                ACCUMULATE CURRENT DIGIT
0000B2 9640 C30E        00336        66          OI    FLAGS,DIGITBIT        INDICATE DIGIT ENCOUNTERED
0000B6 9120 C30E        00336        67          TM    FLAGS,DOTBIT          DECIMAL POINT ENCOUNTERED?
0000BA 4780 C0AA              000D2  68          BZ    PLUS                   NO
0000BE 6C00 C298              002C0  69          MD    0,FLOATTEN            ADJUST DECIMAL PLACE FACTOR
0000C2 47F0 C0AA              000D2  70          B     PLUS                  GO CONTINUE

0000C6 9620 C30E        00336        72 DECIMAL  OI    FLAGS,DOTBIT          SET DECIMAL FLAG
0000CA 47F0 C0AA              000D2  73          B     PLUS                  GO CONTINUE
```

```
SAMPLE ASSEMBLER PROGRAM--SAMPLE9

  LOC  OBJECT CODE    ADDR1 ADDR2  STMT   SOURCE STATEMENT                                                     ASM H V 02 17.00 03/28/89

0000CE 9680 C30E      00336          75 MINUS    OI    FLAGS,SIGNBIT         SET NEGATIVE FLAG
0000D2 8734 C048            00070    77 PLUS     BXLE  3,4,INLOOP            CONTINUE
0000D6 9140 C30E      00336          79          TM    FLAGS,DIGITBIT        ANY DIGITS ENCOUNTERED?
0000DA 4780 C230            00258    80          BZ    ERROR                  NO
0000DE 47F0 C0C2            000EA    81          B     PROCESS               EXIT IF FIELD EXHAUSTED
0000E2 9140 C30E      00336          83 BLANK    TM    FLAGS,DIGITBIT        ANY DIGITS ENCOUNTERED?
0000E6 4780 C0AA            000D2    84          BZ    PLUS                   NO
0000EA 9180 C30E      00336          86 PROCESS  TM    FLAGS,SIGNBIT         NEGATIVE VALUE?
0000EE 4780 C0CC            000F4    87          BZ    POSITIVE               NO
0000F2 1366                          88          LCR   6,6                   NEGATE VALUE (LNR IS EQUIVALENT)
0000F4 5060 C2CC            002F4    90 POSITIVE ST    6,FIXED
0000F8 4170 C36C            00394    91          LA    7,LINE+12             POINT TO OUTPUT POSITION
0000FC 4180 C2CC            002F4    92          LA    8,FIXED               POINT TO BINARY VALUE
000100 4590 C1BC            001E4    93          BAL   9,BINTOHEX            CONVERT TO DISPLAY HEXADECIMAL
000104 D209 C361 C310 00389 00338    94          MVC   LINE+1(10),CARD       MOVE INPUT VALUE
00010A 5760 C2BC            002E4    95          X     6,D2X31+4             REVERSE SIGN BIT
00010E D203 C2C8 C2B8 002F0 002E0    96          MVC   FLOAT,D2X31           SET CHARACTERISTIC
000114 5060 C2CC            002F4    97          ST    6,FIXED               SAVE AS LOW ORDER UNNORMAL F.P. VAL  T
000118 6820 C2C8            002F0    98          LD    2,FLOAT               LOAD UNNORMALIZED VALUE
00011C 6B20 C2B8            002E0    99          SD    2,D2X31               SUBTRACT UNNORMALIZED 2**31
000120 2D20                         100          DDR   2,0                   SET DECIMAL POINT
000122 6020 C2C8            002F0   101          STD   2,FLOAT               SAVE CONVERTED VALUE
000126 4177 0002            00002   102          LA    7,2(7)                POINT TO OUTPUT POSITION
00012A 4180 C2C8            002F0   103          LA    8,FLOAT               POINT TO BINARY VALUE
00012E 4590 C1BC            001E4   104          BAL   9,BINTOHEX            CONVERT TO DISPLAY HEXADECIMAL
000132 4590 C1BC            001E4   105          BAL   9,BINTOHEX            CONVERT TO DISPLAY HEXADECIMAL
000136 4590 C1DC            00204   106          BAL   9,SQRT                GO COMPUTE SQUARE ROOT
00013A 6C20 C2A8            002D0   107          MD    2,D10X7               ALLOW 7 DECIMAL PLACES
00013E 9680 C2A0      002C8         108          OI    FLHALF,X'80'          SET NEGATIVE
000142 9180 C2C8      002F0         109          TM    FLOAT,X'80'           VALUE NEGATIVE?
000146 4710 C126            0014E   110          BO    NEGATIVE               YES
00014A 947F C2A0      002C8         111          NI    FLHALF,X'7F'          FORCE POSITIVE
00014E 6A20 C2A0            002C8   112 NEGATIVE AD    2,FLHALF              ROUND
000152 6020 C2C8            002F0   113          STD   2,FLOAT               STORE SQUARE ROOT * 1000
000156 4177 0002            00002   114          LA    7,2(7)                POINT TO OUTPUT POSITION
00015A 4180 C2C8            002F0   115          LA    8,FLOAT               POINT TO BINARY VALUE
00015E 4590 C1BC            001E4   116          BAL   9,BINTOHEX            CONVERT TO DISPLAY HEXADECIMAL
000162 4590 C1BC            001E4   117          BAL   9,BINTOHEX            CONVERT TO DISPLAY HEXADECIMAL
000166 6B20 C2C0            002E8   118          SD    2,D2X31Z              SUBTRACT 2**31 UNNORMALIZED
00016A 6E20 C2B0            002D8   119          AW    2,D2X32               ADD 2**32 UNNORMALIZED
00016E 6020 C2C8            002F0   120          STD   2,FLOAT               SAVE RESULT
000172 9780 C2CC      002F4         121          XI    FIXED,X'80'           REVERSE SIGN BIT
000176 5800 C2CC            002F4   122          L     0,FIXED               LOAD FIXED POINT VALUE
00017A 1200                         123          LTR   0,0                   WAS INPUT NEGATIVE?
00017C 4740 C190            001B8   124          BM    PRINT                  YES
000180 4E00 C2D0            002F8   125          CVD   0,DOUBLE              CONVERT TO DECIMAL
000184 4177 0002            00002   126          LA    7,2(7)                POINT TO OUTPUT POSITION
000188 4180 C2C8            002F0   127          LA    8,FLOAT               POINT TO BINARY VALUE
00018C 4590 C1BC            001E4   128          BAL   9,BINTOHEX            CONVERT TO DISPLAY HEXADECIMAL
```

```
SAMPLE ASSEMBLER PROGRAM--SAMPLE9

  LOC  OBJECT CODE    ADDR1 ADDR2  STMT   SOURCE STATEMENT                                        ASM H V 02 17.00 03/28/89

000190 4590 C1BC            001E4   129             BAL   9,BINTOHEX            CONVERT TO DISPLAY HEXADECIMAL
000194 D211 7002 C2E8 00002 00310   130             MVC   2(18,7),PATTERN MOVE EDIT PATTERN
00019A DE11 7002 C2D0 00002 002F8   131             ED    2(18,7),DOUBLE  FORMAT VALUE
0001A0 F8F7 C2D8 C2D0 00300 002F8   132             ZAP   P16,DOUBLE            MOVE TO LONG FIELD
0001A6 FCF7 C2D8 C2D0 00300 002F8   133             MP    P16,DOUBLE            COMPUTE SQUARE
0001AC D210 7014 C2FA 00014 00322   134             MVC   20(17,7),PATTERN2     SET EDIT PATTERN
0001B2 DE10 7014 C2DE 00014 00306   135             ED    20(17,7),P16+6

                                    137 PRINT       PUT   PRINTER,LINE          PRINT LINE
0001C6 47F0 C024            0004C   142             B     READLOOP              GO GET NEXT RECORD

                                    144 CARDEOF     CLOSE (CARDS,,PRINTER)      CLOSE FILES

0001DA 58D0 C244            0026C   153 RETURN      L     13,SAVEAREA+4         RESTORE ENTRY REGISTER
                                    154             RETURN (14,12)              RESTORE REGISTERS/RETURN


0001E4 F384 7000 8000 00000 00000   158 BINTOHEX UNPK  0(9,7),0(5,8)            UNPACK NYBLS
0001EA D407 7000 C540 00000 00568   159             NC    0(8,7),=8X'F'         MASK OUT ZONE BITS
0001F0 DC07 7000 C548 00000 00570   160             TR    0(8,7),=C'0123456789ABCDEF' CONVERT TO DISPLAY HEX
0001F6 9240 7008      00008         161             MVI   8(7),C' '             CLEAR BYTE
0001FA 4177 0009            00009   162             LA    7,9(7)                POINT TO NEXT OUTPUT POSITION
0001FE 4188 0004            00004   163             LA    8,4(8)                POINT TO NEXT WORD
000202 07F9                         164             BR    9                     RETURN


                                    166 * THIS SQUARE ROOT IS AN IMPLEMENTATION OF THE TECHNIQUE DESCRIBED IN
                                    167 * "VS FORTRAN: LANGUAGE AND LIBRARY REFERENCE" (IBM FORM SC26-4119).
                                    168 *
                                    169 * IF X=16**(2P-Q)*M 1/16 <= M < 1
                                    170 * THEN SQRT(X)=16**P*4**(-Q)*M
                                    171 *
                                    172 * COMPUTE FIRST APPROXIMATION OF SQRT(X)=Y0 BY
                                    173 *  Y0=16**P*4**(-Q)*0.2202*(M+0.2587)
                                    174 *
                                    175 * APPLY THE NEWTON-RAPHSON ITERATION FOUR TIMES
                                    176 *
                                    177 *       Y(N+1)=(Y(N)+X/Y(N))/2
                                    178 *
                                    179 * THE MAXIMUM RELATIVE ERROR OF Y4 IS THEORETICALLY 2**(-63.23)
000204 2242                         181 SQRT        LTDR  4,2                   SAVE X, IS VALUE > 0?
000206 07D9                         182             BNPR  9                      NO
000208 D200 C30D C2C8 00335 002F0   183             MVC   HALF+1(1),FLOAT       LOAD CHARACTERISTIC
00020E 4810 C30C            00334   184             LH    1,HALF                LOAD CHARACTERISTIC
000212 4B10 C56A            00592   185             SH    1,=H'63'              REMOVE EXCESS 64
000216 4210 C30F            00337   186             STC   1,Q                   SAVE Q BIT
00021A 8A10 0001            00001   187             SRA   1,1                   DIVIDE BY 2
00021E 4A10 C56C            00594   188             AH    1,=H'65'              INSERT EXCESS 64
000222 4210 C288            002B0   189             STC   1,P                   SAVE CHARACTERISTIC
000226 9240 C2C8      002F0         190             MVI   FLOAT,X'40'           SET CHARACTERISTIC (OF M)
00022A 6820 C2C8            002F0   191             LD    2,FLOAT               M
00022E 6A20 C558            00580   192             AD    2,=D'.2587'           M+.2587
000232 6C20 C560            00588   193             MD    2,=D'.2202'           .2202(M+.2587)
000236 6C20 C288            002B0   194             MD    2,P                   16**P*0.2202(M+.2587)
```

```
        SAMPLE ASSEMBLER PROGRAM--SAMPLE9

  LOC  OBJECT CODE     ADDR1 ADDR2  STMT   SOURCE STATEMENT                                     ASM H V 02 17.00 03/28/89

00023A 41F0 0004             00004   195            LA    15,4                NUMBER OF NEWTON-RAPHSON ITERATIONS  NOT GEN
00023E 9101 C30F       00337         196            TM    Q,1                 Q=1 (NOTE ODD IF Q=0, ELSE Q=1)?
000242 4780 C222             0024A   197            BZ    Q1                   YES
000246 2A22                          198            ADR   2,2                 16**P*2**(1-Q)*0.2202(M+2587)
000248 2A22                          199            ADR   2,2                 16**P*4**(1-Q)*0.2202(M+2587)
00024A 2804                          200 Q1         LDR   0,4                 X
00024C 2D02                          201            DDR   0,2                 X/YN
00024E 2A20                          202            ADR   2,0                 YN+X/YN
000250 2422                          203            HDR   2,2                 Y(N+1)=(YN+X/YN)/2
000252 46F0 C222             0024A   204            BCT   15,Q1               CONTINUE FOR 4 ITERATIONS
000256 07F9                          205            BR    9                   RETURN

000258 D214 C360 C56E 00388 00596    207 ERROR      MVC   LINE(21),=C'0INVALID DATA FORMAT '
00025E D24F C375 C310 0039D 00338    208            MVC   LINE+21(80),CARD    MOVE CARD IMAGE
000264 47F0 C190             001B8   209            B     PRINT               GO PRINT ERROR MESSAGE

000268 0000000000000000              211 SAVEAREA   DC    18F'0'
0002B0 4210000000000000              212 P          DC    D'16.'
0002B8 4110000000000000              213 FLOATONE   DC    D'1.'
0002C0 41A0000000000000              214 FLOATTEN   DC    D'10.'
0002C8 4080000000000000              215 FLHALF     DC    D'.5'
0002D0 4698968000000000              216 D10X7      DC    D'10000000.'
0002D8 4E00000100000000              217 D2X32      DC    X'4E00000100000000' UNNORMALIZED 2**32
0002E0 4E00000080000000              218 D2X31      DC    X'4E00000080000000' UNNORMALIZED 2**31
0002E8 4F00000008000000              219 D2X31Z     DC    X'4F00000008000000' UNNORMALIZED 2**31
0002F0                               220 FLOAT      DS    F
0002F4                               221 FIXED      DS    F
0002F8                               222 DOUBLE     DS    D
000300                               223 P16        DS    PL16
000310 4020202020202020              224 PATTERN    DC    C' ',7X'20',X'21',C'.',7X'20',C'-'
000322 402020202020214B20            225 PATTERN2   DC    C' ',4X'20',X'21',C'.',10X'20',C'-'
000334 0000                          226 HALF       DC    H'0'
000336 00                            227 FLAGS      DC    X'0'
                             00080   228 SIGNBIT    EQU   X'80'
                             00040   229 DIGITBIT   EQU   X'40'
                             00020   230 DOTBIT     EQU   X'20'
000337                               231 Q          DS    X
000338                               232 CARD       DS    CL80
000388                       00338   233            ORG   CARD
000338                               234 INPUTA     DS    CL10
000342                               235 INPUTB     DS    CL10
00034C                       00388   236            ORG
000388 F040404040404040              237 LINE       DC    CL133'0'
00040D                       00389   238            ORG   LINE+1
000389                               239 OUTPUTA    DS    CL10
000393                               240 OUTPUTB    DS    CL10
00039D                               241 OUTPUTC    DS    CL10
0003A7                       0040D   242            ORG
00040D F140404040404040              243 HEADING    DC    CL133'1'
000492                       0040E   244            ORG   HEADING+1
00040E 40C4C5C3C9D4C1D3              245            DC    CL11' DECIMAL'
000419 40C2C9D5C1D9E840              246            DC    CL11' BINARY'
000424 4040C6D3D6C1E3C9              247            DC    CL20'  FLOATING POINT'
```

```
        SAMPLE ASSEMBLER PROGRAM--SAMPLE9

  LOC  OBJECT CODE     ADDR1 ADDR2  STMT   SOURCE STATEMENT                                       ASM H V 02 17.00 03/28/89

000438 40F1F0F0F05CE2D8              248            DC    CL21' 1000*SQUARE ROOT'
00044D 4040E4D5D5D6D9D4              249            DC    CL22'  UNNORMALIZED'
000463 4040C4C5C3C9D4C1              250            DC    CL16'  DECIMAL SQRT'
000473 4DC4C5C3C9D4C1D3              251            DC    CL20'(DECIMAL SQRT)**2'
000487                   00492       252            ORG
                                     254 CARDS      DCB   DDNAME=SYSIN,        DATA DEFINITION NAME                 -
                                                          DSORG=PS,            DATA SET ORGNAZIATION=PHYS. SEQ.     -
                                                          MACRF=GM,            MACRO INSTR. FORM=GET,MOVE           -
                                                          EODAD=CARDEOF        END OF DATA ADDRESS
                                     309 PRINTER    DCB   DDNAME=PRINTER,DSORG=PS,                                  -
                                                          MACRF=PM,            MACRO INSTRUCTION FORM=PUT,MOVE      -
                                                          LRECL=133,           LOGICAL RECORD LENGTH                -
                                                          BLKSIZE=133,         BLOCK SIZE                           -
                                                          RECFM=FBA            RECORD FORMAT=FIXED-BLOCKED,FORMAT-A
000022                               363            END   BEGIN
000558 0000033800000001              364                  =A(CARD,1,CARD+72,0)
000568 F0F0F0F0F0F0F0F0              365                  =8X'F'
000570 F0F1F2F3F4F5F6F7              366                  =C'0123456789ABCDEF'
000580 40423A29C779A6B5              367                  =D'.2587'
000588 40385F06F6944674              368                  =D'.2202'
000590 000A                          369                  =H'10'
000592 003F                          370                  =H'63'
000594 0041                          371                  =H'65'
000596 F0C9D5E5C1D3C9C4              372                  =C'0INVALID DATA FORMAT '
```

```
                              CROSS REFERENCE

SYMBOL     LEN     VALUE   DEFN  REFERENCES                                                ASM H V 02 17.00 03/28/89

BEGIN      00002   000022  0019  0363
BINTOHEX   00006   0001E4  0158  0093 0104 0105 0116 0117 0128 0129
BLANK      00004   0000E2  0083  0051
CARD       00080   000338  0232  0042 0094 0208 0233 0364 0364
CARDEOF    00004   0001CC  0146  0276
CARDS      00004   000494  0258  0030 0041 0148
DECIMAL    00004   0000C6  0072  0053
DIGITBIT   00001 00000040  0229  0066 0079 0083
DOTBIT     00001 00000020  0230  0067 0072
DOUBLE     00008   0002F8  0222  0125 0131 0132 0133
D10X7      00008   0002D0  0216  0107
D2X31      00008   0002E0  0218  0095 0096 0099
D2X31Z     00008   0002E8  0219  0118
D2X32      00008   0002D8  0217  0119
ERROR      00006   000258  0207  0059 0061 0080
FIXED      00004   0002F4  0221  0090 0092 0097 0121 0122
FLAGS      00001   000336  0227  0047 0066 0067 0072 0075 0079 0083 0086
FLHALF     00008   0002C8  0215  0108 0111 0112
FLOAT      00004   0002F0  0220  0096 0098 0101 0103 0109 0113 0115 0120 0127 0183 0190 0191
FLOATONE   00008   0002B8  0213  0049
FLOATTEN   00008   0002C0  0214  0069
HALF       00002   000334  0226  0062 0063 0065 0183 0184
HEADING    00133   00040D  0243  0036 0244
INLOOP     00004   000070  0050  0077
INPUTA     00010   000338  0234
INPUTB     00010   000342  0235
LINE       00133   000388  0237  0045 0046 0046 0091 0094 0139 0207 0208 0238
MINUS      00004   0000CE  0075  0057
NEGATIVE   00004   00014E  0112  0110
OUTPUTA    00010   000389  0239
OUTPUTB    00010   000393  0240
OUTPUTC    00010   00039D  0241
P          00008   0002B0  0212  0189 0194
PATTERN    00001   000310  0224  0130
PATTERN2   00001   000322  0225  0134
PLUS       00004   0000D2  0077  0055 0068 0070 0073 0084
POSITIVE   00004   0000F4  0090  0087
PRINT      00004   0001B8  0138  0124 0209
PRINTER    00004   0004F4  0313  0032 0035 0138 0150
PROCESS    00004   0000EA  0086  0081
P16        00016   000300  0223  0132 0133 0135
Q          00001   000337  0231  0186 0196
Q1         00002   00024A  0200  0197 0204
READLOOP   00004   00004C  0041  0142
RETURN     00004   0001DA  0153
SAVEAREA   00004   000268  0211  0023 0024 0153
SIGNBIT    00001 00000080  0228  0075 0086
SQRT       00002   000204  0181  0106
=A(CARD,1,CARD+72,0)
           00004   000558  0364  0048
=C'0INVALID DATA FORMAT '
           00021   000596  0372  0207
=C'0123456789ABCDEF'
           00016   000570  0366  0160
=D'.2202'
           00008   000588  0368  0193
=D'.2587'
           00008   000580  0367  0192
=H'10'     00002   000590  0369  0064
=H'63'     00002   000592  0370  0185
=H'65'     00002   000594  0371  0188
=8X'F'     00001   000568  0365  0159
```

DECIMAL	BINARY	FLOATING POINT	1000*SQUARE ROOT	UNNORMALIZED	DECIMAL SQRT	(DECIMAL SQRT)**2
1234	000004D2	434D2000 00000000	4814F028 A1E7AE77	4E000000 14F028A1	35.1283361	1233.9999971545
1234.56	0001E240	434D28F5 C28F5C28	4814F15F F4989118	4E000000 14F15FF4	35.1363060	1234.5599993256
-1234	FFFFFB2E	C34D2000 00000000	C92DF857 50080000			
.125	0000007D	40200000 00000000	4635F2AE 67EB3538	4E000000 0035F2AE	.3535534	.1250000066
.0625	00000271	40100000 00000000	462625A0 80000000	4E000000 002625A0	.2500000	.0625000000
.03125	00000C35	3F800000 00000000	461AF957 73F59A9C	4E000000 001AF957	.1767767	.0312500016
0	00000000	00000000 00000000	40800000 00000000	4E000000 00000000	.0000000	.0000000000
.1	00000001	40199999 99999999	463040A6 2900CB7E	4E000000 003040A6	.3162278	.1000000214
.01	00000001	3F28F5C2 8F5C28F5	45F42407 FFFFFFFA	4E000000 000F4240	.1000000	.0100000000
4.00	00000190	41400000 00000000	471312D0 08000000	4E000000 01312D00	2.0000000	4.0000000000
40.00	00000FA0	42280000 00000000	473C50CF 1B40FE5E	4E000000 03C50CF1	6.3245553	39.9999997427

The remainder of this appendix contains listings of *IBM 3270 Display System* data stream macros and a sample program that uses these macros. These macros generate data stream orders, attributes, buffer addresses, etc. The macros are:

$BYTE	Produces a valid ASCII or EBCDIC code from a 6-bit code.
$CCC	Generates an IBM 3270 Copy Control Character.
$CENTER	Generates data stream to center text.
$COLOR	Produces an extended color attribute type/value pair.
$EUA	Generates an Erase Unprotected to Address order and buffer address.
$IC	Generates an Insert Cursor order.
$MF	Generates a Modify Field order, count, and extended attribute type/value pair(s).
$NL	Generates data stream to simulate a 'new-line' character.
$PT	Generates a Programmed Tab order.
$RA	Generates a Repeat to Address order, buffer address, and repeat character.
$RJUST	Generates data stream to right justify text to a specific column.
$ROWCOL	Produces a 2-character buffer address for specified row and column.
$SA	Generates a Set Attribute order and extended attribute type/value pair(s).
$SBA	Generates a Start Buffer Address and buffer address.
$SF	Generates a Start Field order and attribute byte.
$SFE	Generates a Start Field Extended order, count, and extended attribute type/value pair(s).
$SYMBOL	Produces a programmed symbol attribute type/value pair.
$TEXT	Generates lower case EBCDIC data. A special case is 'PROPER' which produces text with the first character in upper case.
$WCC	Generates an IBM 3270 Write Control Character.
$XHIGH	Produces an extended highlighting attribute type value/pair.

When the above description begins with "Generates" the text (object code) for the indicated data stream is generated. When "Produced" is used the values are generated and (right) concatenated to the global SETC symbol '&HEX-OUT'. This later case is normally intended for use by the other macro.

```
                        $BYTE                          PAGE: 01 OF 01
START
 COL   ----+----1----+----2----+----3----+----4----+----5----+----6----+----7--

  10           MACRO
   1   &NAME     $BYTE &BYTE,&CODE=EBCDIC
   1   .* THIS MACRO PRODUCES A VALID (8-BIT) CHARACTER FROM THE 6-BIT BINARY
   1   .* PARAMETER.  IF THE 'CODE=ASCII' KEYWORD PARAMETER IS PRESENT THE
   1   .* PRODUCED CHARACTER IS ASCII, ELSE EBCDIC.  THE PRODUCED CHARACTER IS
   1   .* (RIGHT) CONCATANATED TO THE GLOBAL 'SETC' CHARACTER STRING &HEXOUT.
  10             GBLC  &HEX3270,&HEXOUT,&ASC3270
  10             LCLC  &HEX
  10             AIF   (&BYTE GE 0 AND &BYTE LT 64).BYTEOK
  10             MNOTE 4,'INVALID VALUE FOR $BYTE MACRO'
   1   &HEXOUT   SETC  '&HEXOUT'.'00'
  10             MEXIT
   1   .BYTEOK   AIF   ('&CODE' EQ 'ASCII').ASCII
  10             AIF   ('&HEX3270' NE '').NOTFIRST
   1   &HEX3270  SETC  '40C1C2C3C4C5C6C7C8C94A4B4C4D4E4F'   EBCDIC      00-0F
   1   &HEX3270  SETC  '&HEX3270'.'50D1D2D3D4D5D6D7D8D95A5B5C5D5E5F'   10-1F
   1   &HEX3270  SETC  '&HEX3270'.'6061E2E3E4E5E6E7E8E96A6B6C6D6E6F'   20-2F
   1   &HEX3270  SETC  '&HEX3270'.'F0F1F2F3F4F5F6F7F8F97A7B7C7D7E7F'   20-2F
   1   .NOTFIRST ANOP
   1   &HEXOUT   SETC  '&HEXOUT'.'&HEX3270'(2*&BYTE+1,2)
  10             MEXIT
   1   .ASCII    AIF   ('&ASC3270' NE '').NOTFRST
   1   &ASC3270  SETC  '2041424344454647484958B2E3C282B21'   ASCII      00-0F
   1   &ASC3270  SETC  '&ASC3270'.'264A4B4C4D4E4F5051525D242A293B5E'   10-1F
   1   &ASC3270  SETC  '&ASC3270'.'2D2F535455565758595A7C2C255F3E3F'   20-2F
   1   &ASC3270  SETC  '&ASC3270'.'303132333435363738393A2340273D22'   20-2F
   1   .NOTFRST  ANOP
   1   &HEXOUT   SETC  '&HEXOUT'.'&ASC3270'(2*&BYTE+1,2)
  10             MEND
  10             MACRO
   1   &NAME     $CCC  &LIST,&CODE=EBCDIC
   1   .*
   1   .* THIS MACRO GENERATES A COPY CONTROL CHARACTER.  THE KEYWORD PARAME-
   1   .* TER 'CODE=ASCII' OR 'CODE=EBCDIC'(ASSUMED) SPECIFIES THE MODE OF THE
   1   .* GENERATED CHARACTER.  THE FIRST PARAMETER SPECIFIES THE OPTIONS THAT
   1   .* ARE TO BE GENERATED.  VALID OPTIONS ARE 'ATT' TO COPY ONLY ATTRIBUTE
   1   .* CHARACTERS,'PROT' TO COPY ATTRIBUTE CHARACTERS AND PROTECTED FIELDS,
   1   .* 'UNPROT' TO COPY TO ATTRIBUTE CHARACTERS AND UNPROTECTED FIELDS,
   1   .* 'ALL' TO COPY THE ENTIRE BUFFER, 'ALARM' TO ACTIVATE THE AUDIBLE
   1   .* ALARM, 'PRINT' TO ACTIVATE PRINTER AT COMPLETION OF COPY, 40CHAR/
   1   .* '64CHAR'/'80CHAR' TO SET LINE LENGTH TO 40/64/80 BYTES, AND 'NLEM'
   1   .* TO INDICATE THAT LINE LENGTH IS DETERMINED (UP TO 132 COLUMNS) BY
   1   .* NEW-LINE OR END-OF-MESSAGE CONTROL CHARACTERS.  MULTIPLE, NON-
   1   .* MUTUALLY EXCLUSIVE OPTIONS MAY BE SPECIFIED BY ENCLOSING THE
   1   .* PARAMETERS IN PARENTHESES.
   1   .*
  10             GBLC  &HEXOUT
  10             LCLA  &B2,&B3,&B4,&B5,&B6,&B7,&I,&C40,&C64,&C80,&NLEM,&ATT
  10             LCLA  &PROT,&UNPROT,&ALL,&BYTE
   1   &I        SETA  1
```

```
                        $CCC                          PAGE: 02 OF 02
START
 COL  ----+----1----+----2----+----3----+----4----+----5----+----6----+----7--
 10             AIF    (N'&SYSLIST(1) GT 0).LOOP
 10             MNOTE 0,'NULL ''CCC'' LIST'
 10             AGO    .NULL
  1   .LOOP     ANOP
 10             AIF    ('&SYSLIST(1,&I)' EQ 'ATT').ATT
 10             AIF    ('&SYSLIST(1,&I)' EQ 'PROT').PROT
 10             AIF    ('&SYSLIST(1,&I)' EQ 'UNPROT').UNPROT
 10             AIF    ('&SYSLIST(1,&I)' EQ 'ALL').ALL
 10             AIF    ('&SYSLIST(1,&I)' EQ 'ALARM').ALARM
 10             AIF    ('&SYSLIST(1,&I)' EQ 'PRINT').PRINT
 10             AIF    ('&SYSLIST(1,&I)' EQ '40CHAR').C40
 10             AIF    ('&SYSLIST(1,&I)' EQ '64CHAR').C64
 10             AIF    ('&SYSLIST(1,&I)' EQ '80CHAR').C80
 10             AIF    ('&SYSLIST(1,&I)' EQ 'NLEM').NLEM
 10             MNOTE 0,'INVALID ''WCC'' PARAMETER--&SYSLIST(1,&I)'
 10             AGO    .LOOPEND
  1   .ATT      ANOP
  1   &ATT      SETA   1
 10             AGO    .LOOPEND
  1   .UNPROT   ANOP
  1   &UNPROT   SETA   1
  1   &B7       SETA   1
 10             AGO    .LOOPEND
  1   .PROT     ANOP
  1   &PROT     SETA   1
  1   &B6       SETA   1
 10             AGO    .LOOPEND
  1   .ALL      ANOP
  1   &ALL      SETA   1
  1   &B6       SETA   1
  1   &B7       SETA   1
 10             AGO    .LOOPEND
  1   .ALARM    ANOP
  1   &B5       SETA   1
 10             AGO    .LOOPEND
  1   .PRINT    ANOP
  1   &B4       SETA   1
 10             AGO    .LOOPEND
  1   .NLEM     ANOP
  1   &NLEM     SETA   1
 10             AGO    .LOOPEND
  1   .C40      ANOP
  1   &C40      SETA   1
 10             AGO    .SET3
  1   .C64      ANOP
  1   &C64      SETA   1
  1   &B2       SETA   1
 10             AGO    .LOOPEND
  1   .C80      ANOP
  1   &C80      SETA   1
  1   &B2       SETA   1
  1   .SET3     ANOP
  1   &B3       SETA   1
  1   .LOOPEND  ANOP
  1   &I        SETA   &I+1
 10             AIF    (&I LE N'&SYSLIST(1)).LOOP
 10             AIF    (&ALL+&PROT+&UNPROT+&ATT LE 1).NOTC
 10             MNOTE 0,'CONFLICTING ATT/PROT/UNPROT/ALL ''CCC'' PARAMETERS'
  1   .NOTC     ANOP
 10             AIF    (&C40+&C64+&C80+&NLEM LE 1).NULL
 10             MNOTE 0,'CONFLICTING ''CCC'' PRINT FORMATS'
  1   .NULL     ANOP
  1   &BYTE     SETA   &B7+2*(&B6+2*(&B5+2*(&B4+2*(&B3+2*&B2))))
 10             $BYTE  &BYTE,CODE=&CODE
  1   &NAME     DC     X'&HEXOUT'
 10             MEND
  1   *
```

```
                        $CENTER                        PAGE: 01 OF 02
START
 COL  ----+----1----+----2----+----3----+----4----+----5----+----6----+----7--

  10            MACRO
   1  &NAME     $CENTER &LINE,&STRING,&SF,&LABEL=,&TYPE=2,&CASE=UPPER,        -
  16                  &COLOR=,&XHIGH=,&SYMBOL=
   1  .*
   1  .* THIS MACRO CENTERS THE TEXT '&STRING' ON THE SCREEN ROW '&LINE'.
   1  .* IF '&LINE' HAS A PREFIX OF 'A' AN ABSOLUTE LINE NUMBER IS INCICATED,
   1  .* ELSE IT IS RELATIVE TO THE GLOBAL '&ROW'.  IF '&SF' IS PRESENT, THE
   1  .* START FIELD ORDER IS GENERATED WITH THE INDICATED ATTRIBUTES.  IF
   1  .* '&COLOR', '&XHIGH' AND/OR '&SYMBOL' IS PRESENT, THE SET ATTRIBUTE
   1  .* ORDER(S) IS (ARE) GENERATED WITH THE INDICATED ATTRIBUTE TYPE/VALUE
   1  .* PAIRS.  IF '&LABEL' IS
   1  .* PRESENT, IT IS ASSIGNED TO THE LOCATION OF THE STRING.  IF '&NAME'
   1  .* IS PRESENT IT IS ASSIGNED TO THE FIRST GENERATED TEXT (I.E., THE
   1  .* SBA ORDER THAT SPECIFIES THE LOCATION OF THE STRING.  THE NUMBER OF
   1  .* COLUMNS IS DETERMINED BY THE TERMINAL '&TYPE'.  CASE MAY BE UPPER,
   1  .* LOWER, OR PROPER (FIRST CHARACTER UPPER, REMAINDER LOWER)
   1  .*
  10            GBLA  &ROW
  10            GBLC  &HEXOUT
  10            LCLA  &R,&C,&I,&J,&COLS,&K,&TYPES(5)
  10            LCLC  &ALF,&QUOTED
   1  &TYPES(1) SETA  40,80,80,80,132
   1  &K        SETA  &TYPE
  10            AIF   (&TYPE GE 1 AND &TYPE LE 5).TYPEOK
  10            MNOTE *,'INVALID TYPE SPECIFIED, TYPE=2 ASSUMED'
   1  &K        SETA  2
   1  .TYPEOK   ANOP
   1  &COLS     SETA  &TYPES(&K)
   1  &QUOTED   SETC  ''''.'&STRING'.''''
   1  &C        SETA  K'&STRING
  10            AIF   ('&STRING'(1,1) NE '''').COUNTOK
   1  &QUOTED   SETC  '&STRING'
   1  &I        SETA  2
   1  &C        SETA  K'&STRING-2
   1  .QUOTED   AIF   (&I GE &C-1).COUNTOK
   1  &I        SETA  &I+1
  10            AIF   ('&STRING'(&I,2) NE '''''').QUOTED
   1  &I        SETA  &I+1
   1  &C        SETA  &C-1
  10            AGO   .QUOTED
   1  .COUNTOK  ANOP
  10            AIF   (T'&LINE NE 'O').GLINE
  10            MNOTE 0,'NO LINE NUMBER SPECIFIED, SET TO ''0'''
  10            AGO   .CKLEN

   1  .GLINE    ANOP
  10            AIF   ('&LINE'(1,1) NE 'A').REL
   1  &ALF      SETC  '&LINE'(2,2)
   1  &R        SETA  &ALF
  10            AGO   .CKLEN
   1  .REL      ANOP
   1  &R        SETA  &LINE+&ROW
   1  .CKLEN    AIF   (T'&SF EQ 'O').NOADJ
   1  &C        SETA  &C+1
   1  .NOADJ    AIF   (&C LE &COLS).GLEN
```

```
                       $CENTER                         PAGE: 02 OF 02
START
 COL  ----+----1----+----2----+----3----+----4----+----5----+----6----+----7--

 10             MNOTE 0,'STRING LENGTH EXCEEDS LINE LENGTH'
  1   &C        SETA  &COLS-2
  1   .GLEN     ANOP
  1   &C        SETA  (&COLS-&C)/2
  1   &NAME     $SBA  (&R,&C)
 10             AIF   (T'&SF EQ 'O').NOSF
 10             $SF   &SF
  1   .NOSF     ANOP
  1   &HEXOUT   SETC  ''
 10             AIF   (T'&XHIGH EQ 'O').NOXH
  1   &HEXOUT   SETC  '28'
 10             $XHIGH &XHIGH
  1   .NOXH     AIF   (T'&COLOR EQ 'O').NOCL
  1   &HEXOUT   SETC  '&HEXOUT'.'28'
 10             $COLOR &COLOR
  1   .NOCL     AIF   (T'&SYMBOL EQ 'O').NOSYM
  1   &HEXOUT   SETC  '&HEXOUT'.'28'
 10             $SYMBOL &SYMBOL
  1   .NOSYM    AIF   ('&HEXOUT' EQ '').NOSA
 10             DC    X'&HEXOUT'
  1   &HEXOUT   SETC  ''
  1   .NOSA     AIF   ('&CASE' EQ 'UPPER').UPPER
 10             AIF   ('&CASE' EQ 'PROPER').PROPER
 10             AIF   ('&CASE' NE 'LOWER').UPPERX
  1   &LABEL    $TEXT LOWER=&STRING
 10             MEXIT
  1   .PROPER   ANOP
  1   &LABEL    $TEXT PROPER=&STRING
 10             MEXIT
  1   .UPPERX   MNOTE *,'INVALID CASE--CASE=UPPER ASSUMED'
  1   .UPPER    ANOP
  1   &LABEL    DC    C&QUOTED
 10             MEND
```

```
                             $COLOR                         PAGE: 01 OF 01
START
 COL  ----+----1----+----2----+----3----+----4----+----5----+----6----+----7--

 10             MACRO
  1   &NAME     $COLOR &COLOR,&PLANE=
  1   .*
  1   .* THIS MACRO GENERATES AN EXTENDED ATTRIBUTE TYPE/VALUE FOR COLOR.
  1   .* VALID COLORS ARE 'RED', 'BLUE', 'GREEN', 'PINK', 'YELLOW', 'WHITE',
  1   .* 'TURQUOISE', AND 'NORMAL'.  THE PARAMETER 'PLANE=FOREGROUND' OR
  1   .* 'PLANE=BACKGROUND' (ASSUMED) MAY BE SPECIFIED FOR THOSE DEVICES
  1   .* THAT PROVIDE THIS CAPABILITY.
  1   .*
 10             GBLC  &HEXOUT
 10             AIF   ('&PLANE' NE 'FOREGROUND').BACK
  1   &HEXOUT   SETC  '&HEXOUT'.'45'
 11              AGO   .FORE
  1   .BACK     ANOP
  1   &HEXOUT   SETC  '&HEXOUT'.'42'
  1   .FORE     AIF   (N'&SYSLIST(1) LT 1 OR '&COLOR' EQ 'NORMAL').NULL
 10             AIF   ('&COLOR' NE 'BLUE').NOTBLUE
  1   &HEXOUT   SETC  '&HEXOUT'.'F1'
 10             MEXIT
  1   .NOTBLUE  AIF   ('&COLOR' NE 'RED').NOTRED
  1   &HEXOUT   SETC  '&HEXOUT'.'F2'
 10             MEXIT
  1   .NOTRED   AIF   ('&COLOR' NE 'PINK').NOTPINK
  1   &HEXOUT   SETC  '&HEXOUT'.'F3'
 10             MEXIT
  1   .NOTPINK  AIF   ('&COLOR' NE 'GREEN').NOTGREN
  1   &HEXOUT   SETC  '&HEXOUT'.'F4'
 10             MEXIT
  1   .NOTGREN  AIF   ('&COLOR' NE 'TURQUOISE').NOTTURQ
  1   &HEXOUT   SETC  '&HEXOUT'.'F5'
 10             MEXIT
  1   .NOTTURQ  AIF   ('&COLOR' NE 'YELLOW').NOTYELL
  1   &HEXOUT   SETC  '&HEXOUT'.'F6'
 10             MEXIT
  1   .NOTYELL  AIF   ('&COLOR' NE 'WHITE').NOTWHIT
  1   &HEXOUT   SETC  '&HEXOUT'.'F7'
 10             MEXIT
  1   .NOTWHIT  MNOTE 0,'INVALID COLOR, DEFAULT ASSUMED'
  1   .NULL     ANOP
  1   &HEXOUT   SETC  '&HEXOUT'.'00'
 10             MEND
```

```
                             $EUA                           PAGE: 01 OF 01
START
 COL  ----+----1----+----2----+----3----+----4----+----5----+----6----+----7--

 10             MACRO
  1   &NAME     $EUA  &LIST,&CODE=EBCDIC
  1   .*
  1   .* THIS MACRO GENREATES THE 'ERASE UNPROTECTED TO ADDRESS' ORDER AND
  1   .* THE ADDRESS SPECIFIED BY THE FIRST PARAMETER '(ROW,COLUMN)'  THE
  1   .* PARAMETER 'CODE=ASCII' OR 'CODE=EBCDIC' (ASSUMED) SPECIFIES THE
  1   .* MODE OF THE GENERATED VALUES.
  1   .*
 10             AIF   (N'&SYSLIST(1) NE 2).COUNT
  1   &HEXOUT   SETC  '12'
 10             $ROWCOL (&SYSLIST(1,1),&SYSLIST(1,2)),CODE=&CODE
  1   &NAME     DC    X'&HEXOUT'
 10             AGO   .END
  1   .COUNT    ANOP
 10             MNOTE 0,'INVALID ''EUA'' LIST'
  1   .END      ANOP
 10             MEND
```

```
                            $IC                             PAGE: 01 OF 01
START
 COL  ----+----1----+----2----+----3----+----4----+----5----+----6----+----7--
  10            MACRO
   1  &NAME     $IC
   1  .*
   1  .* THIS MACRO GENERATES THE IBM 3270 'INSERT CURSOR' ORDER.
   1  .*
   1  &NAME     DC    X'13'
  10            MEND
   1  *
```

```
                            $MF                             PAGE: 01 OF 01
START
 COL  ----+----1----+----2----+----3----+----4----+----5----+----6----+----7--
  10            MACRO
   1  &NAME     $MF   &COLOR=,&XHIGH=,&SYMBOL=,&COUNT=
   1  .* THIS MACRO GENERATES THE 3270 MODIFY FIELD DATA STREAM ORDER
   1  .*------------------------------------------------------------------
   1  .* EXTENDED HIGHLIGHTING MAY BE SPECIFIED AS:
   1  .*
   1  .*   XHIGH=XXXX (XXXX=REVERSE!BLINK!UNDERLINE (OR _))
   1  .*------------------------------------------------------------------
   1  .* COLOR CAN BE SPECIFIED AS:
   1  .*
   1  .*     COLOR=XXXX (XXXX=REC!BLUE!GREEN!YELLOW!WHITE!TURQUOISE)
   1  .*
   1  .*   OR
   1  .*
   1  .*     COLOR=(XXXX,YYYY) (YYYY=FOREGROUND!BACKGROUND)
   1  .*------------------------------------------------------------------
   1  .* SYMBOLS MAY BE SPECIFIED AS:
   1  .*
   1  .*     SYMBOL=APL (FOR APL CHARACTER SET)
   1  .*
   1  .*   OR
   1  .*
   1  .*     SYMBOL='XX' (XX = HEX VALUE OF LOCAL ID)
   1  .*------------------------------------------------------------------
   1  .* THE NUMBER OF ATTRIBUTE TYPE/VALUE PAIRS IS GENERATED FORM THE ABOVE
   1  .* BUT MAY BE ALTERED BY:
   1  .*
   1  .*     COUNT=XXX (XXX IS A DECIMAL CONSTANT)
   1  .*
  10            GBLC  &HEXOUT
  10            LCLA  &KOUNT
   1  &HEXOUT   SETC  ''
  10            AIF   (T'&XHIGH EQ 'O').NOXHIGH
  10            $XHIGH &XHIGH
   1  &KOUNT    SETA  1
   1  .NOXHIGH  AIF   (T'&COLOR EQ 'O').NOCOLOR
  10            AIF   (T'&COLOR(2) EQ 'O').PLANE
  10            $COLOR &COLOR
  10            AGO   .NOCOLOR
   1  .PLANE    ANOP
  10            $COLOR &COLOR(1),PLANE=&COLOR(2)
   1  .NOCOLOR  AIF   (T'&SYMBOL EQ 'O').NOSYMBL
   1  &KOUNT    SETA  &KOUNT+1
  10            $SYMBOL &SYMBOL
   1  .NOSYMBL  AIF   (T'&COUNT EQ 'O').NOCOUNT
   1  &KOUNT    SETA  &COUNT
   1  .NOCOUNT  ANOP
   1  &NAME     DC    X'2C',AL1(&KOUNT),X'&HEXOUT'
  10            MEND
```

```
                        $NL                          PAGE: 01 OF 01
START
 COL  ----+----1----+----2----+----3----+----4----+----5----+----6----+----7--

 10            MACRO
  1   &NAME    $NL    &NLINES,&CODE=EBCDIC
  1   .*
  1   .* THIS MACRO SIMULATES A 'NEW LINE' CONTROL BY GENERATING THE ADDRESS
  1   .* OF THE FIRST COLUMN OF THE NEXT SCREEN ROW.  THIS ROW IS DETERMINED
  1   .* BY THE VALUE OF THE GLOBAL VARIABLE SYMBOL '&ROW' THAT IS MAINTAINED
  1   .* BY THE OTHER 3270 DATA STREAM MACROS.  ADDITIONAL LINES MAY BE
  1   .* INDICATED BY A POSITIONAL OPERATOR.  THE PARAMETER 'CODE=ASCII' OR
  1   .* 'CODE=ASCII' (ASSUMED) SPECIFIES THE MODE OF THE GENERATED VALUES.
  1   .*
 10            GBLA   &ROW
 10            LCLA   &COUNT,&R
  1   &COUNT   SETA   1
 10            AIF    (T'&NLINES EQ 'O').NOCOUNT
  1   &COUNT   SETA   &NLINES
  1   .NOCOUNT ANOP
  1   &R       SETA   &ROW+&COUNT
  1   &NAME    $SBA   (&R,1),CODE=&CODE
 10            MEND
  1   *
```

```
                        $PT                          PAGE: 01 OF 01
START
 COL  ----+----1----+----2----+----3----+----4----+----5----+----6----+----7--

 10            MACRO
  1   &NAME    $PT    &CODE=EBCDIC
  1   .*
  1   .* THIS MACRO GENERATES THE IBM 3270 'PROGRAMMED TAB' DATA STREAM
  1   .* ORDER.  THE PARAMETER 'CODE=ASCII' OR 'CODE=EBCDIC' (ASSUMED)
  1   .* MAY BE USED TO SPECIFY THE MODE OF THE GENERATED VALUES.
  1   .*
 10            AIF    ('&CODE' EQ 'ASCII').ASCII
  1   &NAME    DC     X'5'
 10            MEXIT
  1   .ASCII   ANOP
  1   &NAME    DE     X'9'
 10            MEND
  1   *
```

```
                           $RA                          PAGE: 01 OF 01
START
 COL   ----+----1----+----2----+----3----+----4----+----5----+----6----+----7--
 10              MACRO
  1    &NAME     $RA    &LIST,&TYPE=2,&CODE=EBCDIC
  1    .*
  1    .* THIS MACRO GENERATES THE IBM 3270 'REPEAT TO ADDRESS' ORDER FOR
  1    .* THE SPECIFIED ADDRESS AND VALUE.  THE FIRST ADDRESS SHOULD BE
  1    .* "(ROW,COLUMN,'CHAR')" OR "(ROW,COLUMN,HEX)".  THE PARAMETER
  1    .* "CODE=ASCII" OR "CODE=EBCDIC" (ASSUMED) SPECIFIES THE MODE OF THE
  1    .* GENERATED VALUES.
  1    .*
 10              GBLC   &HEXOUT
 10              AIF    (N'&SYSLIST(1) NE 3).COUNT
 10              AIF    ('&CODE' EQ 'ASCII').ASCII
  1    &HEXOUT   SETC   X'3C'
 10              AGO    .EBCDIC
  1    .ASCII    ANOP
  1    &HEXOUT   SETC   X'14'
  1    .EBCDIC   ANOP
 10              $ROWCOL (&SYSLIST(1,1),&SYSLIST(1,2)),TYPE=&TYPE,CODE=&CODE
 10              AIF    ('&SYSLIST(1,3)'(1,1) NE '''').HEX
 10              AIF    ('&SYSLIST(1,3)'(3,1) NE '''').FORMAT
  1    &NAME     DC     X'&HEXOUT',C&SYSLIST(3)
 10              MEND
  1    .HEX      ANOP
  1    &NAME     DC     X'&HEXOUT',X'&SYSLIST(3)'
 10              MEND
  1    .COUNT    ANOP
 10              MNOTE  0,'INVALID RA LIST'
 10              AGO    .END
  1    .FORMAT   ANOP
 10              MNOTE  0,'INVALID RA CHARACTER'
  1    .END      ANOP
 10              MEND
  1    *
```

```
                              $RJUST                         PAGE: 01 OF 02
START
 COL   ----+----1----+----2----+----3----+----4----+----5----+----6----+----7--

 10              MACRO
  1    &NAME     $RJUST &LINE,&STRING,&SF,&MARGIN=,&LABEL=,&TYPE=2,           X
 16                    &CASE=UPPER,&COLOR=,&XHIGH=,&SYMBOL=
  1    .*
  1    .* THIS MACRO RIGHT JUSTIVIES THE TEXT '&STRING' ON THE SCREEN ROW
  1    .* '&LINE' SO THAT THE TEXT ENDS AT THE COLUMN SPECIFIED BY '&MARGIN'.
  1    .* IF '&LINE' HAS A PREFIX OF 'A' AN ABSOLUTE LINE NUMBER IS INCICATED,
  1    .* ELSE IT IS RELATIVE TO THE GLOBAL '&ROW'.  IF '&SF' IS PRESENT, THE
  1    .* START FIELD ORDER IS GENERATED WITH THE INDICATED ATTRIBUTES.  IF
  1    .* '&COLOR', '&XHIGH' AND/OR '&SYMBOL' IS PRESENT, THE SET ATTRIBUTE
  1    .* ORDER(S) IS (ARE) GENERATED WITH THE INDICATED ATTRIBUTE TYPE/VALUE
  1    .* PAIRS.  IF '&LABEL' IS
  1    .* PRESENT, IT IS ASSIGNED TO THE LOCATION OF THE STRING.  IF '&NAME'
  1    .* IS PRESENT IT IS ASSIGNED TO THE FIRST GENERATED TEXT (I.E., THE
  1    .* SBA ORDER THAT SPECIFIES THE LOCATION OF THE STRING.  THE NUMBER OF
  1    .* COLUMNS IS DETERMINED BY THE TERMINAL '&TYPE'.  CASE MAY BE UPPER,
  1    .* LOWER, OR PROPER (FIRST CHARACTEI UPPER, REMAINDER LOWER)
  1    .*
 10              GBLA  &ROW
 10              GBLC  &HEXOUT
 10              LCLA  &R,&C,&M,&MA,&J,&K,&COLS,&TYPES(5)
 10              LCLC  &ALF,&QUOTED
  1    &TYPES(1) SETA  40,80,80,80,132
  1    &K        SETA  &TYPE
 10              AIF   (&TYPE GE 1 AND &TYPE LE 5).TYPEOK
 10              MNOTE *,'INVALID TYPE SPECIFIED, TYPE=2 ASSUMED'
  1    &K        SETA  2
  1    .TYPEOK   ANOP
  1    &COLS     SETA  &TYPES(&K)
  1    &QUOTED   SETC  ''''.'&STRING'.''''
  1    &C        SETA  K'&STRING
 10              AIF   ('&STRING'(1,1) NE '''').COUNTOK
  1    &QUOTED   SETC  '&STRING'
  1    &I        SETA  2
  1    &C        SETA  K'&STRING-2
  1    .QUOTED   AIF   (&I GE &C-1).COUNTOK
  1    &I        SETA  &I+1
 10              AIF   ('&STRING'(&I,2) NE '''''').QUOTED
  1    &I        SETA  &I+1
  1    &C        SETA  &C-1
 10              AGO   .QUOTED
  1    .COUNTOK  ANOP
  1    &M        SETA  &COLS
 10              AIF   (T'&LINE NE 'O').GLINE
 10              MNOTE 0,NO LINE NUMBER SPECIFIED, SET TO ''0'''
 10              AGO   .CKLEN
  1    .GLINE    ANOP
 10              AIF   ('&LINE'(1,1) NE 'A').REL
  1    &ALF      SETC  '&LINE'(2,2)
  1    &R        SETA  &ALF
 10              AGO   .CKLEN
  1    .REL      ANOP
  1    &R        SETA  &LINE+&ROW
  1    .CKLEN    ANOP
```

```
                       $RJUST                          PAGE: 02 OF 02
START
 COL  ----+----1----+----2----+----3----+----4----+----5----+----6----+----7--
 10             AIF   (T'&MARGIN EQ 'O').MARG
  1   &M        SETA  &MARGIN
 10             AIF   (&M LE &COLS).MARG
 10             MNOTE 0,'MARGIN EXCEEDS LINE'
  1   .MARG     AIF   (T'&SF EQ 'O').NOADJ
  1   &C        SETA  &C+1
  1   .NOADJ    AIF   (&C LT &M).GLEN
 10             MNOTE 0,'STRING LENGTH EXCEEDS MARGIN'
  1   &C        SETA  &M-1
  1   .GLEN     ANOP
  1   &C        SETA  &M-&C
  1   &NAME     $SBA  (&R,&C)
 10             AIF   (T'&SF EQ 'O').NOSF
 10             $SF   &SF
  1   .NOSF     ANOP
  1   &HEXOUT   SETC  ''
 10             AIF   (T'&XHIGH EQ 'O').NOXH
  1   &HEXOUT   SETC  '28'
 10             $XHIGH &XHIGH
  1   .NOXH     AIF   (T'&COLOR EQ 'O').NOCL
  1   &HEXOUT   SETC  '&HEXOUT'.'28'
 10             $COLOR &COLOR
  1   .NOCL     AIF   (T'&SYMBOL EQ 'O').NOSYM
  1   &HEXOUT   SETC  '&HEXOUT'.'28'
 10             $SYMBOL &SYMBOL
  1   .NOSYM    AIF   ('&HEXOUT' EQ '').NOSA
 10             DC    X'&HEXOUT'
  1   &HEXOUT   SETC  ''
  1   .NOSA     AIF   ('&CASE' EQ 'UPPER').UPPER
 10             AIF   ('&CASE' EQ 'PROPER').PROPER
 10             AIF   ('&CASE' NE 'LOWER').UPPERX
  1   &LABEL    $TEXT LOWER=&STRING
 10             MEXIT
  1   .PROPER   ANOP
  1   &LABEL    $TEXT PROPER=&STRING
 10             MEXIT
  1   .UPPERX   MNOTE *,'INVALID CASE--CASE=UPPER ASSUMED'
  1   .UPPER    ANOP
  1   &LABEL    DC    C&QUOTED
 10             MEND
```

```
                        $ROWCOL                        PAGE: 01 OF 01
START
 COL  ----+----1----+----2----+----3----+----4----+----5----+----6----+----7--

  10           MACRO
   1  &NAME    $ROWCOL &RC,&TYPE=2,&CODE=EBCDIC
   1  .* THIS MACRO COMPUTES THE IBM 3270 BUFFER ADDRESS FROM THE ROW-COLUMN
   1  .* TUPLE POSITIONAL PARAMETER (&RC=(ROW,COLUMN)).  THIS ADDRESS IS
   1  .* DETERMINED BY THE MODEL TYPE 'TYPE=' KEYWORD PARAMETER (A MODEL 2
   1  .* DEVICE IS ASSUMED) AND THIS BUFFER ADDRESS IS CONVERTED TO THE
   1  .* TWO CHARACTER CODE USED BY SBA, EUA, AND RA ORDERS.  THIS FINAL
   1  .* VALUE IS (RIGHT) CONCATANATED TO THE GLOBAL 'SETC' CHARACTER STRING
   1  .* &HEXOUT.  THIS MACRO IS USED BY MACROS $SBA, $EUA, AND $RA.
  10           GBLA  &ROW,&COL
  10           GBLC  &HEXOUT
  10           LCLA  &A,&B,&X,&COLS
  10           LCLC  &Z
   1  &COLS    SETA  40
  10           AIF   ('&TYPE' EQ '1').TYPEOK
   1  &COLS    SETA  80
   5      AIF   ('&TYPE' EQ '2' OR '&TYPE' EQ '3' OR '&TYPE' EQ '4').TYPEOK
   1  &COLS    SETA  132
   1  .TYPEOK  ANOP
   1  &ROW     SETA  &RC(1)
   1  &COL     SETA  &RC(2)
   1  &X       SETA  &COLS*(&ROW-1)+&COL-1
   1  &A       SETA  &X/64
   1  &B       SETA  &X-64*&A
  10           $BYTE &A,CODE=&CODE
  10           $BYTE &B,CODE=&CODE
  10           MEND
```

```
                     $SA                                 PAGE: 01 OF 01
START
 COL  ----+----1----+----2----+----3----+----4----+----5----+----6----+----7--
 10             MACRO                                                     00000000
  1   &NAME     $SA    &COLOR=,&XHIGH=,&SYMBOL=                                      *
 10             GBLC   &HEXOUT                                                       *
 10             LCLA   &I                                                            *
  1   .* THIS MACRO GENERATES THE 3270 SET ATTROBITE DATA STREAM ORDER               *
  1   .*-------------------------------------------------------------------         *
  1   .* EXTENDED HIGHLIGHTING MAY BE SPECIFIED AS:                                  *
  1   .*                                                                             *
  1   .*   XHIGH=XXXX (XXXX=REVERSE!BLINK!UNDERLINE (OR _))                          *
  1   .*-------------------------------------------------------------------         *
  1   .* COLOR CAN BE SPECIFIED AS:                                                  *
  1   .*                                                                             *
  1   .*     COLOR=XXXX (XXXX=REC!BLUE!GREEN!YELLOW!WHITE!TURQUOISE)                 *
  1   .*                                                                             *
  1   .*   OR                                                                        *
  1   .*                                                                             *
  1   .*     COLOR=(XXXX,YYYY) (YYYY=FOREGROUND!BACKGROUND)                          *
  1   .*-------------------------------------------------------------------         *
  1   .* SYMBOLS MAY BE SPECIFIED AS:                                                *
  1   .*                                                                             *
  1   .*     SYMBOL=APL (FOR APL CHARACTER SET)                                      *
  1   .*                                                                             *
  1   .*   OR                                                                        *
  1   .*                                                                             *
  1   .*     SYMBOL='XX' (XX = HEX VALUE OF LOCAL ID)                                *
  1   .*                                                                             *
  1   &HEXOUT   SETC   ''                                                            *
 10             AIF    (T'&XHIGH EQ 'O').NOXHIGH                                     *
  1   .XLOOP    ANOP                                                                 *
  1   &I        SETA   &I+1                                                          *
 10             AIF    ('&XHIGH(&I)' EQ '').NOXHIGH                                  *
  1   &HEXOUT   SETC   '&HEXOUT'.'28'                                                *
 10             $XHIGH &XHIGH(&I)                                                    *
 10             AGO    .XLOOP                                                        *
  1   .NOXHIGH  AIF    (T'&COLOR EQ 'O').NOCOLOR                                     *
  1   &HEXOUT   SETC   '&HEXOUT'.'28'                                                *
 10             AIF    (T'&COLOR(2) EQ 'O').PLANE                                    *
 10             $COLOR &COLOR                                                        *
 10             AGO    .NOCOLOR                                                      *
  1   .PLANE    ANOP                                                                 *
 10             $COLOR &COLOR(1),PLANE=&COLOR(2)                                     *
  1   .NOCOLOR  AIF    (T'&SYMBOL EQ 'O').NOSYMBL                                    *
  1   &HEXOUT   SETC   '&HEXOUT'.'28'                                                *
 10             $SYMBOL &SYMBOL                                                      *
  1   .NOSYMBL  ANOP                                                                 *
  1   &NAME     DC     X'&HEXOUT'                                                    *
 10             MEND                                                                 *
```

```
$SBA                          PAGE: 01 OF 01
START
 COL  ----+----1----+----2----+----3----+----4----+----5----+----6----+----7--

  10           MACRO
   1  &NAME    $SBA   &RC,&TYPE=2,&CODE=EBCDIC
   1  .*
   1  .* THIS MACRO GENERATES THE IBM 3270 'SET BUFFER ADDRESS' ORDER AND
   1  .* ADDRESS SPECIFIED BY THE FIRST PARAMETER '(ROW,COLUMN)'.  THE SCREEN
   1  .* SIZE IS DETERMINED BY THE 'TYPE=MODEL' PARAMETER.  MODELS 1, 2-4,AND
   1  .* 5 INDICATE THAT THE SCREEN HAS 40, 80, OR 132 COLUMNS, RESPECTIVELY.
   1  .* THE PARAMETER 'CODE=ASCII' OR 'CODE=EBCDID' (ASSUMED) SPECIFIES THE
   1  .* MODE FOR THE GENERATED OUTPUT.
   1  .*
  10           GBLC   &HEXOUT
   1  &HEXOUT  SETC   '11'
  10           $ROWCOL &RC,TYPE=&TYPE,CODE=&CODE
   1  &NAME    DC     X'&HEXOUT'
  10           MEND
```

```
                        $SF                              PAGE: 01 OF 02
START
 COL  ----+----1----+----2----+----3----+----4----+----5----+----6----+----7--

 10             MACRO
  1   &NAME     $SF    &LIST,&STRING,&CODE=EBCDIC,&CASE=UPPER
  1   .*
  1   .* THIS MACRO GENERATES THE IBM 3270 'START FIELD' ORDER AND VALUE.  IF
  1   .* NO POSITIONAL PARAMETER IS PRESENT 'UNPROTECTED' IS ASSUMED.  ELSE,
  1   .* 'PROT' SPECIFIES A PROTECTED FIELD, 'NUM' INDICATES A NUMERIC FIELD,
  1   .* 'SKIP' PROVIDES AN AUTO-SKIP FIELD, 'MDT' PROVIDES A MODIFIED DATA
  1   .* TAG, 'HI' INDICATES A HIGH INTENSITY (BRIGHT) FIELD, 'DET' PROVIDES
  1   .* A PEN-DETECTABLE FIELD, AND 'NONDISP' OR 'DARK' PROVIDES A NON-
  1   .* DISPLAYABLE FIELD.  MULTIPLE, NON-MUTUALLY EXCLUSIVE', OPTIONS MAY
  1   .* BE SPECIFIED BY ENCLOSINGING THEM IN PARENTHESES.  'CODE=ASCII' OR
  1   .* 'CODE=EBCDIC' (ASSUMED) SPECIFIES THE MODE OF THE GENERATED VALUES.
  1   .* IF A SECOND POSITIONAL PARAMETER IS PRESENT, IT IS USED TO GENERATE
  1   .* A CHARACTER STRING FOLLOWING THE ABOVE ORDER AND ATTRIBUTE.  THIS
  1   .* STRING SHOULD BE ENCLOSED IN SINGLE QUOTE MARKS IF IT CONTAINS
  1   .* BLANKS OR OTHER NON-ALPHAMERIC SPECIAL CHARACTERS.  THIS STRING MAY
  1   .* BE IN LOWER CASE BY SPECIFING 'CASE=LOWER'.  IF 'CASE=PROPER', THE
  1   .* FIRST CHARACTER IS UPPER CASE AND THE REMAINDER IN LOWER CASE.
  1   .*
 10             GBLC   &HEXOUT
  1   &HEXOUT   SETC   '1D'
 10             LCLA   &B2,&B3,&B4,&B5,&B6,&B7,&I,&SKIP,&NUM,&DET,&NONDISP,&HI
 10             LCLA   &PROT,&BYTE
  1   &I        SETA   1
 10             AIF    (N'&SYSLIST(1) LT 1).NULL
  1   .LOOP     ANOP
 10             AIF    ('&SYSLIST(1,&I)' EQ 'PROT').PROT
 10             AIF    ('&SYSLIST(1,&I)' EQ 'NUM').NUM
 10             AIF    ('&SYSLIST(1,&I)' EQ 'SKIP').SKIP
 10             AIF    ('&SYSLIST(1,&I)' EQ 'MDT').MDT
 10             AIF    ('&SYSLIST(1,&I)' EQ 'HI').HI
 10             AIF    ('&SYSLIST(1,&I)' EQ 'DET').DET
 10             AIF    ('&SYSLIST(1,&I)' EQ 'NONDISP').NONDISP
 10             AIF    ('&SYSLIST(1,&I)' EQ 'DARK').NONDISP
 10             MNOTE  0,'INVALID ''SF'' PARAMETER--&SYSLIST(1,&I)'
 10             AGO    .LOOPEND
  1   .MDT      ANOP
  1   &B7       SETA   1
 10             AGO    .LOOPEND
  1   .NUM      ANOP
  1   &NUM      SETA   1
  1   .SET3     ANOP
  1   &B3       SETA   1
 10             AGO    .LOOPEND
  1   .SKIP     ANOP
  1   &SKIP     SETA   1
  1   &B2       SETA   1
 10             AGO    .SET3
  1   .PROT     ANOP
  1   &PROT     SETA   1
  1   &B2       SETA   1
 10             AGO    .LOOPEND
  1   .DET      ANOP
  1   &DET      SETA   1
```

```
                      $SF                        PAGE: 02 OF 02
START
 COL   ----+----1----+----2----+----3----+----4----+----5----+----6----+----7--

   1   .SET5     ANOP
   1   &B5       SETA  1
  10             AGO   .LOOPEND
   1   .NONDISP  ANOP
   1   &NONDISP  SETA  1
   1   &B4       SETA  1
  10             AGO   .SET5
   1   .HI       ANOP
   1   &HI       SETA  1
   1   &B4       SETA  1
   1   .LOOPEND  ANOP
   1   &I        SETA  &I+1
  10             AIF   (N'&SYSLIST(1) GE &I).LOOP
  10             AIF   (&HI EQ 0).NOTHI
   1   &B5       SETA  0
   1   &DET      SETA  0
   1   .NOTHI    ANOP
  10             AIF   (&PROT+&NUM+&SKIP LE 1).NOTPNS
  10             MNOTE 0,'INVALID PROT/NUM/SKIP ATTRIBUTES'
   1   .NOTPNS   ANOP
  10             AIF   (&HI+&NONDISP+&DET LE 1).NULL
  10             MNOTE 0,'INVALID HI/NONDISP/DET ATTRIBUTES'
   1   .NULL     ANOP
   1   &BYTE     SETA  &B7+2*(&B6+2*(&B5+2*(&B4+2*(&B3+2*&B2))))
  10             $BYTE &BYTE,CODE=&CODE
   1   &NAME     DC    X'&HEXOUT'
  10             AIF   (T'&STRING EQ 'O').END
  10             AIF   ('&CASE' EQ 'LOWER').LOWER
  10             AIF   ('&CASE' NE 'PROPER').UPPER
   1   .         $TEXT PROPER=&STRING
  10             MEXIT
   1   .LOWER    $TEXT LOWER=&STRING
  10             MEXIT
   1   .UPPER    AIF   ('&STRING'(1,1) EQ '''').QUOTE
  10             DC    C'&STRING'
  10             MEXIT
   1   .QUOTE    ANOP
  10             DC    C&STRING
   1   .END      MEND
```

```
                         $SFE                          PAGE: 01 OF 01
START
 COL   ----+----1----+----2----+----3----+----4----+----5----+----6----+----7--
 10              MACRO
  1    &NAME     $SFE  &COLOR=,&XHIGH=,&SYMBOL=,&COUNT=
  1    .* THIS MACRO GENERATES THE 3270 START FIELD EXTENDED DATA STREAM ORDER
  1    .*-------------------------------------------------------------------
  1    .* EXTENDED HIGHLIGHTING MAY BE SPECIFIED AS:
  1    .*
  1    .*   XHIGH=XXXX (XXXX=REVERSE!BLINK!UNDERLINE (OR _))
  1    .*-------------------------------------------------------------------
  1    .* COLOR CAN BE SPECIFIED AS:
  1    .*
  1    .*     COLOR=XXXX (XXXX=REC!BLUE!GREEN!YELLOW!WHITE!TURQUOISE)
  1    .*
  1    .*   OR
  1    .*
  1    .*     COLOR=(XXXX,YYYY) (YYYY=FOREGROUND!BACKGROUND)
  1    .*-------------------------------------------------------------------
  1    .* SYMBOLS MAY BE SPECIFIED AS:
  1    .*
  1    .*     SYMBOL=APL (FOR APL CHARACTER SET)
  1    .*
  1    .*   OR
  1    .*
  1    .*     SYMBOL='XX' (XX = HEX VALUE OF LOCAL ID)
  1    .*-------------------------------------------------------------------
  1    .* THE NUMBER OF ATTRIBUTE TYPE/VALUE PAIRS IS GENERATED FORM THE ABOVE
  1    .* BUT MAY BE ALTERED BY:
  1    .*
  1    .*     COUNT=XXX (XXX IS A DECIMAL CONSTANT)
  1    .*
 10              GBLC  &HEXOUT
 10              LCLA  &KOUNT
  1    &HEXOUT   SETC  ''
 10              AIF   (T'&XHIGH EQ 'O').NOXHIGH
  1    &KOUNT    SETA  1
 10              $XHIGH &XHIGH
  1    .NOXHIGH  AIF   (T'&COLOR EQ 'O').NOCOLOR
  1    &KOUNT    SETA  &KOUNT+1
 10              AIF   (T'&COLOR(2) EQ 'O').PLANE
 10              $COLOR &COLOR
 10              AGO   .NOCOLOR
  1    .PLANE    ANOP
 10              $COLOR &COLOR(1),PLANE=&COLOR(2)
  1    .NOCOLOR  AIF   (T'&SYMBOL EQ 'O').NOSYMBL
  1    &KOUNT    SETA  &KOUNT+1
 10              $SYMBOL &SYMBOL
  1    .NOSYMBL  AIF   (T'&COUNT EQ 'O').NOCOUNT
  1    &KOUNT    SETA  &COUNT
  1    .NOCOUNT  ANOP
  1    &NAME     DC    X'29',AL1(&KOUNT),X'&HEXOUT'
 10              MEND
```

```
                      $SYMBOL                       PAGE: 01 OF 01
START
 COL   ----+----1----+----2----+----3----+----4----+----5----+----6----+----7--

  10              MACRO
   1   &NAME      $SYMBOL &SYMBOL,&HEX=
   1   .*
   1   .* THIS MACRO GENERATES THE IBM 3270 EXTENDED ATTRIBUTE TYPE/VALUE PAIR
   1   .* FOR PROGRAMMED SYMBOLS.  CURRENTLY THE ONLY NAMED SYMBOL SET IS
   1   .* 'APL' AND MAY BE SPECIFIED AS THE FIRST (POSITIONAL) OPERAND.  FOR
   1   .* OTHER SYMBOL SETS IT IS NECESSARY TO SPECIFY THE HEXADECIMAL VALUE
   1   .* BY THE PARAMETER 'HEX=HV'.  THE VALUE IS (RIGHT) CONCATANATED TO THE
   1   .* GLOBAL SYMBOL '&HEXOUT' WHICH IS USED BY OTHER DATA STREAM MACROS.
   1   .*
  10              GBLC  &HEXOUT
  10              LCLC  &VALUE
   1   &HEXOUT    SETC  '&HEXOUT'.'43'
  10              AIF   (T'&HEX EQ 'O').NOTHEX
   1   &HEXOUT    SETC  '&HEXOUT&HEX'
  10              MEXIT
   1   .NOTHEX    ANOP
  10              AIF   (N'&SYSLIST(1) LT 1 OR '&SYMBOL' EQ 'NORMAL').NULL
  10              AIF   ('&SYMBOL' NE 'APL').NOTAPL
   1   &HEXOUT    SETC  '&HEXOUT'.'F1'
  10              MEXIT
   1   .NOTAPL    MNOTE 0,'INVALID SYMBOL, DEFAULT ASSUMED'
   1   .NULL      ANOP
   1   &HEXOUT    SETC  '&HEXOUT'.'00'
  10              MEND
```

```
                          $TEXT                          PAGE: 01 OF 01
START
 COL   ----+----1----+----2----+----3----+----4----+----5----+----6----+----7--

 10              MACRO
  1    &NAME     $TEXT &LOWER=,&PROPER=
  1    .* THIS MACRO GENERATES LOWER CASE CHARACTERS AF FOLLOWS
  1    .*-------------------------------------------------------------------
  1    .* ALL LOWER CASE
  1    .*
  1    .*   $TEXT LOWER=XXXX WHERE XXXX IS A STRING WHICH MAY BE ENCLOSED
  1    .*                 IN SINGLE QUOTE MARKS FOR IMBEDDED SPACES.
  1    .*-------------------------------------------------------------------
  1    .* ALL LOWER CASE EXCEPT THE FIRST CHARACTER
  1    .*
  1    .*   $TEXT PROPER=XXXX WHERE XXXX IS THE SAME AS ABOVE.
  1    .*
 10              LCLC  &UP,&LOW,&IN,&OUT
 10              LCLA  &I,&J,&K,&L
 10              ACTR  32767
  1    &UP       SETC  'ABCDEFGHIJKLMNOPQRSTUVWXYZ'
  1    &LOW      SETC  'abcdefghijklmnopqrstuvwxyz'
 10              AIF   (T'&PROPER EQ 'O').NOTPROP
  1    &I        SETA  1
  1    &K        SETA  K'&PROPER-1
 10              AIF   ('&PROPER'(1,1) NE '''').NOPQ
  1    &I        SETA  2
  1    &K        SETA  K'&PROPER-3
  1    .NOPQ     AIF   (&K LT 1).SMALL
  1    &OUT      SETC  '&PROPER'(&I,1)
  1    &IN       SETC  '&PROPER'(&I+1,&K)
 10              AGO   .CONVERT
  1    .NOTPROP  AIF   (T'&LOWER EQ 'O').NOTLOW
  1    &I        SETA  1
  1    &K        SETA  K'&LOWER
 10              AIF   ('&LOWER'(1,1) NE '''').NOLQ
  1    &I        SETA  2
  1    &K        SETA  K'&LOWER-2
  1    .NOLQ     AIF   (&K LT 0).SMALL
  1    &IN       SETC  '&LOWER'(&I,&K)
 10              AGO   .CONVERT
  1    .SMALL    MNOTE 4,'NULL CHARACTER STRING'
 10              MEXIT
  1    .NOTLOW   MNOTE 4,'INVALID STRING TYPE'
 10              MEXIT
  1    .CONVERT  AIF   (&J GE &K).DONE
  1    &J        SETA  &J+1
  1    &L        SETA  1
  1    .ALOOP    AIF   ('&UP'(&L,1) EQ '&IN'(&J,1)).ALPHA
  1    &L        SETA  &L+1
 10              AIF   (&L LE 26).ALOOP
  1    &OUT      SETC  '&OUT'.'&IN'(&J,1)
 10              AGO   .CONVERT
  1    .ALPHA    ANOP
  1    &OUT      SETC '&OUT'.'&LOW'(&L,1)
 10              AGO   .CONVERT
  1    .DONE     ANOP
  1    &NAME     DC    C'&OUT'
 10              MEND
```

```
                         $WCC                         PAGE: 01 OF 01
START
 COL   ----+----1----+----2----+----3----+----4----+----5----+----6----+----7--

  10            MACRO
   1   &NAME    $WCC   &LIST,&CODE=EBCDIC
   1   .*
   1   .* THIS MACRO GENERATES A WRITE CONTROL CHARACTER.  THE KEYWORD PARAME-
   1   .* TER 'CODE=ASCII' OR CODE=EBCDIC (ASSUMED) SPECIFIES THE MODE OF THE
   1   .* GENERATED CHARACTER.  THE FIRST PARAMETER SPECIFIES THE OPTIONS THAT
   1   .* ARE TO BE GENERATED.  VALID OPTIONS ARE 'RESTORE' TO RESTORE THE
   1   .* KEYBOARD FOR MANUAL INPUT, 'RESET' TO TURN ON THE RESET BIT, 'ALARM'
   1   .* TO ACTIVATE THE AUDIBLE ALARM, 'PRINT' TO ACTIVATE PRINTER AT THE
   1   .* COMPLETION OF COPY, '40CHAR'/'64CHAR'/'80CHAR' TO SET LINE LENGTH TO
   1   .* 40/64/80 CHARACTES, AND 'NLEM' TO INDICATE THAT THE LINE LENGTH IS
   1   .* LENGTH IS DETERMINED (UP TO 132 COLUMNS) BY NEW-LINE OR END-OF-
   1   .* MESSAGE CONTROL CHARACTERS.  MULTIPLE, NON-MUTUALLY EXCLUSIVE
   1   .* OPTIONS MAY BE SPECIFIED BY ENCLOSING THE PARAMETERS IN PARENTHESES.
   1   .*
  10            LCLA   &B2,&B3,&B4,&B5,&B6,&B7,&I,&C40,&C64,&C80,&NLEM
   1   &I       SETA   1
  10            AIF    (N'&SYSLIST(1) GT 0).LOOP
  10            MNOTE  0,'NULL ''WCC'' LIST'
  10            AGO    .NULL
   1   .LOOP    ANOP
  10            AIF    ('&SYSLIST(1,&I)' EQ 'RESTORE').RESTORE
  10            AIF    ('&SYSLIST(1,&I)' EQ 'RESET').RESET
  10            AIF    ('&SYSLIST(1,&I)' EQ 'ALARM').ALARM
  10            AIF    ('&SYSLIST(1,&I)' EQ 'PRINT').PRINT
  10            AIF    ('&SYSLIST(1,&I)' EQ '40CHAR').C40
  10            AIF    ('&SYSLIST(1,&I)' EQ '64CHAR').C64
  10            AIF    ('&SYSLIST(1,&I)' EQ '80CHAR').C80
  10            AIF    ('&SYSLIST(1,&I)' EQ 'NLEM').NLEM
  10            MNOTE  0,'INVALID ''WCC'' PARAMETER--&SYSLIST(1,&I)'
  10            AGO    .LOOPEND
   1   .RESTORE ANOP
   1   &B6      SETA   1
  10            AGO    .LOOPEND
   1   .RESET   ANOP
   1   &B7      SETA   1
  10            AGO    .LOOPEND
   1   .ALARM   ANOP
   1   &B5      SETA   1
  10            AGO    .LOOPEND
   1   .PRINT   ANOP
   1   &B4      SETA   1
  10            AGO    .LOOPEND
   1   .NLEM    ANOP
   1   &NLEM    SETA   1
  10            AGO    .LOOPEND
   1   .C40     ANOP
   1   &C40     SETA   1
  10            AGO    .SET3
   1   .C64     ANOP
   1   &C64     SETA   1
   1   &B2      SETA   1
  10            AGO    .LOOPEND
   1   .C80     ANOP
   1   &C80     SETA   1
   1   &B2      SETA   1
   1   .SET3    ANOP
   1   &B3      SETA   1
   1   .LOOPEND ANOP
   1   &I       SETA   &I+1
  10            AIF    (&I LE N'&SYSLIST(1)).LOOP
  10            AIF    (&C40+&C64+&C80+&NLEM LE 1).NULL
  10            MNOTE  0,'CONFLICTING ''WCC'' PRINT FORMATS'
   1   .NULL    ANOP
   1   &BYTE    SETA   &B7+2*(&B6+2*(&B5+2*(&B4+2*(&B3+2*&B2))))
  10            $BYTE  &BYTE,CODE=&CODE
   1   &NAME    DC     X'&HEXOUT'
  10            MEND
```

```
                        $XHIGH                          PAGE: 01 OF 01
START
 COL   ----+----1----+----2----+----3----+----4----+----5----+----6----+----7--

 10             MACRO                                                          00000000
  1    &NAME    $XHIGH &TYPE                                                          *
  1    .*                                                                             *
  1    .* THIS MACRO GENERATES THE IBM 3270 EXTENDED ATTRIBUTE TYPE/VALUE PAIR        *
  1    .* FOR EXTENDED HIGH LIGHTING.  VALID PARAMETERS ARE 'REVERSE' FOR             *
  1    .* REVERSE VIDEO, 'BLINK' FOR BLINKING, 'UNDERSCORE' OR '_' FOR                *
  1    .* UNDERLINING, AND 'NORMAL' FOR NORMAL.  THE RESULTING 4 HEXADECIMAL          *
  1    .* DIGITS ARE (RIGHT) CONCATNATED TO THE GLOBAL SYMBOL '&HEXOUT'.              *
  1    .*                                                                             *
 10             GBLC  &HEXOUT                                                         *
 10             LCLA  &I                                                              *
  1    .LOOP    ANOP                                                                  *
  1    &I       SETA  &I+1                                                            *
 10             AIF   (&I GT N'&SYSLIST(1)).END                                       *
  1    &HEXOUT  SETC  '&HEXOUT'.'41'                                                  *
 10             AIF   ('&TYPE(&I)' EQ 'NORMAL').NORMAL                                *
 10             AIF   ('&TYPE(&I)' NE 'BLINK').NOTBLNK                                *
  1    &HEXOUT  SETC  '&HEXOUT'.'F1'                                                  *
 10             AGO   .LOOP                                                           *
  1    .NOTBLNK AIF   ('&TYPE(&I)' NE 'REVERSE').NOTRV                                *
  1    &HEXOUT  SETC  '&HEXOUT'.'F2'                                                  *
 10             AGO   .LOOP                                                           *
  1    .NOTRV   AIF   ('&TYPE(&I)' NE 'UNDERSCORE'                            -       *
 16                   AND '&TYPE(&I)' NE '_').NOTUS                                   *
  1    &HEXOUT  SETC  '&HEXOUT'.'F4'                                                  *
 10             AGO   .LOOP                                                           *
  1    .NOTUS   MNOTE 0,'INVALID TYPE, DEFAULT ASSUMED'                               *
  1    .NORMAL  ANOP                                                                  *
  1    &HEXOUT  SETC  '&HEXOUT'.'00'                                                  *
 10             AGO   .LOOP                                                           *
  1    .END     MEND                                                                  *
```

```
DEMO OF 3270 DATA STREAM MACROS

  LOC  OBJECT CODE    ADDR1 ADDR2  STMT   SOURCE STATEMENT                                 ASM H V 02 12.39 03/17/89

                                      2 ***********************************************************************
                                      3 * THIS CICS PROGRAM DISPLAYS A SAMPLE SCREEN THAT DEMONSTRATES THE    *
                                      4 * IBM 3270 DATA STREAM MACROS.  THE OUTPUT IS AS FOLLOWS.             *
                                      5 *                                                                     *
                                      6 * 1) WHEN NO INPUT FOLLOWS THE TRANSID A SCREEN DEMONSTRATING THE     *
                                      7 *    EXTENDED ATTRIBUTES IS DISPLAYED.  THIS SCREEN INCLUDES EXTENDED *
                                      8 *    HIGHLIGNTING (BLINKING AND REVERSE VIDEO), COLORS (BLUE, GREEN,  *
                                      9 *    RED, PINK, YELLOW, TURQUOISE, AND WHITE), AND CHARACTER SETS     *
                                     10 *    (APL).  A VERTICAL DISPLAY OF THE U. S. FLAG IS PRESENTED.       *
                                     11 *                                                                     *
                                     12 * 2) IF THE TRANSID IS FOLLOWED IMMEDIATELY BY A SERIES OF HEXADECIMAL*
                                     13 *    DIGITS, A DATA STREAM CONSISTING OF THE VALUES IS RETURNED (E.G.,*

                                     14 *    11C1C51DC8C1C2C3 WILL RESPOND BY SETTING THE BUFFER ADDRESS TO   *
                                     15 *    5 (ROW 1, COLUMN 6--FROM THE SBA '11C1C5'), DEFINE AN UNPROTECTED*
                                     16 *    FIELD (UNPROTECTED, ALPHAMERIC, HIGH INTENSITY--FROM THE SF 1DC8)*
                                     17 *    AND DISPLAY THE CHARACTERS 'ABC' (C1C2C3).                       *
                                     18 ***********************************************************************
000000                               19 DEMO3270 CSECT                                                          00009
                                     20          PRINT OFF
                                   3873          PRINT ON,NOGEN                                                 00010
000000                             3874 DEMO3270 CSECT
                             00000 3875          USING *,9                 ESTABLISH PROGRAM ADDRESSING
000000 189E                        3876          LR    9,14                LOAD BASE REGISTER FROM VOLATILE REG
000002 58B0 C008             00008 3877          L     TCTTEAR,TCAFCAAA    LOAD TCTTE BASE REGISTER
000006 58A0 B00C             0000C 3878          L     TIOABAR,TCTTEDA     LOAD TIOA BASE ADDRESS REGISTER
00000A 4130 A010             00010 3879          LA    3,TIOADBA+4         LOAD ADDRESS OF TIOA DATA
00000E 4140 0002             00002 3880          LA    4,2                 HEX DIGITS/BYTE
000012 4150 A00A             0000A 3881          LA    5,TIOADBA-2         POINT TO BYTE BEFORE DATA
000016 4A50 A008             00008 3882          AH    5,TIOATDL           POINT TO END OF DATA
                                   3883          DFHSC TYPE=GETMAIN,CLASS=TERMINAL,NUMBYTE=3000,INITIMG=40
00002E 58A0 C05C             0005C 3893          L     TIOABAR,TCASCSA     LOAD TIOA BASE REGISTER
000032 D20C A00C 90C2 0000C 000C2 3894          MVC   TIOADBA(13),=C'INVALID INPUT'
000038 4160 000D             0000D 3895          LA    6,13                SET DEFAULT MESSAGE LENGTH
00003C 9511 A00C       0000C       3896          CLI   TIOADBA,X'11'       FORMATTED SCREEN?
000040 4770 9048             00048 3897          BNE   UNFORMAT             NO
000044 4133 0003             00003 3898          LA    3,3(3)              ALLOW FOR SBA/ADDRESS
000048 1935                        3899 UNFORMAT CR    3,5                 LOW LIMIT < UPPER LIMIT?
00004A 47B0 909C             0009C 3900          BNL   STANDARD             NO
00004E 1766                        3901          XR    6,6                 CLEAR REGISTER
000050 4170 A00C             0000C 3902          LA    7,TIOADBA           POINT TO BEGINNING OF OUTPUT
000054 DC01 3000 90CF 00000 000CF 3903 PACKLOOP TR    0(2,3),HEXTABLE     TRANSLATE CHARACTERS
00005A F212 7000 3000 00000 00000 3904          PACK  0(2,7),0(3,3)       PACK HEX NYBLS
000060 4166 0001             00001 3905          LA    6,1(6)              COUNT OUTPUT BYTE
000064 4177 0001             00001 3906          LA    7,1(7)              COUNT OUTPUT BYTE
000068 8734 9054             00054 3907          BXLE  3,4,PACKLOOP        CONTINUE
00006C 4060 A008             00008 3908 SEND     STH   6,TIOATDL           SET OUTPUT LENGTH
000070 50A0 B00C             0000C 3909          ST    TIOABAR,TCTTEDA     STORE ADDRESS OF CURRENT TIOA
                                   3910          DFHTC TYPE=(WRITE,ERASE)  WRITE DATA

                                   3921 EXIT     DFHPC TYPE=RETURN         RETURN TO CICS                   00029


00009C 4100 A00C             0000C 3931 STANDARD LA    0,TIOADBA           POINT TO 'TO' ADDRESS
0000A0 41E0 91CF             001CF 3932          LA    14,SCREEN           POINT TO 'FROM' ADDRESS
0000A4 4110 0B54             00B54 3933          LA    1,2900              SET MAXIMUM SCREEN LENGTH
```

```
         DEMO OF 3270 DATA STREAM MACROS

  LOC   OBJECT CODE     ADDR1 ADDR2  STMT   SOURCE STATEMENT                                      ASM H V 02 12.39 03/17/89

0000A8 41F0 0B36              00B36  3934            LA    15,LSCREEN           SET SCREEN LENGTH
0000AC 19F1                          3935            CR    15,1                 TOO BIG?
0000AE 47D0 90B4              000B4  3936            BNH   STDOKAY               NO
0000B2 18F1                          3937            LR    15,1                 RESET TO MAXIMUM LENGTH
0000B4 186F                          3938 STDOKAY    LR    6,15                 SAVE OUTPUT LENGTH
0000B6 0E0E                          3939            MVCL  0,14                 MOVE TO TIOA
0000B8 47F0 906C              0006C  3940            B     SEND                 GO DISPLAY STANDARD
0000C0                               3941            LTORG

0000C0 0BB8                          3942                  =AL2(3000)
0000C2 C9D5E5C1D3C9C440              3943                  =C'INVALID INPUT'

0000CF 0000000000000000              3945 HEXTABLE   DC    256X'00'
0001CF                        00190  3946            ORG   HEXTABLE+C'A'
000190 0A0B0C0D0E0F                  3947            DC    X'0A0B0C0D0E0F'
000196                        001BF  3948            ORG   HEXTABLE+C'0'
0001BF 0001020304050607              3949            DC    X'00010203040506070809'
0001C9                        001CF  3950            ORG


                                     3952            PRINT GEN
                                     3953 SCREEN     $SBA  (24,80)
0001CF 115D7F                        3954+SCREEN     DC    X'115D7F'                                                01-$SBA
                                     3955            $SF
0001D2 1D40                          3956+           DC    X'1D40'                                                  01-$SF
                                     3957            $SA   COLOR=BLUE
0001D4 2842F1                        3958+           DC    X'2842F1'                                                01-$SA
                                     3959            $TEXT PROPER='BLUE '
0001D7 C293A48540                    3960+           DC    C'Blue '                                                 01-$TEXT
                                     3961            PRINT NOGEN
                                     3962            $SA   COLOR=RED
                                     3964            $TEXT PROPER='RED '
                                     3966            $SA   COLOR=PINK
                                     3968            $TEXT PROPER='PINK '
                                     3970            $SA   COLOR=GREEN
                                     3972            $TEXT PROPER='GREEN '
                                     3974            $SA   COLOR=TURQUOISE
                                     3976            $TEXT PROPER=TURQUOISE
                                     3978            $SBA  (1,80)
                                     3980            $SF
                                     3982            $SA   COLOR=YELLOW
                                     3984            $TEXT PROPER='YELLOW '
                                     3986            $SA   COLOR=WHITE
                                     3988            $TEXT PROPER='WHITE '
                                     3990            $SA   XHIGH=BLINK,COLOR=BLUE
00021E C2                            3992            DC    C'B'                 B
                                     3993            $SA   COLOR=RED            L
                                     3995            $TEXT LOWER=L
                                     3997            $SA   COLOR=PINK           L
                                     3999            $TEXT LOWER=I
                                     4001            $SA   COLOR=GREEN          N
                                     4003            $TEXT LOWER=N
                                     4005            $SA   COLOR=TURQUOISE      K
                                     4007            $TEXT LOWER='K '
                                     4009            $SA   XHIGH=REVERSE,COLOR=BLUE
000236 D9                            4011            DC    C'R'                 R
```

```
DEMO OF 3270 DATA STREAM MACROS

  LOC  OBJECT CODE    ADDR1 ADDR2  STMT   SOURCE STATEMENT                                          ASM H V 02 12.39 03/17/89
                                   4012          $SA   COLOR=RED
                                   4014          $TEXT LOWER=E              E
                                   4016          $SA   COLOR=PINK
                                   4018          $TEXT LOWER=V              V
                                   4020          $SA   COLOR=GREEN
                                   4022          $TEXT LOWER=E              E
                                   4024          $SA   COLOR=TURQUOISE
                                   4026          $TEXT LOWER=R              R
                                   4028          $SA   COLOR=YELLOW
                                   4030          $TEXT LOWER=S              S
                                   4032          $SA   COLOR=WHITE
                                   4034          $TEXT LOWER=E              E
                                   4036          $SBA  (2,80)
                                   4038          $SF
                                   4040          $SA   XHIGH=NORMAL,COLOR=GREEN
                                   4042 *                 0 1 2 3 4 5 6 7 8 9 A B C D E F
00025A 4041424344454647            4043          DC    X'404142434445464748494A4B4C4D4E4F'   4
                                   4044          $SA   COLOR=YELLOW
00026D 5051525354555657            4046          DC    X'505152535455565758595A5B5C5D5E5F',C' 40-5F'
                                   4047          $SBA  (3,80)
                                   4049          $SF
000288 6061626364656667            4051          DC    X'606162636465666768696A6B6C6D6E6F'   6
                                   4052          $SA   COLOR=GREEN
00029B 7071727374757677            4054          DC    X'707172737475767778797A7B7C7D7E7F',C' 60-7F'
                                   4055          $SBA  (4,80)
                                   4057          $SF
0002B6 8081828384858687            4059          DC    X'808182838485868788898A8B8C8D8E8F'   8
                                   4060          $SA   COLOR=YELLOW
0002C9 9091929394959697            4062          DC    X'909192939495969798999A9B9C9D9E9F',C' 80-8F'
                                   4063          $SBA  (5,80)
                                   4065          $SF
0002E4 A0A1A2A3A4A5A6A7            4067          DC    X'A0A1A2A3A4A5A6A7A8A9AAABACADAEAF'   A
                                   4068          $SA   COLOR=GREEN
0002F7 B0B1B2B3B4B5B6B7            4070          DC    X'B0B1B2B3B4B5B6B7B8B9BABBBCBDBEBF',C' A0-BF'
                                   4071          $SBA  (6,80)
                                   4073          $SF
000312 C0C1C2C3C4C5C6C7            4075          DC    X'C0C1C2C3C4C5C6C7C8C9CACBCCCDCECF'   C
                                   4076          $SA   COLOR=YELLOW
000325 D0D1D2D3D4D5D6D7            4078          DC    X'D0D1D2D3D4D5D6D7D8D9DADBDCDDDEDF',C' C0-DF'
                                   4079          $SBA  (7,80)
                                   4081          $SF
000340 E0E1E2E3E4E5E6E7            4083          DC    X'E0E1E2E3E4E5E6E7E8D9EAEBECEDEEEF'   E
                                   4084          $SA   COLOR=GREEN
000353 F0F1F2F3F4F5F6F7            4086          DC    X'F0F1F2F3F4F5F6F7F8F9FAFBFCFDFE',C'  E0-FE'
                                   4087          $SBA  (9,80)
                                   4089          $SF
                                   4091          $SA   XHIGH=NORMAL,COLOR=GREEN,SYMBOL=APL
                                   4093 *                 0 1 2 3 4 5 6 7 8 9 A B C D E F
000377 4041424344454647            4094          DC    X'40414243444546474849404040404040'   4
                                   4095          $SA   COLOR=YELLOW
00038A 4051525354555657            4097          DC    X'40515253545556575859404040404040'   5
                                   4098          $SBA  (10,80)
                                   4100          $SF
00039F 4040626364656667            4102          DC    X'40406263646566676869404040404040'   6
                                   4103          $SA   COLOR=GREEN
```

```
        DEMO OF 3270 DATA STREAM MACROS

  LOC  OBJECT CODE    ADDR1 ADDR2  STMT   SOURCE STATEMENT                                  ASM H V 02 12.39 03/17/89
0003B2 407172404040404040          4105            DC     X'40717240404040407879404040404040'  7
                                   4106            $SBA   (11,80)
                                   4108            $SF
0003C7 8081828384854040            4110            DC     X'808182838485404040408A8B8C8D8E8F'  8
                                   4111            $SA    COLOR=YELLOW
0003DA 9091929394954040            4113            DC     X'909192939495404040409A9B9C9D9E9F'  9
                                   4114            $SBA   (12,80)
                                   4116            $SF
0003EF A0A1A2A3A4404040            4118            DC     X'A0A1A2A3A440404040AAABACADAEAF'  A
                                   4119            $SA    COLOR=GREEN
000402 B0B1B2B3B440B6B7            4121            DC     X'B0B1B2B3B440B6B7B840BABBBCBDBEBF'  B
                                   4122            $SBA   (13,80)
                                   4124            $SF
000417 C0C1C2C3C4C5C6C7            4126            DC     X'C0C1C2C3C4C5C6C7C840CACB40CD40CF'  C
                                   4127            $SA    COLOR=YELLOW

00042A D0D1D2D3D4D5D6D7            4129            DC     X'D0D1D2D3D4D5D6D7D840DADBDCDDDEDF'  D
                                   4130            $SBA   (14,80)
                                   4132            $SF
00043F 40E1E2E340404040            4134            DC     X'40E1E2E34040404040EAEBECEDEEEF'  E
                                   4135            $SA    COLOR=GREEN
000452 F0F1F2F3F4F5F6F7            4137            DC     X'F0F1F2F3F4F5F6F7F8F940FBFCFDFE'    F
                                   4138            $SBA   (16,80)
                                   4140            $SF    HI
                                   4142            $SA    XHIGH=REVERSE
                                   4144            $SA    SYMBOL=APL
                                   4146 *                   0 1 2 3 4 5 6 7 8 9 A B C D E F
00046C 4041424344454647            4147            DC     X'40414243444546474849404040404040'  4
                                   4148            $SA    COLOR=YELLOW
00047F 4051525354555657            4150            DC     X'40515253545556575859404040404040'  5
                                   4151            $SBA   (17,80)
                                   4153            $SF
000494 4040626364656667            4155            DC     X'40406263646566676869404040404040'  6
                                   4156            $SA    COLOR=GREEN
0004A7 4071724040404040            4158            DC     X'40717240404040407879404040404040'  7
                                   4159            $SBA   (18,80)
                                   4161            $SF
0004BC 8081828384854040            4163            DC     X'808182838485404040408A8B8C8D8E8F'  8
                                   4164            $SA    COLOR=YELLOW
0004CF 9091929394954040            4166            DC     X'909192939495404040409A9B9C9D9E9F'  9
                                   4167            $SBA   (19,80)
                                   4169            $SF
0004E4 A0A1A2A3A4404040            4171            DC     X'A0A1A2A3A440404040AAABACADAEAF'  A
                                   4172            $SA    COLOR=GREEN
0004F7 B0B1B2B3B440B6B7            4174            DC     X'B0B1B2B3B440B6B7B840BABBBCBDBEBF'  B
                                   4175            $SBA   (20,80)
                                   4177            $SF
00050C C0C1C2C3C4C5C6C7            4179            DC     X'C0C1C2C3C4C5C6C7C840CACB40CD40CF'  C
                                   4180            $SA    COLOR=YELLOW
00051F D0D1D2D3D4D5D6D7            4182            DC     X'D0D1D2D3D4D5D6D7D840DADBDCDDDEDF'  D
                                   4183            $SBA   (21,80)
                                   4185            $SF
000534 40E1E2E340404040            4187            DC     X'40E1E2E34040404040EAEBECEDEEEF'  E
                                   4188            $SA    COLOR=GREEN
000547 F0F1F2F3F4F5F6F7            4190            DC     X'F0F1F2F3F4F5F6F7F8F940FBFCFDFE40'  F
                                   4191            $SA    SYMBOL=NORMAL       RESET CHARACTER SET
```

```
        DEMO OF 3270 DATA STREAM MACROS

  LOC  OBJECT CODE    ADDR1 ADDR2  STMT   SOURCE STATEMENT                                      ASM H V 02 12.39 03/17/89
                                   4193          $SBA  (1,40)
                                   4195          $SF
                                   4197          PRINT GEN
                                   4198          $SA   XHIGH=(NORMAL,BLINK),COLOR=WHITE
00055F 2841F12842F7                4199+         DC    X'2841F12842F7'                                      01-$SA
000565 40405C4040405C40            4200          DC    C'  *   *   *   *   *  ' 1 - 5
                                   4201          $SA   XHIGH=REVERSE,COLOR=WHITE
00057A 2841F22842F7                4202+         DC    X'2841F22842F7'                                      01-$SA
                                   4203          PRINT NOGEN
000580 404040                      4204          DC    C'   '                  STRIPE 13
                                   4205          $SA   COLOR=RED                 8
000586 404040                      4207          DC    C'   '
                                   4208          $SA   COLOR=WHITE              12
00058C 404040                      4210          DC    C'   '
                                   4211          $SA   COLOR=RED                11
000592 404040                      4213          DC    C'   '
                                   4214          $SA   COLOR=WHITE              10
000598 404040                      4216          DC    C'   '
                                   4217          $SA   COLOR=RED                 9
00059E 404040                      4219          DC    C'   '
                                   4220          $SBA  (2,40)
                                   4222          $SF
                                   4224          $SA   XHIGH=(NORMAL,BLINK),COLOR=WHITE
0005AC 404040405C404040            4226          DC    C'     *    *    *    *  ' 6 - 9
                                   4227          $SA   XHIGH=REVERSE,COLOR=WHITE
0005C7 404040                      4229          DC    C'   '                     13
                                   4230          $SA   COLOR=RED                 8
0005CD 404040                      4232          DC    C'   '
                                   4233          $SA   COLOR=WHITE              12
0005D3 404040                      4235          DC    C'   '
                                   4236          $SA   COLOR=RED                11
0005D9 404040                      4238          DC    C'   '
                                   4239          $SA   COLOR=WHITE              10
0005DF 404040                      4241          DC    C'   '
                                   4242          $SA   COLOR=RED                 9
0005E5 404040                      4244          DC    C'   '
                                   4245          $SBA  (3,40)
                                   4247          $SF
                                   4249          $SA   XHIGH=(NORMAL,BLINK),COLOR=WHITE
0005F3 40405C4040405C40            4251          DC    C'  *   *   *   *   *  ' 10- 14
                                   4252          $SA   XHIGH=REVERSE,COLOR=WHITE
00060E 404040                      4254          DC    C'   '                     13
                                   4255          $SA   COLOR=RED                 8
000614 404040                      4257          DC    C'   '
                                   4258          $SA   COLOR=WHITE              12
00061A 404040                      4260          DC    C'   '
                                   4261          $SA   COLOR=RED                11
000620 404040                      4263          DC    C'   '
                                   4264          $SA   COLOR=WHITE              10
000626 404040                      4266          DC    C'   '
                                   4267          $SA   COLOR=RED                 9
00062C 404040                      4269          DC    C'   '
                                   4270          $SBA  (4,40)
                                   4272          $SF
                                   4274          $SA   XHIGH=(NORMAL,BLINK),COLOR=WHITE
```

```
DEMO OF 3270 DATA STREAM MACROS                                                                        ASM H V 02 12.39 03/17/89

  LOC  OBJECT CODE    ADDR1 ADDR2  STMT   SOURCE STATEMENT
00063A 404040405C404040            4276          DC    C'   *   *   *   *   ' 15- 18
                                   4277          $SA   XHIGH=REVERSE,COLOR=WHITE
000655 404040                      4279          DC    C'   '                   13
                                   4280          $SA   COLOR=RED               8
00065B 404040                      4282          DC    C'   '
                                   4283          $SA   COLOR=WHITE            12
000661 404040                      4285          DC    C'   '
                                   4286          $SA   COLOR=RED              11
000667 404040                      4288          DC    C'   '
                                   4289          $SA   COLOR=WHITE            10
00066D 404040                      4291          DC    C'   '
                                   4292          $SA   COLOR=RED               9
000673 404040                      4294          DC    C'   '
                                   4295          $SBA  (5,40)
                                   4297          $SF
                                   4299          $SA   XHIGH=(NORMAL,BLINK),COLOR=WHITE
000681 40405C4040405C40            4301          DC    C'  *   *   *   *   *  ' 19- 23
                                   4302          $SA   XHIGH=REVERSE,COLOR=WHITE
00069C 404040                      4304          DC    C'   '                   13
                                   4305          $SA   COLOR=RED               8
0006A2 404040                      4307          DC    C'   '
                                   4308          $SA   COLOR=WHITE            12
0006A8 404040                      4310          DC    C'   '
                                   4311          $SA   COLOR=RED              11
0006AE 404040                      4313          DC    C'   '
                                   4314          $SA   COLOR=WHITE            10
0006B4 404040                      4316          DC    C'   '
                                   4317          $SA   COLOR=RED               9
0006BA 404040                      4319          DC    C'   '
                                   4320          $SBA  (6,40)
                                   4322          $SF
                                   4324          $SA   XHIGH=(NORMAL,BLINK),COLOR=WHITE
0006C8 404040405C404040            4326          DC    C'   *   *   *   *   ' 24- 27
                                   4327          $SA   XHIGH=REVERSE,COLOR=WHITE
0006E3 404040                      4329          DC    C'   '                   13
                                   4330          $SA   COLOR=RED               8
0006E9 404040                      4332          DC    C'   '
                                   4333          $SA   COLOR=WHITE            12
0006EF 404040                      4335          DC    C'   '
                                   4336          $SA   COLOR=RED              11
0006F5 404040                      4338          DC    C'   '
                                   4339          $SA   COLOR=WHITE            10
0006FB 404040                      4341          DC    C'   '
                                   4342          $SA   COLOR=RED               9
000701 404040                      4344          DC    C'   '
                                   4345          $SBA  (7,40)
                                   4347          $SF
                                   4349          $SA   XHIGH=(NORMAL,BLINK),COLOR=WHITE
00070F 40405C4040405C40            4351          DC    C'  *   *   *   *   *  ' 28- 32
                                   4352          $SA   XHIGH=REVERSE,COLOR=WHITE
00072A 404040                      4354          DC    C'   '                   13
                                   4355          $SA   COLOR=RED               8
000730 404040                      4357          DC    C'   '
                                   4358          $SA   COLOR=WHITE            12
000736 404040                      4360          DC    C'   '
```

```
        DEMO OF 3270 DATA STREAM MACROS

  LOC  OBJECT CODE    ADDR1 ADDR2  STMT   SOURCE STATEMENT                                    ASM H V 02 12.39 03/17/89
                                   4361          $SA   COLOR=RED              11
00073C 404040                      4363          DC    C'   '
                                   4364          $SA   COLOR=WHITE            10
000742 404040                      4366          DC    C'   '
                                   4367          $SA   COLOR=RED               9
000748 404040                      4369          DC    C'   '
                                   4370          $SBA  (8,40)
                                   4372          $SF
                                   4374          $SA   XHIGH=(NORMAL,BLINK),COLOR=WHITE
000756 404040405C404040            4376          DC    C'   *   *   *   *   ' 33- 36
                                   4377          $SA   XHIGH=REVERSE,COLOR=WHITE
000771 404040                      4379          DC    C'   '                  13
                                   4380          $SA   COLOR=RED               8
000777 404040                      4382          DC    C'   '
                                   4383          $SA   COLOR=WHITE            12
00077D 404040                      4385          DC    C'   '
                                   4386          $SA   COLOR=RED              11
000783 404040                      4388          DC    C'   '
                                   4389          $SA   COLOR=WHITE            10
000789 404040                      4391          DC    C'   '
                                   4392          $SA   COLOR=RED               9
00078F 404040                      4394          DC    C'   '
                                   4395          $SBA  (9,40)
                                   4397          $SF
                                   4399          $SA   XHIGH=(NORMAL,BLINK),COLOR=WHITE
00079D 40405C4040405C40            4401          DC    C'  *   *   *   *   *  ' 37- 41
                                   4402          $SA   XHIGH=REVERSE,COLOR=WHITE
0007B8 404040                      4404          DC    C'   '                  13
                                   4405          $SA   COLOR=RED               8
0007BE 404040                      4407          DC    C'   '
                                   4408          $SA   COLOR=WHITE            12
0007C4 404040                      4410          DC    C'   '
                                   4411          $SA   COLOR=RED              11
0007CA 404040                      4413          DC    C'   '
                                   4414          $SA   COLOR=WHITE            10
0007D0 404040                      4416          DC    C'   '
                                   4417          $SA   COLOR=RED               9
0007D6 404040                      4419          DC    C'   '
                                   4420          $SBA  (10,40)
                                   4422          $SF
                                   4424          $SA   XHIGH=(NORMAL,BLINK),COLOR=WHITE
0007E4 404040405C404040            4426          DC    C'   *   *   *   *   ' 42- 45
                                   4427          $SA   XHIGH=REVERSE,COLOR=WHITE
0007FF 404040                      4429          DC    C'   '                  13
                                   4430          $SA   COLOR=RED               8
000805 404040                      4432          DC    C'   '
                                   4433          $SA   COLOR=WHITE            12
00080B 404040                      4435          DC    C'   '
                                   4436          $SA   COLOR=RED              11
000811 404040                      4438          DC    C'   '
                                   4439          $SA   COLOR=WHITE            10
000817 404040                      4441          DC    C'   '
                                   4442          $SA   COLOR=RED               9
00081D 404040                      4444          DC    C'   '
                                   4445          $SBA  (11,40)
```

```
        DEMO OF 3270 DATA STREAM MACROS

  LOC  OBJECT CODE    ADDR1 ADDR2  STMT   SOURCE STATEMENT                                ASM H V 02 12.39 03/17/89

                                   4447          $SF
                                   4449          $SA   XHIGH=(NORMAL,BLINK),COLOR=WHITE
00082B 40405C4040405C40            4451          DC    C'  *    *    *    *    *  ' 46- 50
                                   4452          $SA   XHIGH=REVERSE,COLOR=WHITE
000846 404040                      4454          DC    C'   '                 13
                                   4455          $SA   COLOR=RED             8
00084C 404040                      4457          DC    C'   '
                                   4458          $SA   COLOR=WHITE          12
000852 404040                      4460          DC    C'   '
                                   4461          $SA   COLOR=RED            11
000858 404040                      4463          DC    C'   '
                                   4464          $SA   COLOR=WHITE          10
00085E 404040                      4466          DC    C'   '
                                   4467          $SA   COLOR=RED             9
000864 404040                      4469          DC    C'   '
                                   4470          $SBA  (12,40)
                                   4472          $SF
                                   4474          $SA   XHIGH=REVERSE,COLOR=RED
000872 404040                      4476          DC    C'   '                 13
                                   4477          $SA   COLOR=WHITE          12
000878 404040                      4479          DC    C'   '
                                   4480          $SA   COLOR=RED            11
00087E 404040                      4482          DC    C'   '
                                   4483          $SA   COLOR=WHITE          10
000884 404040                      4485          DC    C'   '
                                   4486          $SA   COLOR=RED             9
00088A 404040                      4488          DC    C'   '
                                   4489          $SA   COLOR=WHITE           8
000890 404040                      4491          DC    C'   '
                                   4492          $SA   COLOR=RED             7
000896 404040                      4494          DC    C'   '
                                   4495          $SA   COLOR=WHITE           6
00089C 404040                      4497          DC    C'   '
                                   4498          $SA   COLOR=RED             5
0008A2 404040                      4500          DC    C'   '
                                   4501          $SA   COLOR=WHITE           4
0008A8 404040                      4503          DC    C'   '
                                   4504          $SA   COLOR=RED             3
0008AE 404040                      4506          DC    C'   '
                                   4507          $SA   COLOR=WHITE           2
0008B4 404040                      4509          DC    C'   '
                                   4510          $SA   COLOR=RED             1
0008BA 404040                      4512          DC    C'   '
                                   4513          $SBA  (13,40)
                                   4515          $SF
                                   4517          $SA   XHIGH=REVERSE,COLOR=RED
0008C8 404040                      4519          DC    C'   '                 13
                                   4520          $SA   COLOR=WHITE          12
0008CE 404040                      4522          DC    C'   '
                                   4523          $SA   COLOR=RED            11
0008D4 404040                      4525          DC    C'   '
                                   4526          $SA   COLOR=WHITE          10
0008DA 404040                      4528          DC    C'   '
                                   4529          $SA   COLOR=RED             9
0008E0 404040                      4531          DC    C'   '
```

```
         DEMO OF 3270 DATA STREAM MACROS

  LOC  OBJECT CODE    ADDR1 ADDR2  STMT   SOURCE STATEMENT                              ASM H V 02 12.39 03/17/89

                                   4532            $SA    COLOR=WHITE          8
0008E6 404040                      4534            DC     C'   '
                                   4535            $SA    COLOR=RED            7
0008EC 404040                      4537            DC     C'   '
                                   4538            $SA    COLOR=WHITE          6
0008F2 404040                      4540            DC     C'   '
                                   4541            $SA    COLOR=RED            5
0008F8 404040                      4543            DC     C'   '
                                   4544            $SA    COLOR=WHITE          4
0008FE 404040                      4546            DC     C'   '
                                   4547            $SA    COLOR=RED            3
000904 404040                      4549            DC     C'   '
                                   4550            $SA    COLOR=WHITE          2
00090A 404040                      4552            DC     C'   '
                                   4553            $SA    COLOR=RED            1
000910 404040                      4555            DC     C'   '
                                   4556            $SBA   (14,40)
                                   4558            $SF
                                   4560            $SA    XHIGH=REVERSE,COLOR=RED
00091E 404040                      4562            DC     C'   '               13
                                   4563            $SA    COLOR=WHITE          12
000924 404040                      4565            DC     C'   '
                                   4566            $SA    COLOR=RED            11
00092A 404040                      4568            DC     C'   '
                                   4569            $SA    COLOR=WHITE          10
000930 404040                      4571            DC     C'   '
                                   4572            $SA    COLOR=RED            9
000936 404040                      4574            DC     C'   '
                                   4575            $SA    COLOR=WHITE          8
00093C 404040                      4577            DC     C'   '
                                   4578            $SA    COLOR=RED            7
000942 404040                      4580            DC     C'   '
                                   4581            $SA    COLOR=WHITE          6
000948 404040                      4583            DC     C'   '
                                   4584            $SA    COLOR=RED            5
00094E 404040                      4586            DC     C'   '
                                   4587            $SA    COLOR=WHITE          4
000954 404040                      4589            DC     C'   '
                                   4590            $SA    COLOR=RED            3
00095A 404040                      4592            DC     C'   '
                                   4593            $SA    COLOR=WHITE          2
000960 404040                      4595            DC     C'   '
                                   4596            $SA    COLOR=RED            1
000966 404040                      4598            DC     C'   '
                                   4599            $SBA   (15,40)
                                   4601            $SF
                                   4603            $SA    XHIGH=REVERSE,COLOR=RED
000974 404040                      4605            DC     C'   '               13
                                   4606            $SA    COLOR=WHITE          12
00097A 404040                      4608            DC     C'   '
                                   4609            $SA    COLOR=RED            11
000980 404040                      4611            DC     C'   '
                                   4612            $SA    COLOR=WHITE          10
000986 404040                      4614            DC     C'   '
                                   4615            $SA    COLOR=RED            9
```

```
DEMO OF 3270 DATA STREAM MACROS

  LOC  OBJECT CODE    ADDR1 ADDR2  STMT   SOURCE STATEMENT                                        ASM H V 02 12.39 03/17/89
00098C 404040                      4617            DC    C'  '
                                   4618            $SA   COLOR=WHITE            8
000992 404040                      4620            DC    C'  '
                                   4621            $SA   COLOR=RED              7
000998 404040                      4623            DC    C'  '
                                   4624            $SA   COLOR=WHITE            6
00099E 404040                      4626            DC    C'  '
                                   4627            $SA   COLOR=RED              5
0009A4 404040                      4629            DC    C'  '
                                   4630            $SA   COLOR=WHITE            4
0009AA 404040                      4632            DC    C'  '
                                   4633            $SA   COLOR=RED              3
0009B0 404040                      4635            DC    C'  '
                                   4636            $SA   COLOR=WHITE            2
0009B6 404040                      4638            DC    C'  '
                                   4639            $SA   COLOR=RED              1
0009BC 404040                      4641            DC    C'  '
                                   4642            $SBA  (16,40)
                                   4644            $SF
                                   4646            $SA   XHIGH=REVERSE,COLOR=RED
0009CA 404040                      4648            DC    C'  '                 13
                                   4649            $SA   COLOR=WHITE           12
0009D0 404040                      4651            DC    C'  '
                                   4652            $SA   COLOR=RED             11
0009D6 404040                      4654            DC    C'  '
                                   4655            $SA   COLOR=WHITE           10
0009DC 404040                      4657            DC    C'  '
                                   4658            $SA   COLOR=RED              9
0009E2 404040                      4660            DC    C'  '
                                   4661            $SA   COLOR=WHITE            8
0009E8 404040                      4663            DC    C'  '
                                   4664            $SA   COLOR=RED              7
0009EE 404040                      4666            DC    C'  '
                                   4667            $SA   COLOR=WHITE            6
0009F4 404040                      4669            DC    C'  '
                                   4670            $SA   COLOR=RED              5
0009FA 404040                      4672            DC    C'  '
                                   4673            $SA   COLOR=WHITE            4
000A00 404040                      4675            DC    C'  '
                                   4676            $SA   COLOR=RED              3
000A06 404040                      4678            DC    C'  '
                                   4679            $SA   COLOR=WHITE            2
000A0C 404040                      4681            DC    C'  '
                                   4682            $SA   COLOR=RED              1
000A12 404040                      4684            DC    C'  '
                                   4685            $SBA  (17,40)
                                   4687            $SF
                                   4689            $SA   XHIGH=REVERSE,COLOR=RED
000A20 404040                      4691            DC    C'  '                 13
                                   4692            $SA   COLOR=WHITE           12
000A26 404040                      4694            DC    C'  '
                                   4695            $SA   COLOR=RED             11
000A2C 404040                      4697            DC    C'  '
                                   4698            $SA   COLOR=WHITE           10
000A32 404040                      4700            DC    C'  '
```

```
       DEMO OF 3270 DATA STREAM MACROS

  LOC  OBJECT CODE    ADDR1 ADDR2  STMT   SOURCE STATEMENT                                  ASM H V 02 12.39 03/17/89

                                   4701          $SA   COLOR=RED            9
000A38 404040                      4703          DC    C'   '
                                   4704          $SA   COLOR=WHITE          8
000A3E 404040                      4706          DC    C'   '
                                   4707          $SA   COLOR=RED            7
000A44 404040                      4709          DC    C'   '
                                   4710          $SA   COLOR=WHITE          6
000A4A 404040                      4712          DC    C'   '
                                   4713          $SA   COLOR=RED            5
000A50 404040                      4715          DC    C'   '
                                   4716          $SA   COLOR=WHITE          4
000A56 404040                      4718          DC    C'   '
                                   4719          $SA   COLOR=RED            3
000A5C 404040                      4721          DC    C'   '
                                   4722          $SA   COLOR=WHITE          2
000A62 404040                      4724          DC    C'   '
                                   4725          $SA   COLOR=RED            1
000A68 404040                      4727          DC    C'   '
                                   4728          $SBA  (18,40)
                                   4730          $SF
                                   4732          $SA   XHIGH=REVERSE,COLOR=RED
000A76 404040                      4734          DC    C'   '             13
                                   4735          $SA   COLOR=WHITE         12
000A7C 404040                      4737          DC    C'   '
                                   4738          $SA   COLOR=RED           11
000A82 404040                      4740          DC    C'   '
                                   4741          $SA   COLOR=WHITE         10
000A88 404040                      4743          DC    C'   '
                                   4744          $SA   COLOR=RED            9
000A8E 404040                      4746          DC    C'   '
                                   4747          $SA   COLOR=WHITE          8
000A94 404040                      4749          DC    C'   '
                                   4750          $SA   COLOR=RED            7
000A9A 404040                      4752          DC    C'   '
                                   4753          $SA   COLOR=WHITE          6
000AA0 404040                      4755          DC    C'   '
                                   4756          $SA   COLOR=RED            5
000AA6 404040                      4758          DC    C'   '
                                   4759          $SA   COLOR=WHITE          4
000AAC 404040                      4761          DC    C'   '
                                   4762          $SA   COLOR=RED            3
000AB2 404040                      4764          DC    C'   '
                                   4765          $SA   COLOR=WHITE          2
000AB8 404040                      4767          DC    C'   '
                                   4768          $SA   COLOR=RED            1
000ABE 404040                      4770          DC    C'   '
                                   4771          $SBA  (19,40)
                                   4773          $SF
                                   4775          $SA   XHIGH=REVERSE,COLOR=RED
000ACC 404040                      4777          DC    C'   '             13
                                   4778          $SA   COLOR=WHITE         12
000AD2 404040                      4780          DC    C'   '
                                   4781          $SA   COLOR=RED           11
000AD8 404040                      4783          DC    C'   '
                                   4784          $SA   COLOR=WHITE         10
```

```
        DEMO OF 3270 DATA STREAM MACROS

  LOC  OBJECT CODE    ADDR1 ADDR2  STMT    SOURCE STATEMENT                                    ASM H V 02 12.39 03/17/89
000ADE 404040                      4786           DC    C'     '
                                   4787           $SA   COLOR=RED              9
000AE4 404040                      4789           DC    C'     '
                                   4790           $SA   COLOR=WHITE            8
000AEA 404040                      4792           DC    C'     '
                                   4793           $SA   COLOR=RED              7
000AF0 404040                      4795           DC    C'     '
                                   4796           $SA   COLOR=WHITE            6
000AF6 404040                      4798           DC    C'     '
                                   4799           $SA   COLOR=RED              5
000AFC 404040                      4801           DC    C'     '
                                   4802           $SA   COLOR=WHITE            4
000B02 404040                      4804           DC    C'     '
                                   4805           $SA   COLOR=RED              3
000B08 404040                      4807           DC    C'     '
                                   4808           $SA   COLOR=WHITE            2
000B0E 404040                      4810           DC    C'     '
                                   4811           $SA   COLOR=RED              1
000B14 404040                      4813           DC    C'     '
                                   4814           $SBA  (20,40)
                                   4816           $SF
                                   4818           $SA   XHIGH=REVERSE,COLOR=RED
000B22 404040                      4820           DC    C'     '              13
                                   4821           $SA   COLOR=WHITE           12
000B28 404040                      4823           DC    C'     '
                                   4824           $SA   COLOR=RED             11
000B2E 404040                      4826           DC    C'     '
                                   4827           $SA   COLOR=WHITE           10
000B34 404040                      4829           DC    C'     '
                                   4830           $SA   COLOR=RED              9
000B3A 404040                      4832           DC    C'     '
                                   4833           $SA   COLOR=WHITE            8
000B40 404040                      4835           DC    C'     '
                                   4836           $SA   COLOR=RED              7
000B46 404040                      4838           DC    C'     '
                                   4839           $SA   COLOR=WHITE            6
000B4C 404040                      4841           DC    C'     '
                                   4842           $SA   COLOR=RED              5
000B52 404040                      4844           DC    C'     '
                                   4845           $SA   COLOR=WHITE            4
000B58 404040                      4847           DC    C'     '
                                   4848           $SA   COLOR=RED              3
000B5E 404040                      4850           DC    C'     '
                                   4851           $SA   COLOR=WHITE            2
000B64 404040                      4853           DC    C'     '
                                   4854           $SA   COLOR=RED              1
000B6A 404040                      4856           DC    C'     '
                                   4857           $SBA  (21,40)
                                   4859           $SF
                                   4861           $SA   XHIGH=REVERSE,COLOR=RED
000B78 404040                      4863           DC    C'     '              13
                                   4864           $SA   COLOR=WHITE           12
000B7E 404040                      4866           DC    C'     '
                                   4867           $SA   COLOR=RED             11
000B84 404040                      4869           DC    C'     '
```

```
DEMO OF 3270 DATA STREAM MACROS                                                       ASM H V 02 12.39 03/17/89

  LOC  OBJECT CODE    ADDR1 ADDR2  STMT   SOURCE STATEMENT
                                   4870            $SA   COLOR=WHITE            10
000B8A 404040                      4872            DC    C'   '
                                   4873            $SA   COLOR=RED               9
000B90 404040                      4875            DC    C'   '
                                   4876            $SA   COLOR=WHITE             8
000B96 404040                      4878            DC    C'   '
                                   4879            $SA   COLOR=RED               7
000B9C 404040                      4881            DC    C'   '
                                   4882            $SA   COLOR=WHITE             6
000BA2 404040                      4884            DC    C'   '
                                   4885            $SA   COLOR=RED               5
000BA8 404040                      4887            DC    C'   '
                                   4888            $SA   COLOR=WHITE             4
000BAE 404040                      4890            DC    C'   '
                                   4891            $SA   COLOR=RED               3
000BB4 404040                      4893            DC    C'   '
                                   4894            $SA   COLOR=WHITE             2
000BBA 404040                      4896            DC    C'   '
                                   4897            $SA   COLOR=RED               1
000BC0 404040                      4899            DC    C'   '
                                   4900            $SBA  (22,40)
                                   4902            $SF
                                   4904            $SA   XHIGH=REVERSE,COLOR=RED
                                                                                13
000BCE 404040                      4906            DC    C'   '
                                   4907            $SA   COLOR=WHITE            12
000BD4 404040                      4909            DC    C'   '
                                   4910            $SA   COLOR=RED              11
000BDA 404040                      4912            DC    C'   '
                                   4913            $SA   COLOR=WHITE            10
000BE0 404040                      4915            DC    C'   '
                                   4916            $SA   COLOR=RED               9
000BE6 404040                      4918            DC    C'   '
                                   4919            $SA   COLOR=WHITE             8
000BEC 404040                      4921            DC    C'   '
                                   4922            $SA   COLOR=RED               7
000BF2 404040                      4924            DC    C'   '
                                   4925            $SA   COLOR=WHITE             6
000BF8 404040                      4927            DC    C'   '
                                   4928            $SA   COLOR=RED               5
000BFE 404040                      4930            DC    C'   '
                                   4931            $SA   COLOR=WHITE             4
000C04 404040                      4933            DC    C'   '
                                   4934            $SA   COLOR=RED               3
000C0A 404040                      4936            DC    C'   '
                                   4937            $SA   COLOR=WHITE             2
000C10 404040                      4939            DC    C'   '
                                   4940            $SA   COLOR=RED               1
000C16 404040                      4942            DC    C'   '
                                   4943            $SBA  (23,40)
                                   4945            $SF
                                   4947            $SA   XHIGH=REVERSE,COLOR=RED
                                                                                13
000C24 404040                      4949            DC    C'   '
                                   4950            $SA   COLOR=WHITE            12
000C2A 404040                      4952            DC    C'   '
                                   4953            $SA   COLOR=RED              11
```

```
       DEMO OF 3270 DATA STREAM MACROS

  LOC  OBJECT CODE    ADDR1 ADDR2  STMT    SOURCE STATEMENT                                      ASM H V 02 12.39 03/17/89
000C30 404040                      4955            DC    C'   '
                                   4956            $SA   COLOR=WHITE         10
000C36 404040                      4958            DC    C'   '
                                   4959            $SA   COLOR=RED            9
000C3C 404040                      4961            DC    C'   '
                                   4962            $SA   COLOR=WHITE          8
000C42 404040                      4964            DC    C'   '
                                   4965            $SA   COLOR=RED            7
000C48 404040                      4967            DC    C'   '
                                   4968            $SA   COLOR=WHITE          6
000C4E 404040                      4970            DC    C'   '
                                   4971            $SA   COLOR=RED            5
000C54 404040                      4973            DC    C'   '
                                   4974            $SA   COLOR=WHITE          4
000C5A 404040                      4976            DC    C'   '
                                   4977            $SA   COLOR=RED            3
000C60 404040                      4979            DC    C'   '
                                   4980            $SA   COLOR=WHITE          2
000C66 404040                      4982            DC    C'   '
                                   4983            $SA   COLOR=RED            1
000C6C 404040                      4985            DC    C'   '
                                   4986            $SBA  (24,40)
                                   4988            $SF
                                   4990            $SA   XHIGH=REVERSE,COLOR=RED
000C7A 404040                      4992            DC    C'   '               13
                                   4993            $SA   COLOR=WHITE         12
000C80 404040                      4995            DC    C'   '
                                   4996            $SA   COLOR=RED           11
000C86 404040                      4998            DC    C'   '
                                   4999            $SA   COLOR=WHITE         10
000C8C 404040                      5001            DC    C'   '
                                   5002            $SA   COLOR=RED            9
000C92 404040                      5004            DC    C'   '
                                   5005            $SA   COLOR=WHITE          8
000C98 404040                      5007            DC    C'   '
                                   5008            $SA   COLOR=RED            7
000C9E 404040                      5010            DC    C'   '
                                   5011            $SA   COLOR=WHITE          6
000CA4 404040                      5013            DC    C'   '
                                   5014            $SA   COLOR=RED            5
000CAA 404040                      5016            DC    C'   '
                                   5017            $SA   COLOR=WHITE          4
000CB0 404040                      5019            DC    C'   '
                                   5020            $SA   COLOR=RED            3
000CB6 404040                      5022            DC    C'   '
                                   5023            $SA   COLOR=WHITE          2
000CBC 404040                      5025            DC    C'   '
                                   5026            $SA   COLOR=RED            1
000CC2 404040                      5028            DC    C'   '
                                   5029            $SBA  (23,80)
                                   5031            $SF
                                   5033            $SA   XHIGH=NORMAL
                                   5035            $SA   COLOR=BLUE
000CD0 C9C2D440                    5037            DC    C'IBM '
                                   5038            $SA   COLOR=GREEN
```

```
        DEMO OF 3270 DATA STREAM MACROS

  LOC  OBJECT CODE    ADDR1 ADDR2  STMT   SOURCE STATEMENT                                      ASM H V 02 12.39 03/17/89

000CD7 F3F2F7F040                  5040          DC    C'3270 '
                                   5041          $SA   COLOR=YELLOW
                                   5043          $TEXT LOWER=DATA
                                   5045          $SA   COLOR=RED
                                   5047          $TEXT LOWER=' STREAM '
                                   5049          $SA   XHIGH=BLINK
                                   5051          $SA   COLOR=WHITE
                                   5053          $TEXT LOWER=DEMO
                                   5055          $SA   XHIGH=NORMAL
                                   5057          $SA   COLOR=PINK
                                   5059          $TEXT LOWER=' SCREEN'
                    00B36          5061 LSCREEN  EQU   *-SCREEN                                                      00032
                                   5062          END
```

Appendix E
Sample Storage Dumps

```
ICH70001I SYST002  LAST ACCESS AT 07:52:26 ON FRIDAY, AUGUST 12, 1988
IEF236I ALLOC. FOR SYST002A S1
IEF237I 146  ALLOCATED TO STEPLIB
IEF237I 364  ALLOCATED TO SYS00870
IEF237I JES2 ALLOCATED TO PRINTER
IEF237I JES2 ALLOCATED TO SYSUDUMP
IEF237I JES2 ALLOCATED TO SYSIN
IEA995I SYMPTOM DUMP OUTPUT
 ABEND CODE SYSTEM=0C7  TIME=07.54.18 SEQ=00407 CPU=0000 ASID=0014
 PSW AT TIME OF ERROR  078D0000   00006DEC  ILC 6  INTC 07
   ACTIVE LOAD MODULE=SAMPLE3   ADDRESS=00006CF8  OFFSET=000000F4
   DATA AT PSW  00006DE6 - FC74C13A  C13547F0  C05A4510
   GPR  0-3  00006E62  00006E62  00000040  009ECB24
   GPR  4-7  009ECB00  009FA8A8  009C8FF8  FD000000
   GPR  8-11 009D2DF8  809FAB88  00000000  009FA8A8
   GPR 12-15 40006D20  00006E08  40006D44  12C8B2FC
 END OF SYMPTOM DUMP
IEF472I SYST002A S1 - COMPLETION CODE - SYSTEM=0C7 USER=0000 REASON=00000007
IEF285I   TST1.MVSBATCH.LOADLIB                          KEPT
IEF285I   VOL SER NOS= TOU003.
IEF285I   CATALOG.UCATX08                                KEPT
IEF285I   VOL SER NOS= TOURES.
IEF285I   JES2.JOB04539.S0000102                         SYSOUT
IEF285I   JES2.JOB04539.S0000103                         SYSOUT
IEF285I   JES2.JOB04539.SI000101                         SYSIN
IEF373I STEP /S1      / START 88225.0754
IEF374I STEP /S1      / STOP  88225.0754 CPU    0MIN 01.05SEC SRB    0MIN 00.02SEC VIRT    32K SYS   320K EXT       4K SYS    8896K
IEF375I  JOB /SYST002A/ START 88225.0754
IEF376I  JOB /SYST002A/ STOP  88225.0754 CPU    0MIN 01.05SEC SRB    0MIN 00.02SEC
```

```
    5 +       6 =      11
 1000 -     299 =     701
89999 /      11 =    8181
  100 *      10 =    1000
```

```
JOB SYST002A        STEP S1           TIME 075419   DATE 88225    ID = 000    CPUID = FF1732403090   PAGE 00000001
COMPLETION CODE     SYSTEM = 0C7      REASON CODE = 00000007
PSW AT ENTRY TO ABEND  078D0000 00006DEC       ILC 6   INTC 0007
PSW LOAD MODULE = SAMPLE3   ADDRESS = 00006DEC   OFFSET = 000000F4
 ASCB: 00FBCD80
     +0000  ASCB..... ASCB      FWDP..... 00F9A800  BWDP..... 00F9AC00  CMSF..... 00000000  SVRB..... 009FE9E0
     +0014  SYNC..... 00930E0D  IOSP..... 00000000  TNEW..... 009D2B20  CPUS..... 00000001  ASID..... 0014
     +0026  R026..... 0000      LL5...... 00        HLHI..... 01        DPHI..... 00        DP....... 16
     +002C  TRQP..... 80FDB199  LDA...... 7FF164E8  RSMF..... 00        R035..... 0000      TRQI..... 40
     +0038  CSCB..... 00FBCF48  TSB...... 00000000  EJST..... 00000000  0BD1FE00
     +0048  EWST..... 9EF41784  7AD46E01            JSTL..... 000141DD  ECB...... 809FEF78  UBET..... 9EF3E3F8
     +005C  TLCH..... 00000000  DUMP..... 009FE4A8  AFFN..... FFFF      RCTF..... 00        FLG1..... 00
     +0068  TMCH..... 00000000  ASXB..... 009FF118  SWCT..... 22F8      DSP1..... 00        FLG2..... 00
     +0074  RSV...... 0000      SRBS..... 0000      R078..... 00000000  RCTP..... 009FF338  LOCK..... 00000000
     +0084  LSQH..... 00000000  QECB..... 00000000  MECB..... 40000000  OUCB..... 019E7628  OUXB..... 011A1768
     +0098  FMCT..... 003D      LEVL..... 02        R09B..... 00        XMPQ..... 00000000  IQEA..... 00000000
     +00A4  RTMC..... 00000000  MCC...... 00000000  JBNI..... 00F8D500  JBNS..... 00FBCF58  SRQ1..... 00
     +00B5  SRQ2..... 00        SRQ3..... 00        SRQ4..... 00        VGTT..... 00000000  PCTT..... 020DE5F8
     +00C0  SSRB..... 0000      SMCT..... 00        SRBM..... 07        SWTL..... 00002EF0
     +00C8  SRBT..... 00000000  005BEC00            LSMQ..... 00000000  LSPL..... 00000000  TCBS..... 00000001
     +00DC  TCBL..... 00000000  WPRB..... 009FFA88  NDP...... 16        TNDP..... FF        NTSG..... FF
     +00E7  IODP..... 10        LOCI..... 00000000  CMLH..... 00000000  CMLC..... 00000000  SSO1..... 000000
     +00F7  SSO4..... 00        ASTE..... 00F9D140  LTOV..... 7FFFD000  ATOV..... 7FFFE610  ETC...... 0000
     +0106  ETCN..... 0000      LXR...... 0000      AXR...... 0000      STKH..... 009FFA98  GQEL..... 00000000
     +0114  LQEL..... 02138BA0  GSYN..... 00000000  XTCB..... 009D2B20  CS1...... 00        R121..... 000000
     +0124  GXL...... 00000000  EATT..... 00000000  1A146000            INTS..... 9EF41783  D8A89901
     +0138  LL1...... 00        LL2...... 00        LL3...... 00        LL4...... 00        RCMS..... 00000000
     +0140  IOSC..... 00000007  PKML..... 0000      XCNT..... 01F4      NSQA..... 00000000  ASM...... 0119F760
     +0150  ASSB..... 0119F780  TCME..... 00000000  R158..... 00000000  00000000  00000000  00000000
     +0168  CREQ..... 00000002  RSME..... 0119F740  AVM1..... 00        AVM2..... 00        AGEN..... 0000
     +0174  ARC...... 00000000  RSMA..... 0119F650  DCTI..... 000001D7  TAXT..... 00000000  00000000
     +0188  SAXT..... 00000000  00000000            TCPT..... 00000000  0FC7CD00
     +0198  SCPT..... 00000000  005BEC00

 ASSB: 0119F780
     +0000  ASSB..... ASSB      VAFN..... 00000000  EVST..... 00000000  00000000
     +0010  VFAT..... 00000000  00000000            RSV...... 0000      XMCC..... 0000      XMCT..... 00000000
     +0020  VSC...... 00000000  NVSC..... 0000001B  ASRR..... 00000000  R02C..... 00000000  00000000  00000000
     +0038            00000000  00000000

*** ADDRESS SPACE SWITCH EVENT MASK OFF (ASTESSEM = 0) ***

 TCB: 009D2B20
     +0000  RBP...... 009FE8F0  PIE...... 00000000  DEB...... 009C7330  TIO...... 009C9000  CMP...... 940C7000
     +0014  TRN...... 00000000  MSS...... 7FF160A8  PKF...... 80        FLGS..... 01000000  00
     +0022  LMP...... FF        DSP...... FF        LLS...... 009D2AF0  JLB...... 009FAA48  JPQ...... 009FAA28
     +0030  GPR0-3... 00001000  009BE000  00000000  00000000
     +0040  GPR4-7... 00FDBF30  009BF0C8  00000002  80C791FC
     +0050  GPR8-11.. 81B52360  009C0754  009C07B4  00000008
```

```
JOB SYST002A          STEP S1              TIME 075419   DATE 88225    ID = 000                      PAGE 00000009


SAVE AREA TRACE


INTERRUPT AT 00006DEC


PROCEEDING BACK VIA REG 13
UNKNOWN  WAS ENTERED VIA CALL        AT EP 05..05..01..050.05..05S.0...IGG019DJ12.11.85HDP2230.NONE.............
SA    00006E08  WD1 00000000   HSA 00005FB0   LSA 00000000   RET 40006D44   EPA 12C8B2FC   R0  00006E62
                R1  00006E62   R2  00000040   R3  009ECB24   R4  009ECB00   R5  009FA8A8   R6  009C8FF8
                R7  FD000000   R8  009D2DF8   R9  809FAB88   R10 00000000   R11 009FA8A8   R12 40006D20


REGS AT ENTRY TO ABEND

    FLTR 0-6        0000000000000000       0000000000000000            0000000000000000       0000000000000000

    REGS 0-7        00006E62  00006E62     00000040  009ECB24          009ECB00  009FA8A8     009C8FF8  FD000000
    REGS 8-15       009D2DF8  809FAB88     00000000  009FA8A8          40006D20  00006E08     40006D44  12C8B2FC

ACTIVE LOAD MODULES                                   Load Point                  Entry Point

LPA/JPA MODULE    SAMPLE3
00006CE0                                                              E2C1D4D7 D3C5F360    *                  SAMPLE3.*
00006D00 60C1E2E2 C5D4C2D3 C5C440F0 F861F1F2   61F8F860 F0F74BF5 F20090EC D00C05C0    *.ASSEMBLED 08.12.88.07.52......*
00006D20 50D0C0EC 41D0C0E8 4510C014 00006F38   8F006F98 0A134110 C2184100 C14258F0    *.......Y..............B...A..0*
00006D40 103005EF F248C130 C143F248 C135C14D   F874C13A C130954E C1424780 C0B29560    *....2.A.A.2.A.A.8.A.A...A.......*
00006D60 C1424780 C0BC955C C1424780 C0C6FD74   C13AC135 F872C13A C13AD200 C19DC142    *A.......A....F..A.A.8.A.A.K.A.A.*
00006D80 D209C193 C143D209 C19EC14D D201C1A9   C2D8D207 C1ABC1AA 9221C1B1 9521C1A9    *K.A.A.K.A.A.K.A.BQK.A.A...A...A.*
00006DA0 4770C096 F300C1AA C14196F0 C1AA9240   C1A947F0 C09CDE09 C1A9C13D 4110C278    *....3.A.A..0A...A..0....A.A...B.*
00006DC0 4100C192 58F01030 05EF92F0 C19247F0   C016FA74 C13AC135 47F0C05A FB74C13A    *..A..0.....0A..0....A.A..0....A.*
00006DE0 C13547F0 C05AFC74 C13AC135 47F0C05A   4510C0DC 00006F38 80006F98 0A1458D0    *A..0....A.A..0..................*
00006E00 C0EC98EC D00C07FE 00000000 00005FB0   00000000 40006D44 12C8B2FC 00006E62    *..........................H.....*
00006E20 00006E62 00000040 009ECB24 009ECB00   009FA8A8 009C8FF8 FD000000 009D2DF8    *.........................8......8*
00006E40 809FAB88 00000000 009FA8A8 40006D20   00010000 0F000000 010F0000 00000100    *................................*
00006E60 000C5C40 4040F1F0 F0F0F0F0 40404040   40404040 F1F04040 40404040 40404040    *...   100000          10         *
00006E80 40404040 40404040 40404040 40404040   40404040 40404040 40404040 40404040    *                                *
00006EA0 40404040 40404040 40404040 40404040   4040F040 40404040 40F1F0F0 405C4040    *                  0       100 .  *
00006EC0 40404040 40F1F040 7E404040 404040F1   F0F0F040 40404040 40404040 40404040    *      10 .        1000           *
00006EE0 40404040 40404040 40404040 40404040   40404040 40404040 40404040 40404040    *                                *
      LINE 00006F00    SAME AS ABOVE
00006F20 40404040 40404040 40404040 40404040   40404040 40404000 00000000 00000000    *                         ........*
00006F40 00000000 00000000 00000000 05007E68   00504000 00005F98 06006DF0 90000000    *...............................0...*
00006F60 00685000 009C7E90 12C8B2FC 00C65810   00000001 08090050 00000000 00005E48    *.........H...F..................*
00006F80 00007EC0 00007E70 00000050 00000001   00000000 00000001 00000000 00000000    *................................*
00006FA0 00000000 00000000 00000000 01007DD8   00854000 00005E30 06000001 94000000    *..............Q.................*
00006FC0 00400050 009C7E08 92C8B308 00000001   00000001 08090085 00000000 00005CE0    *.........H......................*
00006FE0 00007E65 00007E65 00000085 00000001   00000000 00000001 40200000 00000000    *................................*

LPA/JPA MODULE    IEAVTRF4
```

```
JOB SYST002A          STEP S1             TIME 075419   DATE 88225    ID = 000                       PAGE 00000031

00005900 C3F64040 404B40F4 C2F4C2F4 C2F4C240    F4C2F4C2 F4C2F4C2 40F4F0C6 F0C6F1C3  *C6      .  4B4B4B4B 4B4B4B4B 40F0F1C*
00005920 5C007D00 0040F0F0 F0F0F5F8 F2F040C6    F2F4F0F4 F0F4F040 F4F0C3F6 F5C3F0F0  *.....  00005820 F2404040 40C65C00*
00005940 40F7C4F0 F0F0F0F4 F040C6F0 C6F0C6F0    C6F04040 4040C6F5 C6F7C3F5 C6F040F4  * 7D000040 F0F0F0F0    F5F7C5F0 4*
00005960 F0C3F6C6 F4C3F340 C6F3C3F6 C6F2C3F6    40C6F4F4 F0C3F6C6 F0404040 5CF24040  *0C6F4C3 F3C6F2C6 F440C6F0    .2  *
00005980 4040C64B 4B4B4B4B 40F0F0F0 F0F5F7C5    F040C6F4 C3F3C6F2 C6F440C6 F05C007D  *   F.....  000057E0 F4C3F2F4 F0...*
000059A0 000040F0 F0F0F0F5 F8F4F040 C3F3C6F6    C3F6C6F4 40C6F4C6 F0F4F0C3 F340C6F6  *..  00005840 C3F6C6F4 F4F040C3 F6*
000059C0 C6F4C6F0 F4F040C3 F3C6F3C3 F6C6F640    404040C3 F3C6F6C3 F6C6F440 F4F0C3F6  *F4F040 C3F3C6F6     C3F6C6F4 40C6*
000059E0 C6F4C3F6 40C6F0C6 F4C6F0C3 F340C6F3    F4F0C3F6 C6F64040 405C4B4B 40F0F0F0  *F4C6 F0F4F0C3 F340C6F6    ...  000*
00005A00 F0F5F8F4 F040C3F3 C6F6C3F6 C6F440C6    F4C6F0F4 F0C3F340 C6F65C00 7D000040  *05840 C3F6C6F4 F4F040C3 F6.....  *
00005A20 F0F0F0F0 F5F9C3F0 40C3F6C6 F4C3F6C6    F040C6F4 C6F0F4F0 C3F340C6 F3C3F6C6  *000059C0 C6F4C6F0 F4F040C3 F3C6F*
00005A40 F3C3F340 C6F6C3F6 C6F6F4F0 40404040    F4F0F4F0 F4F0C3F3 40C6F3C3 F6C6F6C3  *3C3 F6C6F640     404040C3 F3C6F6C*
00005A60 F340C6F6 C3F6C6F4 F4F040C6 F4C6F0C3    F3C6F640 40405CC6 F4C6F0F4 F040C3F3  *3 F6C6F440 F4F0C3F6    .F4F040 C3*
00005A80 C6F3C3F6 C6F64040 4040C3F3 C6F6C3F6    C6F440F4 F0C3F65C 007D0000 40F0F0F0  *F3C6F6     C3F6C6F4 40C6.....  000*
00005AA0 F0F5F9C5 F040C3F6 C6F4C3F3 C6F640F4    F0C3F6C6 F0C3F640 C6F4C3F6 C6F0C3F3  *059E0 C6F4C3F6 40C6F0C6 F4C6F0C3*
00005AC0 40C6F3F4 F0C3F6C6 F3404040 40C6F4C6    F0C3F3C6 F640C3F6 C6F6F4F0 F4F040F4  * F340C6F3     F4F0C3F6 C6F64040 4*
00005AE0 F0F5C3F4 C2F4C240 F4F0C6F0 C6F0C6F0    4040405C C6F4C3F6 40C6F0C6 F4C6F0C3  *05C4B4B 40F0F0F0    .F4C6 F0F4F0C*
00005B00 F340C6F3 F4F0C3F6 C6F64040 404B4B4B    40F0F0F0 5C00E100 7F000000 00200000  *3 F340C6F6    ... 000.............*
00005B20 009D1E68 000054B8 00000000 007D0000    00000000 009D2020 00004040 40CAAEE8  *..............................Y*
00005B40 00E6D81E 000000F8 00005B18 009D1E68    000054B8 000054BC 00005B18 01B71B66  *.WQ....8.......................*
00005B60 009C0268 009C0170 00005B18 00FDBF80    80CAA40E 40CAAC4A 00005B78 7F000000  *................................*
00005B80 00000000 00005B7C 00000000 00000000    00000000 009D1E68 A000004C 00000000  *................................*
00005BA0 00E448D8 52000000 00000000 00000000    2A540008 00000000 00000000 00000000  *.U.Q............................*
00005BC0 00540041 009C7330 92000000 00005AC4    00000000 0660007D 00000000 00000000  *..............D.................*
00005BE0 00000000 C9C7C7F0 F1F9C1C8 00000000    00005B30 00000000 50E6DD7E 00000000  *....IGG019AH...............W....*
00005C00 00000001 00005C38 00005C38 00000078    00005B78 00005A98 00005B98 00005B18  *................................*
00005C20 009D1E68 00000079 000054B8 40E6D85C    00005A9C 00000000 0000014C 00000000  *.............WQ.................*
00005C40 40000000 00000200 00000000 00005A9C    00005B98 00000000 00005A9D 00000000  *................................*
00005C60 20000000 00000000 00000078 00000079    00000000 0000062A 05000006 00000000  *................................*
00005C80 00005C94 00005B78 00000000 00005B18    00000000 00000000 00000000 00000000  *................................*
00005CA0 00000000 00000000 00000000 0000007D    00000000 00000000 00000000 00000000  *................................*
00005CC0 00000000 00005B98 08000000 00000000    04000000 00000000 00000000 00000100  *................................*
00005CE0 00005CE0 7F000000 00000000 00005CE4    00000000 00000000 00000000 00006F98  *..............U.................*
00005D00 A000004C 00000000 00E448D8 52000000    00000000 00000000 4A940008 00000000  *..........U.Q...................*
00005D20 00000000 00000000 00400041 009C7E08    92000000 00005C30 00000000 00850085  *................................*
00005D40 00000000 00000000 00000000 C9C7C7F0    F1F9C1C8 00000000 00006E08 00000000  *............IGG019AH............*
00005D60 50C8B81C 00000000 00000001 00005DA0    00005DA0 00005CE0 00006F98 00006EB2  *.H..............................*
00005D80 00006EB2 0000000C 009D2DF8 00005D00    00000084 92C8B2FC 40006D20 00000000  *..........8.........H...........*
00005DA0 0000014C 00000000 40000000 00000200    00000000 00006EB2 00005D00 00000000  *................................*
00005DC0 00006EB3 00000000 20002000 00000000    00000084 00000085 00000000 000105FD  *................................*
00005DE0 02000004 00000000 00005DFC 00005CE0    00000000 00000000 00000000 00000000  *................................*
00005E00 00000000 00000000 00000000 00000000    00000000 00000000 00000000 00007DE0  *................................*
00005E20 00000000 00000000 00000000 00005D00    08000000 00000000 04000000 00000000  *................................*
00005E40 00000000 00000000 00005E48 7F000000    00000000 00005E4C 00000000 00000000  *................................*
00005E60 00000000 00006F38 A000004C 00000000    00E448D8 54000000 00000000 00000000  *.................U.Q............*
00005E80 48900008 00000000 00000000 00000000    00680041 009C7E90 12000000 00005B80  *................................*
00005EA0 00000000 00500050 00000000 00000000    00000000 C9C7C7F0 F1F9C1C8 00000000  *...................IGG019AH.....*
00005EC0 00006E08 00000000 40C8B3B6 00000000    00000000 00005F08 00005F08 00005E48  *.........H......................*
00005EE0 00006F38 009FA8A8 009C8FF8 FD000000    009D2DF8 809FAB88 00000000 12C8B2FC  *..........8.......8.........H...*
00005F00 40006D20 00000000 0000004C 00000000    40000000 00000200 00000000 00000000  *................................*
00005F20 00005E68 00000000 00006E62 00000000    20000000 00000000 00000050 00000050  *................................*
00005F40 00000000 00000607 07000005 00000000    00005F64 00005E48 00000000 00000000  *................................*
00005F60 00000000 00000000 00000000 00000000    00000000 00000000 00000000 00000000  *................................*
00005F80 00000000 00007E70 00000000 00000000    00000000 00005E68 08000000 00000000  *................................*
00005FA0 04000000 00000000 00000000 00000000    00000000 00000000 00000000 80FDBF80  *................................*
00005FC0 00006D1A FD000008 00005FF8 00000040    009ECB24 009ECB00 009FA8A8 009C8FF8  *..........8....................8*
00005FE0 FD000000 009D2DF8 809FAB88 00000000    009FA8A8 00DC39DA 80005FFE 00000000  *.......8........................*

         |  Register Save Area at Entry to Application Program  |
```

```
JOB SYST002A          STEP S1              TIME 075419   DATE 88225    ID = 000                    PAGE 00000039
                     DUMP INDEX
                     ----------

DATA AREAS                               PAGE NUMBER
----------                               -----------

  ENQ/DEQ CONTROL BLOCKS..................  00000004
  DATA MANAGEMENT CONTROL BLOCKS..........  00000005
  RTM CONTROL BLOCKS......................  00000006
  PCLINK STACKS / SAVE AREAS..............  00000009
  INSTALLATION/SUBSYSTEM AREA.............  00000009
  REGISTERS...............................  00000009
  MODULES.................................  00000009
    AMDPRFMT..............................  00000017
    BLSQALLO..............................  00000019
    BLSQCFMT..............................  00000020
    BLSQIFMT..............................  00000023
    BLSQROUT..............................  00000018
    BLSQTIOF..............................  00000011
    BLSUPUTG..............................  00000016
    BLSUPUT2..............................  00000028
    IEAVTRF2..............................  00000012
    IEAVTRF4..............................  00000009
    IGG019AQ..............................  00000017
    IGG019DJ..............................  00000018
    IGG019DK..............................  00000019
    SAMPLE3...............................  00000009
  USER SUBPOOLS...........................  00000030
  TRACE TABLE.............................  00000032

END OF DUMP
```

```
CUSTOMER INFORMATION CONTROL SYSTEM STORAGE DUMP    CODE=ASRA    TASK=A010       DATE=09/23/88    TIME=14:08:02    PAGE     1

SYMPTOMS= AB/UASRA PIDS/5740XX100 FLDS/F000KC RIDS/KA2250C

CICS/VS LEVEL = 0161

PSW             078D1000   003BF0C0   00060007   00000000
REGS 14-4       50E8F9E2   003BF164   003BFD86   003BF064          003BF0B0   00000005   0027E0E3
REGS 5-11       503C047C   003BD0A8   003BD447   003BD448          003C0432   003BD008   003BD008

TASK CONTROL AREA (USER AREA)          ADDRESS 00279940 TO 0027A03F    LENGTH 000700
00000000   00279800 0068FC0C 016ED8A0 0074DEE0  00279C30 005993BC 43001500 003100A0   *..q.......Q...........l.........*   00279940
00000020   50E7898C 00000000 00000000 00599210  0000002F 00599208 00599070 00599474   *.Xi..........k........k.......m.*   00279960
00000040   60E7749A 00E78499 00E79498 005994B0  00279C98 00000001 50E8F9E2 0027F9B0   *-X...Xdr.Xmg..m....q.....Y9S..9.*   00279980
00000060   40E8F80A C1E2D9C1 003BFD86 00006000  00E90188 00000005 00692DB0 00E8F584   * Y8.ASRA...f..-..Z.h.........Y5d*   002799A0
00000080   FE00F358 00C1D7C4 D6C34040 C1E2D9C1  078D1000 003BF0C0 00060007 00000000   *..3..APDOC  ASRA........0.......*   002799C0
000000A0   50E8F9E2 003BF164 003BFD86 003BF064  003BF0B0 00000005 0027E0E3 503C047C   *.Y9S..1....f..0...0.........T...*   002799E0
000000C0   003BD0A8 003BD447 003BD448 003C0432  003BD008 003BD008 00000000 00000000   *...y..M...M.....................*   00279A00
000000E0   0027F9B0 8C0000A8 24F40000 00000000  00000000 00000000 00E90188 00000000   *..9.....y.4..............Z.h....*   00279A20
00000100   C1D7C4D6 C3404000 27F35CF1 F9F8F800  00000000 00000000 00000000 00000000   *APDOC   ..3*1988................*   00279A40
00000120   00000000 00000000 001B280C 0027A46C  0027ABBC 0027B99C F0F100C1 E3C3E5C1   *...............u.........01.ATCVA*  00279A60
00000140   C4E340F0 F000F000 02000000 05000000  02000000 00001B3B 4CF00001 00000000   *DT 00.0.................0.......*   00279A80
00000160   00000200 00000000 00000000 00000000  00000000 00000000 00000000 00000000   *................................*   00279AA0
00000180   00000000 00000000 00000000 00000000  00000000 00000000 00000000 00000000   *................................*   00279AC0
000001A0   LINES TO 00000240 SAME AS ABOVE                                                                                  00279AE0
00000260   00000000 00000000 8B000028 00279BA8  00000000 006BB024 00000000 00000000   *...............y.....,..........*   00279BA0
00000280   00000000 00000000 00000000 00000000  00000028 00279BA8 00000000 00198FC4   *.......................y.......D*   00279BC0
000002A0   00000001 0018CA5C 00000001 0018C85C  00000001 0018CA9C 00000001 0018F1FC   *.......*......H*..............1.*   00279BE0
000002C0   00000004 0018CF8C 00000001 0018F10C  00000002 00000000 00000000 00000000   *...............1................*   00279C00
000002E0   00000000 00000000 D3C9C6D6 E2E3D6D9  42000068 00000000 FF279C98 50E91754   *........LIFOSTOR............q.Z..*  00279C20
00000300   00E9154C 00000000 00000000 505283AA  005282D4 00528676 5052883C 00279800   *.Z.............c...bM..f...h...q.*  00279C40
00000320   00528277 00528278 00528810 00527F80  0027F070 00279940 0074CEE0 FE279C98   *..b...b...h........0...r.......q*   00279C60
00000340   F000D2C3 00EB4E34 00000000 00000000  00000000 00000000 48000330 00279C30   *0.KC..+.........................*   00279C80
00000360   FF279CF8 00EB4026 00000000 0000C150  00599210 0074F290 001A5350 50EB3F9E   *...8...........A...k...2........*   00279CA0
00000380   00EB4F9E 60E7749A 00E78499 00E79498  005994B0 00279C98 00000001 00279940   *....-X...Xdr.Xmg..m....q......r.*   00279CC0
000003A0   0074CEE0 FE279FC8 F700E3E2 00E751F0  01000000 00000000 80007F80 00C1D7C4   *.......H7.TS.X.0.............APD*   00279CE0
000003C0   D6C34040 00000000 00000000 0074CEE0  80007F80 00C1D7C4 D6C34040 00000000   *OC  ....................APDOC ....*  00279D00
000003E0   00000000 00000000 09220370 00000000  80007F80 00C1D7C4 D6C34040 00000000   *........................APDOC ....*  00279D20
00000400   00000000 00000000 09220370 00000000  90E75724 00000000 80E7E0F8 00000000   *.................X........X.8....*  00279D40
00000420   00000000 00000000 80E7E1C2 00000000  00000000 00000000 80E7E26C 00E803CC   *.........X.B..............XS..Y..*  00279D60
00000440   0018C868 0027990C 00000000 80E7F136  00E803CC 0018F208 0027990C 00000000   *..H...r.......X1..Y.....2...r.....*  00279D80
00000460   00000000 50400000 00000000 00000000  00692E90 00279930 0027990C 00279DC4   *.......................r...r....D*  00279DA0
00000480   0000017C 002799C4 40000101 00000000  006BEDC8 40000000 001BF804 00000000   *.......rD ...........H.....8.....*  00279DC0
000004A0   0018F1FC 00000000 50E774B0 60E774B0  00E803CC 0018C868 A0E77AB8 006C0303   *...1.......X..-X....Y....H..X:.....*  00279DE0
000004C0   60E774B0 80E5DDF6 00279800 40E774B0  00692E90 60E774B0 0027990C 00279940   *-X...V.6..q..X.......-X....r...r.*  00279E00
000004E0   A0E78436 80E78DF8 00000000 50E774B0  006BB024 00000000 001BF804 60E75D1E   *.Xd..X.8....X...,........8.-X).*   00279E20
00000500   00C6CC30 0000C270 0027F358 00000001  00000000 00279800 00000000 00000645   *.F...B...3...............q.........*  00279E40
00000520   00E760AB 00000000 001A4AB0 00279C98  00E750AC 00000000 80E78432 80E7864C   *.X-..............q.X........Xd..Xf.*  00279E60
00000540   00000000 00000000 00000000 00000000  00000000 00000000 80E77AFC 80E77AA4   *..........................X:...X:u*  00279E80
00000560   00000000 00000000 00000000 00000000  00000000 00000000 00000000 00000000   *................................*   00279EA0
00000580   00000000 00000000 A0E78DFC A0E78996  80E78954 80E78E0C 90E7880A 00000000   *..........X...Xio.Xi..X...Xh.....*  00279EC0
000005A0   A0E7843A 00000000 00000000 00000000  80E7879E 00000000 00000000 00000000   *.Xd................Xg...........*   00279EE0
000005C0   80E78DF4 80E78D9C 00000000 00000000  00000000 005993B4 00000000 00000000   *.X.4.X..................l........*  00279F00
```

```
CUSTOMER INFORMATION CONTROL SYSTEM STORAGE DUMP    CODE=ASRA    TASK=A010       DATE=09/23/88    TIME=14:08:02    PAGE    2

TASK CONTROL AREA (USER AREA)            ADDRESS 00279940 TO 0027A03F    LENGTH 000700

000005E0    00000000 00000000 00000000 00000000  00000000 00000000 00000000 00000000   *................................*   00279F20
00000600    00000000 00000000 00000000 00000000  00000000 00000000 00000000 001A4AC0   *................................*   00279F40
00000620    00C1D7C4 D6C34040 00C1D7C4 D6C34040  005994B0 00000000 00000000 00599474   *.APDOC  .APDOC  ..m..........m.*   00279F60
00000640    00000000 005993B4 001A4AB0 001A4AB0  001A4800 000007D4 0000002F 00000000   *......l...............M.........*   00279F80
00000660    00000000 00000000 0000002C 00000200  00000000 00000000 00000000 00000000   *................................*   00279FA0
00000680    00000000 00000000 00000000 00000000  00000000 00000000 00000000 00000000   *................................*   00279FC0
000006A0    LINES TO 000006C0 SAME AS ABOVE                                                                                  00279FE0
000006E0    00000000 00000000 00000000 00000000  00000000 00000000 8A030838 0027F9B0   *..............................9.*   0027A020

TASK CONTROL AREA (SYSTEM AREA)          ADDRESS 00279800 TO 0027993F    LENGTH 000140

00000000    8A030838 0027F9B0 00000000 00000000  0056079C 006CFA88 001A5350 00000000   *......9.................h.......*   00279800
00000020    0074E388 00000000 00000000 00000000  00000000 FE6BBB1C 0027D800 0027D870   *..Th...................,....Q...Q.*   00279820
00000040    0027D860 00279BA8 00000000 0027BB70  00000000 00000000 00000000 00000000   *..Q-...y........................*   00279840
00000060    00000000 00000000 80000000 C1E2D9C1  00000000 00000000 00000000 00000000   *...............ASRA.............*   00279860
00000080    FE279FC8 00000000 FE279C20 FE27A038  0074FE78 00279C30 00000000 00000000   *...H............................*   00279880
000000A0    006ED8A0 00000000 00000000 00000000  C1F0F1F0 00000000 00000000 00000000   *..Q.............A010............*   002798A0
000000C0    C1E2D9C1 00000005 0027F9B0 00000000  00000000 00000000 00000000 00000000   *ASRA.......9....................*   002798C0
000000E0    00000000 00527F80 E3C9E7D2 C3D9C5D8  00000000 00000000 00000000 00000000   *........TIXKCREQ................*   002798E0
00000100    00000000 00527F80 00600000 00279BD8  00000000 00000000 00000000 00000000   *...........-.....Q..............*   00279900
00000120    0C000100 006CFA88 00000000 00279940  01000300 002799C4 006BEDC8 00000000   *.......h......r.......rD.,.H....*   00279920

LIFO STACK ENTRY OWNED BY DFHKCP

00000000    42000068 00000000 FF279C98 50E91754  00E9154C 00000000 00000000 505283AA   *...........q.Z...Z.............c.*   00279C30
00000020    005282D4 00528676 5052883C 00279800  00528277 00528278 00528810 00527F80   *..bM..f...h...q...b...b...h.....*   00279C50
00000040    0027F070 00279940 0074CEE0 FE279C98  F000D2C3 00EB4E34 00000000 00000000   *..0...r........q0.KC..+.........*   00279C70
00000060    00000000 00000000                                                          *........                        *   00279C90

       REGS  0 THRU 15                   ADDRESS 0068FC70 TO 0068FCAF    LENGTH 000040

00000000    003BFD86 003BF064 003BF0B0 00000005  0027E0E3 503C047C 003BD0A8 003BD447   *...f..0...0........T........y..M.*   0068FC70
00000020    003BD448 003C0432 003BD008 003BD008  003BD5A0 0027D870 001B280C 003BF164   *..M................N...Q........1.*   0068FC90

COMMON SYSTEM AREA                       ADDRESS 0074CEE0 TO 0074DEDF    LENGTH 001000

00000000    00000000 00005FA8 0053D220 70F14196  00000000 00000002 00599210 0000002F   *.......y..K..1.o..........k.....*   0074CEE0
00000020    00599208 005993B4 00599474 60E7749A  00E78499 00E79498 005994B0 00279C98   *..k...l...m.-X...Xdr.Xmq..m....q*   0074CF00

00000040    00000001 00279940 8010150C 00279940  1408022F 001A51D0 17700100 00000000   *......r .......r................*   0074CF20
00000060    004DA3E4 00054600 0095AF78 00001EF0  00010000 00006800 00758000 0088267F   *.(tU.....n.....0............h..*   0074CF40
00000080    0074F190 E0FFFFFE 0000001E 007505A8  002323A4 00000000 00187030 E738C616   *..1...............y...u.......X.F.*   0074CF60
000000A0    00000000 001A5410 001DFBC0 001A5150  001A5350 0074E1B8 0074E388 C500FF00   *...........................ThE...*   0074CF80
000000C0    001E000C 00001000 0074DEE0 038402AC  9F2883E2 5AFF8B01 0095AF78 00000000   *...............d....cS.....n......*   0074CFA0

000000E0    40EB3F98 00E89028 00E90188 00EC6078  00F1416E 006EB7E0 00EC1020 00E81018   * ..q.Y...Z.h..-..1...........Y..*   0074CFC0
00000100    00E7506C 006A2BBA 00DC6914 0068FBD0  0074FE00 00E8401C 01E5B4B0 00696A00   *.X.....................Y...V.....*   0074CFE0
00000120    00000000 00000000 006EAAB0 006AB038  006A6A90 00599758 001A4800 0074FBE8   *...........................p.......Y*   0074D000
00000140    00000000 0068FBF0 0073CE98 006B5880  006AA5EC 0068F460 00750560 00000000   *........0...q.,....v..4-...-.....*   0074D020
00000160    0F000000 7FFF0000 00000000 28995609  002441A9 02000000 00000000 00000000   *..................r.....z........*   0074D040

00000180    0074FE00 0074FE04 00000000 0074FE1C  00000000 00000000 05EFD283 0074CE90   *..........................Kc....*   0074D060
000001A0    070E58F0 D19C07FF 00E8EBAC 00E8EE48  00697800 000C0000 E6D6D9D2 C1D9C5C1   *...0J....Y...Y..........WORKAREA*   0074D080
```

```
CUSTOMER INFORMATION CONTROL SYSTEM STORAGE DUMP   CODE=ASRA   TASK=A010      DATE=09/23/88   TIME=14:08:02   PAGE    3

COMMON SYSTEM AREA                               ADDRESS 0074CEE0 TO 0074DEDF    LENGTH 001000

000001C0   0000000C 101C0000 013C030C 56079C35  01996C34 96012C00 0C000C00 0C000C00   *.................r..o...........*   0074D0A0
000001E0   4C043C00 000C0000 0C000C00 0C00000C  00000C00 000C0000 0C00000C 00000C00   *................................*   0074D0C0
00000200   7E97F0F9 61F2F361 F8F80000 00000000  00000000 0000522F 50000000 00000000   *=p09/23/88......................*   0074D0E0
00000220   00000000 00000000 00000000 00000000  00000000 00000000 00000000 00000000   *................................*   0074D100
00000240   LINES TO 00000260 SAME AS ABOVE                                                                                      0074D120
00000280   00C30000 00000000 00000000 00000000  00000000 00000000 00000000 00000000   *.C..............................*   0074D160
000002A0   00000000 00000000 00000000 00000000  00000000 00000000 00000000 00000000   *................................*   0074D180
000002C0   LINES TO 00000440 SAME AS ABOVE                                                                                      0074D1A0
00000460   EE4B8008 004BA008 00000000 EE54AF68  EE3F2E8C 88267F88 0923F8F8 F0F9F2F3   *....................h..h..880923*   0074D340
00000480   00000000 00000000 00000000 00000000  00000000 00000000 00000000 00000000   *................................*   0074D360
000004A0   LINES TO 000004E0 SAME AS ABOVE                                                                                      0074D380
00000500   00000000 00EE0000 C200032A 00000000  00000000 00000000 00000000 00000000   *........B.......................*   0074D3E0
00000520   00000000 00000000 00000000 00000000  00000000 00000000 00000000 00000000   *................................*   0074D400

00000540   LINES TO 000005C0 SAME AS ABOVE                                                                                      0074D420
000005E0   00000000 00000000 00000000 00000000  00000000 00000000 00000000 00000000   *................................*   0074D4C0
00000600   LINES TO 000007E0 SAME AS ABOVE                                                                                      0074D4E0
00000800   00000000 00000000 00000000 00000000  EE000C80 00797FFF 00140001 00640050   *................................*   0074D6E0
00000820   000209C4 03E80001 7FFFC1C1 00000000  00000000 00000000 00000000 00000000   *...D.Y....AA....................*   0074D700
00000840   00000000 00000000 00000000 00000000  0053D8DA EE000000 00000000 00000000   *..................Q.............*   0074D720
00000860   00000000 00000000 00000000 00000000  00000000 00000000 00000000 00000000   *................................*   0074D740
00000880   LINES TO 00000FE0 SAME AS ABOVE                                                                                      0074D760


CSA OPTIONAL FEATURE LIST                        ADDRESS 0074DEE0 TO 0074E13F    LENGTH 000260

00000000   00000000 00000000 0068F430 006A4EC0  00EA9022 00000000 006E8EE0 006E8F62   *..........4...+.................*   0074DEE0
00000020   00E8B26C 006A2520 00EB001C 00188B28  00000000 006E89C0 00000000 00000000   *.Y....................i.........*   0074DF00
00000040   00000000 00000000 00000000 00000000  00EBC116 00000000 00000000 0074FD08   *..................A.............*   0074DF20
00000060   8074FD44 1388F15B 00000000 00000205  00CBFB38 0088267F 00EC501C 0074CEE0   *.....h1$.............h..........*   0074DF40
00000080   0074FE78 00CA3020 00EA5018 00E9D018  00000000 00000000 00000000 00000000   *.............Z..................*   0074DF60
000000A0   00000000 00000000 00ED901C 00F15498  00EC9018 00CA4428 00C94018 00E7DCC8   *.............1.q.........I...X.H*   0074DF80
000000C0   00C62020 00C9A0E8 00E4BBE0 00C61020  006EA840 00C67018 00E88418 006A2380   *.F...I.Y.U...F....y..F...Yd.....*   0074DFA0
000000E0   00DBB560 00DD1C68 006A6540 00E09728  00E47720 00000000 00000000 00C9B030   *...-..........p..U...........I..*   0074DFC0

00000100   00EC7018 00C92018 00C6F018 00DC82A0  00E66018 00E60018 00E5B01C 00E59018   *.....I...F0...b..W-..W...V...V..*   0074DFE0
00000120   00E54018 00E4F018 00E4C018 00DD7342  00E92022 00E96022 00EA7028 00CFB3F2   *.V...U0..U.......Z...Z-........2*   0074E000
00000140   00E95B12 00EA9DA4 00D6D9F2 00DAD908  00CCE342 00CE91B0 00E8F584 00007B78   *.Z$....u.OR2..R...T...j..Y5d....*   0074E020
00000160   00000000 00E7E01C 0069EA40 00E5AEB0  00F28018 00000000 00000000 00C6CC30   *.....X..... .V...2...........F..*   0074E040
00000180   00E72018 00E9154C 00000000 00000000  00000000 00000000 0074FB88 0074E140   *.X...Z.....................h... *   0074E060
000001A0   00692FD0 00722B50 0000C000 00000000  00000000 0068F818 00000000 001A5000   *......................8.........*   0074E080
000001C0   0068F2F0 00000000 00005E60 00009000  00000000 E2E8E2E3 F9F9F840 00000000   *..20......;-........SYST998 ....*   0074E0A0
000001E0   0AD80AD7 00000000 00000000 00000000  00000000 00000000 9F2898F7 24D4E500   *.Q.P......................q7.MV.*   0074E0C0
00000200   9DA334FA 77DB4800 00000000 00000000  00750A68 001B5C40 00000000 00000000   *.t....................* ........*   0074E0E0
00000220   00000000 00000000 00000000 00000000  000185EF 000009C5 00000000 00000000   *..................e....E........*   0074E100
00000240   00000000 00000000 00000000 00000000  00000000 00000000 00000000 00000000   *................................*   0074E120


TRACE TABLE                                      ADDRESS 00696A20 TO 0069EA1F    LENGTH 008000

TRACE HDR          00699B80    00696A20    0069EA00    00000000

   TIME OF DAY    ID  REG 14   REQD TASK   FIELD A  FIELD B  CHARS     RESOURCE  TRACE TYPE                               INTERVAL

14:08:00.302752   F9  406EA2E2 40E5 56054  00000000 001A39A0 ........            JCP RETN GETF
14:08:00.303360   F0  40EC159E 4004 56054  43000000 001DCEF0 .......0            KCP WAIT DCI=IOEVENT                     00.000608
14:08:00.303392   D5  00EB4026 0104 56054  E7D2C3D9 C5D84040 XKCREQ    TIXKCREQ  UEH BEFORE                               00.000032
```

```
CUSTOMER INFORMATION CONTROL SYSTEM STORAGE DUMP   CODE=ASRA   TASK=A010      DATE=09/23/88   TIME=14:08:02   PAGE   17

   TIME OF DAY    ID  REG 14   REQD TASK   FIELD A  FIELD B  CHARS     RESOURCE  TRACE TYPE                                 INTERVAL

14:08:02.114496   F0  40EC159E 4004 56054 43000000 001DCEF0 ........0           KCP WAIT DCI=IOEVENT                        00.000416
14:08:02.114528   D5  00EB4026 0104 56054 E7D2C3D9 C5D84040 XKCREQ    TIXKCREQ  UEH BEFORE                                  00.000032
14:08:02.114560   D5  00EB4026 0204 56054 00000000 001A39A0 ........  TIXKCREQ  UEH AFTER                                   00.000032
14:08:02.193056   FC  40E5B136 1404 TCP   036F0001 006ED8A0 .......Q.           ZCP ZRAC RECEIVE ANY                       *00.078496
14:08:02.193088   FC  50E68112 1304 TCP   00000001 006ED8A0 .......Q.           ZCP ZGET GETMAIN                            00.000032
14:08:02.193120   EE  70E672A4 2314 TCP   036F01A0 016ED8A0 .......Q.           VIO RECEIVE OIC DATA                        00.000032
14:08:02.193152   EE  70E672A4 0024 TCP   00EB7DD4 D311C7E9 ..'ML.GZ            VIO DATA                                    00.000032
14:08:02.193152   F1  50E6761E A504 TCP   001B0100 016ED8A0 .......Q.           SCP GETMAIN CONDITIONAL                     00.000000
14:08:02.193216   C8  50E89802 0004 TCP   001AF240 851B0118 ..2 .....           SCP ACQUIRED TERMINAL STORAGE               00.000064
14:08:02.193504   FC  40DC8614 1103 TCP   00200001 006ED8A0 .......Q.           ZCP ZATT ATTACH                             00.000288
14:08:02.193536   F0  50E5CFD6 1304 TCP   C1E3C3E5 C1F0F1F0 ATCVA010            KCP ATTACH-CONDITIONAL                      00.000032
14:08:02.193568   D5  00EB4026 0104 TCP   E7D2C3D9 C5D84040 XKCREQ    TIXKCREQ  UEH BEFORE                                  00.000032
14:08:02.193568   D5  00EB4026 0204 TCP   00000000 001A39A0 ........  TIXKCREQ  UEH AFTER                                   00.000000
14:08:02.193600   EA  70EB4878 0003 TCP   01040100 0074E420 .......U. A010      TMP PCT LOCATE                              00.000032
14:08:02.193632   EA  40E7F114 0025 TCP   01040100 006CFA88 .........           TMP RETN NORMAL                             00.000032
14:08:02.193664   F1  50EB49F0 EA04 TCP   00080838 016ED8A0 .......Q.           SCP GETMAIN CONDITIONAL INITIMG             00.000032
14:08:02.193728   C8  50E89802 0004 TCP   00279800 8A030838 .........           SCP ACQUIRED TCA STORAGE                    00.000064
14:08:02.193760   D0  50EB57C0 0604 56079 C1E3C3E5 C1F0F1F0 ATCVA010            KCP CREATE                                  00.000032
14:08:02.193792   EA  40EB4E08 0003 TCP   0C000100 006CFA88 ......... A010      TMP PCT TRANSFER                            00.000032
14:08:02.193824   EA  40E7F114 0025 TCP   0C000100 00000000 .........           TMP RETN NORMAL                             00.000032
14:08:02.193824   FC  40E5D104 1125 TCP   0C000100 00000000 .........           ZCP RETN ZATT ATTACH                        00.000000
14:08:02.193856   F0  40E5B1E0 4004 TCP   40000000 0073CE38 .........           KCP WAIT DCI=LIST                           00.000032
14:08:02.193888   D5  00EB4026 0104 TCP   E7D2C3D9 C5D84040 XKCREQ    TIXKCREQ  UEH BEFORE                                  00.000032
14:08:02.193888   D5  00EB4026 0204 TCP   00000000 001A39A0 ........  TIXKCREQ  UEH AFTER                                   00.000000
14:08:02.193920   FC  05E5D6E8 0503 56079 00200001 006ED8A0 .......Q.           ZCP ZSUP START UP TASK                      00.000032
14:08:02.193984   E7  00E5DF1C 0504 56079 00000000 00000000 .........           ERM ENTRY                                   00.000064
14:08:02.193984   E7  00E5DF1C 0504 56079 00000000 000000FF .........           ERM RESPONSE                                00.000000
14:08:02.194016   F2  50E5DF4E 8804 56079 00000000 00000000 ......... KA0100C   PCP XCTL-CONDITIONAL                        00.000032
14:08:02.194016   EA  40E906F6 0003 56079 01000300 002799C4 ........D KA0100C   TMP PPT LOCATE                              00.000000
14:08:02.194048   EA  40E7F114 0005 56079 01000300 006BB2C8 ......,.H           TMP RETN NORMAL                             00.000032
14:08:02.194656   F1  60E913B6 8C04 56079 00000408 016ED8A0 .......Q.           SCP GETMAIN                                 00.000608
14:08:02.194688   C8  50E89802 0004 56079 0027A040 8C000418 .........           SCP ACQUIRED USER STORAGE                   00.000032
14:08:02.194752   F7  50E91754 8003 56079 C1E3C3E5 40404040 ATCV                TSP APPL REQ GET                            00.000064
14:08:02.195328   F0  50E7898C C004 56079 43000000 005993BC .........           KCP WAIT+CANCADDR DCI=IOEVENT               00.000576
14:08:02.195328   D5  00EB4026 0104 56079 E7D2C3D9 C5D84040 XKCREQ    TIXKCREQ  UEH BEFORE                                  00.000000
14:08:02.195360   D5  00EB4026 0204 56079 00000000 001A39A0 ......... TIXKCREQ  UEH AFTER                                   00.000032
14:08:02.195456   F1  40EC3418 4004 56054 001DCE70 017021A0 .........           SCP FREEMAIN                                00.000096
14:08:02.195488   C9  50E89882 0004 56054 001DCE70 9DC00068 .........           SCP RELEASED DWE STORAGE                    00.000032
14:08:02.195520   F1  40EC3372 4004 56054 001DCEE0 017021A0 .........           SCP FREEMAIN                                00.000032
14:08:02.195520   C9  50E89882 0004 56054 001DCEE0 8FC00088 .........           SCP RELEASED FILE STORAGE                   00.000000
14:08:02.195552   F5  40EC1A18 0015 56054 001DCEE0 8FC00088 .........           FCP RETN NORMAL                             00.000032
14:08:02.195616   F5  405345EE 1003 56054 101EB000 00000000 .........           FCP RELEASE                                 00.000064
14:08:02.195616   F1  50EC3372 4004 56054 001EB000 017021A0 .........           SCP FREEMAIN                                00.000000
14:08:02.195648   C9  50E89882 0004 56054 001EB000 8FC00118 .........           SCP RELEASED FILE STORAGE                   00.000032
14:08:02.195680   F5  40EC1A18 0015 56054 001EB000 8FC00118 .........           FCP RETN NORMAL                             00.000032
14:08:02.196544   F2  40534E54 0804 56054 00000000 00000000 ......... VAY001A   PCP DELETE                                  00.000864
14:08:02.196576   EA  40E906F6 0003 56054 01000300 001ED1C4 .......JD VAY001A   TMP PPT LOCATE                              00.000032
14:08:02.196640   EA  40E7F114 0005 56054 01000300 006B5DA0 ......,).           TMP RETN NORMAL                             00.000064
14:08:02.196672   F1  50534E62 4004 56054 001F8F00 017021A0 .........           SCP FREEMAIN                                00.000032
14:08:02.196672   C9  50E89882 0004 56054 001F8F00 8C001778 .........           SCP RELEASED USER STORAGE                   00.000000
14:08:02.196832   F2  50534E70 1004 56054 00000000 00000000 ......... GDBMANGR  PCP RETURN                                  00.000160
14:08:02.196864   F1  60E9075E 4004 56054 001DCE10 017021A0 .........           SCP FREEMAIN                                00.000032
14:08:02.196864   C9  50E89882 0004 56054 001DCE10 891D0058 .........           SCP RELEASED RSA STORAGE                    00.000000
14:08:02.196896   F1  00ED9DB8 4004 56054 001DCD10 017021A0 .........           SCP FREEMAIN                                00.000032
14:08:02.196928   C9  50E89882 0004 56054 001DCD10 8C0000F8 ........8           SCP RELEASED USER STORAGE                   00.000032
```

```
CUSTOMER INFORMATION CONTROL SYSTEM STORAGE DUMP   CODE=ASRA   TASK=A010      DATE=09/23/88   TIME=14:08:02   PAGE  18

  TIME OF DAY   ID  REG 14   REQD TASK   FIELD A  FIELD B  CHARS     RESOURCE  TRACE TYPE                                INTERVAL

14:08:02.196928 E1 503D25E0 00F4 56054 00000000 00000E02 ........            EIP LINK RESPONSE                         00.000000
14:08:02.197216 E1 503D2A6E 0004 56054 001F004C 00000E02 ........            EIP LINK ENTRY                            00.000288
14:08:02.197248 F2 00C9A114 8204 56054 00000000 00000000 ........  GDBMANGR  PCP LOCATE                                00.000032
14:08:02.197280 EA 40E906F6 0003 56054 01000300 001ED1C4 ......JD  GDBMANGR  TMP PPT LOCATE                            00.000032
14:08:02.197312 EA 40E7F114 0005 56054 01000300 006BA8AC ........            TMP RETN NORMAL                           00.000032
14:08:02.197344 F1 00ED9DB8 CC04 56054 000000F0 017021A0 ...0....            SCP GETMAIN INITIMG                       00.000032
14:08:02.197376 C8 50E89802 0004 56054 001DCD10 8C0000F8 .......8            SCP ACQUIRED USER STORAGE                 00.000032
14:08:02.197376 F2 00EDA0E6 8104 56054 00000000 00000000 ........  GDBMANGR  PCP LINK-CONDITIONAL                      00.000000
14:08:02.197408 EA 40E906F6 0003 56054 01000300 001ED1C4 ......JD  GDBMANGR  TMP PPT LOCATE                            00.000032
14:08:02.197440 EA 40E7F114 0005 56054 01000300 006BA8AC ........            TMP RETN NORMAL                           00.000032
14:08:02.197472 F1 40E90306 8904 56054 001D0050 017021A0 ...&....            SCP GETMAIN                               00.000032
14:08:02.197472 C8 50E89802 0004 56054 001DCE10 891D0058 ........            SCP ACQUIRED RSA STORAGE                  00.000000
14:08:02.197536 F2 40532366 0404 56054 00000000 00000000 ........  VAY001A   PCP LOAD                                  00.000064
14:08:02.197536 EA 40E906F6 0003 56054 01000300 001ED1C4 ......JD  VAY001A   TMP PPT LOCATE                            00.000000
14:08:02.197600 EA 40E7F114 0005 56054 01000300 006B5DA0 .....).            TMP RETN NORMAL                           00.000064
14:08:02.197600 F1 6053238E CC04 56054 00001766 017021A0 ........            SCP GETMAIN INITIMG                       00.000000
14:08:02.197792 C8 50E89802 0004 56054 001F8F00 8C001778 ........            SCP ACQUIRED USER STORAGE                 00.000192
14:08:02.198048 F5 40534868 8403 56054 00000000 00000000 ........  VAOCCUR   FCP GET-UPDATE                            00.000256
14:08:02.198048 EA 40EC1AF2 0003 56054 01000500 001ED1C4 ......JD  VAOCCUR   TMP FCT LOCATE                            00.000000
14:08:02.198112 EA 40E7F114 0055 56054 01000500 006B49B0 ........            TMP RETN NORMAL                           00.000064
14:08:02.198112 F1 70EC338A 9D04 56054 00C00054 017021A0 ........            SCP GETMAIN                               00.000000
14:08:02.198144 C8 50E89802 0004 56054 001DCE70 9DC00068 ........            SCP ACQUIRED DWE STORAGE                  00.000032
14:08:02.198176 F1 40EC3190 8F04 56054 00C00084 017021A0 ........            SCP GETMAIN                               00.000032
14:08:02.198176 C8 50E89802 0004 56054 001DCEE0 8FC00098 ........            SCP ACQUIRED FILE STORAGE                 00.000000
14:08:02.198208 F1 40EC3190 8F04 56054 00C0001E 017021A0 ........            SCP GETMAIN                               00.000032
14:08:02.198240 C8 50E89802 0004 56054 001DCF80 8FC00028 ........            SCP ACQUIRED FILE STORAGE                 00.000032
14:08:02.198240 F0 50EC3F7C 0104 56054 1E1DCF88 00000000 ........            KCP ENQUEUE                               00.000000
14:08:02.198272 D5 00EB4026 0104 56054 E7D2C3D9 C5D84040 XKCREQ    TIXKCREQ  UEH BEFORE                                00.000032
14:08:02.198272 D5 00EB4026 0204 56054 00000000 001A39A0 ........  TIXKCREQ  UEH AFTER                                 00.000000
14:08:02.198304 F1 70EC3372 4004 56054 001DCF80 017021A0 ........            SCP FREEMAIN                              00.000032
14:08:02.198336 C9 50E89882 0004 56054 001DCF80 8FC00028 ........            SCP RELEASED FILE STORAGE                 00.000032
14:08:02.198336 F1 40EC3190 8F04 56054 001D0108 017021A0 ........            SCP GETMAIN                               00.000000
14:08:02.198368 C8 50E89802 0004 56054 001EB000 8F1D0118 ........            SCP ACQUIRED FILE STORAGE                 00.000032
14:08:02.198816 F0 40EC159E 4004 56054 43000000 001DCEF0 .......0            KCP WAIT DCI=IOEVENT                      00.000448

14:08:02.198848 D5 00EB4026 0104 56054 E7D2C3D9 C5D84040 XKCREQ    TIXKCREQ  UEH BEFORE                                00.000032
14:08:02.198848 D5 00EB4026 0204 56054 00000000 001A39A0 ........  TIXKCREQ  UEH AFTER                                 00.000000
14:08:02.211616 F1 40E757FC AE04 56079 00270738 016ED8A0 ......Q.            SCP GETMAIN CONDITIONAL                   00.012768
14:08:02.211648 C8 50E89802 0004 56079 0027A460 8E270748 ........            SCP ACQUIRED TEMPSTRG STORAGE             00.000032
14:08:02.211712 F7 40E75D68 0005 56079 0027A460 8E270748 ...-....            TSP RETN APPL RESP NORMAL                 00.000064
14:08:02.211776 F7 50E91754 8003 56079 C1E3C3E5 C9D5E2D9 ATCVINSR            TSP APPL REQ GET                          00.000064
14:08:02.212896 F0 50E7898C C004 56079 43000000 005993BC ........            KCP WAIT+CANCADDR DCI=IOEVENT             00.001120
14:08:02.212928 D5 00EB4026 0104 56079 E7D2C3D9 C5D84040 XKCREQ    TIXKCREQ  UEH BEFORE                                00.000032
14:08:02.212960 D5 00EB4026 0204 56079 00000000 001A39A0 ........  TIXKCREQ  UEH AFTER                                 00.000032
14:08:02.228064 F1 40E757FC AE04 56079 00270DCB 016ED8A0 ......Q.            SCP GETMAIN CONDITIONAL                  *00.015104
14:08:02.228224 C8 50E89802 0004 56079 0027ABB0 8E270DD8 .......Q            SCP ACQUIRED TEMPSTRG STORAGE             00.000160
14:08:02.228320 F7 40E75D68 0005 56079 0027ABB0 8E270DD8 .......Q            TSP RETN APPL RESP NORMAL                 00.000096
14:08:02.228352 F7 50E91754 8003 56079 C1E3C3E5 C1C4E340 ATCVADT             TSP APPL REQ GET                          00.000032
14:08:02.228416 F1 40E757FC AE04 56079 002701CD 016ED8A0 ......Q.            SCP GETMAIN CONDITIONAL                   00.000064
14:08:02.228448 C8 50E89802 0004 56079 0027B990 8E2701D8 .......Q            SCP ACQUIRED TEMPSTRG STORAGE             00.000032
14:08:02.228480 F7 40E75D68 0005 56079 0027B990 8E2701D8 .......Q            TSP RETN APPL RESP NORMAL                 00.000032
14:08:02.228544 FA 50E91754 0003 56079 00000525 00000000 ........            BMS MAP MAPSET SAVE MAP-FROM IN           00.000064
14:08:02.228544 F1 40EA9188 CC04 56079 000002FC 016ED8A0 ......Q.            SCP GETMAIN INITIMG                       00.000000
14:08:02.228576 C8 50E89802 0004 56079 0027BB70 8C000308 ........            SCP ACQUIRED USER STORAGE                 00.000032
14:08:02.228640 F1 60DD79DC CC04 56079 000000A4 016ED8A0 ......Q.            SCP GETMAIN INITIMG                       00.000064
14:08:02.228640 C8 50E89802 0004 56079 0027BE80 8C0000B8 ........            SCP ACQUIRED USER STORAGE                 00.000000
```

```
CUSTOMER INFORMATION CONTROL SYSTEM STORAGE DUMP   CODE=ASRA   TASK=A010      DATE=09/23/88   TIME=14:08:02   PAGE   19

  TIME OF DAY     ID  REG 14   REQD TASK   FIELD A  FIELD B  CHARS    RESOURCE  TRACE TYPE                                  INTERVAL

14:08:02.228672  F2 40EAA3B2 8404 56079 00000000 00000000 ........ KAEP1PCM  PCP LOAD-CONDITIONAL                           00.000032
14:08:02.228704  EA 40E906F6 0003 56079 01000300 002799C4 .......D KAEP1PCM  TMP PPT LOCATE                                00.000032
14:08:02.228736  EA 40E7F114 0405 56079 01000304 00000000 ........           TMP RETN NOT FOUND                            00.000032
14:08:02.228768  F2 40EAA3F4 0404 56079 00000000 00000000 ........ KAEP1PC   PCP LOAD                                     00.000032
14:08:02.228768  EA 40E906F6 0003 56079 01000300 002799C4 .......D KAEP1PC   TMP PPT LOCATE                               00.000000
14:08:02.228800  EA 40E7F114 0005 56079 01000300 006BB024 ......,.           TMP RETN NORMAL                               00.000032
14:08:02.228864  F1 60E96D0A C504 56079 000002B4 016ED8A0 ......Q.           SCP GETMAIN INITIMG                           00.000064
14:08:02.228896  C8 50E89802 0004 56079 001B3B40 850002C8 .......H           SCP ACQUIRED TERMINAL STORAGE                 00.000032
14:08:02.229056  FA 40EA9F78 0005 56079 00000000 00000000 ........           BMS RETN                                      00.000160
14:08:02.229088  F2 50E91754 0104 56079 00000000 00000000 ........ KA0250C   PCP LINK                                     00.000032
14:08:02.229120  EA 40E906F6 0003 56079 01000300 002799C4 .......D KA0250C   TMP PPT LOCATE                               00.000032
14:08:02.229152  EA 40E7F114 0005 56079 01000300 006BB330 ......,.           TMP RETN NORMAL                               00.000032
14:08:02.229152  F1 40E90306 8904 56079 001B0050 016ED8A0 ...&.'Q.           SCP GETMAIN                                   00.000000
14:08:02.229184  C8 50E89802 0004 56079 0027BF40 891B0058 ........           SCP ACQUIRED RSA STORAGE                      00.000032
14:08:02.229216  F1 60E913B6 8C04 56079 002702F8 016ED8A0 ...8..Q.           SCP GETMAIN                                   00.000032
14:08:02.229344  C8 50E89802 0004 56079 0027BFA0 8C270308 ........           SCP ACQUIRED USER STORAGE                     00.000128
14:08:02.229376  F1 50E91754 CC04 56079 00000064 016ED8A0 ......Q.           SCP GETMAIN INITIMG                           00.000032
14:08:02.229408  C8 50E89802 0004 56079 0027C2B0 8C000078 ..B.....           SCP ACQUIRED USER STORAGE                     00.000032
14:08:02.229440  F2 50E91754 0104 56079 00000000 00000000 ........ KUPFAOC   PCP LINK                                     00.000032
14:08:02.229440  EA 40E906F6 0003 56079 01000300 002799C4 .......D KUPFAOC   TMP PPT LOCATE                               00.000000
14:08:02.229504  EA 40E7F114 0005 56079 01000300 006BEDC8 ......,H           TMP RETN NORMAL                               00.000064
14:08:02.229504  F1 40E90306 8904 56079 00270050 016ED8A0 ...&.'Q.           SCP GETMAIN                                   00.000000
14:08:02.229536  C8 50E89802 0004 56079 0027C330 89270058 ..C.....           SCP ACQUIRED RSA STORAGE                      00.000032
14:08:02.229536  F1 60E913B6 8C04 56079 00270260 016ED8A0 ...-..Q.           SCP GETMAIN                                   00.000000
14:08:02.229568  C8 50E89802 0004 56079 0027C390 8C270268 ..C.....           SCP ACQUIRED USER STORAGE                     00.000032
14:08:02.229600  F1 50E91754 CC04 56079 00000064 016ED8A0 ......Q.           SCP GETMAIN INITIMG                           00.000032
14:08:02.229632  C8 50E89802 0004 56079 0027C600 8C000078 ..F.....           SCP ACQUIRED USER STORAGE                     00.000032
14:08:02.229664  F7 50E91754 8003 56079 00C1D7E3 C4C5D4D6 .APTDEMO           TSP APPL REQ GET                              00.000032
14:08:02.230208  F0 50E7898C C004 56079 43000000 005993BC ........           KCP WAIT+CANCADDR DCI=IOEVENT                 00.000544
14:08:02.230240  D5 00EB4026 0104 56079 E7D2C3D9 C5D84040 XKCREQ   TIXKCREQ  UEH BEFORE                                   00.000032
14:08:02.230240  D5 00EB4026 0204 56079 00000000 001A39A0 ........ TIXKCREQ  UEH AFTER                                    00.000000
14:08:02.250720  F1 40E757FC AE04 56079 00270E04 016ED8A0 ......Q.           SCP GETMAIN CONDITIONAL                      *00.020480
14:08:02.250752  C8 50E89802 0004 56079 0027C680 8E270E18 ..F.....           SCP ACQUIRED TEMPSTRG STORAGE                 00.000032
14:08:02.250848  F7 40E75D68 0005 56079 0027C680 8E270E18 ..F.....           TSP RETN APPL RESP NORMAL                     00.000096
14:08:02.250880  F1 50E91754 4004 56079 0027C600 016ED8A0 ..F...Q.           SCP FREEMAIN                                  00.000032
14:08:02.250912  C9 50E89882 0004 56079 0027C600 8C000078 ..F.....           SCP RELEASED USER STORAGE                     00.000032
14:08:02.250912  F2 50E91754 1004 56079 00000000 00000000 ........ KUPFAOC   PCP RETURN                                   00.000000
14:08:02.250944  F1 60E90A4E 4004 56079 0027C390 016ED8A0 ..C...Q.           SCP FREEMAIN                                  00.000032
14:08:02.250944  C9 50E89882 0004 56079 0027C390 8C270268 ..C.....           SCP RELEASED USER STORAGE                     00.000000
14:08:02.250976  F1 60E9075E 4004 56079 0027C330 016ED8A0 ..C...Q.           SCP FREEMAIN                                  00.000032
14:08:02.251008  C9 50E89882 0004 56079 0027C330 89270058 ..C.....           SCP RELEASED RSA STORAGE                      00.000032
14:08:02.251104  F2 50E91754 0104 56079 00000000 00000000 ........ KUPFAOC   PCP LINK                                     00.000096
14:08:02.251104  EA 40E906F6 0003 56079 01000300 002799C4 .......D KUPFAOC   TMP PPT LOCATE                               00.000000
14:08:02.251168  EA 40E7F114 0005 56079 01000300 006BEDC8 ......,H           TMP RETN NORMAL                               00.000064
14:08:02.251168  F1 40E90306 8904 56079 00270050 016ED8A0 ...&.'Q.           SCP GETMAIN                                   00.000000
14:08:02.251200  C8 50E89802 0004 56079 0027D4A0 89270058 ..M.....           SCP ACQUIRED RSA STORAGE                      00.000032
14:08:02.251328  F1 60E913B6 8C04 56079 00270260 016ED8A0 ...-..Q.           SCP GETMAIN                                   00.000128
14:08:02.251360  C8 50E89802 0004 56079 0027D500 8C270268 ..N.....           SCP ACQUIRED USER STORAGE                     00.000032
14:08:02.251392  F1 50E91754 CC04 56079 00000064 016ED8A0 ......Q.           SCP GETMAIN INITIMG                           00.000032
14:08:02.251424  C8 50E89802 0004 56079 0027D770 8C000078 ..P.....           SCP ACQUIRED USER STORAGE                     00.000032
14:08:02.251424  F7 50E91754 8003 56079 00C1D7E3 C5D4D740 .APTEMP            TSP APPL REQ GET                              00.000000
14:08:02.251968  F0 50E7898C C004 56079 43000000 005993BC ........           KCP WAIT+CANCADDR DCI=IOEVENT                 00.000544
14:08:02.252000  D5 00EB4026 0104 56079 E7D2C3D9 C5D84040 XKCREQ   TIXKCREQ  UEH BEFORE                                   00.000032
14:08:02.252032  D5 00EB4026 0204 56079 00000000 001A39A0 ........ TIXKCREQ  UEH AFTER                                    00.000032
14:08:02.264128  F1 40E757FC AE04 56079 002700D0 016ED8A0 ......Q.           SCP GETMAIN CONDITIONAL                       00.012096
```

```
CUSTOMER INFORMATION CONTROL SYSTEM STORAGE DUMP   CODE=ASRA   TASK=A010      DATE=09/23/88   TIME=14:08:02   PAGE   20

  TIME OF DAY    ID  REG 14   REQD TASK   FIELD A  FIELD B  CHARS    RESOURCE  TRACE TYPE                             INTERVAL

14:08:02.264192  C8 50E89802 0004 56079 0027D7F0 8E2700D8 ..PO...Q           SCP ACQUIRED TEMPSTRG STORAGE          00.000064
14:08:02.264224  F7 40E75D68 0005 56079 0027D7F0 8E2700D8 ..PO...Q           TSP RETN APPL RESP NORMAL              00.000032
14:08:02.264256  F1 50E91754 4004 56079 0027D770 016ED8A0 ..P...Q.           SCP FREEMAIN                           00.000032
14:08:02.264288  C9 50E89882 0004 56079 0027D770 8C000078 ..P.....           SCP RELEASED USER STORAGE              00.000032
14:08:02.264288  F2 50E91754 1004 56079 00000000 00000000 ........ KUPFAOC   PCP RETURN                             00.000000
14:08:02.264320  F1 60E90A4E 4004 56079 0027D500 016ED8A0 ..N...Q.           SCP FREEMAIN                           00.000032
14:08:02.264320  C9 50E89882 0004 56079 0027D500 8C270268 ..N.....           SCP RELEASED USER STORAGE              00.000000
14:08:02.264352  F1 60E9075E 4004 56079 0027D4A0 016ED8A0 ..M...Q.           SCP FREEMAIN                           00.000032
14:08:02.264384  C9 50E89882 0004 56079 0027D4A0 89270058 ..M.....           SCP RELEASED RSA STORAGE               00.000032
14:08:02.264512  F1 50E91754 4004 56079 0027C680 016ED8A0 ..F...Q.           SCP FREEMAIN                           00.000128
14:08:02.264512  C9 50E89882 0004 56079 0027C680 8E270E18 ..F.....           SCP RELEASED TEMPSTRG STORAGE          00.000000

14:08:02.264640  F1 50E91754 4004 56079 0027D7F0 016ED8A0 ..PO..Q.           SCP FREEMAIN                           00.000128
14:08:02.264672  C9 50E89882 0004 56079 0027D7F0 8E2700D8 ..PO...Q           SCP RELEASED TEMPSTRG STORAGE          00.000032
14:08:02.264800  F1 50E91754 4004 56079 0027C2B0 016ED8A0 ..B...Q.           SCP FREEMAIN                           00.000128
14:08:02.264800  C9 50E89882 0004 56079 0027C2B0 8C000078 ..B.....           SCP RELEASED USER STORAGE              00.000000
14:08:02.264832  F2 50E91754 1004 56079 00000000 00000000 ........ KA0250C   PCP RETURN                             00.000032
14:08:02.264832  F1 60E90A4E 4004 56079 0027BFA0 016ED8A0 ......Q.           SCP FREEMAIN                           00.000000
14:08:02.264864  C9 50E89882 0004 56079 0027BFA0 8C270308 ........           SCP RELEASED USER STORAGE              00.000032
14:08:02.264928  F1 60E9075E 4004 56079 0027BF40 016ED8A0 ... ..Q.           SCP FREEMAIN                           00.000064
14:08:02.264960  C9 50E89882 0004 56079 0027BF40 891B0058 ... ....           SCP RELEASED RSA STORAGE               00.000032
14:08:02.264992  FA 50E91754 0003 56079 00000525 00000000 ........           BMS MAP MAPSET SAVE MAP-FROM IN        00.000032
14:08:02.265056  F1 60E96D0A C504 56079 000001FE 016ED8A0 ......Q.           SCP GETMAIN INITIMG                    00.000064
14:08:02.265088  C8 50E89802 0004 56079 001B2800 85000218 ........           SCP ACQUIRED TERMINAL STORAGE          00.000032
14:08:02.265312  FA 40EA9F78 0005 56079 00000000 00000000 ........           BMS RETN                               00.000224
14:08:02.265344  F2 50E91754 0104 56079 00000000 00000000 ........ KA2250C   PCP LINK                               00.000032
14:08:02.265376  EA 40E906F6 0003 56079 01000300 002799C4 .......D KA2250C   TMP PPT LOCATE                         00.000032
14:08:02.265408  EA 40E7F114 0005 56079 01000300 006BBB1C ........           TMP RETN NORMAL                        00.000032
14:08:02.265440  F1 40E90306 8904 56079 001B0050 016ED8A0 ...&..Q.           SCP GETMAIN                            00.000032
14:08:02.265568  C8 50E89802 0004 56079 0027D800 891B0058 ..Q.....           SCP ACQUIRED RSA STORAGE               00.000128
14:08:02.265600  F1 60E913B6 8C04 56079 00270368 016ED8A0 ......Q.           SCP GETMAIN                            00.000032
14:08:02.265632  C8 50E89802 0004 56079 0027D860 8C270378 ..Q-....           SCP ACQUIRED USER STORAGE              00.000032
14:08:02.265664  F1 50E91754 CC04 56079 00000096 016ED8A0 ......Q.           SCP GETMAIN INITIMG                    00.000032
14:08:02.265696  C8 50E89802 0004 56079 0027DBE0 8C0000A8 ........           SCP ACQUIRED USER STORAGE              00.000032
14:08:02.265696  F2 50E91754 0104 56079 00000000 00000000 ........ KUPFAOC   PCP LINK                               00.000000
14:08:02.265728  EA 40E906F6 0003 56079 01000300 002799C4 .......D KUPFAOC   TMP PPT LOCATE                         00.000032
14:08:02.265760  EA 40E7F114 0005 56079 01000300 006BEDC8 .......H           TMP RETN NORMAL                        00.000032
14:08:02.265792  F1 40E90306 8904 56079 00270050 016ED8A0 ...&..Q.           SCP GETMAIN                            00.000032
14:08:02.265792  C8 50E89802 0004 56079 0027DC90 89270058 ........           SCP ACQUIRED RSA STORAGE               00.000000
14:08:02.265824  F1 60E913B6 8C04 56079 00270260 016ED8A0 ...-..Q.           SCP GETMAIN                            00.000032
14:08:02.265856  C8 50E89802 0004 56079 0027DCF0 8C270268 ...O....           SCP ACQUIRED USER STORAGE              00.000032
14:08:02.265888  F1 50E91754 CC04 56079 00000064 016ED8A0 ......Q.           SCP GETMAIN INITIMG                    00.000032

14:08:02.265888  C8 50E89802 0004 56079 0027DF60 8C000078 ...-....           SCP ACQUIRED USER STORAGE              00.000000
14:08:02.265920  F7 50E91754 8003 56079 00C1D7E3 C4C5E2C3 .APTDESC           TSP APPL REQ GET                       00.000032
14:08:02.266496  F0 50E7898C C004 56079 43000000 005993BC ........           KCP WAIT+CANCADDR DCI=IOEVENT          00.000576
14:08:02.266496  D5 00EB4026 0104 56079 E7D2C3D9 C5D84040 XKCREQ   TIXKCREQ  UEH BEFORE                             00.000000
14:08:02.266528  D5 00EB4026 0204 56079 00000000 001A39A0 ........ TIXKCREQ  UEH AFTER                              00.000032
14:08:02.273344  F1 40E757FC AE04 56079 00270922 016ED8A0 ......Q.           SCP GETMAIN CONDITIONAL                00.006816
14:08:02.273504  C8 50E89802 0004 56079 0027DFE0 8E270938 ........           SCP ACQUIRED TEMPSTRG STORAGE          00.000160
14:08:02.273568  F7 40E75D68 0005 56079 0027DFE0 8E270938 ........           TSP RETN APPL RESP NORMAL              00.000064
14:08:02.273600  F1 50E91754 4004 56079 0027DF60 016ED8A0 ...-..Q.           SCP FREEMAIN                           00.000032
14:08:02.273600  C9 50E89882 0004 56079 0027DF60 8C000078 ...-....           SCP RELEASED USER STORAGE              00.000000
14:08:02.273632  F2 50E91754 1004 56079 00000000 00000000 ........ KUPFAOC   PCP RETURN                             00.000032
14:08:02.273664  F1 60E90A4E 4004 56079 0027DCF0 016ED8A0 ...O..Q.           SCP FREEMAIN                           00.000032
14:08:02.273664  C9 50E89882 0004 56079 0027DCF0 8C270268 ...O....           SCP RELEASED USER STORAGE              00.000000
14:08:02.273696  F1 60E9075E 4004 56079 0027DC90 016ED8A0 ......Q.           SCP FREEMAIN                           00.000032
```

```
CUSTOMER INFORMATION CONTROL SYSTEM STORAGE DUMP   CODE=ASRA   TASK=A010      DATE=09/23/88   TIME=14:08:02   PAGE   21

  TIME OF DAY    ID  REG 14   REQD TASK   FIELD A  FIELD B  CHARS    RESOURCE  TRACE TYPE                             INTERVAL
14:08:02.273696  C9  50E89882 0004 56079 0027DC90 89270058 ........           SCP RELEASED RSA STORAGE                00.000000
14:08:02.273792  F2  50E91754 0104 56079 00000000 00000000 ........  KUDATOA  PCP LINK                                00.000096
14:08:02.273824  EA  40E906F6 0003 56079 01000300 002799C4 .......D KUDATOA  TMP PPT LOCATE                          00.000032
14:08:02.273856  EA  40E7F114 0005 56079 01000300 006BECB0 ....'...           TMP RETN NORMAL                         00.000032
14:08:02.273888  F1  40E90306 8904 56079 00270050 016ED8A0 ...&..Q.           SCP GETMAIN                             00.000032
14:08:02.273888  C8  50E89802 0004 56079 0027E920 89270058 ..Z.....           SCP ACQUIRED RSA STORAGE                00.000000
14:08:02.273920  F1  50528DCC CC04 56079 00000032 016ED8A0 ......Q.           SCP GETMAIN INITIMG                     00.000032
14:08:02.273952  C8  50E89802 0004 56079 0027E980 8C000048 ..Z.....           SCP ACQUIRED USER STORAGE               00.000032
14:08:02.273984  F1  60528E0E 4004 56079 0027E980 016ED8A0 ..Z...Q.           SCP FREEMAIN                            00.000032
14:08:02.273984  C9  50E89882 0004 56079 0027E980 8C000048 ..Z.....           SCP RELEASED USER STORAGE               00.000000
14:08:02.274016  F2  50528E1C 1004 56079 00000000 00000000 ........  KUDATOA  PCP RETURN                              00.000032
14:08:02.274016  F1  60E9075E 4004 56079 0027E920 016ED8A0 ..Z...Q.           SCP FREEMAIN                            00.000000
14:08:02.274048  C9  50E89882 0004 56079 0027E920 89270058 ..Z.....           SCP RELEASED RSA STORAGE                00.000032
14:08:02.274080  F2  50E91754 0104 56079 00000000 00000000 ........  KUDATOA  PCP LINK                                00.000032
14:08:02.274080  EA  40E906F6 0003 56079 01000300 002799C4 .......D KUDATOA  TMP PPT LOCATE                          00.000000
14:08:02.274144  EA  40E7F114 0005 56079 01000300 006BECB0 ....'...           TMP RETN NORMAL                         00.000064
14:08:02.274144  F1  40E90306 8904 56079 00270050 016ED8A0 ...&..Q.           SCP GETMAIN                             00.000000
14:08:02.274176  C8  50E89802 0004 56079 0027E9D0 89270058 ..Z.....           SCP ACQUIRED RSA STORAGE                00.000032
14:08:02.274176  F1  50528DCC CC04 56079 00000032 016ED8A0 ......Q.           SCP GETMAIN INITIMG                     00.000000
14:08:02.274208  C8  50E89802 0004 56079 0027EA30 8C000048 ........           SCP ACQUIRED USER STORAGE               00.000032
14:08:02.274240  F1  60528E0E 4004 56079 0027EA30 016ED8A0 ......Q.           SCP FREEMAIN                            00.000032
14:08:02.274240  C9  50E89882 0004 56079 0027EA30 8C000048 ........           SCP RELEASED USER STORAGE               00.000000
14:08:02.274272  F2  50528E1C 1004 56079 00000000 00000000 ........  KUDATOA  PCP RETURN                              00.000032
14:08:02.274272  F1  60E9075E 4004 56079 0027E9D0 016ED8A0 ..Z...Q.           SCP FREEMAIN                            00.000000
14:08:02.274304  C9  50E89882 0004 56079 0027E9D0 89270058 ..Z.....           SCP RELEASED RSA STORAGE                00.000032
14:08:02.274400  F1  50E91754 4004 56079 0027DFE0 016ED8A0 ......Q.           SCP FREEMAIN                            00.000096
14:08:02.274432  C9  50E89882 0004 56079 0027DFE0 8E270938 ........           SCP RELEASED TEMPSTRG STORAGE           00.000032
14:08:02.274592  F2  50E91754 0104 56079 00000000 00000000 ........  KUPFAOC  PCP LINK                                00.000160
14:08:02.274592  EA  40E906F6 0003 56079 01000300 002799C4 .......D KUPFAOC  TMP PPT LOCATE                          00.000000
14:08:02.274656  EA  40E7F114 0005 56079 01000300 006BEDC8 ....'..H           TMP RETN NORMAL                         00.000064
14:08:02.274656  F1  40E90306 8904 56079 00270050 016ED8A0 ...&..Q.           SCP GETMAIN                             00.000000
14:08:02.274784  C8  50E89802 0004 56079 0027F000 89270058 ..O.....           SCP ACQUIRED RSA STORAGE                00.000128
14:08:02.274816  F1  60E913B6 8C04 56079 00270260 016ED8A0 ....-.Q.           SCP GETMAIN                             00.000032
14:08:02.274848  C8  50E89802 0004 56079 0027F060 8C270268 ..O-....           SCP ACQUIRED USER STORAGE               00.000032
14:08:02.274880  F1  50E91754 CC04 56079 00000064 016ED8A0 ......Q.           SCP GETMAIN INITIMG                     00.000032
14:08:02.274880  C8  50E89802 0004 56079 0027F2D0 8C000078 ..2.....           SCP ACQUIRED USER STORAGE               00.000000
14:08:02.274912  F7  50E91754 8003 56079 00C1D7C4 D6C34040 .APDOC              TSP APPL REQ GET                        00.000032
14:08:02.275456  F0  50E7898C C004 56079 43000000 005993BC ........           KCP WAIT+CANCADDR DCI=IOEVENT           00.000544
14:08:02.275488  D5  00EB4026 0104 56079 E7D2C3D9 C5D84040 XKCREQ   TIXKCREQ  UEH BEFORE                              00.000032
14:08:02.275488  D5  00EB4026 0204 56079 00000000 001A39A0 ........ TIXKCREQ  UEH AFTER                               00.000000
14:08:02.277728  F9  50EC3CB0 0103 56054 01018001 001F8E60 .......-           JCP WRITE                               00.002240
14:08:02.277792  F9  406EA2E2 84E5 56054 00000000 001A39A0 ........           JCP RETN                                00.000064
14:08:02.277792  F5  40EC1A18 0015 56054 00000000 001A39A0 ........           FCP RETN NORMAL                         00.000000
14:08:02.278592  F5  405348A2 4003 56054 00000000 00000000 ........ VAOCCUR   FCP PUT                                 00.000800
14:08:02.278624  F9  60EC3CCE 0203 56054 01008002 001F8E60 .......-           JCP WAIT                                00.000032
14:08:02.278944  F0  606E99A2 0804 56054 001A6140 FF00D1D1 ../...JJ           KCP RESUME                              00.000320
14:08:02.278976  F0  406E96D0 4004 56054 88000000 006E8C64 ........           KCP WAIT DCI=CICS                       00.000032
14:08:02.279008  D5  00EB4026 0104 56054 E7D2C3D9 C5D84040 XKCREQ   TIXKCREQ  UEH BEFORE                              00.000032
14:08:02.279008  D5  00EB4026 0204 56054 00000000 001A39A0 ........ TIXKCREQ  UEH AFTER                               00.000000
14:08:02.279040  F0  406E9E62 4004 JJJ   43000000 006E8C74 ........           KCP WAIT DCI=IOEVENT                    00.000032
14:08:02.279072  D5  00EB4026 0104 JJJ   E7D2C3D9 C5D84040 XKCREQ   TIXKCREQ  UEH BEFORE                              00.000032
14:08:02.279072  D5  00EB4026 0204 JJJ   00000000 001A39A0 ........ TIXKCREQ  UEH AFTER                               00.000000
14:08:02.283712  F1  40E757FC AE04 56079 00270645 016ED8A0 ......Q.           SCP GETMAIN CONDITIONAL                 00.004640
14:08:02.283776  C8  50E89802 0004 56079 0027F350 8E270658 ..3&....           SCP ACQUIRED TEMPSTRG STORAGE           00.000064
14:08:02.283840  F7  40E75D68 0005 56079 0027F350 8E270658 ..3&....           TSP RETN APPL RESP NORMAL               00.000064
```

```
CUSTOMER INFORMATION CONTROL SYSTEM STORAGE DUMP   CODE=ASRA   TASK=A010       DATE=09/23/88   TIME=14:08:02   PAGE   22

 TIME OF DAY    ID  REG 14   REQD TASK   FIELD A  FIELD B  CHARS     RESOURCE  TRACE TYPE                                INTERVAL

14:08:02.283872 F1 50E91754 4004 56079 0027F2D0 016ED8A0 ..2...Q.            SCP FREEMAIN                               00.000032
14:08:02.283872 C9 50E89882 0004 56079 0027F2D0 8C000078 ..2.....            SCP RELEASED USER STORAGE                  00.000000
14:08:02.283904 F2 50E91754 1004 56079 00000000 00000000 ........ KUPFAOC    PCP RETURN                                 00.000032
14:08:02.283936 F1 60E90A4E 4004 56079 0027F060 016ED8A0 ..0-..Q.            SCP FREEMAIN                               00.000032
14:08:02.283936 C9 50E89882 0004 56079 0027F060 8C270268 ..0-....            SCP RELEASED USER STORAGE                  00.000000
14:08:02.283968 F1 60E9075E 4004 56079 0027F000 016ED8A0 ..0...Q.            SCP FREEMAIN                               00.000032

14:08:02.283968 C9 50E89882 0004 56079 0027F000 89270058 ..0.....            SCP RELEASED RSA STORAGE                   00.000000
14:08:02.284288 F2 80E8B6E0 6004 56079 C1E2D9C1 00000000 ASRA....            PCP ABEND                                  00.000320
14:08:02.284320 F1 40E8F80A CC04 56079 000000A0 016ED8A0 ......Q.            SCP GETMAIN INITIMG                        00.000032
14:08:02.284352 C8 50E89802 0004 56079 0027F9B0 8C0000A8 ..9.....            SCP ACQUIRED USER STORAGE                  00.000032
14:08:02.284352 F4 50E8F9E2 FE04 56079 00000000 C1E2D9C1 ....ASRA            DCP TRANSACTION                            00.000000
14:08:02.297920 F0 40F1506C 4004 56079 80000000 0068FD5C .......*            KCP WAIT DCI=SINGLE                       *00.013568
14:08:02.297952 D5 00EB4026 0104 56079 E7D2C3D9 C5D84040 XKCREQ   TIXKCREQ   UEH BEFORE                                 00.000032
14:08:02.297952 D5 00EB4026 0204 56079 00000000 001A39A0 ........ TIXKCREQ   UEH AFTER                                  00.000000
14:08:02.299680 F0 406E99E8 0404 JJJ   10000000 00000000 ........            KCP SUSPEND NON-DISPATCHABLE               00.001728
14:08:02.299712 D5 00EB4026 0104 JJJ   E7D2C3D9 C5D84040 XKCREQ   TIXKCREQ   UEH BEFORE                                 00.000032
14:08:02.299712 D5 00EB4026 0204 JJJ   00000000 001A39A0 ........ TIXKCREQ   UEH AFTER                                  00.000000
14:08:02.299776 F9 406EA2E2 40E5 56054 00000000 001A39A0 ........            JCP RETN GETF                              00.000064
14:08:02.299776 F9 40EC3CEC 0303 56054 04018003 001F8E60 ........            JCP PUT                                    00.000000
14:08:02.300096 F0 606E99A2 0804 56054 001A8140 FF00D1D1 ......JJ            KCP RESUME                                 00.000320
14:08:02.300128 F0 406E96D0 4004 56054 88000000 006E8C68 ........            KCP WAIT DCI=CICS                          00.000032
14:08:02.300160 D5 00EB4026 0104 56054 E7D2C3D9 C5D84040 XKCREQ   TIXKCREQ   UEH BEFORE                                 00.000032
14:08:02.300160 D5 00EB4026 0204 56054 00000000 001A39A0 ........ TIXKCREQ   UEH AFTER                                  00.000000
14:08:02.300192 F0 406E9E62 4004 JJJ   43000000 006E8E34 ........            KCP WAIT DCI=IOEVENT                       00.000032
14:08:02.300224 D5 00EB4026 0104 JJJ   E7D2C3D9 C5D84040 XKCREQ   TIXKCREQ   UEH BEFORE                                 00.000032
14:08:02.300224 D5 00EB4026 0204 JJJ   00000000 001A39A0 ........ TIXKCREQ   UEH AFTER                                  00.000000
14:08:02.319904 F0 406E99E8 0404 JJJ   10000000 00000000 ........            KCP SUSPEND NON-DISPATCHABLE              *00.019680
14:08:02.319904 D5 00EB4026 0104 JJJ   E7D2C3D9 C5D84040 XKCREQ   TIXKCREQ   UEH BEFORE                                 00.000000
14:08:02.319936 D5 00EB4026 0204 JJJ   00000000 001A39A0 ........ TIXKCREQ   UEH AFTER                                  00.000032
14:08:02.319968 F9 406EA2E2 40E5 56054 00000000 001A39A0 ........            JCP RETN GETF                              00.000032
14:08:02.320576 F0 40EC159E 4004 56054 43000000 001DCEF0 .......0            KCP WAIT DCI=IOEVENT                       00.000608
14:08:02.320608 D5 00EB4026 0104 56054 E7D2C3D9 C5D84040 XKCREQ   TIXKCREQ   UEH BEFORE                                 00.000032
14:08:02.320608 D5 00EB4026 0204 56054 00000000 001A39A0 ........ TIXKCREQ   UEH AFTER                                  00.000000

TRANSACTION STORAGE -USER                ADDRESS 0027F9B0 TO 0027FA5F    LENGTH 0000B0

00000000   8C0000A8 0027F350 00000000 00001840  C4C6C8E3 C1C3C240 80600000 C1E2D9C1   *...y..3........ DFHTACB .-..ASRA*   0027F9B0
00000020   D2C1F2F2 F5D6C340 00000000 00000000  00000000 00000000 00000000 00000000   *KA2250C .......................*   0027F9D0
00000040   00000000 00000000 D9C5C7E2 50D7E2E6  003BFD86 003BF064 003BF0B0 00000005   *........REGS.PSW...f..0...0.....*   0027F9F0
00000060   0027E0E3 503C047C 003BD0A8 003BD447  003BD448 003C0432 003BD008 003BD008   *...T.......y..M...M.............*   0027FA10
00000080   00279940 0074CEE0 001B280C 003BF164  078D1000 003BF0C0 00060007 00000000   *..r ...........1.......0........*   0027FA30
000000A0   00000000 00000000 8C0000A8 0027F350                                        *...........y..3.               *   0027FA50

TRANSACTION STORAGE -TS                  ADDRESS 0027F350 TO 0027F9AF    LENGTH 000660

00000000   8E270658 0027DBE0 06450000 C1D7C4D6  C3404005 32377C00 1E000600 0B000E00   *..........APDOC   ............*   0027F350
00000020   00D4C5C4 4040D4C5 C4C9C3C9 D5C54040  40404040 40404040 40404040 404040E2   *.MED  MEDICINE               S*   0027F370
00000040   E4D94040 E2E4D9C7 C5D9E840 40404040  40404040 40404040 40404040 40C4C5D5   *UR  SURGERY               DEN*   0027F390
00000060   4040C4C5 D5E3C9E2 E3D9E840 40404040  40404040 40404040 404040D6 C2404040   *  DENTISTRY              OB   *   0027F3B0
00000080   D6C2E2E3 C5E3D9C9 C3E24050 40C7E8D5  C5C3D6D3 D6C7E840 40D6D9E3 4040D6D9   *OBSTETRICS . GYNECOLOGY  ORT  OR*   0027F3D0
000000A0   E3C8D6D7 C5C4C9C3 E2404040 40404040  40404040 404040D7 E2E84040 D7E2E8C3   *THOPEDICS             PSY  PSYC*   0027F3F0
000000C0   C8C9C1E3 D9E84050 40D5C5E4 D9D6D3D6  C7E84040 40D7C5C4 4040D7C5 C4C9C1E3   *HIATRY . NEUROLOGY   PED  PEDIAT*   0027F410
000000E0   D9C9C3E2 40404040 40404040 40404040  404040E4 D9D64040 E4D9D6D3 D6C7E840   *RICS                URO  UROLOGY *   0027F430
```

```
CUSTOMER INFORMATION CONTROL SYSTEM STORAGE DUMP   CODE=ASRA   TASK=A010      DATE=09/23/88   TIME=14:08:02   PAGE   24

TRANSACTION STORAGE -USER              ADDRESS 0027D860 TO 0027DBDF    LENGTH 000380

00000000   8C270378 0027D800 00000000 00000000  00300000 00692DB8 00000000 503BEF96   *....Q..........................o*   0027D860
00000020   00E9154C 003BFE50 00000000 003BEF06  00000005 0027E0E3 503C047C 003BD0A8   *.Z.....................T.......y*   0027D880
00000040   003BD447 003BD448 003C0432 003BD008  003BD008 003BD5A0 2002204B 00000000   *..M..M..................N.......*   0027D8A0
00000060   00000000 003BDB0A 00000000 154C0000  00000000 00000000 00000000 503C0418   *................................*   0027D8C0
00000080   0059A37A 803C03C4 0000002F 00006688  003BD5B4 00000004 00692DB8 00272000   *..t...D.......h..N..............*   0027D8E0
000000A0   803C03C4 803BD014 003C0432 003BD008  003BD008 003BD5A0 00000000 00000000   *...D..................N.........*   0027D900
000000C0   00000000 00000000 8059A49E 00000000  00000000 00000000 00000000 00000000   *..........u.....................*   0027D920
000000E0   00000000 00000000 00000000 00000000  00000000 00000000 00000000 00000000   *................................*   0027D940
00000100   LINES TO 000001A0 SAME AS ABOVE                                                                                 0027D960
000001C0   003BD008 00000000 00006688 E2E8E2D6  E4E34040 E300000C 003BD090 00000000   *..........hSYSOUT  T...........*   0027DA20
000001E0   00000000 00000000 00000000 00000000  00000000 00000000 00000000 00000000   *................................*   0027DA40
00000200   00000000 00000000 00000000 00000000  003BD0A8 00000000 00000000 00C9699F   *..................y.........I...*   0027DA60
00000220   00000000 00000000 00000000 00000000  00000000 00000000 0027DA98 0074CEE0   *..........................q.....*   0027DA80
00000240   00000000 00279940 016ED8A0 001B280C  00000000 0027A46C 0027B99C 0027DFEC   *......r..Q...........u..........*   0027DAA0
00000260   0027F35C 0027DBE0 00000000 00000000  00000000 01880913 091E0294 022200AE   *..3*..................h....m....*   0027DAC0
00000280   017900A2 03840636 0641001E 011E016C  00000000 0027E18B 0027E41F 0027E641   *...s.d......................U..W.*   0027DAE0
000002A0   0027E6EF 0027E868 0027F6F5 0027F713  0027F831 0027F99D 0027E0E3 003BFFB8   *..W...Y...65..7...8...9...T.....*   0027DB00
000002C0   003C0006 003BF9FE 003BFAA4 003BFE50  00000000 003BFD86 00000000 00000000   *.......9....u.........f.........*   0027DB20
000002E0   003BFA4E 003BFAF4 00000000 003BFEA0  00000000 003BFFB8 003BFFB8 00000000   *...+...4........................*   0027DB40
00000300   003C0006 00000000 003BF9FE 00000000  003BFAA4 00000000 003BFE50 00000000   *.........9............u.........*   0027DB60
00000320   003BF958 00000000 003BFD86 00000000  003BFF78 00000000 003BF9A8 00000000   *..9.........f...............9y..*   0027DB80
00000340   003BFA4E 00000000 003BFAF4 00000000  003BFDFA 00000000 003BFEA0 00000000   *...+.......4....................*   0027DBA0
00000360   00000000 00000000 00000000 00000000  00000000 00000000 8C270378 0027D800   *..............................Q.*   0027DBC0

TRANSACTION STORAGE -RSA               ADDRESS 0027D800 TO 0027D85F    LENGTH 000060

00000000   891B0058 0027BE80 00000000 FE6BB2C8  00000000 0027A050 0027A040 00000000   *i.............,.H...........p...*   0027D800
00000020   50E91754 00E9154C 00000000 00000000  005297B7 00000040 005297BF 5052E420   *.Z...Z..........p.......p...U.*   0027D820
00000040   00279800 0052A11F 0052A120 0052E3D6  00529310 0027A050 891B0058 0027BE80   *..q...........TO..l......i......*   0027D840

TRANSACTION STORAGE -USER              ADDRESS 0027BE80 TO 0027BF3F    LENGTH 0000C0

00000000   8C0000B8 0027BB70 C4C6C8E3 E3D7C4E2  D4D40000 00000000 00010001 00010000   *........DFHTTPDSMM..............*   0027BE80
00000020   00000000 00000000 00000000 003C4808  00000000 00000000 FFFFFFFF 00000000   *................................*   0027BEA0
00000040   00000000 D2C1C5D7 F1D7C340 00000000  00000000 00000000 18500000 40000001   *....KAEP1PC ....................*   0027BEC0
00000060   01015000 00000000 07800000 00000000  00000000 00000000 00000000 00000000   *................................*   0027BEE0
00000080   00000000 00000000 00000000 00000000  00000000 016ED8A0 00404000 00000000   *.......................Q.. .....*   0027BF00
000000A0   00000000 00000000 FFFFFFFF 00000000  00000000 00000000 8C0000B8 0027BB70   *................................*   0027BF20

TRANSACTION STORAGE -USER              ADDRESS 0027BB70 TO 0027BE7F    LENGTH 000310

00000000   8C000308 0027B990 C4C6C8D6 E2D7E6C1  40EA963E 00DD7320 40EAB308 00E96022   *........DFHOSPWA .o..... ....Z-.*   0027BB70
00000020   00000000 00000000 00000000 00000000  00000000 00000000 00000000 00000000   *................................*   0027BB90
00000040   00000000 00000000 00000000 00000000  00000525 00000000 C5D4D740 00000000   *.........................EMP ....*   0027BBB0
00000060   D2C1C5D9 C7D7C340 D2C1C5D7 F1D7C340  40401754 0040404C 00000000 00000000   *KAERGPC KAEP1PC   ... ..........*   0027BBD0
00000080   00529797 00000020 0052979F 00000000  00000000 00000000 00000000 00000000   *..pp.....p......................*   0027BBF0
000000A0   00000000 00000000 0027BE80 0027BE80  00000000 00000000 00000000 00000000   *................................*   0027BC10
000000C0   00000000 006ED8AC 00000000 00000000  00000000 00000000 00000000 00000000   *.....Q..........................*   0027BC30
000000E0   00000000 00000000 1C6BB2C8 00004040  00000001 00000000 00000000 00000000   *..........,.H..  ...............*   0027BC50
00000100   00000000 00100000 00000000 00000000  00000000 00000000 00000000 00000000   *................................*   0027BC70
00000120   00000000 00000000 00000000 00000000  00000000 00000000 00000000 00000000   *................................*   0027BC90
00000140   00000000 00000000 00000000 00000000  00000000 00000000 A0EAA0D8 70EAB0A2   *..........................Q...s*   0027BCB0
```

```
CUSTOMER INFORMATION CONTROL SYSTEM STORAGE DUMP    CODE=ASRA    TASK=A010       DATE=09/23/88   TIME=14:08:02   PAGE   30

TERMINAL STORAGE                              ADDRESS 001B3B40 TO 001B3E0F    LENGTH 0002D0

00000000    850002C8 001AF240 02AD0000 00000000  00000000 00000000 00000000 00000000   *e..H..2 ........................*   001B3B40
00000020    00000000 00000000 0000F000 00000000  00000000 00000000 00000000 00000000   *..........O.....................*   001B3B60
00000040    00000000 00000000 00000000 00000000  00000000 00000000 00000000 00000000   *................................*   001B3B80
00000060    LINES TO 000000E0 SAME AS ABOVE                                                                                  001B3BA0
00000100    00000000 00000000 00000000 00000000  00000000 00000000 0000F000 00000000   *..........................O.....*   001B3C40
00000120    00000000 0600D5D6 D5C54040 0000F000  000000FF FF00D9C5 E3C9D9C5 C4404040   *......NONE  ..O.......RETIRED   *   001B3C60
00000140    40404040 40404040 40404040 40404000  00F00000 00000000 00000000 00000000   *               ..O..............*   001B3C80
00000160    00000000 00000000 00000000 00000000  00000000 00F00000 00000000 00000000   *.....................O..........*   001B3CA0
00000180    00000000 00000000 00000000 00000000  00000000 00000000 00000000 00F00000   *.............................O..*   001B3CC0
000001A0    00000000 00000000 00000000 00000000  00000000 00000000 00000000 00000000   *................................*   001B3CE0
000001C0    000000F0 00000000 00000000 00000000  00000000 00000000 00000000 00000000   *...O............................*   001B3D00
000001E0    000000F0 00000000 00000000 00F00000  00000000 00000000 00000000 00000000   *...O.........O..................*   001B3D20
00000200    F0000000 00000000 00000000 00000000  00000000 00000000 00000000 F0000040   *O...........................O.. *   001B3D40
00000220    00000000 00000000 00F00000 00000000  00000000 00000000 00000000 00000000   *.........O......................*   001B3D60
00000240    00000000 00000000 F0000000 00000000  00000000 0000F000 00000000 00000000   *........O.............O.........*   001B3D80
00000260    00000000 00000000 00000000 00000000  F0000000 00000000 00000300 C3C1E300   *................O...........CAT.*   001B3DA0
00000280    00F00000 00000000 00000000 00000000  00000000 00000000 00000000 00000000   *.O..............................*   001B3DC0
000002A0    00000000 00000000 00000000 00F00000  00000000 00000000 00000000 00000000   *.............O..................*   001B3DE0
000002C0    00000000 00000000 850002C8 001AF240                                        *........e..H..2                 *   001B3E00

TERMINAL STORAGE                              ADDRESS 001AF240 TO 001AF35F    LENGTH 000120

00000000    851B0118 006ED8A4 00E8DFF0 11C7E9D5  D6D5C540 4011C7F5 D9C5E3C9 D9C5C440   *e.....Qu.Y.O.GZNONE  .G5RETIRED *   001AF240
00000020    40404040 40404040 40404040 40404040  40114CE9 C3C1E311 4FD2C4C9 C1C2C5E3   *                 ..ZCAT..KDIABET*   001AF260
00000040    C9C36BD7 D6E2E340 C3E5C16B 40D34BC5  C1D940C9 E240C2D3 C5C5C4C9 D5C74040   *IC,POST CVA, L.EAR IS BLEEDING  *   001AF280
00000060    40404040 40404040 40404040 40404040  11505CF0 F911505F F2F31150 E2F8F811   *                ..*09...23..S88.*   001AF2A0
00000080    506CF0F2 11506FF0 F71150F2 D711D4D2  5CF9F6F9 F911D47D F111D54C F711D5E2   *..02...07..2P.MK*9699.M'1.N.7.NS*   001AF2C0
000000A0    C311D6F2 F0F911D6 F5F2F311 D6F8F8F8  11D7C3F0 F211D7C6 F0F711D7 C9D7115A   *C.0209.0523.0888.PC02.PF07.PIP..*   001AF2E0
000000C0    5DD5D6D5 C5404040 40404040 40404040  40404040 40404040 4040115B E7E6C1D3   *)NONE                    .$XWAL*   001AF300
000000E0    D2C5C440 40404040 40404040 40404040  40404040 00000000 00000000 00000000   *KED                 ............*   001AF320
00000100    00000000 00000000 00000000 00000000  00000000 00000000 851B0118 006ED8A4   *........................e.....Qu*   001AF340

PROGRAM STORAGE                               ADDRESS 003BD008 TO 003C04BF    LENGTH 0034B8

00000000    90ECD00C 185D05F0 4580F010 D2C1F2F2  F5D6C340 E5E2D9F1 0700989F F02407FF   *.....).O..O.KA225OC VSR1..q.O...*   003BD008
00000020    96021034 07FE41F0 000107FE 003C0432  003BD008 003BD008 003BD5A0 0027D870   *o......O..................N...Q.*   003BD028
00000040    003BDB0A 003C037C 00000000 503C0498  00006688 003BD5B4 003BFEA0 503C047C   *.................q...h..N.......*   003BD048
00000060    003BD0A8 003BD447 003BD448 003C0432  003BD008 003BD008 003BD5A0 0027D870   *...y..M...M...............N...Q.*   003BD068
00000080    00E91360 003BD468 F1F04BF4 F34BF0F7  C6C5C240 F1F76B40 F1F9F8F8 00000000   *.Z.-..M.10.43.07FEB 17, 1988....*   003BD088
000000A0    D4C5C4C9 D7C1C340 6040C3D6 D7E8D9C9  C7C8E340 D4C5C4C9 C6D3C5E7 40E2E8E2   *MEDIPAC - COPYRIGHT MEDIFLEX SYS*   003BD0A8
000000C0    E3C5D4E2 40C3D6D9 D74B4040 6040F1F9  F8F10000 00000000 004C0025 00110256   *TEMS CORP.  - 1981..............*   003BD0C8
000000E0    05040084 07380DCB 02D0016C 01CD0AFC  00680036 003601E0 00400000 00000000   *...d............................*   003BD0E8
00000100    000C0050 00100014 0008000C 0008000C  000C0060 00880000 1915F040 5060C84C   *.....................-.h...O.-H.*   003BD108
00000120    C161F1F8 80FF2842 4341C0C1 003FFFFF  F1F2F3F4 F5F6F7FF FFF1F2F4 0402064D   *A/18.......A....1234567..124...(*   003BD128
00000140    C9D1D95D E86C0105 03077C00 00000000  C1C9D5C4 E2E3D7E3 C4C5E2C3 5BE3D9D4   *IJR)Y...........AINDSTPTDESC$TRM*   003BD148
00000160    E3C1C2E2 E3D9D4E3 C2D7E3C4 C5D4D6D7  E3C3D5E3 E8D7E3C5 D4D740E4 D5C3E3D9   *TABSTRMTBPTDEMOPTCNTYPTEMP UNCTR*   003BD168
00000180    D3C1C3C3 D4C9C6C8 E2D7E2D9 E5C1C4E3  C3D6D5C1 C4E3C540 40C9D5C6 C4E2D7D7   *LACCMIFHSPSRVADTCONADTE  INFDSPP*   003BD188
000001A0    C2F0F140 40D7C2F0 F24040D7 C2F0F340  40D7C2F0 F44040D7 C2F0F540 40D7C2F0   *B01  PB02  PB03  PB04  PB05  PBO*   003BD1A8
000001C0    F64040D7 C2F0F740 40D7C2F1 F64040C9  E2F0F140 40D6D7E2 C5C340D7 D4C6D5C3   *6  PB07  PB16  IS01  OPSEC PMFNC*   003BD1C8
000001E0    E2D4D4C6 D5C3E2D6 D5C6D3C5 40D7C4D6  C34040D7 C2F3F840 40D4D9C6 D5C3E2D4   *SMMFNCSONFLE PDOC  PB38  MRFNCSM*   003BD1E8
00000200    D9F0F140 40D4D9F0 F24040D4 D9F0F340  40D4D9F0 F44040D4 D9F0F540 40D4D9F0   *R01  MR02  MR03  MR04  MR05  MRO*   003BD208
00000220    F64040D4 D9F0F740 40D4D9F0 F84040D4  D9F0F940 40000000 00300000 00692DB8   *6  MR07  MR08  MR09  ...........*   003BD228
00000240    00000000 00000000 00000000 00000000  00000000 00000000 00000000 00000000   *................................*   003BD248
```

```
CUSTOMER INFORMATION CONTROL SYSTEM STORAGE DUMP   CODE=ASRA   TASK=A010       DATE=09/23/88   TIME=14:08:02   PAGE   31

PROGRAM STORAGE                                  ADDRESS 003BD008 TO 003C04BF    LENGTH 0034B8

00000260    00000000 00000000 00000000 00000000  00000000 00000000 00000000 00000000  *................................*  003BD268
00000280    2002204B 00000000 00000000 003BDB0A  00000000 00000000 00000000 00000000  *................................*  003BD288
000002A0    00000000 503C0418 0059A37A 803C03C4  0000002F 00006688 003BD5B4 00000004  *..........t...D.......h..N......*  003BD2A8
000002C0    00692DB8 00272000 803C03C4 803BD014  003C0432 003BD008 003BD008 003BD5A0  *..........D..................N..*  003BD2C8
000002E0    00000000 00000000 00000000 00000000  8059A49E 00000000 00000000 00000000  *...................u............*  003BD2E8
00000300    00000000 00000000 00000000 00000000  00000000 00000000 00000000 00000000  *................................*  003BD308
00000320    LINES TO 000003C0 SAME AS ABOVE                                                                                    003BD328
000003E0    00000000 00000000 003BD008 00000000  00006688 E2E8E2D6 E4E34040 E300000C  *...................hSYSOUT  T...*  003BD3E8
00000400    003BD090 00000000 00000000 00000000  00000000 00000000 00000000 00000000  *................................*  003BD408
00000420    00000000 00000000 00000000 00000000  00000000 00000000 003BD0A8 00000000  *............................y...*  003BD428
00000440    00000000 00000000 00000000 00000000  00000000 00000000 00000000 00000000  *................................*  003BD448
00000460    LINES TO 00000500 SAME AS ABOVE                                                                                    003BD468
00000520    003BFFB8 00000000 003C0006 00000000  003BF9FE 00000000 003BFAA4 00000000  *...................9.......u....*  003BD528
00000540    003BFE50 00000000 003BF958 00000000  003BFD86 00000000 003BFF78 00000000  *..........9.......f.............*  003BD548
00000560    003BF9A8 00000000 003BFA4E 00000000  003BFAF4 00000000 003BFDFA 00000000  *..9y.......+.......4.............*  003BD568
00000580    003BFEA0 00000000 00000000 00000000  00000000 00000000 000061BA 00E9154C  *........................../..Z..*  003BD588
000005A0    0000B852 0000B64A 000061BE C9D3C2D6  E2D9E5F0 C9D3C2D6 E6E3C2F0 C9D3C2D6  *........../.ILBOSRVOILBOWTBOILBO*  003BD5A8
000005C0    C4E3C5F0 C9D3C2D6 E2D9E5F1 003BDC7E  003BEF44 003BF00C 003BF232 003BF6CC  *DTEOILBOSRV1...=......0...2...6.*  003BD5C8
000005E0    003BF902 003BF958 003BF9A2 003BF9A8  003BF9FE 003BFA48 003BFA4E 003BFAA4  *..9...9...9s..9y..9........+...u*  003BD5E8
00000600    003BFAEE 003BFAF4 003BFC88 003BFD44  003BFD80 003BFD86 003BFDF4 003BFDFA  *.......4...h..........f...4.....*  003BD608
00000620    003BFE50 003BFE9A 003BFEA0 003BFF72  003BFF78 003BFFB8 003C0000 003C0006  *................................*  003BD628
00000640    003C0040 003C01D2 003C0324 003C032C  003C0334 003C033C 003C0344 003C034C  *.......K........................*  003BD648
00000660    003C0354 003C035C 003C0364 003C036C  003C0374 003BDB8C 003BDBCE 003BDD14  *.......*........................*  003BD668
00000680    003BDD0E 003BDD38 003BDD70 003BDD6A  003BDE00 003BDDC8 003BDDB0 003BDDF8  *......................H........8*  003BD688
000006A0    003BDE76 003BDEA2 003BDED4 003BDECC  003BDEFC 003BDF7A 003BDF42 003BDF9A  *.......s...M....................*  003BD6A8
000006C0    003BDFBA 003BDFDA 003BE040 003BE01C  003BE0B8 003BE032 003BE056 003BE092  *...............................k*  003BD6C8
000006E0    003BE0B0 003BE12E 003BE16C 003BE1FC  003BE1BC 003BE21C 003BE23C 003BE2A2  *......................S...S...Ss*  003BD6E8
00000700    003BE27E 003BE33C 003BE294 003BE2E6  003BE316 003BE308 003BE3B2 003BE3EA  *..S=..T...Sm..SW..T...T...T...T.*  003BD708
00000720    003BE3E4 003BE40E 003BE442 003BE43C  003BE4CE 003BE496 003BE482 003BE4C6  *..TU..U...U...U...U...Uo..Ub..UF*  003BD728
00000740    003BE53C 003BE560 003BE598 003BE592  003BE5BC 003BE5F0 003BE5EA 003BE67C  *..V...V-..Vq..Vk..V...VO..V...W.*  003BD748
00000760    003BE644 003BE630 003BE674 003BE6EA  003BE70E 003BE746 003BE740 003BE76A  *..W...W...W...W...X...X...X...X.*  003BD768
00000780    003BE79E 003BE798 003BE82A 003BE7F2  003BE7DE 003BE822 003BE898 003BE8BC  *..X...Xq..Y...X2..X...Y...Yq..Y.*  003BD788
000007A0    003BE8F4 003BE8EE 003BE918 003BE94C  003BE946 003BE9D8 003BE9A0 003BE98C  *..Y4..Y...Z...Z...Z...ZQ..Z...Z.*  003BD7A8
000007C0    003BE9D0 003BEA46 003BEA6A 003BEA96  003BEB0E 003BEABE 003BEAE8 003BEB2E  *..Z............o............Y...*  003BD7C8
000007E0    003BEB08 003BEB26 003BEB92 003BEBBE  003BEC36 003BEBE6 003BEC10 003BEC56  *..........k..........W..........*  003BD7E8
00000800    003BEC30 003BEC4E 003BECBA 003BECE6  003BED68 003BED0E 003BED42 003BED88  *.......+.......W...............h*  003BD808
00000820    003BED62 003BED80 003BEDEC 003BEE0A  003BEE1C 003BEE8E 003BEE44 003BEE6E  *................................*  003BD828
00000840    003BEEF2 003BEF06 003BEF5C 003BF03C  003BF164 003BF064 003BF0B0 003BF17C  *...2.......*..0...1...0...0...1.*  003BD848
00000860    003BF0EA 003BF132 003BF15E 003BF1E0  003BF1F4 003BF252 003BF2C2 003BF282  *..0...1...1;..1...14..2...2B..2b*  003BD868
00000880    003BF2A6 003BF2E4 003BF348 003BF3F0  003BF41E 003BF4AE 003BF454 003BF48C  *..2w..2U..3...30..4...4...4...4.*  003BD888
000008A0    003BF49A 003BF4C6 003BF530 003BF5A2  003BF608 003BF60E 003BF668 003BF694  *..4...4F..5...5s..6...6...6...6m*  003BD8A8
000008C0    003BF6F4 003BF730 003BF75E 003BF7E8  003BF7AE 003BF7BC 003BF800 003BF816  *..64..7...7;..7Y..7...7...8...8.*  003BD8C8
000008E0    003BF81E 003BF882 003BF89A 003BF920  003BF94A 003BF9C6 003BF9F0 003BFA6C  *..8...8b..8...9...9...9F..90....*  003BD8E8
00000900    003BFA96 003BFB16 003BFB58 003BFBBC  003BFBC2 003BFC28 003BFC3C 003BFCD8  *...o................B..........Q*  003BD908
00000920    003BFD28 003BFDAE 003BFDEE 003BFE18  003BFE42 003BFEC4 003BFF18 003BFF4A  *......................D.........*  003BD928
00000940    003BFF34 003BFF3A 003BFF6A 003BFFD8  003BFFF8 003BDDE2 003BE4B0 003BE65E  *..............Q...8...S...U...W;*  003BD948
00000960    003BE80C 003BE9BA 003BF106 003C0078  003C006C 003BD008 003C00B8 003C00AC  *..Y...Z...1.....................*  003BD968
00000980    003BD008 003C00F8 003C00EC 003BD008  003C0138 003C012C 003BD008 003C0178  *.......8........................*  003BD988
000009A0    003C016C 003BD008 003C01B8 003C01AC  003C020A 003C01FE 003BD008 003C024A  *................................*  003BD9A8
000009C0    003C023E 003BD008 003C028A 003C027E  003BD008 003C02CA 003C02BE 003BD008  *...............=................*  003BD9C8
000009E0    003C030A 003C02FE 003BFFB8 00000000  003C0006 00000000 003BF9FE 00000000  *...........................9....*  003BD9E8
00000A00    003BFAA4 00000000 003BFE50 00000000  003BF958 00000000 003BFD86 00000000  *...u...........9.........f......*  003BDA08
00000A20    003BFF78 00000000 003BF9A8 00000000  003BFA4E 00000000 003BFAF4 00000000  *..........9y.......+.........4...*  003BDA28
00000A40    003BFDFA 00000000 003BFEA0 00000000  CC009600 00000100 00000002 1CFFFF0F  *...................o............*  003BDA48
00000A60    F0F00000 0C99999C 79697C79 698C7969  9C100C01 000C0115 9C01259C 01200C10  *00...rr.........................*  003BDA68
```

```
CUSTOMER INFORMATION CONTROL SYSTEM STORAGE DUMP    CODE=ASRA    TASK=A010        DATE=09/23/88    TIME=14:08:02    PAGE    35

PROGRAM STORAGE                                   ADDRESS 003BD008 TO 003C04BF    LENGTH 0034B8

00001F20    1B119640 D04958F0 C00405EF 94BFD049   40F0D05C 58F0D1B8 50D0F080 58E0D23C   *..o ...O....m... O.*.OJ...O...K.*    003BEF28
00001F40    4830E12E 4930C4BC 58F0C2B0 077F5810   C03C07F1 58E0D234 58F0D244 D200E100   *.......D..OB.........1..K..OK.K..*    003BEF48
00001F60    F00ED205 E101614D D201E080 C4BED206   E084C508 9240E08B 58F0D22C D203E0F8   *O.K.../(K...D.K..dE.k....OK.K..8*    003BEF68
00001F80    F0E81B11 9640D049 58F0C004 05EF94BF   D04940F0 D05C58F0 D1B850D0 F08058E0   *OY..o ...O....m... O.*.OJ...O...*    003BEF88
00001FA0    D22858F0 D234D203 E028F107 58E0D254   92F1E03F 58E0D250 D201E00B E00B5820   *K..OK.K...1...K.k1....K.K.......*    003BEFA8
00001FC0    C0C80522 58E0D250 D201E00D E00D5820   C0CC0522 58E0D250 D201E00F E00F5820   *.H....K.K..............K.K.......*    003BEFC8
00001FE0    C0D00522 58E0D250 D201E011 E0115820   C0D40522 58E0D250 D201E013 E0135820   *......K.K.........M....K.K.......*    003BEFE8
00002000    C0D80522 58E0D254 92F0E00C 5820C2B4   58E0D23C 9500E130 078258E0 D25492F1   *.Q....K.kO....B...K.n....b..K.k1*    003BF008
00002020    E00C58E0 D23C58F0 D244F342 E131F6CD   96F0E135 58E0D23C 4830E12E 4930C4BC   *.....K..OK.3....6.oO....K.......D.*    003BF028
00002040    58F0C2B8 078F5800 D3185000 D2C45800   C2BC5000 D3185810 C06C07F1 5800D2C4   *.OB......L...KD..B...L......1..KD*    003BF048
00002060    5000D318 5820C2C0 58E0D254 95F1E009   077258E0 D23CF274 D208E131 58E0D244   *..L...B...K.n1........K.2.K.....K.*    003BF068

00002080    F822E6CD D20D94F0 E6CF960C E6CF58F0   D254D218 E6D0F012 58E0D23C D218E139   *8.W.K.mOW.o.W..OK.K.W.O...K.K...*    003BF088
000020A0    F0125810 C2C407F1 58E0D23C F274D208   E131F922 D20DC4D0 58F0C2C8 078FF274   *O...BD.1..K.2.K...9.K.D..OBH..2.*    003BF0A8
000020C0    D208E131 F922D20D C4D358F0 C2C8078F   F274D208 E131F922 D20DC4D6 58F0C2CC   *K...9.K.DL.OBH..2.K...9.K.DO.OB.*    003BF0C8
000020E0    077F5810 C3D05820 C2CC58E0 D23C9540   E1390742 0721D517 E13AE139 07D258E0   *....C...B...K.n ......N......K..*    003BF0E8
00002100    D23CF274 D208E131 58E0D244 F822E6CD   D20D94F0 E6CF960C E6CF58F0 D23CD218   *K.2.K.....K.8.W.K.mOW.o.W..OK.K.*    003BF108
00002120    E6D0F139 5810C2C4 07F158E0 D25492F1   E00C5820 C2D058E0 D23C9540 E1310772   *W.1...BD.1..K.k1....B...K.n.....*    003BF128
00002140    D503E132 E1310772 58F0D244 F342E131   F6CD96F0 E1355810 C2C407F1 58E0D244   *N........OK.3....6.oO....BD.1..K.*    003BF148
00002160    F920E6CD C4C758F0 C2C4077F 58E0D254   92F1E00C 5820C2D4 58E0D254 95F1E00C   *9.W.DG.OBD.....K.k1....BM..K.n1..*    003BF168
00002180    077258E0 D23CD200 E11C6083 58E0D248   4140E002 58E0D244 F870D208 E0044F30   *....K.K....-c..K.........K.8.K.....*    003BF188
000021A0    D2085C20 C4C01A43 5B40C4C0 F870D208   C4C4FA21 D20D4000 F8114000 D20E5040   *K.*.D...$ D.8.K.DD..K...8....K...*    003BF1A8
000021C0    D2A892F1 E00658E0 D23CD201 E12EC4C5   58E0D234 92F1E138 5820C2D8 58E0D254   *Kyk1.....K.K....DE...K.k1.....BQ..K.*    003BF1C8
000021E0    95F1E03F 07825810 C04007F1 58E0D228   5830E028 4B30606A 58E0D234 5030E05C   *n1...b.....1..K.........-....K.....**    003BF1E8
00002200    9240E05C 58F0D22C D203E0F8 F0E41B11   9640D049 58F0C004 05EF94BF D04940F0   *k ..*.OK.K...8OU..o ...O....m...O*    003BF208
00002220    D05C58F0 D1B850D0 F08058E0 D25492F0   E00C5820 C2DC58E0 D23C9500 E1B90782   *.*.OJ...O....K.kO.....B...K.n....b*    003BF228
00002240    58E0D244 D201E5DA C4CB58E0 D23C4830   E1B74930 C4BC58F0 C2E0078F 5820C008   *...K.K.V.D....K.........D..OB.......*    003BF248
00002260    DD02E1BA 20005810 C2E40781 58E0D254   92F1E00C 5810C2E0 07F158E0 D23CF272   *..........BU.a..K.k1.....B..1..K.2.*    003BF268
00002280    D208E1BA F911D20E C4D958F0 C2E807DF   58E0D254 92F1E00C 5810C2E0 07F158E0   *K...9.K.DR.OBY.....K.k1.....B...1...*    003BF288
000022A0    D23CF272 D208E1BA 58E0D244 F811E5DA   D20E94F0 E5DB960C E5DB58E0 D244F910   *K.2.K.....K.8.V.K.mOV.o.V...K.9.*    003BF2A8
000022C0    E5DAC4C7 58F0C2EC 07DF5820 C2EC9540   E5D90772 58E0D254 92F1E00C 5820C2F0   *V.DG.OB......B.n VR.....K.k1.....BO*    003BF2C8
000022E0    58E0D254 95F1E00C 077258E0 D23CD200   E1A66083 58E0D248 4140E002 58E0D244   *...K.n1.........K.K...w-c..K.........K.*    003BF2E8
00002300    F870D208 E0044F30 D2085C20 C4C01A43   5B40C4C0 F870D208 C4C4FA21 D20D4000   *8.K.......K.*.D...$ D.8.K.DD..K...*    003BF308
00002320    F8114000 D20E5040 D2A892F1 E00658E0   D23CD201 E1B7C4C5 58E0D234 92F1E138   *8...K... Kyk1....K.K...DE..K.k1..*    003BF328
00002340    58E0D254 92F0E00C 5820C2F4 58E0D248   95E8E116 077258E0 D23C4830 E1D04930   *...K.kO.....B4...K.nY.......K.........*    003BF348
00002360    C4BC58F0 C2F4077F 4830E1D5 4930C4BC   58F0C2F4 077F4830 E1DA4930 C4BC58F0   *D..OB4.......N..D..OB4...........D..O*    003BF368
00002380    C2F4077F 58E0D244 F920E709 C4C758F0   C2F4077F 5820C2F4 D503E000 C5040772   *B4.....K.9.X.DG.OB4.....B4N....E....*    003BF388
000023A0    4100D218 58F0C00C 05EF58E0 D254D207   E037D218 58E0D23C 58F0D254 D201E1D3   *...K...O.........K.K....K....K...OK.K...L*    003BF3A8
000023C0    F03796F0 E1D4D201 E1D8F03A 96F0E1D9   D201E1DD F03D96F0 E1DE58E0 D24458F0   *O.oO.MK...QO.oO.RK....O.oO.......K...O*    003BF3C8
000023E0    D248F822 E709F1BA 58E0D23C 4830E1D0   4930C4BC 58F0C2F8 077F4830 E1D54930   *K.8.X.1....K..........D..OB8.....N...*    003BF3E8
00002400    C4BC58F0 C2F8077F 4830E1DA 4930C4BC   58F0C2FC 078F58E0 D25458F0 D23CD201   *D..OB8...........D..OB......K..OK.K.*    003BF408
00002420    E02FF1D3 D201E031 F1D8D201 E035F1DD   D201E033 C5155800 D3205000 D2C85800   *...1LK....1QK....1.K....E....L....KH...*    003BF428
00002440    C3005000 D3205810 C09007F1 5800D2C8   5000D320 58E0D234 F922E102 C4CD58F0   *C....L...........1..KH...L....K.9....D...O*    003BF448
00002460    C304078F 58F0D248 F922E102 F1BD58F0   C304074F 58F0D248 F922E102 F1BA58F0   *C.....OK.9....1...OC......OK.9....1...O*    003BF468
00002480    C30807DF 58E0D254 92F1E00C 5810C30C   07F158E0 D24458F0 D234F822 E709F102   *C.......K.k1......C...1...K...OK.8.X.1.*    003BF488
000024A0    5810C30C 07F158E0 D244F920 E709C4C7   58F0C30C 077F58E0 D25492F1 E00C5820   *...C...1...K.9.X.DG.OC.........K.k1.....*    003BF4A8
000024C0    C31058E0 D25495F1 E00C0772 58E0D23C   D200E1BF 608358E0 D2484140 E00258E0   *C....K.n1..........K.K.....-c...K..........*    003BF4C8
000024E0    D244F870 D208E004 4F30D208 5C20C4C0   1A435B40 C4C0F870 D208C4C4 FA21D20D   *K.8.K.......K.*.D...$ D.8.K.DD...K..*    003BF4E8
00002500    4000F811 4000D20E 5040D2A8 92F1E006   58E0D23C D201E1D0 C4C558E0 D23492F1   * .8....K... Kyk1.....K.K....DE...K.k1*    003BF508
00002520    E1385810 C31407F1 5820C314 58E0D244   D503E000 C5040772 58F0D248 F922E709   *......C...1...C....K.N....E......OK.9.X.*    003BF528
00002540    F1C058F0 C31407AF 58E0D23C D200E1BF   608358E0 D2484140 E00258E0 D244F870   *1...OC.........K.K.....-c...K.........K.8.*    003BF548
00002560    D208E004 4F30D208 5C20C4C0 1A435B40   C4C0F870 D208C4C4 FA21D20D 4000F811   *K.......K.*.D...$ D.8.K.DD...K....8..*    003BF568
00002580    4000D20E 58E0D23C D201E1D0 C4C55040   D2A858E0 D23492F1 E13858E0 D25492F0   * .K....K.K....DE. Ky...K.k1.......K.kO*    003BF588
000025A0    E00C5820 C31858E0 D24895E8 E1160772   58E0D23C 4830E1E9 4930C4BC 58F0C318   *.....C.....K.nY.........K.....Z...D...OC.*    003BF5A8
000025C0    077F4830 E1EE4930 C4BC58F0 C318077F   4830E1F3 4930C4BC 58F0C318 077F58E0   *...........D...OC...........3...D...OC.......*    003BF5C8
000025E0    D244F920 E70CC4C7 58F0C318 077F5820   C318D503 E000C504 07725810 C31C07F1   *K.9.X.DG.OC.........C.N....E.......C...1*    003BF5E8
```

```
    1      //AUXTRACE JOB 12345,'SYSTEMS',MSGCLASS=H,MSGLEVEL=(1,1)              JOB 7739
    2      //JOBLIB    DD   DSN=CICS161.LOADLIB,DISP=SHR
    3      //          EXEC PGM=DFHTUP,PARM='TERMID=ACCH'
           ***
           *** POSSIBLE CONTROL CARD SUGGESTIONS
           *** PARM='TERMID=????'
           *** PARM='TRANID=????'
           *** PARM='TRANID=????,TERMID=????'
           *** PARM='ALL'
           *** PARM='TASKID=????'
           *** PARM='TIMERG=(HHMMSS-HHMMSS)'
           *** PARM='ALL'
           ***
    4      //DFHAUXT  DD DSN=CICS.AUXTRACE,DISP=SHR
    5      //DFHAXPRT DD SYSOUT=*
ICH70001I SYST002  LAST ACCESS AT 10:44:11 ON MONDAY, SEPTEMBER 26, 1988
IEF236I ALLOC. FOR AUXTRACE
IEF237I 367  ALLOCATED TO JOBLIB
IEF237I 157  ALLOCATED TO SYS04596
IEF237I 145  ALLOCATED TO DFHAUXT
IEF237I JES2 ALLOCATED TO DFHAXPRT
IEF142I AUXTRACE - STEP WAS EXECUTED - COND CODE 0000
IEF285I   CICS161.LOADLIB                              PASSED
IEF285I   VOL SER NOS= TOUSPL.
IEF285I   CATALOG.UCATXS1                              KEPT
IEF285I   VOL SER NOS= TOU020.
IEF285I   CICS.AUXTRACE                                KEPT
IEF285I   VOL SER NOS= TOU002.
```

```
      CUSTOMER INFORMATION CONTROL SYSTEM  -  T R A C E   U T I L I T Y   P R O G R A M          PAGE    1
  SELECTION PARAMETERS:     TERMID=ACCH
AUXILIARY TRACE ACTIVATED AT -  10:41:15.37
  TIME OF DAY    ID  REG 14   REQD TASK   FIELD A  FIELD B  CHARS    RESOURCE  TRACE TYPE                          INTERVAL

10:41:16.214816  D0  50EB57C0 0604 26930  C1C3C3C8 D4C3D6D7 ACCHMCOP           KCP CREATE
10:41:16.215008  D0  50EB66FA 0504 26930  00000000 00000000 ........           KCP DISPATCH                        00.000192
10:41:16.215008  FC  05E5D6E8 0503 26930  00200001 006F56A0 ........           ZCP ZSUP START UP TASK              00.000000
10:41:16.215072  E7  00E5DF1C 0504 26930  00000000 00000000 ........           ERM ENTRY                           00.000064
10:41:16.215072  E7  00E5DF1C 0504 26930  00000000 000000FF ........           ERM RESPONSE                        00.000000
10:41:16.215104  F2  50E5DF4E 8804 26930  00000000 00000000 ........ SECUR005  PCP XCTL-CONDITIONAL                00.000032
10:41:16.215136  EA  40E906F6 0003 26930  01000300 002109C4 .......D SECUR005  TMP PPT LOCATE                      00.000032
10:41:16.215168  EA  40E7F114 0005 26930  01000300 006CA384 ........           TMP RETN NORMAL                     00.000032
10:41:16.215200  F1  50E913B6 8C04 26930  00008F2C 016F56A0 ........           SCP GETMAIN                         00.000032
10:41:16.215424  C8  50E89802 0004 26930  00286000 8C008F38 ..-.....           SCP ACQUIRED USER STORAGE           00.000224
10:41:16.216096  E1  504EB596 0004 26930  0028604C 00000204 ..-.....           EIP HANDLE-CONDITION ENTRY          00.000672
10:41:16.216096  F1  00ED9DB8 CC04 26930  000000F2 016F56A0 ...2....           SCP GETMAIN INITIMG                 00.000000
10:41:16.216160  C8  50E89802 0004 26930  00211250 8C000108 ...&....           SCP ACQUIRED USER STORAGE           00.000064
10:41:16.216192  F1  00ED9DB8 CC04 26930  00000040 016F56A0 ........           SCP GETMAIN INITIMG                 00.000032
10:41:16.216192  C8  50E89802 0004 26930  00211360 8C000048 ...-....           SCP ACQUIRED USER STORAGE           00.000000
10:41:16.216352  E1  504EB596 00F4 26930  00000000 00000204 ........           EIP HANDLE-CONDITION RESPONSE       00.000160
10:41:16.216384  E1  504EB610 0004 26930  0028604C 00000204 ..-.....           EIP HANDLE-CONDITION ENTRY          00.000032
10:41:16.216384  F1  00ED9DB8 CC04 26930  00000040 016F56A0 ........           SCP GETMAIN INITIMG                 00.000000
10:41:16.216416  C8  50E89802 0004 26930  002113B0 8C000048 ........           SCP ACQUIRED USER STORAGE           00.000032
10:41:16.216448  F1  00ED9DB8 CC04 26930  0000012E 016F56A0 ........           SCP GETMAIN INITIMG                 00.000032
10:41:16.216448  C8  50E89802 0004 26930  00211400 8C000138 ........           SCP ACQUIRED USER STORAGE           00.000000
10:41:16.216480  F1  00ED9DB8 4004 26930  00211250 016F56A0 ...&....           SCP FREEMAIN                        00.000032
10:41:16.216512  C9  50E89882 0004 26930  00211250 8C000108 ...&....           SCP RELEASED USER STORAGE           00.000032
10:41:16.216544  E1  504EB610 00F4 26930  00000000 00000204 ........           EIP HANDLE-CONDITION RESPONSE       00.000032
10:41:16.216544  E1  504EB6FC 0004 26930  0028604C 00001204 ..-.....           EIP ENQ ENTRY                       00.000000
10:41:16.216576  F0  00C610E0 0104 26930  08286066 00000000 ..-.....           KCP ENQUEUE                         00.000032
10:41:16.216608  D5  00EB4026 0104 26930  E7D2C3D9 C5D84040 XKCREQ   TIXKCREQ  UEH BEFORE                          00.000032
10:41:16.216608  D5  00EB4026 0204 26930  00000000 001A39A0 ........ TIXKCREQ  UEH AFTER                           00.000000
10:41:16.216640  D0  50EB66FA 0504 26930  00000000 00000000 ........           KCP DISPATCH                        00.000032
10:41:16.216672  E1  504EB6FC 00F4 26930  00000000 00001204 ........           EIP ENQ RESPONSE                    00.000032
10:41:16.216768  E1  504EB77C 0004 26930  0028604C 00000A04 ..-.....           EIP READQ-TS ENTRY                  00.000096
10:41:16.216800  F7  00E7DD8E 8903 26930  E2C9C7D5 E3C1C2D3 SIGNTABL           TSP APPL REQ GETQ                   00.000032
10:41:16.216864  F1  40E757FC AE04 26930  00216CA8 016F56A0 ........           SCP GETMAIN CONDITIONAL             00.000064
10:41:16.217088  C8  50E89802 0004 26930  0028EF40 8E216CB8 ... ....           SCP ACQUIRED TEMPSTRG STORAGE       00.000224
10:41:16.217696  F7  40E75D68 0005 26930  0028EF40 8E216CB8 ... ....           TSP RETN APPL RESP NORMAL           00.000608
10:41:16.218112  F1  00ED9DB8 4004 26930  0028EF40 016F56A0 ... ....           SCP FREEMAIN                        00.000416
10:41:16.218144  C9  50E89882 0004 26930  0028EF40 8E216CB8 ... ....           SCP RELEASED TEMPSTRG STORAGE       00.000032
10:41:16.218464  E1  504EB77C 00F4 26930  00000000 00000A04 ........           EIP READQ-TS RESPONSE               00.000320
10:41:16.221472  E1  504EC8EA 0004 26930  0028604C 00001002 ..-.....           EIP ASKTIME ENTRY                   00.003008
10:41:16.221504  F3  00E4BC32 1303 26930  13210D00 00000000 ........           ICP GETIME                          00.000032
10:41:16.221504  F3  40EC61CA 0025 26930  0028604C 00001002 ..-.....           ICP RETN NORMAL                     00.000000
10:41:16.221536  E1  504EC8EA 00F4 26930  00000000 00001002 ........           EIP ASKTIME RESPONSE                00.000032
10:41:16.222208  E1  504EC810 0004 26930  0028604C 00000A02 ..-.....           EIP WRITEQ-TS ENTRY                 00.000672
10:41:16.222240  F1  00ED9DB8 8E04 26930  00286CA8 016F56A0 ........           SCP GETMAIN                         00.000032
10:41:16.222528  C8  50E89802 0004 26930  0028EF40 8E286CB8 ........           SCP ACQUIRED TEMPSTRG STORAGE       00.000288
10:41:16.223488  F7  00E7DD8E 5D03 26930  E2C9C7D5 E3C1C2D3 SIGNTABL           TSP APPL REQ PUTQ-REPLACE           00.000960
10:41:16.223552  F1  40E752A4 0004 26930  B017F804 47210FE8 ..8....Y           SCP GETMAIN CONDITIONAL ANY         00.000064
10:41:16.223872  C8  50E89802 0004 26930  02625340 9C006CC0 ... ....           SCP ACQUIRED EXTENDED STORAGE       00.000320
```

```
        CUSTOMER INFORMATION CONTROL SYSTEM  -  T R A C E   U T I L I T Y   P R O G R A M                PAGE    2
    TIME OF DAY    ID  REG 14   REQD TASK   FIELD A  FIELD B  CHARS    RESOURCE  TRACE TYPE                                INTERVAL

10:41:16.223904  F1 60E75AC0 0004 26930 4000F800 47210FE8  .8....Y             SCP FREEMAIN                              00.000032
10:41:16.224864  C9 50E89882 0004 26930 025CA340 9C006CC0 .*. ....             SCP RELEASED EXTENDED STORAGE             00.000960
10:41:16.225792  F7 40E75D68 0005 26930 025CA340 9C006CC0 .*. ....             TSP RETN APPL RESP NORMAL                 00.000928
10:41:16.225824  F1 00ED9DB8 4004 26930 0028EF40 016F56A0 ... ....             SCP FREEMAIN                              00.000032
10:41:16.225856  C9 50E89882 0004 26930 0028EF40 8E286CB8 ... ....             SCP RELEASED TEMPSTRG STORAGE             00.000032
10:41:16.226112  E1 504EC810 00F4 26930 00000000 00000A02 ........             EIP WRITEQ-TS RESPONSE                    00.000256
10:41:16.226144  E1 504EC85E 0004 26930 0028604C 00001206 ..-.....             EIP DEQ ENTRY                             00.000032
10:41:16.226176  F0 00C610E0 0204 26930 08286066 00000000 ..-.....             KCP DEQUEUE                               00.000032
10:41:16.226208  D5 00EB4026 0104 26930 E7D2C3D9 C5D84040 XKCREQ    TIXKCREQ   UEH BEFORE                                00.000032
10:41:16.226208  D5 00EB4026 0204 26930 00000000 001A39A0 ........  TIXKCREQ   UEH AFTER                                 00.000000
10:41:16.226240  D0 50EB66FA 0504 26930 00000000 00000000 ........             KCP DISPATCH                              00.000032
10:41:16.226240  E1 504EC85E 00F4 26930 00000000 00001206 ........             EIP DEQ RESPONSE                          00.000000
10:41:16.226272  E1 504EC8EA 0004 26930 0028604C 00001002 ..-.....             EIP ASKTIME ENTRY                         00.000032
10:41:16.226304  F3 00E4BC32 1303 26930 13210D00 00000000 ........             ICP GETIME                                00.000032
10:41:16.226336  F3 40EC61CA 0025 26930 0028604C 00001002 ..-.....             ICP RETN NORMAL                           00.000032
10:41:16.226336  E1 504EC8EA 00F4 26930 00000000 00001002 ........             EIP ASKTIME RESPONSE                      00.000000
10:41:16.227392  E1 504EE002 0004 26930 0028604C 00000E04 ..-.....             EIP XCTL ENTRY                            00.001056
10:41:16.227392  F2 00C9A114 8204 26930 00000000 00000000 ........  KHNMCBC    PCP LOCATE                                00.000000
10:41:16.227424  EA 40E906F6 0003 26930 01000300 002109C4 .......D  KHNMCBC    TMP PPT LOCATE                            00.000032
10:41:16.227488  EA 40E7F114 0005 26930 01000300 006BCA94 .....,..             TMP RETN NORMAL                           00.000064
10:41:16.227840  F1 00ED9DB8 4004 26930 00211360 016F56A0 ...-....             SCP FREEMAIN                              00.000352
10:41:16.227840  C9 50E89882 0004 26930 00211360 8C000048 ...-....             SCP RELEASED USER STORAGE                 00.000000
10:41:16.227904  F1 00ED9DB8 4004 26930 002113B0 016F56A0 ........             SCP FREEMAIN                              00.000064
10:41:16.227904  C9 50E89882 0004 26930 002113B0 8C000048 ........             SCP RELEASED USER STORAGE                 00.000000
10:41:16.227936  F1 00ED9DB8 4004 26930 00211400 016F56A0 ........             SCP FREEMAIN                              00.000032
10:41:16.227936  C9 50E89882 0004 26930 00211400 8C000138 ........             SCP RELEASED USER STORAGE                 00.000000
10:41:16.227968  F2 00EDA0E6 0204 26930 00000000 00000000 ........  KHNMCBC    PCP XCTL                                  00.000032
10:41:16.228000  F1 60E90A4E 4004 26930 00286000 016F56A0 ..-.....             SCP FREEMAIN                              00.000032
10:41:16.228000  C9 50E89882 0004 26930 00286000 8C008F38 ..-.....             SCP RELEASED USER STORAGE                 00.000000
10:41:16.228320  EA 40E906F6 0003 26930 01000300 002109C4 .......D  KHNMCBC    TMP PPT LOCATE                            00.000320
10:41:16.228352  EA 40E7F114 0005 26930 01000300 006BCA94 .....,..             TMP RETN NORMAL                           00.000032
10:41:16.228384  F5 404C82AC 8403 26930 00000000 00000000 ........  MEDMSTR    FCP GET-UPDATE                            00.000032
10:41:16.228416  EA 40EC1AF2 0003 26930 01000500 002109C4 .......D  MEDMSTR    TMP FCT LOCATE                            00.000032
10:41:16.228448  EA 40E7F114 0045 26930 01000500 006ABC08 ........             TMP RETN NORMAL                           00.000032
10:41:16.228480  F1 70EC338A 9D04 26930 00800054 016F56A0 ........             SCP GETMAIN                               00.000032
10:41:16.228512  C8 50E89802 0004 26930 00211250 9D800068 ...&....             SCP ACQUIRED DWE STORAGE                  00.000032
10:41:16.228512  F1 40EC3190 8F04 26930 00800084 016F56A0 ........             SCP GETMAIN                               00.000000
10:41:16.228544  C8 50E89802 0004 26930 002112C0 8F800098 ........             SCP ACQUIRED FILE STORAGE                 00.000032
10:41:16.228576  F1 40EC3190 8F04 26930 00800198 016F56A0 ........             SCP GETMAIN                               00.000032
10:41:16.228576  C8 50E89802 0004 26930 00211360 8F8001A8 ...-....             SCP ACQUIRED FILE STORAGE                 00.000000
10:41:16.229056  F0 40EC159E 4004 26930 43000000 002112D0 ........             KCP WAIT DCI=IOEVENT                      00.000480
10:41:16.229088  D5 00EB4026 0104 26930 E7D2C3D9 C5D84040 XKCREQ    TIXKCREQ   UEH BEFORE                                00.000032
10:41:16.229088  D5 00EB4026 0204 26930 00000000 001A39A0 ........  TIXKCREQ   UEH AFTER                                 00.000000
10:41:16.328544  D0 50EB66FA 0504 26930 00000000 00000000 ........             KCP DISPATCH                             *00.099456
10:41:16.328576  F5 40EC1A18 0025 26930 00000000 00000000 ........             FCP RETN NORMAL                           00.000032
10:41:16.328672  F5 604C82E0 2803 26930 00000000 00000000 ........  MEDMSTR    FCP GETAREA                               00.000096
10:41:16.328672  EA 40EC1AF2 0003 26930 01000500 002109C4 .......D  MEDMSTR    TMP FCT LOCATE                            00.000000
10:41:16.328736  EA 40E7F114 0025 26930 01000500 006ABC08 ........             TMP RETN NORMAL                           00.000064
10:41:16.328736  F1 40EC31A0 CF04 26930 00000198 016F56A0 ........             SCP GETMAIN INITIMG                       00.000000
10:41:16.328768  C8 50E89802 0004 26930 00211510 8F0001A8 ........             SCP ACQUIRED FILE STORAGE                 00.000032
10:41:16.328800  F5 40EC1A18 0025 26930 00211510 8F0001A8 ........             FCP RETN NORMAL                           00.000032
10:41:16.328832  F5 404C830E 4403 26930 00000000 00000000 ........  MEDMSTR    FCP PUT-NEW                               00.000032
10:41:16.328832  F1 70EC338A 9D04 26930 00150054 016F56A0 ........             SCP GETMAIN                               00.000000
```

```
       CUSTOMER INFORMATION CONTROL SYSTEM  -  T R A C E   U T I L I T Y   P R O G R A M                 PAGE     3

   TIME OF DAY     ID   REG 14  REQD TASK   FIELD A  FIELD B  CHARS    RESOURCE  TRACE TYPE                                        INTERVAL

10:41:16.328864    C8  50E89802 0004 26930 002116C0 9D150068 ........            SCP ACQUIRED DWE STORAGE                           00.000032
10:41:16.328896    F1  40EC3190 8F04 26930 0015007C 016F56A0 ........            SCP GETMAIN                                        00.000032
10:41:16.328896    C8  50E89802 0004 26930 00211730 8F150088 ........            SCP ACQUIRED FILE STORAGE                          00.000000
10:41:16.345824    F0  40EC159E 4004 26930 43000000 00211740 ........            KCP WAIT DCI=IOEVENT                              *00.016928
10:41:16.345856    D5  00EB4026 0104 26930 E7D2C3D9 C5D84040 XKCREQ   TIXKCREQ  UEH BEFORE                                         00.000032
10:41:16.345856    D5  00EB4026 0204 26930 00000000 001A39A0 ........ TIXKCREQ  UEH AFTER                                          00.000000
10:41:16.489856    D0  50EB66FA 0504 26930 00000000 00000000 ........            KCP DISPATCH                                      *00.144000
10:41:16.489952    F0  40EC2E1A 4004 26930 88000000 006ABC21 ........            KCP WAIT DCI=CICS                                  00.000096
10:41:16.489984    D5  00EB4026 0104 26930 E7D2C3D9 C5D84040 XKCREQ   TIXKCREQ  UEH BEFORE                                         00.000032
10:41:16.489984    D5  00EB4026 0204 26930 00000000 001A39A0 ........ TIXKCREQ  UEH AFTER                                          00.000000

END OF AUXILIARY TRACE DATA -     TOTAL TIME ACTIVE       00:00:26.14
                                  TRACE RECORDS READ          38,399
                                  TRACE RECORDS SELECTED         111
```

Bibliography

IBM Corporation. IBM System/370 Extended Architecture: Reference Summary. IBM Form GX20-0157.

———. IBM System/370 Extended Architecture: Principles of Operation. IBM Form SA22-7085.

———. Assembler H Version 2: Language Reference. IBM Form GC26-4037.

———. Assembler H Version 2: Programming Guide. IBM Form GC26-4036.

———. MVS/Extended Architecture System Programming Library: Supervisor Services and Macro Instruction. IBM Form GC28-1154.

———. MVS/Extended Architecture System Programming Library: Macros and Facilities, Volume 1. IBM Form GC28-1150.

———. MVS/Extended Architecture System Programming Library: Macros and Facilities, Volume 2. IBM Form GC28-1151.

———. MVS/Extended Architectur Data Administration: Macro Instructionse. IBM Form GC26-4141.

———. MVS/Extended Architecture Data Administration Guide. IBM Form GC26-4140.

Index